Heroes and Hero Cults in Latin America

Heroes & Hero Cults in Latin America

Edited by Samuel Brunk & Ben Fallaw

University of Texas Press ⌄ Austin

Requests for permission to reproduce material from this work should be sent to:
 Permissions
 University of Texas Press
 P.O. Box 7819
 Austin, TX 78713-7819
 www.utexas.edu/utpress/about/bpermission.html

∞ The paper used in this book meets the minimum requirements of ANSI/NISO Z39.48-1992 (R1997) (Permanence of Paper).

Library of Congress Cataloging-in-Publication Data

Heroes and hero cults in Latin America / edited by Samuel Brunk and Ben Fallaw.—1st ed.
 p.   cm.
Includes bibliographical references and index.

ISBN 13: 978-0-292-71481-6

1. Hero worship—Latin America—History.   2. Politicians—Latin America—Public opinion.   3. Statesmen—Latin America—Public opinion.   4. Public opinion—Latin America.   I. Brunk, Samuel, 1959–   II. Fallaw, Ben, 1966–
 F1408.3.H49   2006
 980—dc22
                                    2006012990

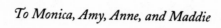

To Monica, Amy, Anne, and Maddie

Contents

Heroes and Hero Cults in Latin America

Introduction

Heroes and Their Cults in Modern Latin America

BEN FALLAW AND SAMUEL BRUNK

Modern Latin American history is brimming with heroes. Since the independence movements of the early nineteenth century, the politics of the region have been profoundly personalistic, as attested to by the many groups that have coalesced around leaders with a strong personal draw: the Zapatistas, Porfirians, Peronistas, Sandinistas. Some storied Latin American heroes of the past have, in death, transcended their national settings to become international icons, emblems of the region: Frida Kahlo, Che Guevara, Pancho Villa, Chico Mendes, and Evita Perón spring quickly to mind, but there are many others. And some figures whom we must consider at least potential heroes are with us still—witness the charisma with which Brazil's Luis Inácio "Lula" da Silva—pursued and ultimately won the presidency of that nation, the symbolic flair of the ski-masked rebel Subcomandante Marcos in the Mexican state of Chiapas, or the success with which Fidel Castro has persisted in Cuba and the singular legacy he will leave.

What exactly is a hero? Our definition is that a hero is a person to whom remarkable courage, talent, and other noble, even godlike traits are attributed by members of a community and who thus acquires a lasting place of importance in that community's culture. No one, of course, is likely to be granted such qualities by everyone in a given group of people. Indeed, the best that most heroes can hope for, especially those who are involved in politics, is to win the enduring affection of many and the enmity of a few. Still, most cultures—probably all cultures—have produced individuals who have achieved that lasting place of importance despite the dissent.

One thing a hero surely needs is charisma. Indeed, sociologist Max Weber's classic definition of charisma is quite similar to ours. Charisma,

Weber wrote, is "a certain quality of an individual personality by virtue of which he is set apart from ordinary men and treated as endowed with supernatural, superhuman, or at least specifically exceptional powers or qualities."[1] Charisma, then, is what makes heroes heroic, but what exactly are the qualities or traits that charismatic individuals possess? Judging from the evidence in this book, they vary widely. Venezuelan independence leader Simón Bolívar was an energetic visionary and a good speaker; Mexican revolutionary Emiliano Zapata had an impressive gaze; Yucatecan peasant organizer Felipe Carrillo Puerto demonstrated *cariño*—empathy— for his Mayan constituents; Argentine populist Evita Perón was sincerely concerned for those in need and knew how to use her good looks to political effect.

Such elements of charisma—if that is what they are—are historical contingencies, and historians often refer to French philosopher Blaise Pascal's famous remark about Cleopatra's nose when they want to talk about such contingencies. Pascal was discussing the *je ne sais quoi* (the unknowable quality) of love. Love, he wrote, "is such a tiny thing that we cannot even recognize it. [But it] rocks the world, thrones, armies, the whole of creation to their foundation. The nose of Cleopatra: if it had been shorter, the face of the earth would have changed."[2] But what if Cleopatra's nose had risen stately over Zapata's moustache? Would that visage also have changed history? The problem is the *je ne sais quoi*. What does a historian do with something that cannot be recognized, cannot be described?

Did Bolívar or Evita Perón have greater charisma, and could either match George Washington's share? It is difficult to know. Although Bolívar, Perón, and Washington might each have been endowed with cause, character, and good looks, Weber's definition implies that charisma exists only when there is an audience receptive to the particular traits of the individual in question. This is where the "cult"—the veneration of a person by a group of admirers—of this book's title comes in. In some cases an individual might serendipitously have a trait or behavior that is widely admired in his or her society; Cleopatra's nose fits here. In other instances, resonant characteristics are intentionally cultivated, as when Perón and Zapata made decisions about how to wear their hair. Either way, charisma as we use the term in this book is a relationship between an individual and her or his adherents that is conditioned by their shared culture. Bolívar had charisma only because he had a following that was receptive to his qualities, and as this relationship flourished, it increasingly set him "apart from ordinary men."[3] We would go so far in stressing the importance of the audience as to suggest that charisma often survives even when the person who supposedly possesses it has died and so can do nothing more to earn admiration.[4]

But to attribute someone's heroic stature to charisma still begs the question. To understand a hero we need to explore the conditions that produce charisma in the community in which that hero operates.

What kinds of communities, then, have heroes? Both in life and as the sacred, charismatic dead, heroes serve as a kind of cultural glue that helps hold together many kinds of communities—tribal, local, regional, national, international, religious, and ethnic. Our contributors explore heroes of the post-independence or national era of Latin America, from 1810 to the present. During this period the idea of the nation emerged and gathered strength in other parts of the world as well, and heroes played prominent roles in these nation-building processes. In his book, *Imagined Communities*, Benedict Anderson argues that people have "imagined" national communities by conceiving of unity for specific populations based on what they believe to be shared histories and cultures.[5] This imagining of nations has generally included what can best be described as a form of ancestor worship in which heroes—ancestors of national communities—represent supposedly shared cultural characteristics and historical events that are accepted as being critical to the creation of a nation. The use of such departed heroes helps simplify nations, which is necessary because national communities are, in reality, far too large and complex to be easily understood and envisioned; one cannot, for instance, know everyone by sight in a nation as one might in a small town. In this way, heroes help large numbers of people identify with a nation and internalize and accept as natural its basic principles and laws, thus producing greater unity in a population.

This unity is often cultivated and exploited by officials seeking to extend state power into people's daily lives, where a state is defined as the civil and military bureaucracies of a territory and the officials those who, in different branches and at various levels, control those bureaucracies.[6] States presumably benefit from the national identity that heroes can help produce because people who feel themselves to be part of a single community may be less fractious and thus more easily governable than people who do not. But more than that, political leaders often invoke heroes in an effort to bolster their legitimacy through association with admired predecessors, or in the hope of making citizens more virtuous and productive by giving them models of behavior to follow. Heads of state generally want their constituents to perceive state and nation as one and the same, so that, for example, a Brazilian thinking of the Brazilian nation would automatically think of the Brazilian president, the head of state, as the most obvious embodiment of and spokesperson for the nation. A head of state who links himself to a heroic figure can draw on the hero's national unifying power to consolidate his own power as head of state.

Heads of state cannot, however, just shape heroes and nations according to their own designs. A useful caution against taking the concept of the nation as an imagined community too far comes from Anthony D. Smith, who stresses that although nations are relatively modern constructions, they are generally built on older ethnic traditions.[7] Anderson's reference to ancestor worship, after all, brings to mind images of tribally organized peoples remembering departed elders, and when a national hero is called a founding father, it is an evocation both of the family community and of the ancestor cult. The many Christian cults of saints and martyrs that emerged during Europe's Middle Ages and carried over strongly into Latin America produced another kind of hero long before there were Latin American nations, and during the nineteenth and twentieth centuries leaders in many countries consciously sought to bolster national identification by adopting heroes with religious evocations, especially those understood to have become martyrs for their nations, in order to capture for the state some of the sense of the sacred at work within religious communities.[8] For example, in Chapter 9 David Nugent demonstrates that Víctor Raúl Haya de la Torre represented himself as a martyr for the Peruvian people and his cadre of organizers as a priesthood of democracy. Those who become heroes of nations, then, often have popular roots that predate the origins of the nation and limit what leaders of modern states can do with them.

Another factor limiting state manipulation of heroes is that new heroes with little relationship to states, such as sports and entertainment figures, are constantly being born. And it is also possible for heroic figures to embody concepts of identity and nationality that are apart from, and in opposition to, the images crafted by internationally recognized nations. A good example here is the ethnic nationalism of the Chicano, black, and American Indian movements in the United States in the 1960s and 1970s, which produced its own heroes and flourished in their light.

Furthermore, it is difficult to separate a state from the society in which it operates. Modern states are not highly unified structures. Rather, having metastasized into multiple branches, levels, ministries, and committees, they are generally unable to present consistent messages, and nearly always must consider the interests of people who work at cross-purposes with one another on behalf of different constituencies that may use heroes in conflicting ways.[9] At a minimum, for heroes and nations to be heroes and nations people have to accept them as such, and in so doing people also participate in the creation of nations and heroes, adapting them to their personal needs or those of the smaller communities in which they live. These needs might be in opposition to the needs of the state, however, and the heroic figures might in this way be manipulated to serve two masters simultaneously. Thus, although the building of state power and institutions and the forging of nations have been profoundly interconnected because governing elites have had good reason to create and manipulate national myths and the heroes that are part of them, the making of nations and heroes is both a collective endeavor and one that can be opposed.

Nineteenth-Century Latin American Heroes

BETWEEN 1810 AND 1825, most Latin American countries fought and won wars of independence from Spain. As the former colonies struggled to form themselves into nation-states even as they sought liberation through martial efforts, it is not surprising that heroic figures dominated the process. The most prominent among them were men of action—strongmen or warlords, called *caudillos*, who led armies against Spanish troops or, at times, against each other in battles to settle the boundaries of the nations. Through martial prowess and force of personality, they often dominated their countries once independence was achieved. Two Mexican priests, Miguel Hidalgo and José María Morelos, lost rebellions for independence yet still became prominent in Mexico's national pantheon. In Spanish South America, the two great liberators were Simón Bolívar of Venezuela and José de San Martín of Argentina, both of whom fought their way to Peru to drive the Spanish army from the continent. Their supporting cast included Venezuelans Francisco de Miranda and José Antonio Páez; Colombian Francisco de Paula Santander; Antonio José de Sucre, who finished off the Spanish forces and became Bolivia's first president; and Uruguayan José Gervasio Artigas. In Brazil the independence process was more peaceful and thus produced no heroes of the sword, but there was one heroic gesture. In 1822, Emperor Pedro I established Brazilian independence from Portugal by issuing what became known as the Cry of Ipiranga: "Independence or Death."

While the period from independence until about 1870 was characterized by military competition for power between caudillos, some of the strongmen of the early and middle nineteenth century have been remembered as effective—and thus perhaps heroic—statesmen. Chilean conservative Diego Portales, for instance, constructed durable economic and political frameworks for his country, and José Gaspar Rodríguez de Francia kept Paraguay self-sufficient and separate from its menacing neighbor, Argentina, until his death in 1840. What Portales and Rodríguez de Francia had in common with the warriors of the period was a close association between their persons and the governments they led, their authoritarian personalism tending to transcend the constitutional trappings with which their new nations were endowed.

This less warlike, more constructive bearing was, in some respects, a model for Latin American leaders who came on the scene after 1870. During the last decades of the nineteenth century, Latin America became more integrated into the world economy through railroads, steamships, and the telegraph. At the same time, the industrialization of parts of Europe and the United States heightened demand for the region's raw materials. Exports boomed. This stronger connection to global markets gave some caudillos the financial means to build stronger states. It also gave elites powerful incentives to unite in creating such states, since the greatest profits would come only when political stability encouraged foreign investments. These newly stable states were generally limited in the services they offered. Latin American governments of the Gilded Age concentrated on regulating markets and servicing public debts, generally addressing social problems through more effective methods of repression, which export-led prosperity made possible by fattening police forces and militaries. In some countries the new political arrangements underwritten by export booms included elections that merely rotated members of the elite among the positions of power. In others, individual caudillos simply suppressed or bought off their rivals, sometimes holding power for decades at a time. Dictators such as Porfirio Díaz in Mexico, Antonio Guzmán Blanco in Venezuela, Rafael Núñez in Colombia, and José Santos Zelaya in Nicaragua emerged as a new breed of strongmen, caudillos who spoke the language of economic growth but who still relied on force to put down rivals and restive populations. Historian John Lynch has called them "modernizing dictators."[10]

The last three decades of the nineteenth century were an era of liberal ascendancy across the region, which meant belief in pursuing progress and modernization through laissez-faire capitalism. It also meant the need to pay at least lip service to republican institutions: members of the new set of dictators often held elections intended to cloak their authoritarian rule in republican forms. When they felt it necessary, however, they rigged those elections, and they did their best to centralize authority in their own persons rather than submit to checks and balances. Instead of seeking to project a sense of personal connectedness to the citizens of their countries, these dictators generally kept their distance symbolically, seeking to manipulate public opinion by glorifying themselves. One way to do that was to associate themselves with the arrival of relative peace, order, and prosperity after the turmoil of the pre-1870 period. Another was to identify with past heroes of their nations. Guzmán Blanco, for instance, was a vain man who liked to be called "the Illustrious American" and linked himself to Bolívar through his father, Antonio Leocadio Guzmán, whom he touted as one of Bolívar's most valued collaborators. Bolívar's birthdays were celebrated in the capital, Caracas, with cries of "Long Live Bolívar! Glory to Guzmán!"[11] Guzmán Blanco also took pains to display—and take credit for—the progress and prosperity of Venezuela under his rule. A great admirer of all things European, he reconstructed Caracas in the Parisian mode and filled it with new buildings, monuments, and statues of himself.

Similar events were taking place in Porfirio Díaz's Mexico (1876–1911), as discussed in Chapter 4. Díaz promised peace and prosperity to foreign investors and privileged Mexicans while using an army he could move quickly by railroad to suppress unruly indigenous groups on Mexico's northern and southern borders, as well as peasants and workers who resisted his economic policies. To court public opinion, demonstrate his successes, and legitimize his rule through association with heroes of the past, Díaz lined the Paseo de la Reforma, a new Mexico City thoroughfare, with the statues of such prominent Mexicans as Aztec resistance hero Cuauhtémoc, independence leader Hidalgo, and Reform-era president Benito Juárez. The Porfirian regime also projected its heroes internationally in its exhibits at the world fairs.[12]

Of course, not every end-of-the-century leader was cut from the same cloth, and one who was not, Cuba's José Martí, bears mention here. Martí was a prominent player in Cuba's struggle for independence from Spain, but he died, tragically, before it was achieved in 1898. Consequently, Martí operated in a far different historical context than the modernizing dictators who presided over countries that had thrown off their colonial shackles decades earlier. It is not surprising, then, that Martí's program also differed from those of other Latin American leaders of the period. In his Cuba Libre (Free Cuba) he envisioned democracy, civil government, and an end to foreign interference. While leading an attack on the Spanish in 1895, he became a martyr to that vision. Since then he has become perhaps the most renowned Latin American hero of the nineteenth century and one of the most studied individuals in all of Latin American history.[13]

Revolutionaries, Populists, and Other Twentieth-Century Strongmen

BY THE FIRST DECADE OF THE TWENTIETH CENTURY, the age of Latin American warlords seemed to be on the wane. Although caudillos remained at the helm in many countries, most nations had become constitutional republics whose fates increasingly depended on economic growth overseen by swelling middle classes with democratic leanings. At the same time, urban workers, clustered together in the region's burgeoning cities, increased in number. Literacy expanded along with the urban centers and—especially in Argentina, Brazil, and Uruguay—immigration. Then as now, the future seemed likely to be shaped by economic laws of supply and demand, not the gloved fist of caudillos. But the triple shocks of World War I, the Russian Revolution, and the Great Depression shook the region to its foundations and undermined both the trend toward democracy, where it existed, and the import-export emphasis of liberal economics. Many began to argue that Latin American countries should focus on autonomous economic development, prescribing an interventionist state that would invest in infrastructure to nurture growing industries. As faith in democracy waned during the Depression, new ideological models, such as communism and fascism, seemed to offer more promising ways of including the increasingly restive urban masses politically. Rising to preside over the changed landscape in the middle decades of the twentieth century was a new kind of personalist leader, and thus would-be hero, the populist.

Populism was a style, not an ideological position. Practitioners combined the *don de gente* (popular touch) and elements of popular culture (the tango, the samba, the Mexican folksong called the *corrido*) with modern technology, using the airplane and automobile to extend their political appeals into the remotest corners of their countries and using mass media such as the radio and motion pictures to reach populations that remained substantially illiterate. Beginning with Mexican revolutionaries such as Carrillo Puerto, they courted the growing middle classes as well as traditionally marginalized groups—organized labor, the urban poor, young people, women, and sometimes even indigenous populations. By the 1930s, populists of many stripes had emerged as dominant leaders in their countries. On the right were military dictators such as Rafael Trujillo of the Dominican Republic, Anastasio Somoza García of Nicaragua, and Fulgencio Batista in Cuba; on the left were men like Presidents Lázaro Cárdenas of Mexico and Arturo Alessandri of Chile. These populists shared certain characteristics—such as a proclivity toward authoritarian leadership—with nineteenth-century warlords, but mass media and modern travel gave them the chance to develop cults of personality on a scale that the classic caudillo could only have envied. Even authoritarian leaders on the far right of the political spectrum, who did not cultivate mass followings with the patrician-baiting reformism characteristic, say, of Juan and Evita Perón, tried to woo lower-class groups. A good example is Somoza, who ruled Nicaragua from 1936 to 1956. Somoza sought labor support to shore up his control over national politics through *obrerismo* ("workerism"), a strategy in which he promoted labor organization, portrayed himself as "the guarantor of labor's aspirations," and made sure that some of labor's demands were met.[14]

For this reason, it is often difficult to separate left-leaning, democratic populism from right-wing authoritarianism, and many leaders never saw the need to do so. One great ideological chameleon was José María Velasco Ibarra of Ecuador, perennial presidential contender who was in and out of power so many times that his unofficial slogan became, "Give me a balcony and I will return to the Presidency." Velasco Ibarra got his start with backing from the conservative elite in the 1930s and then, while in power from 1944 to 1947, formed an alliance with the left-leaning Popular Front before turning against the left. During his last campaign, in 1960, he made free use of radical rhetoric lifted from the Cuban Revolution.[15] With evidence like this, one might easily conclude that the personalism of *caudillismo*—the dominance of the strongman or warlord—tamed and co-opted modern ideologies rather than being displaced by them.

As the only country in Latin America to experience a bloody social revolution in the first half of the twentieth century, Mexico is markedly different from the rest of the region. The Mexican Revolution (fought 1910–1920) provided the context for a whole new set of martial caudillos, some with rather traditional attributes. Pancho Villa, Emiliano Zapata, and Alvaro Obregón, among many others, now became candidates for entry into that nation's pantheon. Elsewhere in the region, revolutionary heroes did not turn up until the cold war. Most notably, the Cuban Revolution of 1959 made both Fidel Castro and Argentine physician-turned-revolutionary Ernesto "Che" Guevara leftist icons, not only in Latin America but throughout the world.[16]

Heroes Outside of High Politics

ALTHOUGH THIS BOOK is largely about "high" politics, we do not want to ignore other varieties of heroism, which often had political dimensions of their own. In the late nineteenth century, for instance, bandits drew as much attention as caudillos. For some observers bandits were nothing more than common thieves who had to be stamped out so that order and progress could be more deeply embedded. For others they were like Robin Hood, admirable in their willingness to buck the period's modernizing trends. In Mexico the bandits "Chucho el Roto" and Heraclio Bernal drew praise, or at least quiet admiration, for their ability to taunt the Porfirian regime. Their exploits were recorded in corridos and sometimes in the print media as well.[17] In Argentina, as political conflict died down and a government intent on greater centralization moved to control the feared *gauchos* of the rich pampas grasslands, some people responded with romantic defenses of these celebrated Argentine horsemen. Most famous is José Hernández's epic, *Martín Fierro*, a work with tremendous resonance in that nation. In Brazil the backlands (the *sertão*) were full of bandits with serious reputations who sometimes became symbolic focal points of protest at the national level. There the "good thief," Antonio Silvino, was a particularly prominent Robin Hood figure around the start of the twentieth century.[18]

The blooming of mass culture in the first half of the twentieth century revolutionized ideas about who could be considered heroic. Another plebeian icon, the working-class hero, began to appear, in part the creation of populist leaders who tapped into popular culture to attract the support of urban labor. Former radio actress Evita Perón's melodramatic political speeches on behalf of workers (see Chapter 10), for example, bore a strong resemblance to the radio dramas she had starred in, with foreign interests and the Argentine elite substituting for the villain. Samba and carnival joined soccer as symbols of Brazilian nationalism during the era of Getúlio Vargas (1930–1954). But political uses of worker heroes and "low" culture often involved sanitizing them for elite, and foreign, consumption. Samba songs initially celebrated both the virtues and vices of the *malagrado*, the street-smart hustler; but during the Vargas regime this figure inexplicably gave up hustling for hard work and respectability.[19] In Mexico, Mario "Cantinflas" Moreno adapted the similar *pelado* character, a fixture of the tent theater of Mexico City's famous Garibaldi Square, to the movie screen. Unfortunately, the pelado did not fare well in his new medium. Like the malagrado, he had been admired for his heroic ability to mock authority figures, both plutocrat and politician. Under the guiding hand of the postrevolutionary Mexican state, however, which had considerable interest in the propaganda power of movies, he evolved from a marginalized figure into an upright symbol of the new regime and its supposed successes.[20]

Twentieth-century media also facilitated the emergence of female heroes. Women who might be considered heroic have always been present in Latin America, but in part because they have not usually held political office, women's heroism has often gone unrecognized, both by the societies in which they lived and by historians. In the twentieth century, however, the Mexican Revolution's *soldadera* (female soldier or camp follower) emerged as a national icon, even though individual soldaderas and such popular leaders of the postrevolutionary era as María de la O and Felipa Poot were rarely remembered.[21] Painter Frida Kahlo, the subject of Chapter 8, emerged as a cultural hero years after her death, and her interest in elements of Mexico's Precolumbian past helped foster modern nationalism. The journals of

Carolina Maria de Jesus, an Afro-Brazilian woman from the city of São Paulo, meanwhile, chronicled her struggles against poverty, racial discrimination, and, often, her own family. After the publication of her first book, which was a tremendous success, she enjoyed a kind of heroic, emblematic stature for a time, but also encountered a great deal of controversy. Another Afro-Brazilian woman, Benedita da Silva, who emerged from a *favela* (shantytown) of Rio de Janeiro to become Brazil's first black woman in the senate, recently drew greater attention to her accomplishments by publishing her life story as well. Other such accounts include those of Rosa Isolde Reuque Paillalef, a Mapuche Indian activist from Chile, and Domitila Barrios de Chungara, the wife of a Bolivian miner, who became involved in labor and political disputes.[22]

A New Look at Latin American Heroes

ONE OF THE GOALS OF THIS BOOK is to make a case for returning the study of individuals—in this case, prominent ones—to the center of historical analysis. Obviously, Latin American leaders and others who might qualify as heroes have not been ignored by historians. In fact, before the 1960s scholars often adopted the "great man" approach, implying that elite men who wielded formal political power, commanded armies, and wrote books were the primary architects of history.[23] Over the past forty years or so that kind of interpretation has drawn heavy criticism, and the role of privileged individuals has been of less concern for most historians. From the 1960s to the 1980s, historians were instead interested primarily in social and economic structures. During roughly the past fifteen years, they have turned hard toward the examination of culture, often focusing more on political discourse, symbols, and ritual than on individuals. Most historians of recent decades have viewed the concept of the hero skeptically, both because they do not believe that leaders have been the fundamental makers of history and because they recognize that those who have claimed heroic stature or have had such claims made for them have often been deeply flawed.

But though historians sometimes scoff, the phenomenon of personalism has continued to demand a share of scholarly attention. During the era in which the focus was socioeconomic, caudillos, populists, and more local political bosses (often called *caciques* in Mexico) all drew notice from historians. Scholars of this period were generally most concerned with categorizing their subjects and examining their relationships to larger structures.[24] The comparative perspective offered in Michael Conniff's edited volumes, for instance, deepened our knowledge of the leaders of the populist era.[25] David Brading's collection on the Mexican Revolution, meanwhile, explored the bonds between caudillos and their followers. The contributors debated how long caudillos continued to exist, whether there were caudillos of different types, and how caudillos were related to the process of institutionalizing the revolution.[26]

The more recent students of culture have been concerned with questions of agency and identity, emphases that have nudged historical inquiry away from structural determinism and given it a more biographical quality. To the extent that cultural historians have been interested in individuals, however, they have not been especially interested in renowned leaders but rather in people, or groups of people, that previous historians had overlooked.[27] Still, there has been some examination of the prominent and their impact on national histories through the cultural lens, focusing on the ways that they, in life and death, were linked to national identity through architecture, public ritual, and propagandistic literature. One pioneering work of this kind is Charles Weeks's *The Juárez Myth in Mexico*, which examines memories of Benito Juárez, the Zapotec Indian who rose to power in the mid-nineteenth century, led the Liberal Party to victory over its Conservative foes, and contributed greatly to the Constitution of 1857.[28] Weeks traces the ways in which the Mexican state, since Juárez's death in 1872, has made him a secular hero who could compete with the powerful religious image of the Virgin of Guadalupe and thus promote a nationalism more effectively linked to the government. Another pathbreaking work on the posthumous careers of Mexican heroes is Ilene O'Malley's *The Myth of the Revolution*.[29] Focusing on the years between 1920 and 1940, O'Malley discusses how the mainly middle- and upper-class winners of the Mexican Revolution portrayed deceased revolutionaries as founding fathers of the new, postrevolutionary order. As they did so, O'Malley argues, they attached to popular leaders such as Zapata messages of nationalism and patriarchalism meant to pacify and otherwise manipulate the Mexican people.

More recently, there have been several important works on heroes and culture in other parts of Latin America. In *Mañana es San Perón: A Cultural History of Peron's Argentina*, Mariano Plotkin closely examines Juan Perón's propaganda efforts in Argentina between 1946 and 1955, with attention to political rituals and education programs. Plotkin maintains that Perón built Peronism into a political religion, placing himself at the center of conceptions of nationalism.[30] Lauren Derby has recently argued, meanwhile, that Dominican dictator Trujillo used beauty pageants and popularly accepted macho stereotypes (he was known as "the Goat") to increase the identification of poor Dominicans with his regime.[31] Finally, books on nineteenth-century caudillos by John Chasteen (author of Chapter 1) and Ariel de la Fuente have explored the concept of charisma, stressing the notion that charisma is about the relationship between leaders and followers. They thus move the focus from the inherent characteristics of leaders to the characteristics that members of a particular society expect of their leaders.[32] De la Fuente in particular pays great attention to oral tradition—folksongs and stories—in rooting this out.

Despite the existence of these works, historians have not always given heroes (and individuals in general) the attention they merit. They deserve better, in part because of the way people often receive history and the uses they have for it. Historian David Thelen recently surveyed 1,453 randomly selected people in the United States about their uses of the past.[33] Thelen's report notes that the greatest challenge identified by the people he contacted was that historians "pay more attention to individuals both as interpreters of and actors in the past." This was important to the interviewees because they wanted to use the past to establish identity, to pass on knowledge to their children as preparation for the future, or "to find and hold on to other people, and to make a difference in their lives and those of others." In other words, they had intensely personal uses for history. Based on those discussions, Thelen suggests that there is a popular ethic about history in the United States, the crux of which is that people can do much to shape their destinies, despite the constraints under which they live, and that the ways in which historical actors have shaped their lives hold important lessons for us.

Thelen's findings probably do not completely apply to Latin America, of course, but as we have suggested, Latin Americans have amply demonstrated a similar need for exemplary lives; indeed, most authorities would say that personalism has been stronger in Latin America than in the United States. At any rate, it is that relationship between individuals and groups that enables heroes to serve as windows into the societies in which they live, and it is that relationship that the chapters in this book explore. We are writing, in other words, not primarily about the policy or electoral campaigns or battles that make up the sometimes dry chronology of politics. Rather, we are interested in political culture, the ties that bind leaders and followers—the methods of organization, the mechanics of patronage, the rituals and rhetorical practices, the symbols and myths that help explain why some people gain political power or influence and why we remember some leaders and quickly forget many others. Anthropologist Katherine Verdery writes that to study political culture is to "enchant" or "enliven" politics "with a richer sense of what it might consist of."[34] It is also to study societies instead of just politicians.

This book, then, examines leaders during the nineteenth and twentieth centuries, with attention to caudillos, populists, revolutionaries, an artist, and the relationship between such figures, their admirers, and the processes of identity creation, state formation, and nation building. For comparative purposes, we decided not to limit our focus to those who achieved the lasting stature demanded by our definition of hero. Instead, the book's content reflects our understanding that incipient hero cults can take many different trajectories by considering a group of people who were at least candidates for heroism, some attaining it, others celebrated as heroic only at particular moments in their lives, then largely forgotten after their deaths or marked down in memory as villains. The cases of those who did not reach the ultimate status help us identify the variables that seem necessary to the making of a Latin American hero.

John Chasteen begins our scrutiny of the independence era with a close look at Simón Bolívar in Chapter 1. During his life, Chasteen observes, Bolívar did not always seem heroic; he was not, for instance, an especially effective military leader. He was, however, a persistent and daring visionary, as well as a gifted communicator highly attentive to the cultivation of his own image. Based on those strengths Bolívar became, after his death, an example for others to follow and the center of an official state cult in Venezuela "with pronounced religious resonances." Charles Walker's subject in Chapter 2 is Peruvian Agustín Gamarra, another independence-era hero who was, in retrospect, merely one of a throng of somewhat prominent caudillos of his era. During his lifetime, though, his image sometimes flourished despite limited military talents. Perhaps this was because he shared with Bolívar what military historian John Keegan terms the "mask of command," gaining credit by managing and administering long and grueling campaigns, stringing together political coalitions, corresponding effectively with subordinates, and maintaining morale in difficult circumstances—skills sometimes as valuable as battlefield prowess.[35] Be that as it may, Walker reveals that, unlike Bolívar, Gamarra was not successful in generating a hero cult that outlived him, partly because it was impossible to see him in unambiguous terms and partly because of his failure to establish a mass following.

In describing Santa Anna honoring his amputated leg, Shannon Baker in Chapter 3 demonstrates that attempts to solidify national power in newly independent Latin America could be comical. On the more serious side, the success of those efforts was limited by civil wars, economic difficulties, and the lack of powerful national institutions, such as centralized armies or educational systems. Baker also believes that Santa Anna's personalism was a problem, because it undermined more viable sources of national identity, while his uneven record as military leader and chief executive was insufficient to make him the embodiment of the nation he hoped to become.

Despite moments such as the defeat of the French in 1838, during which he appeared heroic to many, he was generally perceived as being too self-serving and thus did not become the center of a lasting hero cult. In fact, he has become one of the principal villains of Mexican history, largely because of his association with the loss of national territory to the United States at mid-century.

In Chapter 4, Victor Macias presents the very different Mexico of Porfirio Díaz. Like Santa Anna, Díaz first achieved power through military means, but while Santa Anna came to represent the disorder of the post-independence period, Díaz presided over the late-nineteenth-century trend toward political order and economic growth. Although Díaz did hold (and fix) the regular elections called for by the Constitution of 1857, he balanced his feints at republicanism with the projection of a regal image through architecture and the etiquette and ceremony of presidential audiences. Anthropologist Clifford Geertz has noted that people tend to build cults around rulers as a reflection of their personification of power.[36] Díaz's regal strategy, which distanced him from the throng and enhanced his embodiment of power, seems to have been calculated to achieve such an effect. But Díaz's pseudo-monarchical airs did not age well. Since the Mexican Revolution ended his dictatorship in 1911, he has fared poorly in Mexican memory.

Our coverage of the twentieth century starts with two chapters on prominent actors in the Mexican Revolution. In his essay on Emiliano Zapata, Samuel Brunk in Chapter 5 finds that Zapata's image, both in life and after death, was shaped by the interaction of national and more local impressions and memories. Brunk argues that Zapata's strong presence in both local and national imaginations may help explain his considerable symbolic power throughout much of Mexico's twentieth century. The career of Felipe Carrillo Puerto, with its greater regional limitations, is scrutinized by Ben Fallaw in Chapter 6. In life, Carrillo Puerto led a revolutionary transformation of the southeastern Mexican state of Yucatán, yet his posthumous hero cult, crafted by politicians, an ambitious brother, and entertainment maven Manuel Cirerol Sansores, served to legitimize a status quo that was far from radical. Perhaps because memories of him were sometimes so shamefully manipulated, Carrillo Puerto's cult has faded over time.

Richard Grossman in Chapter 7 takes us to Nicaragua for a discussion of Augusto César Sandino. Sandino first came to national and international attention during the late 1920s when he initiated a guerrilla war against the U.S. Marines who had been sent to intervene in Nicaragua and the national leaders who accepted their presence. In the course of this struggle, Grossman discovers, Sandino developed a dual image as an anti-imperialist

warrior and a Nicaraguan patriarch. He outlasted the U.S. forces, who left
his country in 1933, but was assassinated soon afterward by the Nicaraguan
National Guard, commanded by Anastasio Somoza García, who was on his
way to establishing a family dictatorship that would last for more than four
decades. Sandino was not, however, forgotten, and eventually the rebels who
toppled the Somoza regime in 1979, the most important of which were allied
with the Sandinista National Liberation Front (Frente Sandinista de
Liberación Nacional, or FSLN), made him a social revolutionary icon and
the founding father of a newly conceptualized Nicaraguan nation.

Chapter 8 raises several new issues, both because it concerns a woman,
the Mexican artist Frida Kahlo, and because Kahlo was not a politician.
Nancy Deffebach demonstrates that Kahlo crafted an image of herself in
her paintings to explore how one could be "female, Mexican, modern, and
powerful." Despite her many physical ailments, she did not depict herself as
a martyr but rather as a secular pilgrim who used elements of Christian
iconography to "negotiate her way through the special problems facing
women artists in Mexico." This did not win her much renown during her
lifetime, but since her death in 1954 at the age of only 47, and despite her
own disdain for hero worship, her work and her image have attracted a
broad and still-growing international following. Deffebach contends that
this has occurred precisely because she "fills a need and a niche" that more
traditional heroic types cannot.

David Nugent in Chapter 9 takes on populist Haya de la Torre of Peru,
exploring how Haya's American Popular Revolutionary Alliance (Alianza
Popular Revolucionaria Americana, or APRA) party reached out to potential adherents through a combination of charisma and institutions. Haya's
charisma was considerable, Nugent argues, but he was also a stickler for
organization and discipline. Without the party structures he fashioned and
the assistance those structures offered people who joined the party, his
charisma would not have been felt in such remote regions of the nation as
Chachapoyas, in the northern department of Amazonas. In showing how
APRA magnified and extended Haya's charisma, then, Nugent provides the
crucial insight that a given hero's success may not be explicable through cultural considerations alone and hints that the charismatic relationship may
sometimes be forged through rather mundane means.

Chapter 10 is Linda Hall's study of the career of a second heroine, Evita
Perón. Unlike Kahlo, Perón was a politician, although rather than holding
her own political office she benefited from opportunities to wield power
because her husband occupied the presidency. Hall follows Perón's rise from
provincial obscurity and the evolution of her public persona: how her choice

of dress and hairstyle, combined with her willingness to literally and figuratively embrace the poor and the sick, helped make her appealing to workers, women, and children. Like Kahlo, Evita Perón fashioned her image after Christian symbols, ultimately making herself a sort of secular Virgin Mary. In part because she continued to be a polarizing figure after her death, her history remains more complex than that of any of the other subjects of this book.

In Chapter 11, the concluding chapter, we consider what general lessons can be drawn about Latin American heroes. As is readily apparent, Latin American heroes have generally been male, though being female does not rule out heroism. We also find that they portray themselves as problem solvers in difficult times, that they tend to hold liberal or progressive ideas (though they are rarely ideologically orthodox), and that those whose reputations have flourished most did not rise to executive power in their nations. Finally, many of them came to a tragic end. Although that description does not make the region's heroes unique, we argue that the heroes of individual nations within Latin America might be unique at one level of analysis, and that by studying a given nation's heroic pantheon, we can come to new understandings about how that nation is conceptualized.

Notes

1. Max Weber, *On Charisma and Institution Building*, ed. S. N. Eisenstadt (Chicago: University of Chicago Press, 1968), 48.

2. Blaise Pascal, *Pensées*, trans. Martin Turnell (New York: Harper and Row, 1962), 133.

3. Douglas Madsen and Peter G. Snow, *The Charismatic Bond: Political Behavior in Time of Crisis* (Cambridge, Mass.: Harvard University Press, 1991).

4. At this point there is at least a tendency for charisma to become routine, or institutionalized. On this process see Weber, *On Charisma*, 54–61.

5. Benedict Anderson, *Imagined Communities: Reflections on the Origin and Spread of Nationalism*, rev. ed. (New York: Verso, 1991), 4–12. Anderson defines a nation as "an imagined political community—and imagined as both inherently limited and sovereign."

6. Nora Hamilton, *The Limits of State Autonomy: Post-Revolutionary Mexico* (Princeton, N.J.: Princeton University Press, 1982), 7.

7. Anthony D. Smith, *Myths and Memories of the Nation* (New York: Oxford University Press, 1999), 8–19.

8. For a French example, see Mona Ozouf, *Festivals and the French Revolution* (Cambridge, Mass.: Harvard University Press, 1988).

9. Joel S. Migdal, *State in Society: Studying How States and Societies Transform and Constitute One Another* (New York: Cambridge University Press, 2001).

10. John Lynch, *Caudillos in Spanish America, 1800–1850* (Oxford: Oxford University Press, 1992), 427–428.

11. George S. Wise, *Caudillo: A Portrait of Antonio Guzmán Blanco* (Westport, Conn.: Greenwood Press, 1951), 166, 170–171.

12. Barbara A. Tenenbaum, "Streetwise History: The Paseo de la Reforma and the Porfirian State, 1876–1910," in *Rituals of Rule, Rituals of Resistance: Public Celebrations and Popular Culture in Mexico*, ed. William H. Beezley, Cheryl English Martin, and William E. French (Wilmington, Del.: Scholarly Resources Books, 1994), 135–146; Mauricio Tenorio-Trillo, "1910 Mexico City: Space and Nation in the City of the Centenario," in *¡Viva Mexico! Viva La Independencia: Celebrations of September 16*, ed. William H. Beezley and David E. Lorey (Wilmington, Del.: Scholarly Resources, 2001), 167–197; and Matthew D. Esposito, "Death and Disorder in Mexico City: The State Funeral of Manuel Romero Rubio," in *Latin American Popular Culture*, ed. William H. Beezley and Linda A. Curcio-Nagy (Wilmington, Del.: Scholarly Resources, 2000), 88.

13. Notable recent English-language studies of Martí include John Kirk, *José Martí, Inventor of the Cuban Nation* (Tampa: University of Florida Press, 1983), and Christopher Abel and Nissa Torrents, eds., *José Martí, Revolutionary Democrat* (Durham, N.C.: Duke University Press, 1986).

14. Jeffrey Gould, *To Lead as Equals: Rural Protest and Political Consciousness in Chinandega, Nicaragua, 1912–1979* (Chapel Hill: University of North Carolina Press, 1990), 15, 47–50.

15. Agustín Cueva, *The Process of Political Domination in Ecuador*, trans. Danielle Salti (New Brunswick, N.J.: Transaction Books, 1982); David W. Schodt, *Ecuador: An Andean Enigma* (Boulder, Colo.: Westview Press, 1987); and Carlos de la Torre, *Populist Seduction in Latin America: The Ecuadorian Experience* (Athens: Ohio State University Press, 2000).

16. As testimony to his lasting appeal, in 1997 alone nonacademic presses published three biographies of Guevara: Jorge G. Castañeda, *Compañero: The Life and Death of Che Guevara*, trans. Marina Castañeda (New York: Alfred A. Knopf, 1997); John Lee Anderson, *Che Guevara: A Revolutionary Life* (New York: Grove Press, 1997); and Paco Ignacio Taibo II, *Guevara, Also Known as Che*, trans. Martin Michael Roberts (New York: Thomas Dunne, 1997).

17. Paul J. Vanderwood, *Disorder and Progress: Bandits, Police, and Mexican Development*, rev. ed. (Wilmington, Del.: Scholarly Resources, 1992), 90.

18. Linda Lewin, "The Oligarchical Limitations of Social Banditry in Brazil: The Case of the 'Good' Thief Antonio Silvino," in *Bandidos: The Varieties of Latin American Banditry*, ed. Richard W. Slatta (New York: Greenwood Press, 1987), 67–69, 76, 84–85.

19. Lisa Shaw, *The Social History of the Brazilian Samba* (Brookfield, Vt.: Ashgate, 1999); Simon Webb, "Masculinities at the Margins: Representations of the Malandro and the Pachuco," in *Imagination Beyond Nation: Latin American Popular Culture*, ed. Eva P. Bueno and Terry Caesar (Pittsburgh: University of Pittsburgh Press, 1998), 238–248.

20. Jeffrey Pilcher, *Cantinflas and the Chaos of Mexican Modernity* (Wilmington, Del.: Scholarly Resources, 2001).

21. Ben Fallaw, "The Life and Deaths of Felipa Poot," *Hispanic American Historical Review* 82, no. 4 (November 2002): 645–684; and Nélida Flores Arellano and América Inces Román, *Doña María de la O, una mujer ejemplar* (Mexico City: Universidad Autónoma de Guerrero and Centro de Estudios Históricos del Agrarismo en México, 1992).

22. Carolina Maria de Jesus, *Child of the Dark: The Diary of Carolina Maria de Jesus,*

trans. David St. Clair (New York: Dutton, 1962); Carolina Maria de Jesus, *The Unedited Diaries of Carolina Maria de Jesus*, trans. Nancy P. S. Naro and Cristina Mehrtens (New Brunswick, N.J.: Rutgers University Press, 1999); Rosa Isolde Reuque Paillalef, *When a Flower Is Reborn: The Life and Times of a Mapuche Feminist*, trans., ed., and with an introduction by Florencia Mallon (Durham, N.C.: Duke University Press, 2002); Medea Benjamin and Maisa Mendonça, *Benedita da Silva: An Afro-Brazilian Woman's Story of Politics* (Monroe, Ore.: Food First Books, 1997); and Domitila Barrios de Chungara, *Let Me Speak! Testimony of Domitila, a Woman of the Bolivian Mines* (New York: Monthly Review Press, 1978).

23. See John J. Johnson, "One Hundred Years of Historical Writing on Modern Latin America by United States Historians," *Hispanic American Historical Review* 65 (1985): 747–749.

24. Eric Van Young, "Recent Anglophone Scholarship on Mexico and Central America in the Age of Revolution (1750–1850)," *Hispanic American Historical Review* 64 (1985): 733–734. Examples include John Lynch, *Argentine Dictator: Juan Manuel de Rosas, 1829–1852* (New York: Oxford University Press, 1981); Paul Friedrich, *Agrarian Revolt in a Mexican Village* (Englewood Cliffs, N.J.: Prentice Hall, 1970); Brian McBeth, *Juan Vicente Gómez and the Oil Companies in Venezuela, 1908–1935* (New York: Cambridge University Press, 1983); Linda Hall, *Alvaro Obregón: Power and Revolution in Mexico, 1911–1920* (College Station: Texas A&M University Press, 1981); and Fernando Díaz y Díaz, *Caudillos y Caciques: Antonio López de Santa Anna y Juan Álvarez* (Mexico City: El Colegio de México, 1972).

25. Michael Conniff, ed., *Latin American Populism in Comparative Perspective* (Albuquerque: University of New Mexico Press, 1982); and Michael Conniff, ed., *Populism in Latin America* (Tuscaloosa: University of Alabama Press, 1999).

26. David Brading, ed., *Caudillo and Peasant in the Mexican Revolution* (Cambridge: Cambridge University Press, 1980).

27. This development can be seen in some of the attention to nonelite women noted above, as well as in works such as William H. Beezley and Judith Ewell, eds., *The Human Tradition in Modern Latin America* (Wilmington, Del.: Scholarly Resources, 1997), and Judith Adler Hellman, *Mexican Lives* (New York: New Press, 1994).

28. Charles A. Weeks, *The Juárez Myth in Mexico* (Tuscaloosa: University of Alabama Press, 1987).

29. Ilene V. O'Malley, *The Myth of the Revolution: Hero Cults and the Institutionalization of the Mexican State, 1920–1940* (New York: Greenwood Press, 1986). Another book that touches on similar themes, though without addressing individuals as directly, is Thomas Benjamin, *La Revolución: Mexico's Great Revolution as Memory, Myth, and History* (Austin: University of Texas Press, 2000).

30. Mariano Plotkin, *Mañana es San Perón: A Cultural History of Perón's Argentina*, trans. Keith Zahniser (Wilmington, Del.: Scholarly Resources, 2002).

31. Robin Derby, "The Dictator's Seduction: Gender and State Spectacle during the Trujillo Regime," in *Latin American Popular Culture*, ed. William H. Beezley and Linda Curcio-Nagy (Wilmington, Del.: Scholarly Resources, 2000), 213–240.

32. John Charles Chasteen, *Heroes on Horseback: A Life and Times of the Last Gaucho Caudillos* (Albuquerque: University of New Mexico Press, 1995); and Ariel de la Fuente, *Children of Facundo: Caudillo and Gaucho Insurgency During the Argentine State Formation Process (La Rioja, 1853–1870)* (Durham, N.C.: Duke University Press, 2000). The point about charisma being relational is made in Madsen and Snow, *The Charismatic Bond*.

33. David Thelen, "Popular Uses of History in the United States: Individuals in History," *Perspectives* (American Historical Association newsletter) 38, no. 5 (May 2000): 22–25.

34. Katherine Verdery, *The Political Lives of Dead Bodies: Reburial and Postsocialist Change* (New York: Columbia University Press, 1999), 26.

35. John Keegan, *The Masks of Command* (New York: Penguin Books, 1988).

36. Clifford Geertz, "Centers, Kings, and Charisma: Reflections on the Symbolics of Power," in *Rites of Power: Symbolism, Ritual, and Politics Since the Middle Ages*, ed. Sean Wilentz (Philadelphia: University of Pennsylvania Press, 1985), 31.

1

Simón Bolívar

Man and Myth

JOHN CHASTEEN

Who is tall as the cedar and strong as a rock
to resist, dominate, and calm the storm?

From *Description of the Funerary Honors
of the Liberator Simón Bolívar*, 1842

Metaphors in praise of Simón Bolívar proliferate, and sometimes lurch out of control, but perhaps that is not odd. This most celebrated Spanish American hero on horseback is the very epitome of rhetorical heroes, patterned explicitly, in the eyes of many contemporaries, on Napoleon. In 1842, when the ashes of Bolívar were repatriated to Venezuela, "all Caracas" turned out to see the funeral pomp of the fallen Venezuelan hero—no longer, alas, in the words of the published *Description of the Funerary Honors of the Liberator Simón Bolívar*, "strong as a Lion, swift as an Eagle." Caracas had been Bolívar's hometown, where he had been alternately loved and hated during his life. Even in Caracas, where "the sacred urn of the ashes of Bolívar" was reburied, his life already a decade over, Bolívar the man had begun to disappear behind Bolívar the myth. The description of the funerary honors mentions a milling crowd of "rich and poor" who "rushed forward to gaze at the tomb, and with fervor gathered loose earth from it to keep as a relic." Meanwhile, the air hung heavy with oratory. Bolívar was remembered as the Liberator, whose image "called forth valor, wisdom, and the heroic defense of liberty," the maker of independence, who "magically attracted the astonished multitude to follow." The orators made Bolívar, above all, an example to his countrymen. "Surrounded with glory, power, and majesty," the Bolívar of their vision "inspired beauty, nobility, and grandeur." He moved "the hidden fibers of the heart" and also "explored the highest regions of intelligence." He was an "immortal genius on a celestial mission."[1]

And so it was, but only in retrospect. Such rhetorical tributes to the Liberator exemplify the "great man" theory of history, intellectually fashionable in 1842, that attributed overwhelming significance to individual leadership. Leaders such as Bolívar and Napoleon were believed to alter the course of history thanks to their individual genius and force of character. The great man idea remained influential through the rest of the nineteenth century and into the twentieth. It is understandable, therefore, that a figure like the Liberator became viewed as the greatest of men, an example constantly held up for inspiration and imitation, and even the center of an official, state-sponsored civic cult with pronounced religious resonances. During the years 1850–1950, this civic cult of the Liberator developed not only in Venezuela but also in Colombia, Ecuador, Peru, and Bolivia, the five countries in which Bolívar's armies had overthrown Spanish colonial rule. Library shelves groan with the weight of the Bolivarian bibliography produced in those years.[2]

In all five countries, Bolívar is a national independence hero, a "founding father" (to put it in U.S. terms) like George Washington, whom today we tend to remember as the first U.S. president but who was also, of course, the winning general of U.S. independence. Like George Washington, founding fathers everywhere have become the center of state-sponsored great man cults. In an important way, great men were replacements for the hereditary monarchs ousted by republican revolutions, such as Spanish America's wars of independence. The difference was that monarchs had gained their legitimacy from their dynastic bloodlines. Monarchs did not have to be great.[3] Leaders like Bolívar or Washington, on the other hand, supposedly earned their leadership status through "glory." Their glory had to be constructed in people's minds through stories and images. Together, such stories and images may be said to constitute a powerful hero myth, something essential to understanding figures like Bolívar or Washington.[4] This chapter introduces readers to both the man and the myth. First, the real person named Simón Bolívar (his entire given name was actually Simón José Antonio de la Santísima Trinidad), who was born in Caracas in 1783.

Never was anyone more truly born with a silver spoon in his mouth. In the 1500s, an *encomienda*—an early grant of indigenous labor, commonly believed to be a taproot of Latin America's age-old pattern of social inequality—also became the root of the Bolívar family fortune. That fortune later expanded into mines and plantations worked by African slaves.

In general, plantation slavery provided the wealth for the entire elite class of Caracas, the haughty and opulent "Mantuanos" (in reference to their elegant apparel), to which the Bolívar family belonged. In fact, the infant Simón Bolívar received several plantations with slaves as baptismal gifts in 1784. The Bolívar family did not have an aristocratic title, but during Simón's childhood they were trying to buy one. Given the Bolívar family's affluence and the Spanish Crown's indebtedness, it was not an unreasonable goal.[5]

Although Simón Bolívar lost both parents by the age of nine, a blow that could have sunk a child not so buoyed up by wealth and privilege, he quickly became a headstrong boy who challenged the authority of his guardians. He was only sixteen years old in 1799 when he sailed to Europe for the first time. On the way his ship stopped in Mexico, where the rich and assertive young Mantuano made a courtesy call at the viceroy's palace. In Madrid, Simón went to live with a relative well connected at the Spanish royal court, and he may have socialized a bit with young Prince Fernando, his future adversary. There is even a story, recounted by Bolívar himself in later years, that he knocked Prince Fernando's hat off while playing a game, then refused to apologize.[6] There is no evidence to corroborate the story, but the free-spending young Simón Bolívar of 1800 did move in Madrid's most exclusive social circles.[7] Few descriptions of Bolívar from this time on fail to mention his delight in the company of women and his enthusiasm for dancing, two passions that lasted his entire life. In 1803, on another European tip, Bolívar made an extensive walking tour of France and Italy in the company of his tutor, and when in Rome, they supposedly called on the Pope. Again, the evidence, Bolívar's later story about refusing to kiss the cross on the Pope's sandal, sounds suspiciously self-promoting, but it could have happened.[8] The story told more often about Bolívar's Rome trip, his swearing on his knees to make Venezuela independent, is corroborated by letters exchanged with his tutor in later years.[9]

Simón Bolívar returned from Europe as the most sophisticated and self-confident of the young Mantuanos, conversant with the new political philosophies of the French Revolution and a first-hand witness to the rise of Napoleon.[10] Like Napoleon, he was a small man and also a skilled horseman who, unlike Napoleon, involved himself in the actual fighting of his battles. General José Antonio Páez, another of Latin America's most famous *caudillos* (generals on horseback), a man of humble background and Bolívar's strong right arm during crucial campaigns in the wars of independence, later wrote of the Mantuano leader, "He liked combat, maybe even a little too much, and he remained quite calm through it all. When his soldiers seemed ready to turn and run, he freely used his voice, his example, and his sword to dissuade them."[11] No one, not even Bolívar's enemies, called him greedy for money (which he disregarded as only silver-spoon people can do), but few could doubt his thirst for glory. The sad, dying Bolívar of 1830—emaciated by tuberculosis, facing exile, and fearing that he had "plowed the sea," as he watched the republics he had created fall apart—cared much what history would think of him.

In strictly military terms, history had little reason to be impressed. Bolívar was not a notable battlefield commander or a great strategist. His only important military command during the first Venezuelan republic was the 1812 disaster at Puerto Cabello, from which only he and a handful of his officers escaped.[12] His next military campaign, the 1813–1814 "War to the Death" against the Spanish reoccupation of Caracas, did succeed, but only at the cost of tremendous bloodshed. In effect, Bolívar made the war against Spain into a war against Venezuela's tiny but powerful Spanish minority. Mass executions became common on both sides. This campaign created a second Venezuelan republic, which Bolívar ruled as a wartime dictator. But the second Venezuelan republic did not last much longer than the first and ended badly when a fearsome force of plainsmen called *llaneros* decided that they preferred a Spanish king to the dictatorship of a republican Mantuano. In 1815, Bolívar escaped from Venezuela a second time with a few followers and spent more than a year in exile in New Granada (modern Colombia), Jamaica, and Haiti.[13]

In 1816, he returned to Venezuela, this time to a remote eastern region populated by many people of African descent, the region where resistance to Spanish control was most tenacious. Joining forces with these eastern patriot guerrillas (though his forces, at this point, were only himself and his ego), Bolívar led an ill-advised amphibious assault on Ocumare, in central Venezuela, an assault that failed in eight days. Bolívar managed to escape, leaving much of his hapless army and precious munitions abandoned on the beach. He returned via a circuitous route to Haiti, where he spent several more months in exile. Then the eastern patriot guerrillas, notable among them a black general named Manuel Piar, invited the humiliated Mantuano leader back once more.[14]

The years 1817–1819 saw Bolívar's great triumph, but the campaign owed little to his gifts as a military strategist. Piar was already leading patriot guerrillas into the eastern Orinoco plains, home of the llaneros, and Bolívar, too, finally embraced this strategy of using the Orinoco river for access to outside support and building strength on the Orinoco plains away from Caracas. Gathering llanero forces and learning to navigate the difficult environment of the Orinoco plains, which flood widely during part of every year, Bolívar established his capital at the small river port of Angostura and called a "congress" to confer institutional legitimacy on his military action. He then made a move so daring it verged on foolishness: he marched his army hundreds of miles west across the Orinoco plains, all the way out of Venezuela, toward Bogotá, capital of Spanish-controlled New Granada, *during flood season*, fording dozens of swollen rivers, sometimes walking for long periods through waist-high water. Emerging half-naked from the water (llaneros wore only light clothing at best—sandals instead of boots, for example), the army climbed into Andean heights so frigid that many troops died of exposure. But when they reached the high plateau at the rear approach to Bogotá, they took the Spanish so utterly by surprise that victory followed easily, and three days later, Bolívar's army occupied the viceregal capital. Piar, executed for insubordination to Bolívar months before, did not live to see the victory he had helped make possible.[15]

Here is a substantial stain on Bolívar's record. The execution of one's own generals is a highly unusual procedure. Why Piar? Piar had disobeyed Bolívar, but he had never betrayed the patriot cause. Therefore, Bolívar's fear of a rival comes irresistibly to mind. In addition, Piar's color made him both vulnerable and threatening to a Mantuano like Bolívar. Pardos constituted the bulk of Bolívar's manpower, and Piar was executed for a "treachery" that came down to accusing Bolívar of color discrimination. The harsh treatment of Piar stands in marked contrast to Bolívar's preference for British officers who joined the Orinoco campaign as mercenaries and whose occasional insubordination he pardoned easily enough. Few historians justify the execution of General Manuel Piar.[16] The execution raises the matter of Bolívar's views on race and society, to which we will turn after concluding a brief overview of his military career.

After the capture of Bogotá in August 1819, Bolívar's new resources and momentum enabled him to consolidate his control of New Granada, then retake Caracas in 1821. His protégé, General Antonio José de Sucre, captured Quito in 1822, putting Ecuador in patriot hands. The Ecuadorian port of Guayaquil now became the scene of a famous meeting between the greatest of Spanish America's independence-era heroes on horseback—Bolívar, on the one hand, and San Martín, liberator of Argentina and Chile, on the other. Like Bolívar, General José de San Martín had lived many years in Europe. Like Bolívar, San Martín had marched an army across Andean heights to make a decisive surprise attack against the forces of Spanish king Fernando VII—in San Martín's case, the march was from Argentina to Spanish-controlled Chile. Then, from Chile, San Martín took his army north to the last holdout of Spanish power in South America, Peru. Peru's capital, Lima, fell to San Martín's army in 1821, and the Peruvian viceroy fled to the old seat of Inca power in the high Andes. The

Andean campaign would be the last of the wars of independence, but it would not be an easy one.[17]

When Bolívar and San Martín met to discuss that campaign in 1822, they seemed unable to work together. Conflicting accounts of the meeting exist, but the outcome is beyond doubt. San Martín withdrew, and turned over leadership of the Andean campaign to Bolívar. Bolívar spent most of the next few years in Lima, reigning politically and socially as the Liberator. Sucre, not Bolívar, led the patriot army in the decisive final battle of Ayacucho where the last Spanish viceroy was captured in 1824. Bolivia bears Bolívar's name, but it was Sucre who first decreed the country's independence in 1825. Bolívar wrote a constitution for the newly independent Bolivian republic, but it did not last. Nor did Bolívar's constitution last long in Peru, which accepted it under pressure in 1826. Colombia, where Bolívar returned in 1827, also resisted his constitution, and the resistance became ugly. He barely escaped an assassination attempt, leaping from a window on a cold night in Bogotá to hide for several hours in the icy water underneath a bridge. Thereafter his physical and political decline accelerated, and he was on his way to forced exile in 1830 when he died on the Colombian coast, prevented from returning to Caracas by a decree of the Venezuelan government.[18]

Bolívar's post-1830 hero myth therefore represents the posthumous comeback of a reputation that was at a low ebb when he died. How did this comeback occur? And how did Bolívar become the mythic Liberator in the first place, if his gifts as a military commander were not great?

Understanding the trajectory of Bolívar's reputation requires some knowledge of hero myths. Hero myths are stories about individual people who come to be regarded as embodiments of something transcendental. To say the stories are mythic in this sense is not to say they are untrue, only that they take on meanings that transcend the literal truth of the story. Some myths, of course, are completely made up. Most, however, have some basis in fact. The myth-making then resides in how the story is used and how it is received.[19] There is a range of possibilities that will become clear as we go along. So let us begin. What was heroic about Bolívar?

Sometimes heroes have a vision that brings their followers' own aspirations into focus. Bolívar's wide reading and travels gave him a vision of Latin American independence well before 1810, when that vision was still uncommon, and he never wavered. He was willing to sacrifice anything for that vision—anything except his own central position in it, as his execution of Manuel Piar and his inability to work with San Martín both demonstrate. Moreover, Sucre would have been the official liberator of Bolivia had Bolívar not delayed in confirming Sucre's decree of Bolivian independence until Bolívar could travel from Lima to take the credit himself. But if Bolívar's jealousy of Sucre showed on more than one occasion, the dying Liberator still thought Sucre was the best leader for the independent "Bolivarian" republics after he was gone. Sucre's assassination in July 1830 contributed greatly to the dying leader's despondency.[20]

Bolívar's early and unwavering vision of Latin American independence is certainly crucial to his heroic status, but it had limitations. The Liberator's vision definitely brought no democratic aspirations into focus, for example, as one can see in the constitution that he authored and promoted so insistently. The Liberator's constitution was a main cause of his loss of popularity in the new republics, and for good reason. It was an authoritarian document that instituted a president for life with almost monarchical powers and gave no significant role at all to popular elections. The Liberator might evoke fervent shows of support among black and indigenous people who embraced independence, but his ideas on race were completely unenlightened. To an English visitor in March 1825 he said, "Of all lands, South America is perhaps least suited to the republican form of government, because the population consists of Indians and Negroes who are even more ignorant than the Spanish from whom we have liberated ourselves."[21] This did not make Bolívar more racist than others in his position, of course, only equally and unheroically so. If Haitian hospitality and aid inspired him to free slaves in Venezuela, he freed them only into the ranks of his army. And he argued at one point that freeing slaves to join the patriot ranks was beneficial partly because their deaths on the battlefield would reduce the black population.[22] Yet Bolívar once reportedly jumped off his horse during a parade to embrace the slave woman Hipólita, who had breast-fed him and whom he always called "mother," carefully providing for her welfare all her life. His ideas on race were those of a Mantuano who tussled with slave playmates as a child and then finished his education in Europe around 1800. That is, he grew up with racial hierarchies, saw them confirmed in Enlightenment writings, and never questioned them. Ironically, though, Bolívar's family tree contained a great grandmother who was of humble status and, it seems probable, partly of African descent.[23]

Bolívar's unwavering vision of independence also included the ideal of Spanish American unity, perhaps the most salient meaning of Bolívar's heroic image today. Mistrusting the expansionist penchant of the United States (as well as the recolonizing threat of Europe's reactionary monarchist Holy Alliance) Bolívar called a not-very-well-attended diplomatic meeting, the 1826 Congress of Panama, which failed to form the hemispheric federation he proposed. Most people's political imaginations were already taxed by the creation of new nations, it seems, without the additional creation of supranational federations. Bolívar's subsequent attempt to form a more limited Federation of the Andes, with himself as lifetime president, also attracted little support. Indeed, the trend in the 1830s and 1840s was in the other direction, toward further political fragmentation. Many years after Bolívar's death, however, in 1898, the ideal of Spanish American unity and brotherhood reemerged in response to the U.S. occupation of Cuba. During the 1900s, that ideal became the most celebrated part of the Bolivarian vision. Late-twentieth-century presidents of Venezuela, Colombia, Ecuador, Peru, and Bolivia invoked this Bolivarian vision in speech after speech when gathering to create an Andean Pact trading zone. Meanwhile, the leftist guerrillas of the region cooperated, at least rhetorically, in a Bolivarian alliance.

Thus, the hero myth of Simón Bolívar evolved significantly in the twentieth century. In the 1820s, Bolívar's vision of Spanish American unity had seemed above all to express his own towering ambitions. But people who invoked Bolivarian unity in the twentieth century preferred to forget that, and to forget, too, that he had once proposed making all Latin America a protectorate of Great Britain. They recalled his vision of Spanish American solidarity and made it mean more than it had in Bolívar's time.[24] There are several factors at work here. If heroes make believers by what they do, believers also make heroes by what they believe. Crafted and recrafted in a process of selective remembrance, hero myths respond to people's changing psychological needs. In addition, members of the educated elite manipulate hero myths for political ends. Let us first consider how Bolívar inspired followers, then how his followers (and subsequently writers, politicians, and schoolteachers) embroidered the Bolivarian myth.

Bolívar contributed actively to the creation of his myth. His greatest skill as a leader, in fact, was his ability to project his own heroic image, to which he was tirelessly attentive. He considered the public impact of every action and did many things primarily for effect. For example, he may never have expected his unity initiatives to succeed, saying at one point, "I called the Congress of Panama in order to create a sensation. It was my ambition to bring the names of Colombia and the other South American republics to the attention of the whole world."[25] There are countless other examples of Bolívar's conscious manipulation of his image. Personal descriptions of him always emphasize his social graces and his tremendous nervous energy. Most of that energy went into his relationships with other people, near and far, individually and collectively. His train of famous love affairs can be understood at least partly in the context of his overall vocation as a charmer.[26] Not much of a drinker, he nevertheless adored parties and had the habit of filling the glasses of those seated by him and offering many eloquent toasts, sometimes standing on a chair to do so. Bolívar was also a master of long-distance personal relations. Pacing back and forth with his arms crossed, he listened to and dictated letters by the thousand, year after year, until his correspondence filled dozens of thick volumes. Sometimes he dictated several letters at once because his dictation was faster than his secretaries' writing. His letters explained, inspired, cajoled, flattered, admonished, and exhorted.[27] Very frequently, they bent the facts. He well understood how to confuse the enemy with misinformation, and he could never resist the desire to improve on the truth in matters pertaining to his own image. The stories he told about himself not kissing the Pope's sandal or knocking off Prince Fernando's hat are typical of the way he elaborated his own myth. He was likewise eager to link himself symbolically with Napoleon, but Napoleon had finally become the most famous tyrant of the age, so the matter was sensitive. Bolívar at one point said explicitly that he avoided the comparison for that reason. Nonetheless, he claimed to have seen Napoleon crowned emperor at Notre Dame in 1804, even though his tutor wrote that neither he nor the young Bolívar had left their Paris hotel that day. For mythic purposes, how could the Liberator of South America be in Paris during Napoleon's coronation without seeing it?[28]

Bolívar was keenly attuned to political spectacle. He was never so happy as when crowned with laurels and pulled through the streets of Caracas in a Roman-style triumphal chariot by a dozen daughters of the city's patrician families after his successful campaign of 1813.[29] Bolívar's own associates in the second Venezuelan republic soon accused him of organizing "an assembly or, in other and better words, a theatrical presentation" where he planted orators to call "spontaneously" for a Bolivarian dictatorship.[30] The orchestration of political theater was Bolívar's strong suit. Political meetings were opportunities for his stirring oratory and grand gestures. A biographer of the 1930s describes the following scene at Angostura, where Bolívar called a congress and sought support for the decisive Orinoco campaign of 1818:

> At a long table a banquet was served to all the officers, civilian officials, and their ladies. After toasts were drunk and while dessert was being served, the Liberator was called upon to speak. He was brilliantly dressed for the occasion in a uniform which had been sent him as a sample by a merchant in Trinidad. From his place at the head of the table, he made a typically fiery and eloquent speech. Then, when he had brought his audience to a high pitch of excitement, he suddenly jumped upon the table, and oblivious of the wine bottles and flowers and crystal that crashed under his great boots, he strode the length of the board. "Thus," he cried, "as I cross this table

from one end to the other, I shall march from the Atlantic to the Pacific, from Panamá to Cape Horn, until the last Spaniard is expelled!" Then, turning, he strode back. "And thus," he shouted, "I shall return, without having done harm to a single soul save those who oppose the completion of my sacred mission."[31]

The Liberator's great Colombian political adversary of later years, Francisco de Paula Santander, who opposed Bolívar's constitutional ideas, proclaimed openly that Bolívar should be barred from the 1828 National Assembly because he was simply too persuasive: "His influence and the secret power of his will are such that I, myself, have been amazed a thousand times. No one can contradict General Bolívar face to face."[32] Simon Bolívar was both a man of action and a man of words. Furthermore, some of his most famous actions were gestures—that is, signs that sent a message to be observed and recounted. Two anecdotes, from Venezuela and Peru, illustrate his extraordinary ability to turn events into political coin.

When two valiant patriot officers from New Granada died heroically during the desperate fighting in Venezuela, Bolívar promoted their heroism to win further support in New Granada. One of the young heroes was Antonio Ricaurte, who became a martyr by blowing himself up to prevent patriot powder stores from falling into Spanish hands. Ricaurte's self-sacrifice, "flying into atoms," got him into his country's national anthem, but Bolívar later said that he had made up the story of Ricaurte's martyrdom "to frighten the enemy and create a lofty impression of the soldiers of New Granada." Ricaurte had been shot and lanced, he explained.[33] The other New Granadan hero was Atanasio Girardot, killed while raising the republican banner over an enemy position. Bolívar sent Girardot's body back to New Granada but took his heart to Caracas, where a procession of flaming torches conveyed it to the cathedral for burial in a golden urn. "His memory will live in the hearts of all Americans," wrote Bolívar to the boy's father.[34]

Bolívar made Ricaurte and Girardot into martyrs to promote a feeling of American solidarity, rhetorically uniting all people born in the New World—white, black, and indigenous, and anywhere in between—in the patriot cause. These were gestures of the 1813–1814 War to the Death, a period when Bolívar ordered many executions of Spanish prisoners—the most efficacious gesture of all. Bolívar spared Americans (even those captured on the Spanish side) and executed Spaniards as a matter of policy, to draw a line in blood between all Americans and all Spaniards in people's minds. Atrocities were committed on both sides, it must be said, and some of Bolívar's executions were paybacks. But etching the Spanish/American divide deeply was a prerequisite for independence, and Bolívar's well-publicized policy of leniency for Americans and no mercy for Spaniards created that divide.[35]

The situation was quite different ten years later in Peru when one of Bolívar's officers violated the honor of an upper-class Spaniard's daughter by entering her chamber at night. The young woman's royalist mother discovered them and killed the offending patriot officer. It was 1824, the last year of fighting, and Bolívar's reaction was pure politics. He praised the "worthy matron" for defending her family's honor, and he publicly reprimanded the officer's battalion, one of his best. With the Spanish on the run, a bloody line between friend and foe was no longer advantageous, so Bolívar's gestures defined him now not as the implacable insurgent but as the magnanimous victor. It must be remembered, too, that most of Bolívar's soldiers were Venezuelans and Colombians—outsiders, viewed with some suspicion in Peru—extra reason to display military discipline there. So the dead patriot officer's sword was broken over his grave in a standard military ritual of humiliation. "Long live the Liberator!" shouted the formerly royalist matron—or so the story was remembered and told in later years.[36] Finally, there could be no clearer example of sending a message than Bolívar's rejection of an imperial crown during his last days in Peru. When the crown was offered him (according to a Cartagena newspaper many years later) Bolívar staged a grand gesture of what made him different from Napoleon, placing the crown under the door of the coach that would carry him from Lima and stepping on the jewel-encrusted object as he climbed in.[37]

Now for the other angle, the way that believers make heroes. Evidence of people's need to believe in a heroic liberator is clear in many stories. Each town in the path of Bolívar's armies conserved its own obscure anecdote about the Liberator's acts there. Often, the stories show a person of heroic proportions that exceed probability or even credibility, clearly revealing the storyteller's will to believe in a hero. Could this Mantuano aristocrat really "shoe a horse like the best blacksmith or cut a suit of clothes like the finest tailor," as the stories said?[38] It seems highly unlikely, but the storytellers wanted their hero to be good at everything, the exemplary person. At the moment of Bolívar's christening, did the priest suddenly change the child's intended name? According to one story, they had wanted to name him Pedro José Bolívar.

—Do not call him Pedro José, said the priest, because I have given him another name. You shall call him Simón.
—And why that change?

Figure 1.1. Anonymous portrait of Bolívar, Quito school, c. 1825. Local painters who had never actually seen Bolívar copied well-known portraits of him to meet the popular demand for the Liberator's image in the 1820s. Ecuador, Ministerio de Gobierno.

—I cannot explain why, but I have heard a voice inside, no doubt an inspiration from on high, saying that this child will one day be the Simon Macabee of America.[39]

It seems improbable, to put it mildly, that this really occurred—that the Liberator was named after the biblical "revolutionary" Simon Macabee, who led a Hebrew resistance to Roman imperial domination. After all, Bolívar's own ancestor, the first to settle in Caracas, had been named Simón de Bolívar. Rather, the story of the priestly vision seems a clear case of "heroic foreshadowing"—the well-known tendency, present in almost all hero myths, to provide a supernatural announcement of the hero's destiny at the moment of birth.

In a third example, did Bolívar pursue and mesmerize the daughter of a high Spanish official, the lovely Aurora Pardo, during a dance in Lima? This seems less incredible. There are many stories about Bolívar's adventures with women. But the truth of the anecdote is not the point. Supposedly Aurora did not recognize Bolívar and asked his name only after the dance had begun:

—Simón Bolívar, your servant, obedient to your slightest caprice . . . Aurora.

A slight shudder passed through her body, and she reflexively tried to pull away from Bolívar, who kept her pressed gently to his chest. Aurora fixed her wide, beautiful eyes on the Liberator's in surprise. Their looks met like arrows colliding in infinite sweetness. Aurora lowered her eyes then and said softly:

—Long live Spain! But if you are the Liberator, then long live Glory, too![40]

Manuela Sáenz, the Ecuadorian woman who abandoned her English merchant husband to follow Bolívar, seems to have been struck in similar fashion by an amorous Bolivarian thunderbolt. Naturally, "Manuelita" became the object of tremendous scandal, but retrospective accounts present her as Bolívar's worthy partner and a heroine in her own right, lingering on her boldness and savvy, and particularly on the way that she confronted the Liberator's would-be assassins and gave him time to escape on that cold night in Bogotá, close to the end of his life.[41]

Among the virtues consistently attributed to Bolívar in these stories is his generosity to followers, a trait confirmed by all the evidence. Generosity to followers is a cardinal virtue in societies where patronage plays a central role. Bolívar emerges here as a lenient landowner, canceling the debts of his plantation workers, and a military patriarch, using his own salary to provide for patriot widows and orphans.[42] He is a commander deserving the loyalty of brave men. In one representative story that began circulating in 1883, the much celebrated centenary of the Liberator's birth, a soldier is caught slaughtering a cow against orders. Bolívar calls the soldier before him and asks, "Are you not aware that I have prohibited, on pain of flogging, that anyone kill cows?" "Sir," replies the soldier, "I was so hungry I could not contain myself." An officer standing nearby informs Bolívar that this soldier is among the bravest in the patriot army. "Give him another cow," decides Bolívar.[43] In another centennial story, one of Bolívar's sergeants is caught leaving the barracks without permission, but for a laudable reason: to escort a young woman to her father's deathbed. Compelled to uphold military discipline Bolívar calls for the sergeant's execution, but then, dressed incognito, he arranges for the firing squad to fire blanks. The sergeant pretends to fall dead, and Bolívar arranges his escape with the young woman.[44] Perhaps the most frequent anecdotes about Bolívar's generosity to followers involve his shirts. For example, noticing that one of his British mercenaries buttoned his uniform jacket to the throat, Bolívar guessed the cause: "Colonel Rook, you have no shirt!" Bolívar instructed his orderly to give one of his own shirts to Rook. "That's impossible, Your Excellency. You have only one shirt left," came the reply. "Then give him that one," Bolívar insisted. "That's impossible, sir. You have it on."[45]

What, then, is the final balance sheet of our accounting? How did Bolívar become Spanish America's most celebrated great man? For starters, the Mantuano leader possessed a lot of cultural capital, beginning his career at the summit of colonial society, as a traveled and cultured young aristocrat of immense wealth, on speaking terms with viceroys. In this respect, from the class-conscious perspective of the time, Bolívar seemed born to lead. Second, he was driven by an insatiable desire for the glory that defined a great man. Perhaps no other personal quality is so remarkable as the sheer tenacity of his ambition during his relentless, twenty-year struggle from 1810 to 1830. Third, Bolívar was a true master of political communications. He could inspire or intimidate, clarify or obfuscate, with equal facility. (No wonder metaphors and anecdotes and gestures swirl so breathlessly around him. They were always his natural medium.) Finally, and perhaps most important, Bolívar became a hero because generations of Spanish Americans needed one—or rather, as many as they could get—to fill the void left by the ouster of the Spanish monarchy from America. In the years after his death, he became the center of both fervent popular devotion and official hero cults.

Figure 1.2. Bogotá, Palace of San Carlos. Many years after his death, statues of Bolívar (many, like this one, clad in Roman togas) were erected in town squares (often renamed the Plaza de Bolívar) throughout Colombia.

Already by 1877, when a Venezuelan author began to publish his multivolume *Biographies of Notable Spanish Americans*, he pronounced Bolívar too great to enter it, too important to stand alongside anyone else.[46] In the 1990s, saintlike figurines of the Liberator appeared in popular Venezuelan religious devotions, and Venezuelan president Hugo Chávez made his country officially a "Bolivarian republic." Colombia, with its countless Plazas de Bolívar in virtually any city or town, is the second most devoted to the hero. In Ecuador, Peru, and Bolivia (despite its name), Bolívar has always been seen somewhat as an outsider. Even so, these countries' contributions to Bolivarian iconography and bibliography are substantial. Bolívar may have died fearing that he had "plowed the sea." In the end, though, history has remembered Simón Bolívar as a great man. He would have found that no small consolation.

Notes

1. Fermín Toro, "Descripción de los honores funebres consagrados a los restos del Libertador Simón Bolívar en cumplimiento del decreto legislativo de 30 de abril de 1842. Hecha por orden del gobierno por Fermín Toro," reprinted in Fermín Toro, *La doctrina conservadora, Fermín Toro* (Caracas: Pensamiento Político Venezolano del Siglo XIX, 1960), 321–355 passim.

2. Simón Aljure Chalela, *Bibliografía Bolivariana* (Bogota: Banco de la República/Biblioteca Luis Angel Arango, 1983), for example, offers many thousands of titles in poetry and prose.

3. The "great man" theory of history is associated most especially with influential lectures given by Thomas Carlyle in 1840. Although Carlyle's Lecture VI is titled "The Hero as King," he argues that only a natural great man, the wisest, fittest, and most able, deserves kingship. Those who inherit kingship are merely *"called* Kings." *The Works of Thomas Carlyle in Thirty Volumes*, vol. 5, *On Heroes, Hero-Worship, and the Heroic in History* (New York: AMS Press, 1969), 199.

4. For the case of George Washington's hero myth, see Daniel J. Boorstin, *The Americans: The National Experience* (New York: Random House, 1965). Spanish America is full of similar myths associated with heroes-of-independence-cum-founding-fathers called *próceres*. The political careers of many such heroes continued into the first years of independence and set an enduring pattern of political leadership. Caudillos—generals on horseback—became a commonplace of nineteenth-century history throughout Spanish America. See John Lynch, *Caudillos in Spanish America, 1800–1850* (Oxford: Clarendon Press, 1992).

5. Salvador de Madariaga, *Bolívar*, 2 vols. (Mexico City: Editorial Hermes, 1951), 1:64–67. Madariaga's two-volume work is unusually critical and therefore valuable. Patriotic praise dominates most biographical writing on Bolívar.

6. The story as told by Bolívar many years later, then reported, years later again, in the memoirs of one of his generals, the caudillo Tomás Cipriano de Mosquera, *Memorias sobre la vida del General Simón Bolívar* (Caracas, 1983).

7. A close associate of Bolívar's uncle, with whom the boy lived during part of the

time in Madrid, was even, for a time, whispered to be the queen's lover. Madariaga, *Bolívar*, 117.

8. The story was told by Bolívar more than ten years later, as recalled by his Irish secretary. Daniel Florencio O'Leary, *Memorias del General Daniel Florencio O'Leary, Narración*, trans. and ed. Robert F. McNerney, Jr. *Bolívar and the War of Independence*, Texas Pan American Series (Austin: University of Texas Press, 1970), 1:23.

9. Madariaga, *Bolívar*, 154.

10. There is conflicting evidence about whether or not he saw Napoleon famously crown himself emperor. Bolívar described seeing the coronation in later years, and he was definitely in Paris at the time, but Bolívar's tutor Simon Rodriguez wrote that, in a spirit of republican protest, neither he nor his student attended Napoleon's coronation.

11. José Antonio Paez, *Autobiografía del General José Antonio Paez* (New York, 1867): 1:139.

12. Gerhard Masur, *Simón Bolívar*, rev. ed. (Albuquerque: University of New Mexico Press, 1969), 101–102. Bolívar's summary execution in later years of the man responsible for this catastrophe gives a good indication of how deeply the disgrace stung him.

13. This is an extremely compressed account of five years that most biographies narrate in several hundred pages. See, for example, Tomás Polanco Alcántara, *Simón Bolívar: Ensayo de interpretación biográfica a través de sus documentos* (Caracas: Academia Nacional de la Historia, 1994), 237–536; and Indalecio Liévano Aguirre, *Bolívar* (Botogá: Oveja Negra, 1979), 59–213.

14. The most accessible summary in English, though not a scholarly one, is Thomas Rourke, *Man of Glory: Simón Bolívar* (New York: William Morrow, 1939).

15. This decisive campaign is among the most fully, frequently, and enthusiastically narrated parts of the story; a good example is Rourke, *Man of Glory*, 208–227. The same spirit moves more scholarly versions by Colombian Liévano Aguirre (*Bolívar*, 215–226) or Venezuelan Polanco Alcántara (*Simón Bolívar: Ensayo de interpretación biográfica*, 541–565). For a more comprehensive view, see Rebecca A. Earle, *Spain and the Independence of Colombia 1810–1825* (Exeter: University of Exeter Press, 2000).

16. Piar's fate is emphasized here far more than in most accounts, however.

17. José de San Martín remains, in death as in life, Bolívar's greatest rival for the laurels of Spanish American liberator. For a recent scholarly account, see Patricia Pasquali, *San Martín: La fuerza de la misión y la soledad de la gloria* (Buenos Aires: Planeta, 1999). In English, there is a translation of *San Martín, Knight of the Andes* (New York: Cooper Square, 1967) by early-twentieth-century Argentine writer Ricardo Rojas.

18. It was the obscure final months of Bolívar's life that Gabriel García Márquez chose to fill with an imaginative recreation in novel form in *The General in His Labyrinth*, trans. Edith Grossman (New York: Alfred A. Knopf, 1990).

19. This view of myth owes much to Roland Barthes, *Mythologies* (New York: Hill and Wang, 1972). For another example of this approach applied to Latin American political heroes, see Ilene V. O'Malley, *The Myth of the Revolution: Hero Cults and the Institutionalization of the Mexican State, 1920–1940* (New York: Greenwood Press, 1986).

20. A firm commitment to independence dating from 1810 (and even before), while not unique, was unusual among the early patriot leadership. For a standard synthesis, see Jay Kinsbruner, *Independence in Spanish America: Civil Wars, Revolutions, and Underdevelopment*, Diálogos series (Albuquerque: University of New Mexico Press, 1994).

21. Masur, *Bolívar*, 403.

22. Masur, *Bolívar*, 275.

23. Bolívar's phenotype was fully compatible with a small degree of African descent. Very occasionally, those who wished to insult him might make racial insinuations, calling him *"amulatado."* Juan Manuel Saldarriaga Betancur, *Anecdotário del Libertador* (Medellin: Tipografía Olympia, 1953), 201. Madariaga is among the few biographers to make the point: *Bolívar*, 57–59.

24. Visions of Bolivarian unity have often competed with (or against) U.S. visions of hemispheric unity: Arthur Preston Whitaker, *The Western Hemisphere Idea: Its Rise and Decline* (Ithaca, N.Y.: Cornell University Press, 1954).

25. Masur, *Bolívar*, 415.

26. Bolívar married in his early twenties, before his political career began, but his wife died after only a few months. There are entire books dedicated to Bolívar's love life.

27. A good source on Bolívar the letter writer is the memoir of his Irish aide, O'Leary, *Bolívar and the War of Independence*.

28. Masur, *Bolívar*, 37.

29. Mariano R. Martínez, *Simón Bolívar Intimo* (Paris: Casa Editorial Hispano-Americana, n.d.), 80.

30. Madariaga, *Bolívar*, 1:467.

31. Rourke, *Man of Glory*, 209–210. Rourke evidently further dramatizes the scene.

32. Cornelio Hispano, *Los cantores de Bolívar* (Bogota: Minerva, 1930), 116.

33. Madariaga, *Bolívar*, 431.

34. Masur, *Bolívar*, 142.

35. The ruthless War to the Death was a winning strategy but a controversial one. Biographers typically dedicate at least one chapter to it, for or against. Opposite positions are assumed in the matter by Venezuelan Polanco Alcántara, *Simón Bolívar,* 59–214, 334–341, and the Spaniard Madariaga, *Bolívar*, 313–466.

36. Ricardo Palma, "Justicia de Bolívar," from his *Tradiciones peruanas* (Estella, Navarra: Salvat Editores, 1984), 178–181. Palma's *Tradiciones,* which began to appear in 1872, are a centerpiece of Peruvian literature, many times reprinted. Timothy E. Anna, *The Fall of the Royal Government in Peru* (Lincoln: University of Nebraska Press, 1979), provides a more sober view of Bolívar's Peruvian adventures.

37. This anecdote appeared in a Cartagena newspaper, *El Heraldo,* 24 July 1883, during the centennial commemorations of Bolívar's birth, and was reprinted in Saldarriaga Betancur, *Anecdotario del Libertador*, 124.

38. Saldarriaga Betancur, *Anecdotario del Libertador,* collects anecdotes scattered in many obscure sources. The present story (110–111), from a nineteenth-century potpourri called *Archivo de historia y variedade,* tells how Bolívar personally found a source of needed tin for the army in 1824.

39. From the *Almanaque anuario de Rojas Hermanos* (1884), collected by Cornelio Hispano, *El libro de oro de Bolívar* (Paris: Garnier Hermanos, 1925), 29–32.

40. This story was apparently taken from an unpublished private album of the sort in which nineteenth-century women collected personal memorabilia. Saldarriaga Betancur, *Anecdotario del Libertador*, 152–153.

41. Manuela Sáenz is finally getting the attention she deserves from serious historians of Latin America: Sarah C. Chambers, "Republican Friendship: Manuela Sáenz Writes Women into the Nation, 1835–1836," *Hispanic American Historical Review* 81, no. 2 (2001): 225–257; and Pamela Murray, "'Loca' or 'Libertadora': Manuela Sáenz in the Eyes of History and Historians, 1900–c. 1990," *Journal of Latin American Studies* 33, no. 2 (2001): 291–310.

42. While the first of the following accounts is merely a story (repeated by Emilio Constantino Guerrero, *Los heroes de la epopeya: Faces y rasgos* (Rio de Janeiro: Typografia do Jornal do Commércio, n.d., 22), the latter actions are well substantiated by Bolívar's written orders to use his salary for the purpose (Saldarriaga Betancur, *Anecdotario del Libertador*, 46–48).

43. *Papel periódico ilustrado* (1881), excerpted in Saldarriaga Betancur, *Anecdotario del Libertador*, 123.

44. *Primer Centenario del Natalicio del Libertador Simón Bolívar en 1883*, 355, excerpted in Saldarriaga Betancur, *Anecdotario del Libertador*, 50.

45. *Los heroes de la epopeya*, 129, excerpted in Saldarriaga Betancur, *Anecdotario del Libertador*, 39–40.

46. Ramón Aspúrua, *Biografías de hombres notables de Hispanoamérica* (Caracas: Imprenta Nacional, 1877), 1:7–8.

2

Remembering and Forgetting Agustín Gamarra

The Life and Legacy of the Cuzco Caudillo

CHARLES F. WALKER

Father Ortiz "turned to the Indian market woman and told her in
Quechua 'Ulacai yuyanquichu Jeneralninchismanta. . . .' Ulaca, do
you remember that only you and I cried for our General [Gamarra]."

José María Blanco, *Diario del viaje del
Presidente Orbegoso al sur del Perú*

For better or worse, the study of *caudillos* (warlords, generals on horse-back) and military heroes and antiheroes has a promising future.[1] On
the one hand, important studies in recent years have uncovered new infor-
mation and proposed novel or radically reworked interpretations. For example, in his study of La Rioja, Argentina, Ariel de la Fuente shows that
understanding the *cliente* side of the patron-client relationship is not only a
logical product of "social history from below" but a rich entryway into the
difficult transition from colony to republic in Spanish America. In doing so,
he breathes new life into the concept of charisma. Cristóbal Aljovín brings
together two elements that many would incorrectly have thought mutually
incompatible: caudillos and constitutions. His study of early republican
Peru confirms that caudillos and *caudillismo* operated within republican
structures and cannot be interpreted as aberrations or "failures."[2] Víctor
Peralta and Marta Irurozqui have refuted Alcides Arguedas's enduring
interpretation that divided Bolivian caudillos into *letrados* and *bárbaros*—
good and bad. They show that the diverse pretenders to and holders of
power in nineteenth-century Bolivia presented cohesive programs, counted
on extensive social bases, and, once in power, created a postcolonial state

and, arguably, a citizenry.[3] The essays in this book testify to the innovations and significance of recent studies of Latin American heroes and hero cults.

In this essay, I examine the life of Agustín Gamarra, the most important figure in Peruvian politics from independence in 1821 until his death in 1841. He was a significant but not particularly competent commander in the war of independence, president for two terms (1829–1833 and 1838–1841), and key conspirator against or supporter of regimes until his death in battle in 1841. As a military officer and politician, he visited just about every region of Peru, as well as its neighbors, Bolivia, Colombia, and Ecuador, and had his hand in seemingly every political event of the period. Although a ham-fisted authoritarian, he encountered great opposition and was not able to operate at will. Nonetheless, at the time of his martyrdom on the battlefields of Bolivia, he was the leader of a vast movement or movements, both in his native Cuzco and in Lima. His reputation as a triumphant caudillo who counted on followers from the Indian markets of the Andes to the elite salons of Lima stretched throughout the Andes. Yet in the following decades he lost this aura of a mythical military leader, to the point that he is now just one more name in the long list of generals who temporarily ran the Peruvian state. This chapter explores his rise and calamitous fall.

At the core of this discussion are two related questions: why did Gamarra fail in institutionalizing his movement, the most dominant in Peru for two decades, but which quickly vanished upon his death, and why has he been a relatively forgotten caudillo? In other words, why was there no *Gamarrismo* without Gamarra, and why has he not been transformed into a mythical hero or villain, as was the case with other leading "men on horseback" from the period? His reputation or aura declined quickly after his death. I show that his life and death give us important clues to why he is not in the pantheon of heroic or mythical caudillos.

This chapter therefore begins with a review of Gamarra's life and the complex political alliance that he created. Not only did he have solid support in the cities of Lima and Cuzco, which were bitterly opposed to one another at this time, but military campaigns extended his fame throughout Peru and into Ecuador and Bolivia. Nonetheless, he was not able to gain a mass Indian base, a key explanation for his failure to become a heroic icon of the early republic. Furthermore, upon his death, former supporters remembered that he had backed the "other side," and abandoned him. Finally, the twentieth century was not kind to Conservative caudillos; Gamarra and his cohort were blamed more than venerated. The reasons for his failure to enter the pantheon of heroes are found both in his active life and in the historical memory of the era.

El Angel Negro

DISAGREEMENTS ABOUT GAMARRA begin with the circumstances of his birth in Cuzco on August 27, 1785. Most biographers agree that his parents were Fernando Gamarra, a notary, and Josefa Petronila Messía. Some contemporaries contended that his mother was an Indian—an allegation made during his lifetime with clear pejorative intent—while others claimed that he was the son of a priest, Father Saldívar.[4] Educated in one of Cuzco's best schools, he entered the San Francisco Convent but left in 1809 to join the royalist army. He fought against the rebels in Charcas or Upper Peru (what became Bolivia) and Arequipa. In his native region of Cuzco, he helped put down a massive uprising led by members of the city's middle class and supported by Indians, the misnamed Pumacahua Rebellion (1813–1815). The uprising was brutally repressed—in some small towns all men were forced into the plaza and one-fifth of them were executed—and the Spanish went to great lengths to stop any further insurgency in Cuzco. Gamarra did not participate in this violent aftermath. By 1818, Viceroy Pezuela suspected that he had ties with the rebels who sought independence from Spain. In January 1821, Gamarra presented himself to the commander in chief of the rebel forces in Peru, José de San Martín. His experience and knowledge of the indigenous language Quechua made him an important convert.

As he rose in the Patriot army, he proved himself to be a more able conspirator than commander. Months after Gamarra switched sides, the rebel general Juan Antonio Alvarez de Arenales blamed him for allowing the royalist troops, led by General José Carratalá, to recapture the important Mantaro Valley to the east of Lima. This was not his last dubious action as a commander. The life of Gamarra demonstrates that for the generation that fought in the war of independence and then took important posts in the republican period, brilliance on the battlefield was not an absolute requirement.[5] On the political front, he helped weaken the governing junta of José de la Riva Agüero, which prompted the arrival of Simón Bolívar in September 1823. Gamarra was named Bolívar's chief of staff, and with the defeat of the Spanish in December 1824, he became Cuzco's first prefect. At this point he was already moving toward the side of Bolívar's opponents.

At the time of independence, Cuzco was Peru's second city, the center of a trans-Andean economy that revolved around commerce among Cuzco, the Lake Titicaca area, and Potosí, but also extended to Buenos Aires and Lima. The city of Cuzco had approximately 30,000 people at this point, compared with the 50,000 in Lima. It had been the capital of the Inca Empire, the great civilization that had awed the conquistadors in the sixteenth century. Although the Incas had been subjugated by the Spanish, their language, Quechua, was still spoken by millions of people in the nineteenth century (as it is today), and they represented a crucial symbol for Andean Indians. Laudatory depictions of Gamarra almost invariably stressed his knowledge of Quechua (much as Felipe Carrillo Puerto, subject of Chapter 6, would rely on his knowledge of Yucatec Maya). Many of the rebellions that took place in the eighteenth and nineteenth centuries called for a return of the Incas. Cuzco was seen as the core of "Indian" Peru, while Lima, located on the coast, was viewed as, or saw itself as, the more Western center. Whereas Cuzco was predominantly Indian, Lima was multi-ethnic, including people of European, African, and Indian descent (as well as a small Asian population) and a large "mixed" population. The tensions between these two cities marked the political struggles of the era.[6]

Prefect of Cuzco was not a minor post. Gamarra used Cuzco as his base to become president in 1829 and relied heavily on his native land throughout his career. Although a questionable military commander, he was an outstanding administrator. As Cuzco's first prefect, he faced the challenges that republican state builders confronted throughout Latin America with the defeat of the Spanish. The long wars of independence had damaged mines, mills, and haciendas and prompted the exodus of capital. The republics were deeply in debt before the Spanish departed. Although by 1825 calls for a constitutional monarchy had abated and most agreed that Peru would become a republic, great doubts existed about the nature and geographical extent of postcolonial Peru. For example, were Bolivia and Ecuador to be part of Peru or to become independent nations? In social terms, the role of Indians and the future of black slavery were pressing questions. At a more mundane level, Gamarra and others had to rebuild fiscal, legal, and other administrative structures. He confronted these challenges, ensuring stability with surprising speed and creating institutions that would last for decades. This success in Cuzco was at the center of his political ascent. Administrative abilities, however, are not usually a key ingredient of the legends and myths that create heroes.

The Caudillo State

GAMARRA LED MILITARY CAMPAIGNS in Peru, Ecuador, and Bolivia in the early republic, and, after assuming the presidency through elections in 1829 for the first time, he again became president in 1839 after overthrowing the Peru-Bolivia Confederation. Military power was important to him and other caudillos. Nonetheless, a focus on the use of force by caudillos and on the instability of the period has meant a relative inattention to how the caudillo state functioned. His adroit creation of republican structures in

Cuzco and his ability to count on them in his political campaigns ultimately proved more important than his military strength. In understanding Gamarrismo, the structures of the nascent state play a greater role than the military. He did not operate outside the regional and national state but used them to solidify his position. In fact, the military campaigns were an important element of both state-making and mythmaking, specifically as they helped diffuse the notion of Gamarra as an omnipotent leader who transcended regional and class divisions.[7]

Gamarra arrived in Cuzco on December 24, 1824. Within a matter of weeks the legal system functioned, taxes were collected, and municipal authorities met. Those in charge of the new republic recognized the danger of a chaotic transition. It threatened to provide opportunities to the more radical members of the independence movement or to the Spanish themselves and their abundant supporters. Gamarra hastily and successfully launched the republican administration. Continuity more than change characterized the transition as Gamarra and other figures tinkered with rather than overhauled the bureaucratic systems left by the Spanish. The economic crisis, as well as Gamarra's conservatism, discouraged radical reform. Even Bolívar's efforts to weaken the presence of the Church and to initiate a weak social welfare system (hospitals and schools, essentially) floundered in the face of strong opposition and minimal resources. Gamarra himself learned firsthand the cost of confronting the Church, and quickly eschewed anticlericalism.[8]

The new republican state urgently needed revenue, and the fiscal system was at the center of Peruvian political debates for decades. From the 1820s to mid-century, Liberals sought to abolish or weaken the Indian head tax, the linchpin of the Andean caste system, but failed. Gamarra defended what had been in the colonial period called "the tribute" and was at this point renamed "the contribution," in part because he deemed it necessary to force Indians to sell their goods and their labor and in part because the state desperately needed the revenue. Cuzco underwent major changes in this period, most noticeably elections and the development of a free and very active press. But in terms of administrative structures, Gamarra did not orchestrate any radical changes.

Historical work and fiction on this period often focus on instability. Civil wars were common, and regimes changed with alarming frequency. Many scholars have noted that Peru averaged more than one president per year in this period, a statistic that denotes chaos and random violence. Nonetheless, the examination of Gamarrismo in Cuzco demonstrates a surprising strength and coherence of the early republican state, even in a region distant from Lima. The courts, the fiscal system, and other governmental entities functioned despite political uncertainty and frequent battles. Liberals and Conservatives fought to control the state, although a certain level of autonomy can be seen. That is, the frequent regime changes in Lima did not mean a concomitant housecleaning of state institutions in Cuzco. Treasury officers, for example, usually remained.[9]

Gamarra placed trusted supporters in important positions and used the state to promote his vision of Cuzco, and Peru in general. He recruited an eclectic group of backers, many of them loyalists until the departure of the Spanish. Subprefects, militia leaders, and members of the military monitored Cuzco's extensive and varied geography and made sure that revenue from the head tax reached Cuzco. The correspondence between Gamarra and his subprefects confirms the absolute centrality of finances in state formation. Both the regional state (Cuzco) and the national state in Lima relied heavily on the Indian head tax, and thus subprefects and other local authorities were in no way obscure or unimportant figures.[10] Militia leaders and military officers also served as significant representatives of the state in local society. They became even more important in times of civil war. Gamarra ably created republican institutions, placing his supporters in the city and the provinces.

Economic malaise and political uncertainty foster patronage. The state needed representatives, and individuals in Cuzco and beyond saw this as an attractive opportunity. Many figures rose within Gamarrismo. But economic gain was not the only rationale for supporting Gamarra and pursuing a political (or politically endorsed) career. Gamarra created a sophisticated ideological platform that drew a wide band of supporters within Cuzco. The attraction and limitations of this platform—why he was a hero to some and an enemy to others—explain in large part the fate of his movement.

The Gamarra Platform: Cuzco First

AGUSTÍN GAMARRA was Peru's most important Conservative from independence in the 1820s until his death in 1841. In office (as prefect of Cuzco and later president of Peru) and in the opposition he led the battle against the other leading political coalition, the Liberals. He espoused the primary causes of nineteenth-century conservatives: centralization, protectionism, severe social control, xenophobia, and the continuation of racial hierarchies, which in Peru meant black slavery and the Indian head tax. The Conservatives were also deemed "the authoritarians," an appropriate label. Gamarra and his followers stressed his effective authoritarianism and contrasted it to the unrealistic focus on institutions espoused by the Liberals, which purportedly prompted social anarchy. A key explanation for

Gamarra's importance was his ability to link the Conservatives, a Lima-based coalition, with his base in his native Cuzco. He developed a unique ideology for this regional movement.

In Cuzco, Gamarrismo stressed the benefits of a strong government but also touted his attributes as a native son and his efforts to recapture Cuzco's former grandeur. In the press, Gamarra supporters cast the Liberals as elitist, unrealistic dreamers who sought to impose European models and to aid a small minority. Pro-Gamarra newspapers presented the Liberals as an exclusive club or clique.[11] Liberal journalists, in turn, castigated the Conservatives for returning Peru to colonial despotism and treated Gamarra as a corrupt tyrant. The often sensational and personalistic attacks presented him as a venal social climber and in some cases as a foolish Indian or mestizo.[12]

Gamarra and his ideologues developed a special platform for Cuzco that was different from that of the Conservatives based in Lima. They emphasized Gamarra's concern for his native land and the painful contrast between the region's glories under the Incas, who ruled for approximately two centuries before the arrival of the Spanish in the early 1500s, and its stagnation in the nineteenth century. While treating the three centuries of colonial rule gingerly, they blamed outsiders for Cuzco's decline, particularly political forces from Bolivia, the other southern Andean city of Arequipa, and Lima. Gamarra propaganda never tired of repeating his allegiance to his native land. For example, in 1835 a pamphlet that announced his return to Cuzco declared, "COMPATRIOTS: Today I have stepped onto the sacred soil of my birthplace after a year of absence. Everywhere, even in the midst of extreme danger, you always remained in my memory and in my heart. Crossing over from Bolivia, I was instructed that the cradle of the Incas was occupied by an insolent soldiery and suffered unmerited humiliations; I decided to fulfill the most gratifying of my duties."[13] His supporters emphasized that Cuzco's Quechua-speaking native son would return their city to its former grandeur. They wrapped him in the Inca flag, casting the Inca Empire as a model of hierarchy and social control. While using the Incas to symbolize the region's grandiose past, the Gamarristas sought to maintain the important place that Cuzco had enjoyed in the colonial administration and economy, a system largely based on the exploitation of Indians. The historian Cecilia Méndez has accurately deemed this enduring tendency to extol the pre-Hispanic past and overlook the status of contemporary Indians as "Incas Yes, Indians No."[14]

Gamarra constantly reminded the Cuzco population of the benefits of having a loyal native son in office during volatile times. He directed business to the region's textile mill owners and tailors. The mill owners saw free trade as the cause of their economic difficulties and avidly supported Gamarra.[15] Yet British industrialists constituted an excessively vague enemy for this highland region, particularly because textile production was not that important by the early nineteenth century. Instead, Gamarristas condemned Cuzco's Andean neighbors, Bolivia and Arequipa, as well as Lima.

Bolivia, formerly part of the viceroyalty of Peru, loomed large because it was the base of Gamarra's key opponent, Andrés de Santa Cruz, and had important economic connections to Cuzco. Gamarra led the military opposition to the Peru-Bolivia Confederation (1836–1839) crafted by Santa Cruz, stressing in Cuzco that the region should not play second fiddle to Bolivia and casting the confederation's representatives (political and military) as evil invaders. Arequipa, an important base for the Liberals, was also seen as a threat to Cuzco's place as the center of the Peruvian Andes. Gamarra supporters in Cuzco also took advantage of widespread anti-Lima sentiments. This was particularly impressive (or duplicitous) because as a national leader of the Conservatives, Gamarra had an important political base in the capital and resided there when president.

Both the Gamarra forces and their opponents, the Liberals, used the press, public festivities, elections, and the frequent times of political instability to weaken the enemy and highlight their platform. For example, Gamarra took advantage of the military campaigns to spread his doctrine, giving speeches in the towns that he passed. He also recognized Cuzco's taste for festivals. The celebration of his birthday in August 1832 lasted for days and included speeches, skits, dances, banquets, and bullfights. In the inaugural mass, the priest noted that Cuzco had a savior in heaven as well as one on earth. In a skit, a young man "dressed as an Inca" thanked Gamarra in Quechua for protecting Cuzco, while bullfighters carried floral arrangements that spelled out his name. Replicating the frenzied pace of Andean religious festivals, increasingly boisterous popular celebrations took place alongside more stodgy banquets and speeches. These different acts emphasized Gamarra's loyalty to Cuzco, its traditions and needs. Above all, they reiterated a key trope of Gamarrismo: a militaristic state based on the (invented) traditions of the Incas. This was at the core of Gamarra's myth: an effective leader whose power spread from Cuzco to Lima and beyond, yet whose heart and program remained in the Inca homeland.[16]

In contrast to the Gamarristas, Liberals emphasized republican institutions such as Congress and the courts. They sought a less centralized state, with sharp restrictions on the president, and favored free trade. In the early republic they led an energetic struggle against Gamarra and his supporters, but remained the minority party. Numerous yet ultimately related explanations come to mind for the superiority of Gamarra in Cuzco. These include the structural weakness of professional groups that supported the Liberals elsewhere, the ability of Gamarra to form a broad coalition, and the ideological attraction of Gamarrismo. The Liberals proposed abstract solutions, while Gamarra never refrained from emphasizing his immediate, concrete efforts and his deep ties to the Andes. This platform worked spectacularly in his lifetime but subsequently was tarnished. Few remembered him as an effective or omnipotent leader, and even fewer recalled his Inca invocations. The base of his heroic stature melted away quickly after death.

Gamarra's Social Base: Success Except with the Majority (Indians)

URBAN PROFESSIONALS constituted the single most important group of Liberals, and thus Gamarra opponents. Many resented Gamarra's favoritism to his followers, believing that they deserved positions in the state or governmental contracts. Liberal writers mentioned members of the Supreme Court, the municipality, the mint, the printing press, and teachers as bastions of Gamarra opponents, many of them in danger of losing their positions because of this opposition. Yet the urban professional class, with a certain intellectual savvy and a disposition to free trade politics and constitutionalism, was weak in Cuzco in this period. Several possible reasons suggest themselves. First, Cuzco had been an important colonial center and, as was the case with Lima, many members of the Spanish-speaking middle and upper sectors worried about the radical overthrow of colonial structures such as racial stratification. The economy relied on the exploitation of Indians, and few members of the middle class rallied against the abolition of the head tax.[17] Although Cuzqueños decried Lima centralization, the city had been an important colonial center, and the rise of Arequipa and other Andean competitors was of concern. Gamarra used this concern to develop Cuzco's opposition to the Peru-Bolivia Confederation.

Cuzco's unique late colonial history also had weakened the potential base for Liberals. Cuzco had been the center of two massive anticolonial uprisings, the Tupac Amaru Rebellion (1780–1783) and the Pumacahua Rebellion. Brutal repression followed the defeat of both, weakening and disillusioning radical groups in the city and countryside. The Spanish had controlled the region from 1816 to 1824, preventing the emergence of a broad anticolonial coalition. In sum, structural reasons (the region's "colonialness" and weak economy), as well as the defeat of massive insurgent movements, meant that the Liberals had a small pool of supporters among the urban middle and upper classes.

Gamarra pressured and recruited the opposition masterfully. In the press and in public festivities, Gamarristas cast the Liberals either as hopeless dreamers, importers of unrealistic European schemes, or as cynics who used their rhetorical adherence to the constitution and other platforms to disguise their efforts to place themselves in positions of power. He made life difficult for many key Liberals but in general allowed them to operate. In doing so, he kept the doors open for them. While key Gamarristas included former colonial authorities, mill owners, and the chain of authorities who depended on the Indian head tax (collectors, subprefects, and prefects are just three links in the long chain that stretched from the Indian community to the Cuzco state), his movement also counted on the urban professional middle class, which should have been the bastion of the Liberals. With his ability to create a regional state and redistribute its benefits to his supporters, as well as his skill in crafting a region-specific and coherent ideology, Gamarra created a loyal coalition of supporters in the city of Cuzco and provincial capitals. He did not have the same success in the countryside.

Indians constituted approximately 80 percent of the Department of Cuzco's population in the early 1820s, about 200,000 out of 250,000 total.[18] The postcolonial state quickly abandoned any egalitarian leanings and retained the foundation of racial definitions in the Andes, the Indian head tax. This semiannual payment by Indian men financed the regional and national states into the second half of the nineteenth century, decades after independence. It did more than provide funds for the state, as it anchored social and economic hierarchies. Questions about who was an Indian ultimately reverted to who paid the tribute or contribution. Local authorities in Indian communities, Indians and non-Indians, used it to accumulate power and money. Indians saw it as a means to defend their rights to land and to obtain a degree of self-rule. Throughout the colonial period, the payment of the head tax by Indians had been understood as part of a "contract" that allowed them to maintain their land (held collectively and individually) and granted them the right to have local, Indian authorities.[19]

Gamarra recognized the importance of Indians in Cuzco and for his political aspirations. He efficiently collected and spent the Indian head tax to implement his Cuzco-based coalition. He also recognized that Indians represented a very powerful potential social base: they could provide money, soldiers, a geographical base, and an ideological support. He would truly be the father of the Cuzco fatherland—an image he propagated extensively—if Quechua speakers massively supported him. Gamarra perceived something evident in other chapters of this book, that a full-fledged caudillo needed a mass base.[20] However, while efficient in creating a Cuzco coalition and in fighting in the courts, in the streets, and on the battlefields in Peru and Bolivia, he failed to gain the mass support of Cuzco Indians.

Gamarra and other Conservatives never considered Indians as potential citizens. Although journalists and political ideologues were notably silent about the Quechua population, Cuzco's subprefects and their dependents sent frequent reports about Indians. They consistently presented them as backward, lazy inferiors who would revert to heathen, unproductive ways if not forced by the state to pay taxes and thus sell their labor and goods. Esteban de Navia, a tax agent in Qusipicanchis, to the south of Cuzco, wrote, "Indians are not capable of improving their agriculture because, since they don't have any other necessities than eating and dressing very poorly, the little that their work produces is enough for them."[21] These authors expressed no confidence that the market could rectify Indians' behavior and insisted that they, non-Indian state authorities, had to mediate to make sure that Indians paid their taxes and avoided heathen ways. These reports nourished the largely successful efforts at the regional and national levels to recreate the colonial relationship between the state and the indigenous population. This view of the Indian as a backward "other" was at the heart of Gamarrismo.

Therefore, when Gamarra and his backers recruited Indians, they sought soldiers for the frequent civil wars and not any sort of enduring ally; they wanted troops, but did not want to convert them into long-term supporters, let alone full-fledged citizens. Although pro-Gamarra journalists stressed the caudillo's knowledge of Quechua and wrapped him in the flag of the Inca Empire, they and their leader did not pretend to lead a pro-Indian campaign. At the heart of the Gamarrista coalition were the multiple layers of authorities, hacienda and textile-mill owners, and others who lived off Indians' taxes, labor, and consumption. At the core of their ideology was the recreation of a strong Cuzco-based state and colonial racial hierarchies. They demonstrated no inclination to tamper with the Indians' subordinate position in Andean society—they lived off and firmly believed in it. Furthermore, they remembered the massive uprisings that had spread throughout Cuzco in the 1780s and 1810s, when Indians had violently seized haciendas and expelled or even murdered those seen as Europeans. This memory discouraged them from arming Indians. Nonetheless, they would turn to them in times of need, that is, civil war.

Gamarra thus attempted to recruit Indian guerrillas into the civil wars of the 1830s but, to his great frustration, failed. In August 1835, he lost a costly and humiliating battle to the Santa Cruz forces in Lake Yanacocha to the south of Cuzco, his bastion, largely because of the low numbers and poor performance of his Indian troops.[22] This defeat led to his temporary exile in Costa Rica and the emergence of the Santa Cruz-led Peru-Bolivia Confederation. It also reflected, in part, the extremely limited role that he and his followers envisioned for Indians.

The frustrated coalition between Gamarra and Cuzco Indians must also be understood from the perspective of the latter. We do not count on direct sources that explain why Indians by and large declined offers to fight for the Gamarristas. But explanations emerge. First, the situation of the Indians was not that bad in the early republic, at least in comparison with subsequent periods. The depressed economy and unstable politics meant that outsiders—that is, non-Indians—were not inclined or able to usurp Indians' resources, land in particular. In fact, low operating costs meant that Indians were able to compete well with estates in times of low prices. The "liberal assault" on Indians' land and labor would occur only in the latter half of the nineteenth century. Second, Gamarra did not have much to offer. His coalition did not conceive of Indians as potential citizens but only as soldiers—informal guerrillas, in fact. If they could not be dragooned—as was frequently the case—the Gamarristas offered them low pay or the possibility of plunder. This could provide groups of temporary soldiers in times of battle, but not long-term support.

Finally, the historical experience of Cuzco Indians must be considered. The region had been the site of two massive rebellions, Tupac Amaru and Pumacahua, as well as countless riots and revolts. These had been followed by periods of brutal repression, and residents of the Cuzco countryside knew well the cost of losing a war. Although Gamarra might offer them aid in a legal battle and some money, his opponents would punish them once Gamarra was defeated. In light of the brutality that followed the rebellions and the frequent turnover in caudillo politics, the Cuzco Indians apparently made a smart decision in not massively backing Agustín Gamarra. How this decision was made and whether they understood the derision that the Gamarristas held for them is impossible to confirm, but their hesitance makes great sense in the context of post-independence Cuzco. Although Gamarra was a Quechua-speaking native son, the distance between the state and Indians remained enormous (see Chapter 9 for the continuation of this problem in the twentieth century). Gamarra could not or did not want to bridge that gulf, which helps explain his military defeats and perhaps even his death in battle in 1841. It also helps explain why his movement disappeared upon his martyrdom. A loyal mass base seems to be fundamental not only to gaining and retaining power but also to creating a historical legacy.

Death and Beyond

IN THE LATE 1830s, Gamarra directed the successful efforts to overthrow the Santa Cruz-led Peru-Bolivia Confederation. He became president for the second time, the head of the staunchly conservative Regeneration regime. In November 1841 he found himself again in Bolivia, leading his forces to impede the return of Andrés de Santa Cruz. He also contemplated the idea of creating a Peruvian-led, more conservative confederation. On November 18, the Bolivian forces routed the Peruvians. Gamarra strove to rouse his troops but was shot and killed. Some believe that his own forces shot him. In 1873, a dying Peruvian told intellectual Manuel González Prada that he, not the Bolivians, had fired the shot. Alfredo González Prada, Manuel's son, elaborated this story in a book published in New York in 1941.[23]

Gamarra was Peru's most important political figure in its first fifteen years of independence and would seem to have had all of the qualifications for hero status. He stood out in Cuzco, where he established a regional movement based on his ties to his native land; in Lima, where he was president for two terms; and on the battlefield throughout Peru and into Ecuador and Bolivia. In other words, his fame extended from one end of Peru to the other, overcoming sharp geographical and ethnic differences among groups, and he seemed to have had the charisma and the career to become a hero. He is granted substantial space in books on modern Peru, although often in the shadow of General Ramón Castilla, president from 1845 to 1851 and again from 1855 to 1862. In Cuzco a medium-sized statue portrays his rigid face in the Plaza San Francisco. His name is now commonly heard in Lima because "Gamarra" is a bustling textile market where family operations produce cotton and other textile products for national consumption and for export. Yet probably only a small percentage of the people who frequent this market could explain who it was named after. While not forgotten, Agustín Gamarra is certainly not venerated. His name does not have the historical resonance of other early republican caudillos, such as Santa Anna in Mexico (see Chapter 3) or Juan Manuel de Rosas in Argentina. Within Peru, the two non-Peruvian leaders of the war of independence, Simón Bolívar (see Chapter 1) and José de San Martín; the Bolivian caudillo (and Gamarra's occasional ally and frequent enemy) Andrés de Santa Cruz; and the mid-nineteenth-century caudillo, Ramón Castilla, attract more attention and are more widely recognized by nonspecialists. What explains this relative obscurity or forgetting?

In order to explain why Gamarra is not a hero, both his legacy in the decade or so following his death and his allure for historians and activists in more recent times must be examined. Gamarra did not create a mass base. His death shocked his followers and began a new round of jostling for power in Peru, including Cuzco. But mourners did not descend from the Andes, and religious invocations did not occur. Gamarra's inability to develop a mass base among Cuzco's Indians proved costly in life, death, and beyond. In terms of national politics, different caudillos fought for the control of the movement, yet none presented himself explicitly as a descendent of Gamarra. Leaders such as Manuel Ignacio de Vivanco had their own programs and supporters, and the name of the Cuzco caudillo apparently did not bring sufficient status or cachet to prompt a continuation of Gamarrismo without Gamarra. In other words, the movement that he had led largely disavowed or forgot him after his death.

In intellectual terms, Father Bartolomé Herrera became the leading ideologue of the Conservatives in the 1840s, in part because of his sermon at Gamarra's funeral, which was later widely disseminated. After describing Peru's decline after its rupture "with the vast monarchy of which it formed part," he explained why this had occurred: "the principle of authority was lost in the struggle for emancipation." He castigated Peruvians for their lack of discipline and order and called for supreme obedience to God, an obvious jab at the Liberals and their emphasis on the legal system and the constitution. He drew a parallel between Gamarra's death and that of Jesus, and cast him as a great Peruvian martyr. Yet this imagery did not develop into any sort of hero cult, and Herrera himself expanded his own particularly reactionary views and in no way was a mere defender of Gamarra's legacy.[24] In 1845 Ramón Castilla took control of the Peruvian state and, financed by the astonishingly lucrative export of guano (bird droppings used as a fertilizer, primarily in Europe), brought relative stability and oversaw a number of reforms, such as the abolition of slavery and of the Indian head tax. He presented his government as a novelty and did not employ Gamarra as a martyred precursor. In sum, following his death, Agustín Gamarra did not have a strong symbolic presence among Conservatives and their regimes.[25]

Perhaps Gamarra's ability, unique in this period of Andean history, to bridge the Andes and Lima detracted from his image. In Lima, opponents presented him as a brutish Andean arriviste who took power in order to enrich himself and his closest allies. Although the most venomous racist diatribes were aimed at the Bolivian Andrés de Santa Cruz, Gamarra also was a target, specifically of attacks from Liberal writers. Conservatives in Lima had recognized him as their maximum leader during his lifetime but abandoned him as a symbol of their movement, perhaps in part because of their discomfort with his Andean background. In Cuzco, his ties with Lima Conservatives or "authoritarians" cast shadows on him, weakening the shine of the "son of the homeland" argument. This explanation is speculative—why leaders do not become mythical figures after death is a difficult proposition to study—but, perhaps ironically, his greatest political attribute worked against him. His Conservative Cuzco-Lima alliance shattered after his death, and each region recalled the negative implications of his ties to the other.

In the twentieth century, no "neo-Gamarra" movement emerged. Agustín Gamarra operated in a period of great instability when Peru lost its privileged position as the colonial center in Spanish South America to become a much smaller republic, one of many. Nationalist historians have little to praise other than the fact that Peru did not further disintegrate. He did not lead any great military, economic, or political resurgence, and his defenders have had to stress his achievements in terms of "it could have been worse." His greatest accomplishments were as an administrator, skills that historians have largely overlooked and that are not the stuff of which legends are made, though Chapter 9 will make the case that organizational skills were a crucial underpinning of the charisma of twentieth-century Peruvian politician Víctor Raúl Haya de la Torre.[26]

Moreover, few if any historically attuned thinkers turn to the early republican Conservatives for possible icons. His political project finds few adherents today. He was a very capable iconoclastic Conservative or perhaps even reactionary. Although he developed his home base in the Andes, spoke Quechua, and created a broad coalition of supporters, he ultimately led a movement that longed for the stability of colonial days and defended slavery, the Indian head tax, and minimal change with independence. Unlike Bolívar or Cuzco's own Tupac Amaru II—whose name has been used by guerrilla groups in Uruguay and Peru, as well as the late rap singer Tupac Shakur—modern political movements have little incentive to invoke his name. Although authoritarians have certainly risen, none has declared himself or his movement Gamarrista.

Finally, most writing on Gamarra has been ambivalent. He has not received the waves of one-sided hyperbole (positive and negative) that other heroes discussed in this book have attracted. Even his greatest critics recognized his erudition and honesty, while his loyal followers pointed out his weakness on the battlefield and his exasperating conflicts with Lima-based Liberals and Andrés de Santa Cruz. Some hyperbole can be found, of course, in his numerous biographies. In the mid-nineteenth century, Felipe Pardo y Aliaga described him as "affable, generous, well-educated and eloquent to the point that with one word in Quechua, he could make 12,000 Indians suddenly kneel down," underlining his purported command over Indians. In contrast, José María Valega wrote in the 1920s that "the psychology of this Cuzco soldier indicates, politically, the terrible defect of his race that psychiatrists call moral weakness."[27] Nonetheless, accounts that lean toward hagiography point out some faults, while very critical accounts usually mention some positive traits.

One author captured this discrepancy by deeming Gamarra Cuzco's "Black Angel," black referring to his pitfalls and perhaps to his mestizo heritage.[28] Gamarra symbolized the energy of caudillismo but also its grave danger, defeat on the battleground. He does not represent otherworldly invincibility. Those critical of the Cuzco caudillo, meanwhile, usually note some positive attributes.[29] True heroes require clearly polarized perspectives in which they are treated as villains or heroes. This explains why he provides such a wonderful entry into early republican Peru but perhaps also why he has not entered the pantheon of famed caudillos.

Notes

* This chapter's epigraph is from José María Blanco, *Diario del viaje del Presidente Orbegoso al sur del Perú* (Lima: PUC, Instituto Riva-Agüero, 1974), 255. The quotation refers to Gamarra's departure and exile in 1835, not his death, but underlines how Gamarra was forgotten.

1. An earlier version of some of the material presented here was published in Charles F. Walker, *Smoldering Ashes: Cuzco and the Creation of Republican Peru, 1780–1840*, (Durham, N.C.: Duke University Press, 1999), which provides more detailed citations.

2. Ariel de la Fuente, *Children of Facundo: Caudillo and Gaucho Insurgency During the Argentine State-Formation Process (La Rioja, 1853–1870)* (Durham, N.C.: Duke University Press, 2000); and Cristóbal Aljovín Losada, *Caudillos y constituciones: Perú: 1821–1845* (Lima: Pontificia Universidad Católica, Fondo de Cultura Económica, 2000), esp. chap. 2.

3. Víctor Peralta Ruíz and Marta Irurozqui Victoriano, *Por la concordia, la fusión y el unitarismo: Estado y caudillismo en Bolivia, 1825–1880* (Madrid: CSIC, Departamento de Historia de América, 2000).

4. The allegations about Father Saldívar are from Pruvonena (José de la Riva Agüero), *Memorias y documentos para la historia de la independencia del Perú*, 2 vols. (Paris: Librería de Garnier Hermanos, 1858), 1:372–373.

5. Pedro de Angelis, prologue to *Segunda campaña a la sierra del Perú en 1821*, by José I. Arenales (Buenos Aires: Vaccaro, 1920), 64–67.

6. On the memory of the Incas, see Alberto Flores Galindo, *Buscando un Inca*, 4th ed. (Lima: Editorial Horizonte, 1994). See also Tom Cummins, "A Tale of Two Cities: Cuzco, Lima and the Construction of Colonial Representation," in *Converging Cultures: Art and Identity in Spanish America*, ed. Diana Fane (New York: Brooklyn Museum, 1997), 157–170.

7. This is changing, as the books by Aljovín Losada, *Caudillos y constituciones*, and Peralta and Irurozqui, *Por la concordia*, indicate.

8. Horacio Villanueva Urteaga, *Gamarra y la iniciación de la república en el Cuzco*

(Lima: Banco de los Andes, 1981), 114–130; and Walker, *Smoldering Ashes*, 133–135.

9. On the post-independence state, Jorge Basadre is still outstanding. Jorge Basadre, *La Iniciación de la república*, 2 vols. (Lima: F. y E. Rosay, 1929).

10. Therefore, the "Subprefectura" and "Prefectura" holdings in the Archivo Departamental del Cuzco are particularly valuable sources on local society, particularly relations between the state and Indians.

11. On the active Cuzco press, see Fructuoso Cahuata Corrales, *Historia del periodismo cuzqueño* (Lima: SAGSA, 1990); Donato Amado and Luis Miguel Glave, *Periódicos cuzqueños del siglo XIX: Estudio y catálogo de Fondo de Archivo Departamental del Cuzco* (Madrid: Fundación Histórica Tavera, 1999); and Charles F. Walker, "La orgía periodística: Prensa y cultura política en el Cuzco durante la joven república," *Revista de Indias* 61, no. 221 (2001): 7–26.

12. For examples of the attacks on Gamarra, see Walker, "Orgía Periodística." One apocryphal account was entitled "The New Natural History of Tyranny in Peru" (Cuzco, 1834) and called Gamarra an "Indian quadruped and animal."

13. Agustín Gamarra, *El Gran Mariscal Don Agustín Gamarra a los cuzqaueños*, Cuzco, June 9, 1935 (pamphlet). This is one of many examples of pamphlets and newspaper articles that stressed his native ties.

14. Cecilia Méndez, *Incas sí, indios no: Apuntes para el estudio del nacionalismo criollo en el Perú* (Lima: IEP, 1993).

15. On *obrajes*, see Neus Escandell-Tur, *Producción y comercio de tejidos coloniales: Los obrajes y chorrillos del Cuzco 1570–1820* (Cuzco: Centro Bartolomé de Las Casas, 1997). On free trade, see Paul Gootenberg, *Between Silver and Guano: Commercial Policy and the State in Postindependence Peru* (Princeton, N.J.: Princeton University Press, 1989).

16. Walker, *Smoldering Ashes*, chap. 6.

17. Studies on the head tax in the Andes include Víctor Peralta Ruíz, *En pos del tributo: Burocracia estatal, elite regional y comunidades indígenas en el Cuzco rural (1826–1854)* (Cuzco: Centro Bartolomé de Las Casas, 1991); Tristan Platt, *Estado boliviano y ayllu andino: Tierra y tributo en el norte de Potosí* (Lima: IEP, 1982); Nuria Sala I Vila, *Y se armó el tole tole: Tributo indígena y movimientos sociales en el virreinato del Perú, 1784–1814* (Lima: IER José María Arguedas, 1996); and George Kubler, *The Indian Caste of Peru, 1795–1940: A Population Study Based upon Tax Records and Census Reports*, Smithsonian Institution of Social Anthropology Publications, no. 14 (Washington, D.C.: Smithsonian Institution, 1952).

18. On early republican demographics, see Paul Gootenberg, "Population and Ethnicity in Early Republican Peru: Some Revisions," *Latin American Research Review* 26, no. 3 (1991): 109–157; Thomas Krüggeler, "El mito de la 'despoblación': Apuntes para una historia demográfica del Cuzco (1791–1940)," *Revista Andina* 16, no. 1 (1998): 119–137.

19. Platt, *Estado*; and Walker, *Smoldering Ashes*, chap. 7. See also Nils Jacobsen, "Liberalism and Indian Communities in Peru, 1821–1920," in *Liberals, the Church, and Indian Peasants: Corporate Lands and the Challenge of Reform in Nineteenth-Century Spanish America*, ed. Robert H. Jackson (Albuquerque: University of New Mexico Press, 1997), 123–170; and, for the independence period, Christine Hünefeldt, *Lucha por la tierra y protesta indígena: Las comunidades indígenas del Perú entre colonia y república* (Bonn: Bonner Amerikanische Studien, 1982).

20. This is also a key argument of the important book by John Lynch, *Caudillos in Spanish America, 1800–1850* (Oxford: Clarendon Press, 1992).

21. Archivo Departamental del Cuzco, ATP, Tributacion, Legajo 67, 1826–1830.

22. On the Battle of Yanacocha, Black Lake in Quechua, see Carlos Dellepiane, *Historia Militar del Perú*, 2 vols. (Lima: Librería e Imprenta Gil, 1931), I:336–337; Jorge Basadre, *Historia de la República del Perú*, 7th ed., 11 vols. (Lima: Editorial Universitaria, 1983), 2:38–39. On Indian guerrillas in the war of independence, among many studies see Flores Galindo, *Buscando un Inca*, chap. 7, "Soldados y montoneros."

23. Abraham Valdelomar, *La Mariscala: Doña Francisca Zubiaga y Bernales de Gamarra* (Lima: Taller de la Penitenciaría, 1914), and Alfredo González Prada, *Un crimen perfecto: El asesinato del Gran Mariscal Don Agustín Gamarra, Presidente del Perú* (New York: H. Wolff, 1941). The dean of modern Peuvian historians, Jorge Basadre, refuted this allegation at length. Basadre, *Historia*, 2:148–152.

24. Bartolomé Herrera, *Escritos y discursos*, 2 vols. (Lima: Biblioteca de la República, 1929), 1:14–34. The quotation is from p. 17.

25. For the 1840s in Peru and the rise of Ramón Castilla, see the many works of Jorge Basadre, including *Historia*, vol. 2; Paul Gootenberg, *Imagining Development: Economic Ideas in Peru's "Fictitious Prosperity" of Guano, 1840–1880* (Berkeley and Los Angeles: University of California Press, 1993); and Natalia Sobrevilla Perea, "The Influence of the European 1848 Revolution in Peru," in *The European Revolutions of 1848 and the Americas*, ed. Guy Thomson (London: Institute of Latin American Studies, 2002), 191–216.

26. Basadre, *La Iniciación*, 1:126–130. Basadre emphasizes the comparatively humble origins of this first generation of caudillos. On Gamarra's administrative skills, see Villanueva Urteaga, *Gamarra*.

27. Felipe Pardo y Aliaga, "Semblanzas peruanas," *Boletín de la Academia Chilena de la Historia* 33 (1945): 6; and José María Valega, *República del Perú* (Lima: Librería e Imprenta Don Miranda, 1927), 16.

28. Luis Alayza Paz Soldán, *El Gran Mariscal José de la Mar* (Lima: Gil, 1941), 109

29. Biographies on Gamarra include N. Andrew Cleven, "Dictators Gamarra, Orbegoso, Salaverry, and Santa Cruz," in *South American Dictators During the First Century of Independence*, ed. A. Curtis Wilgus (Washington, D.C.: George Washington University Press, 1937), 289–333; Manuel de Mendiburu, *Biografías de generales republicanos* (Lima: Instituto Histórico del Perú, Academia Nacional de la Historia, 1963); Miguel A. Martínez, *El Mariscal de Piquiza, Don Agustín Gamarra* (Lima: Librería e Imprenta D. Miranda, 1946); Alberto Tauro, "Agustín Gamarra, fundador de la independencia nacional," in *Historia del Perú*, ed. César Pacheco Vélez, no. 7, *Biblioteca de Cultura Peruana Contemporánea* (Lima: Ediciones del Sol, 1963), 507–518; and Horacio Villanueva Urteaga, *Gamarra y la iniciación de la república en el Cuzco* (Lima: Banco de los Andes, 1981).

3

Antonio López de Santa Anna's Search for Personalized Nationalism

Shannon Baker

After gaining independence in 1821, Mexicans struggled to bolster a weakened economy, create an effective government, and foster a sense of loyalty to the newly formed nation. New Spain had been the most prosperous Spanish colony in 1800, but the wars for independence generated incalculable property damage throughout the area. Mining—vitally important to the economy—agriculture, industry, and investments all suffered. The various national governments proved unable to recover adequately from this devastation or to devise a functional tax system to support the country's needs. Citizens endured political as well as economic problems. Throughout the years of the early republic (1824–1855), Mexicans witnessed many changes in government as politicians and military officers disputed, sometimes violently, whether a president or a dictator, a federalist or a centralist constitution, would best suit Mexico. Such debates and battles focused not only on what type of national leader to have but also on how much power should be granted to the individual states. While centralists, also referred to as traditionalists, argued that the national government should be strong, federalists posited that the states should have more local control. And although centralists frequently believed that the president should have a wide range of powers, federalists typically asserted that executive authority should be more limited. Politicians from both factions often appealed to the middle sectors as well as to their fellow elites, because they believed that each group played a role in national politics. They attempted to attract followers and create alliances through the use of ceremonies and symbols that communicated their different ideas about Mexico. Statesmen also believed these rituals encouraged stability and fostered nation building, which engendered a sense of identity and citizenship among newly independent Mexicans, the elites and masses alike. The observances, such as the October 4 commemoration of the Constitution of 1824, commonly promoted pride in Mexico rather than in any one individual. Yet Antonio López de Santa Anna, one of the most noted figures of the era, believed that personalistic ceremonies that stressed his heroism would augment his popularity at the same time that they increased citizens' esteem for Mexico.[1]

Santa Anna began his military career fighting for both sides during the wars for independence. He joined the military in 1810 at the age of sixteen, confronting the rebels in northern Mexico. But like many other creole officers, he switched allegiances and joined the insurgency after Agustín de Iturbide announced the Plan of Iguala in 1821. This plan embraced new, more inclusive and moderate goals for Mexico than previous plans had, including promises that Mexico would be independent and Catholic and that Spaniards who chose to remain in the new country would not be harmed. Santa Anna emerged as a prominent figure in national politics following independence. In 1822 he announced the Plan of Veracruz, calling for an end to Iturbide's brief reign as emperor of Mexico. Six years later he incited a revolution against the presidential election of political moderate Manuel Gómez Pedraza in favor of Vicente Guerrero, who, as a radical, attracted more support from the popular classes. After Santa Anna thwarted Spanish efforts to reconquer Mexico with an 1829 victory at Tampico, he was assured a position among the pantheon of independence heroes and guaranteed an expanded role in national politics.[2]

Santa Anna assumed control of Mexico sporadically between 1833 and 1853, yet he could not maintain power for extended periods of time. The economic and political weaknesses of Mexico surely hindered his ability to stay in office for lengthy terms and achieve order, but his own actions were also to blame. Rather than using his authority as president to solve the myriad difficulties facing the new nation, Santa Anna often retired to his hacienda and left interim presidents to resolve the most challenging problems. He vacated the presidency still more ingloriously when public opinion turned against him and coups forced him from office. These coups frequently occurred on those occasions when Santa Anna failed to keep the support of important groups such as the Catholic Church and the military.[3]

Even though Santa Anna failed to maintain power for long terms, he exhibited an amazing ability not only to regain control but also to reemerge as a hero in the hearts and minds of Mexicans. In order to accomplish these goals, he demonstrated many of the characteristics associated with *caudillo*

leadership and discussed in the previous two chapters: regionalism, opportunism, personalism, and elements of *machismo*. He employed his military
office and popularity in his home state of Veracruz during various efforts to
attain control of the nation or to thwart foreign invasions. The caudillo
(warlord, general on horseback) likewise attempted to gain and preserve
control by appealing to important interest groups, which frequently included the army, the Catholic Church, and wealthy citizens proffering military
and monetary support in return for favored treatment. He claimed to be a
federalist when it suited his needs, yet his centralist nature surfaced during
nearly all of his presidencies. He utilized the political disarray in the years
following independence to his own benefit. He took advantage of the relative power vacuum created by the elimination of colonial authority. Because
Mexicans were accustomed to the personalistic leadership associated with a
monarchy, Santa Anna attempted to gain the loyalty of the population by
appearing to be as seemingly indispensable to the welfare of the nation as
the king had been. He buttressed his popularity by posing as a hero during
many of the seemingly endless critical moments in early republican Mexico.

Santa Anna also unsuccessfully attempted to control national politics by
promoting allegiance to himself through the creation of ceremonies
designed to remind citizens that he had ensured the sovereignty of Mexico.
These rituals, including the September 11 commemoration of his 1829 victory and the 1842 funeral for his leg (lost fighting the French, who had
invaded in 1838), portrayed him as a selfless and heroic patriot who acted in
the interest of preserving and strengthening the Mexican state. Indeed, they
frequently represented Santa Anna as the human embodiment of Mexico.
The observances also characterized him as a *macho*—a powerful, assertive,
and almost invulnerable masculine figure. In addition, they suggested that
Mexico would not have survived without his indispensable presence.
Santanistas (Santa Anna supporters) believed that highlighting the
strength and heroism of the caudillo would inspire public confidence and
pride; these politicians therefore thought that such personalistic ceremonies
performed the function of nation building. Other national leaders did not
support these efforts; they believed that festivities honoring him subverted
the creation of national loyalty because the rituals focused too much attention on one seemingly unpredictable individual. Santa Anna's opponents
need not have worried that holidays honoring the caudillo alone would win
over the Mexican people; such pomp and circumstance, as well as his
actions while in power, actually contributed to the citizens' perception of
Santa Anna as a villain rather than a hero.[4]

Mexicans' exuberant praise for Santa Anna after his victory at Tampico
demonstrated that citizens did not always share the politicians' concerns

about personalism. This dubious triumph elevated him to a heroic status. During the late 1820s, Spanish spies had been informing the Spanish monarch, King Ferdinand VII, about the weaknesses that plagued the newly independent country. The king believed that Spanish forces could easily reconquer Mexico, allowing him to reassert control over the former colony. He therefore ordered Brigadier General Isidro Barradas to invade Mexico. On July 16, 1829, Barradas landed near the gulf port of Tampico with 2,600 men. Santa Anna, serving as the governor and commanding general of Veracruz, responded to the challenge, ringing Veracruz's church bells to gather all the men in the plaza and rouse them to action. After apprising residents of the situation and filling their minds with images of victory, he organized a force of 2,000 men. Santa Anna's plan for a direct attack against the Spaniards at Tampico failed, but he maintained a siege that led to victory. Beleaguered by yellow fever and a hurricane rather than the might of Mexican arms, Barradas surrendered to Santa Anna and General Manuel de Mier y Terán, the other Mexican commander, on September 11, 1829, agreeing to recognize Mexican independence and evacuate the country.[5]

Citizens lauded the caudillo with spontaneous celebrations as news of the victory spread to Mexico City. President Vicente Guerrero received a communication from Santa Anna while attending the theater on September 20. He announced the victory to the audience, proclaiming "Brigadier Santa Anna has forced Barradas to surrender in Tampico, he has conquered him, saving the honor of the nation." The theatergoers exploded in applause and *vivas* to Santa Anna and Terán as they spilled into the streets, where city residents ignited fireworks in jubilation. Published articles and proclamations also bore witness to the Spanish defeat. *El boletín oficial*, the government newspaper, printed Santa Anna's notice of the capitulation on the following day, confirming his heroic service to the nation. The editors depicted the caudillo as intrepid and described Barradas as a ruthless invader when they referred to him as "the second Hernán Cortés." Such a comparison further strengthened Santa Anna's image: by defeating Barradas, he had succeeded where the Aztecs had failed. Guerrero, perhaps trying to deflect attention from Santa Anna and refocus citizens' attention on the nation itself, alluded to the national symbol of Mexico when he proclaimed that the lion of Spain had succumbed to the Mexican eagle.[6]

Mexico City residents also took part in planned festivities commemorating the caudillo's victory. José María Tornel y Mendívil, governor of the Federal District and a Santanista, designated September 25–27 as days of celebration on which the public could demonstrate its joy and gratitude. Representatives from the three branches of the federal government attended a mass at the sanctuary of the Virgin de Guadalupe on September 27, arriving amid a large parade of the citizenry. The procession to the church proved more spectacular than the service itself. City children rode in carriages expensively decorated by the various neighborhoods. Carlos María de Bustamante, who wrote about the event, estimated that 200,000 people joined in Mexico City to rejoice. Mexicans, still accustomed to venerating kings, demonstrated a level of enthusiasm for personalistic heroes such as Santa Anna that they did not readily display for abstract notions of patriotism. Yet the government attempted to place the caudillo's victory in a context of nationalism rather than personalism when it again commemorated the triumph during October 4 festivities observing the anniversary of the Constitution of 1824. On the balcony of the national palace, the Mexican flag waved triumphantly above a copy of the Constitution, two Spanish standards, and a flag that Santa Anna had captured from the Spaniards.[7]

In the year that followed, Santa Anna built a strong base of support, receiving accolades that threatened to interfere with many federalists' objectives of nation building. Various cities presented him with jeweled swords and medals while proclaiming him a "citizen of honor." He grew accustomed to being referred to as "Savior of the Country" and "Conqueror of Tampico." Such sobriquets boosted his popularity by reinforcing the caudillo's macho image and heroic status; they portrayed him as a powerful and aggressive figure capable of saving the nation from foreign conquest. On the one-year anniversary of the defeat, municipal officials in Jalapa organized a procession and mass and ordered residents to decorate and illuminate their houses. The festivities at Jalapa demonstrated that Santa Anna maintained solid backing in his home state, an essential objective for caudillos with national aspirations. The national government, wary of the general's growing popularity, refrained from awarding him lasting honors—at least for a time.[8]

Nevertheless, Santa Anna and the soldiers of the Tampico campaign continued to be admired in Mexico City on the victory's first and second anniversaries. In September 1830, the minister of foreign relations gave a toast at an independence day function in which he praised Miguel Hidalgo y Costilla, the priest who had initiated the independence movement in 1810, and concluded by saying that the victory at Tampico affirmed and consolidated sovereignty. The government newspaper, *Registro oficial*, included the event in an 1831 editorial about the independence movement, claiming that the triumph had secured Mexican sovereignty. It named Hidalgo, Iturbide, and Santa Anna as the primary protagonists in the struggle for liberty, thus elevating the caudillo to the highest level in the pantheon of Mexican heroes. This comparison became all the more powerful because Santa Anna was the only member of this lofty trio still alive to be venerated. That same year the Junta Patriótica, the group of citizens responsible for planning independence celebrations, donated a portion of its customary charitable funds to widows and orphans of men who had lost their lives fighting in 1829 and to soldiers wounded during that campaign.[9]

The acclaim that Santa Anna received from the national government predictably increased after his 1833 election to the presidency, a position he assumed in a manner that augmented his prestige without jeopardizing his popularity. Rather than accept the political risks associated with his new office, the caudillo claimed to be ill and shrewdly allowed his vice president, federalist Valentín Gómez Farías, to take the oath of office and act as president. The vice president, best remembered for controversial radical legislation reducing the power of the Catholic Church and army, used his authority to officially honor Santa Anna and the soldiers who fought at Tampico. Gómez Farías hoped to increase Mexicans' loyalty to the state by reminding the nation that the army and the president were a powerful force capable of defeating the former mother country. During his first month in office the vice president mandated that a monument be erected at Tampico on the spot where the Spanish had surrendered, featuring the national arms and an inscription reading, "The Mexican nation triumphed over its invaders, conquering the Spanish." While the planned monument did honor Santa Anna's victory, the inscription emphasized the federalists' broad-based efforts at nation-building ideals by giving credit to the "Mexican nation" rather than to the caudillo himself.[10]

In September 1833, Gómez Farías was still serving as acting president while Santa Anna commanded troops against a traditionalist insurrection. The goals of the rebellion characterized the beliefs of the traditionalists, or centralists: their movement aimed to restore customary powers to the army and the clergy and, ironically, to give Santa Anna dictatorial powers. The caudillo utilized the September 11 anniversary of his victory at Tampico to address his troops in a speech reflecting federalist ideals and nation building rather than personalistic aggrandizement. Published in the official national newspaper, now named *El telégrafo*, the speech reached a much wider audience. In this impassioned oration, Santa Anna reminded the soldiers of Mexico's (perceived, at least) military prowess, bolstered their spirits, reinforced the importance of their present charge, and defended federalism. Much as the editors of *Registro oficial* had done in 1831, he elevated September 11, 1829, to the status of an independence day when he asserted that it was a "glorious" day on which the Mexican army had ensured independence. He referred to the soldiers of 1829 as "our eagles," comparing them to the national symbol of Mexico. He argued that the Spaniards had continued to "sow discord" by inspiring those involved in the uprising to support centralism and dictatorship, ideas akin to Spanish monarchy. The president assured the soldiers that they were fighting to defend federalist institutions that had been adopted freely by the nation, and he concluded that history would remember their actions with "tenderness and respect."[11]

Although Santa Anna retained the presidency, by the following September the political landscape had changed dramatically. Gómez Farías and the ideas of the radical Congress had fallen into disfavor with Santa Anna and his followers; in April the president resumed control of the executive branch, and the following month the vice president left the country. On May 25, 1834, traditionalists in many provinces had announced adherence to the Plan of Cuernavaca, which called for "Religion, *fueros*, and Santa Anna." This traditionalist plan asked that Santa Anna assume extraordinary powers as president in order to reverse radical policies, including the laws that stripped the Catholic Church and military of their *fueros*, or special legal privileges. Reacting to these sentiments in June, Santa Anna dismissed his vice president's advisors, closed the radical-dominated Congress, and revoked many of its laws.[12]

Transformations in the observance of September 11 accompanied the shift that had occurred in government; the celebration reflected the increased power that Santa Anna had assumed in recent months and became more personalistic, extolling Santa Anna as a hero who was indispensable to the survival of the Mexican state. Tornel y Mendívil, once again serving as Federal District governor, used this position to decree that Mexico City residents officially commemorate September 11 in 1834. This act amended the calendar of civic rituals associated with independence, which previously had included only the September 16 holiday in honor of Hidalgo's Grito de Dolores. In his mandate, Tornel y Mendívil wrote that Santa Anna had demonstrated to the world that despite civil discord, Mexicans would cooperate to defeat foreign aggressors. He echoed the sentiments of many Santanistas and other politicians when he claimed that the September 11 triumph had consolidated sovereignty. Tornel y Mendívil raised his president once again to the exalted status of an independence hero. His words also suggested that as a strong leader, Santa Anna was capable of fostering unity, a feat acknowledged by nearly everyone in such contentious times as being essential for national success. The governor ordered city residents to decorate and illuminate their homes and mandated that the *ayuntamiento*, or city council, adorn the public buildings, as was the long-standing custom on civic holidays. The editors of *El telégrafo*, not surprisingly, announced the creation of the holiday with excitement, describing Santa Anna as an "immortal hero" and writing that Mexicans would remember "the triumph of Tampico" for centuries.[13]

Santa Anna observed the new holiday with a variety of activities. Accompanied by government functionaries, he attended a Te Deum to thank God for the defeat of the Spanish. In the afternoon he conducted a general review of the troops in the Paseo Nuevo. After the review the first magistrate of the ayuntamiento presented each soldier with a one-peso gift from the city and awarded the men who had served at Tampico with two pesos in recognition of their important service to the country. In the early evening the authorities met at the Ciudadela, the chief military garrison in the city, to offer congratulations to "the Conqueror of Tampico." Poems also appeared in the papers, extolling the president as "the savior of Mexico" and "a glorious CAUDILLO." The festivities reflected the ideas of both the traditionalists and the Santanistas by emphasizing the importance of a powerful military and the significance of strong leadership that Santa Anna himself represented on this holiday. Mexico City residents continued to observe September 11 in future years whenever the caudillo was in power.[14]

In the years between 1834 and 1842, Santa Anna experienced enormous fluctuations in popularity, suffered a serious injury on the field of battle, and reassumed the title of president. In 1836, he became a traitor in the minds of most Mexicans because after he suffered defeat at the hands of the rebellious Texans at the Battle of San Jacinto in April and was taken prisoner, he signed the Treaties of Velasco, which essentially guaranteed Texas independence. The humiliated caudillo returned to Mexico in February 1837 and retired to his hacienda at Manga de Clavo, claiming that he had left public life. Yet in 1838 he seized an opportunity to regain the admiration of the Mexican people and to renew his heroic status when a European power once again endangered national sovereignty in an event known as the Pastry War. The French threatened to attack Mexico for its refusal to pay 600,000 pesos in claims for damages—including the losses incurred by a pastry chef—suffered by French citizens living in the chaotic environment of early republican Mexico during the previous ten years. On December 5, Santa Anna awoke in the predawn hours to hear the enemy forcing the Veracruz city gates open. As the recently appointed commander, the caudillo swiftly organized soldiers and citizens to fight the invaders. He pursued the retreating intruders to the waterfront, where the French fired a concealed cannon at the charging forces. The general was struck with grapeshot and wounded so severely that doctors had to amputate his left leg below the knee. The sacrifice of his limb rejuvenated Santa Anna's popularity and reminded citizens that Mexico's welfare depended on his presence. At the same time that Mexicans honored the maimed caudillo for his bravery, many criticized traditionalist President Anastasio Bustamante, who faced insurrections against his leadership. In August 1841, Santa Anna joined the rebels and forced Bustamante from office. The caudillo took the oath of office to serve as provisional president with temporary dictatorial powers on October 10, 1841. Santa Anna and his supporters hoped that a brief dictatorship would help restore order to the country. He led a centralistic, personalistic, and at times nearly despotic government until December 1844.[15]

The 1842 independence ceremonies reflected the values of Santa Anna's current regime by glorifying strong leadership and elevating the caudillo to a still more prominent position among his fellow independence heroes. An earlier expansion of the independence calendar also helped communicate the increasingly traditionalist inclinations of Santa Anna. Beginning in 1837, with traditionalists in power but Santa Anna temporarily out of favor, the Junta Patriótica planned festivities for September 27 to immortalize Iturbide, whose triumphant entry into Mexico City in 1821 had signified the accomplishment of independence and whose brief tenure as emperor provided a model of strong leadership to the few traditionalists who favored dictatorial rule. This new holiday reflected the ideas of the traditionalists more effectively than the customary September 16 ceremony in honor of Hidalgo did. It praised Iturbide's Plan of Iguala, which had called for a strong central government (albeit a monarchy), the defense of Catholicism, and the equal treatment of Spanish citizens. These objectives coincided with the traditionalists' goal of leading a powerful national government that would produce an orderly society that respected the power of the Church and the military. Those who favored permanent dictatorial rule would even use the holiday to honor Iturbide as emperor of Mexico, a fact that more moderate politicians ignored.[16]

Mexico City residents began the 1842 independence holiday season on September 11 by reading laudatory newspaper articles about the president in the city newspapers. *El siglo XIX* hailed the president for his 1829 triumph, urging all citizens to unite and applaud the memory of Santa Anna, whose very name had become a "title of glory." The article extolled him as "the common father" of the republic. This sobriquet implied that he would defend and take care of the country as he would his family and reinforced his *macho* image as a protector of *la familia*. Such praise undermined more broad-based efforts at nation building by defining the Mexican state as Santa Anna's family rather than connecting the image of Mexico to general concepts of liberty or republic as earlier federalist leaders had done.[17]

Organized festivities took place throughout the day. In the morning Santa Anna left the national palace to review 4,000 troops who stood in formation to honor him at the Paseo Nuevo. Accompanied by generals and government officials, the president and his retinue presented a consolidation of power to those assembled. After giving a speech, Santa Anna returned to the Plaza Mayor, where he stood on the palace balcony to observe the troops that marched by to acknowledge his authority. He later received esteemed visitors who had been invited to a banquet in his honor. The guests gathered in a room lavishly decorated with silk walls and a gilded ceiling. Santa Anna sat regally on a raised platform surrounded by his advisors. The president concluded celebrations with a ball for his officials and distinguished citizens.[18]

On September 16, citizens enjoyed traditional festivities to honor Hidalgo's Grito de Dolores, despite the rain that persisted for much of the day. A soggy crowd gathered at the Alameda to listen to the customary oration, in which Manuel Gómez Pedraza attempted to bolster national pride by reminding those assembled that Mexico's abundant natural resources could provide wealth to resurrect the weak national economy. He not only praised Hidalgo but also complimented Iturbide for his heroic role in the independence movement. The speech thus demonstrated the current government's fondness for the traditionalist values and strong leadership that the emperor had embodied and that Santa Anna now represented.[19]

The independence season concluded on September 27 when Mexicans remembered Iturbide's triumphant 1821 march into Mexico City. Government and church functionaries began the festive day by attending a commemorative mass at the cathedral, where they gave thanks for their "happy emancipation" from Spanish rule. Following the service they marched to the Alameda, where they sat in front of the central fountain and listened to the discourse of Rafael Espinosa, a member of Congress. The orator urged the functionaries to celebrate the 1821 victory, asserting that it had guaranteed the advancement of civil and political rights. He praised the Plan of Iguala, recalling that all Mexicans had embraced it and even European politicians had commended it. Espinosa concluded by proclaiming that Iturbide would live as king in people's hearts because he had achieved independence.[20]

The focus of attention shifted from Iturbide to Santa Anna that afternoon when people attended a strange event designed to remember the president's bravery: a funeral for the leg that he had lost fighting the French in 1838. Both the wealthy and poor watched a marvelous procession from the Alameda to the Santa Paula Cemetery for the service. Shaded by veils that customarily hung above the streets for civic and religious processions, government and army officials led the parade, demonstrating their respect for Santa Anna's sacrifice. Behind these representatives sergeants carried the honored leg on a platform. The limb had been preserved in an adorned crystal urn within a box; the actual spectacle of the gruesome appendage would have made the funeral seem ridiculous, and perhaps offensive, to some. Two regiments of infantry and a squadron of cavalry solemnly followed the pallbearers and an artillery detachment formed the rear of the distinguished line, which reinforced the military's respect for its leader's sacrifice.[21]

Santa Paula, located in the suburbs on the west side of the city, was the oldest, most prestigious, and most picturesque burial ground in Mexico City. Albert Gilliam, author of a travel narrative, described the cemetery as a beautiful area enclosed by a tall brick wall. A garden lay between its entrance and the chapel, located at the middle of the grounds. Gilliam noted that although some graves bore few markings, others were "fantastically decorated." The cemetery had served as a hospital burial ground until 1836, when it opened to the public and became the resting place of many prominent citizens. Santa Anna's leg would be buried among Mexico City's elite to emphasize his important place in society.[22]

Arriving at Santa Paula, the group, which included Santa Anna, assembled around the imposing monument that Minister of War Antonio María Esnaurrizar had ordered constructed to honor the leg. The column to house the leg bore an inscription that Santa Anna himself had composed, in which he professed that he had lost his limb fighting for his home and country and that he now offered it as a testament of his love for Mexico. Consular insignias of Rome embossed the base of the column. On top of the cannon that formed part of the structure perched a statue of an eagle with a snake in its mouth, the national symbol of Mexico. Above the entire structure waved a Mexican flag.[23]

The remainder of the ceremony took place at the monument. Esnaurrizar placed the box containing the limb in the statue, then Ignacio Sierra y Rosso, Santa Anna's close friend and political ally, delivered an ardent eulogy, praising the president's glorious contributions to Mexico. Asking onlookers to define their feelings regarding this reverent celebration of their national leader, Sierra y Rosso admitted that he was overcome with emotion on this solemn occasion. He opined that Santa Anna's sacrifice to the country was "sweet" and should be commemorated with enthusiasm, declaring that the president had earned the love of the nation and "civic crowns." While Iturbide had won sovereignty, Santa Anna had ensured— at the cost of his own leg—continued independence for Mexico. The president was, in fact, the savior of independence. Presenting the caudillo with a Mexican flag, Sierra y Rosso again reminded those gathered of the president's heroic and important actions when he proclaimed that in the hands of Santa Anna, the banner was an "emblem of victory." The funeral concluded when the minister of war presented the urn's key to Santa Anna.[24]

Festivities extended into the afternoon and evening. The intrepid attended a running of the bulls in one of the capital's plazas, while the less courageous attended a comedy at the Teatro de Nuevo-México. The president and citizens who gathered at the Paseo de Bucareli enjoyed the entertainment of musicians. Santa Anna returned to the Santa Paula Cemetery later in the day accompanied by troops and functionaries, who again paid homage at the monument. While the president watched, government officials and soldiers showed their respect to the memorial as they would pay homage to a king. That evening some Mexicans gathered at the Plaza Mayor to watch fireworks, and others proceeded to celebrations at the opera.[25]

The personalistic funeral subverted the federalists' goals of nation building, displayed Santa Anna's authoritarian tendencies and demonstrated his machismo. By having the funeral on September 27, Santa Anna became the focal point of two of the three major independence holidays and identified himself with Mexico's only autocratic leader to date, Iturbide. The monument at Santa Paula Cemetery reinforced the idea that Santa Anna had played a singular role in history that had rendered him indispensable to the national welfare. The inscription emphasized his patriotism, generosity, and machismo because it reminded citizens that he had bravely sacrificed a leg to defend Mexico. The Roman insignias implied that, in the hands of Santa Anna, Mexico was as powerful as Rome, and the eagle and flag characterized the caudillo (or at least his limb) not only as representative of all Mexicans but as the human embodiment of the nation. Few republican leaders become the center of a civic ceremony to the extent that Santa Anna did at this event, where he heard himself eulogized. The oration again suggested that the caudillo had consolidated independence, not only with his 1829 victory but also with his 1838 sacrifice. It reiterated that Santa Anna's presence was vital to the nation. He likely hoped that the funeral would strengthen his macho image and thus reinforce his suitability to be president of Mexico.

Although the funeral impressed Santa Anna's friends and supporters, the bizarre memorial incited protest among his detractors, who expressed disdain toward the dictator for a variety of reasons. A compulsory military draft rankled the lower classes, and increased taxes continued to alienate both the poor and the wealthy. The president had also infuriated citizens when he called in outstanding copper coins but failed to reimburse people. While the government remained bankrupt, Santa Anna's personal wealth grew; and while federal officials went unpaid, the president constructed statues in his own honor. His disregard of his supporters' interests alarmed Mexicans, who feared that the will of the citizens did not interest him. The regal September celebrations of 1842 increased suspicions that he planned to establish a permanent dictatorship.[26]

Protesting the funeral, critics performed satires and otherwise denigrated the event for days in poems that circulated throughout the city. Someone even left a poem titled "Protest of the Dead Bodies of the Cemetery against the Reception of the Limb Among Them" at the burial ground, criticizing the memorial as well as Santa Anna's leadership. The anonymous poet disparaged the president's exorbitance when he described the monument as a sepulchral mansion and the burial as an act of "vain adulation." Because "Santa Anna [was] the stick / from which the splinter left," revolutionary germs had infected the limb. The dead therefore feared that the leg would contaminate them, ending their serene existence. They implored the "prudent congress" to prohibit its entrance to heaven. The poet criticized the president's tendency to incite revolution by implying that the leg had the power to wreak havoc even when detached from the caudillo's body.[27]

In the face of such taunts, a member of the Junta Patriótica dissociated himself from the memorial. A. F. Carvajal wrote to the editors of *El siglo XIX* that although he had attended all of the association's meetings, he had never heard anyone mention the ceremony. He admitted that he might have fallen asleep during a conversation or forgotten a discussion regarding the funeral, implying that he had not helped organize the event. Defining the Junta as a group created "with only the patriotic objective of celebrating September 16," he declared that the committee did not have the responsibility to plan the service.[28]

By the summer of 1844, Santa Anna faced personal as well as political turmoil that proved to be more significant than taunts regarding the memorial to his leg. His wife, Doña Inés García de Santa Anna, who had been ill since 1842, died at Puebla on August 23, 1844, at the age of thirty-three. Capital residents had admired Doña Inés even when their respect for her husband faltered, and they joined Santa Anna in mourning her death. On August 24, cannon blasts preceded the announcement that she had died. The *Diario del gobierno* printed the news and described her as a "loving and obedient daughter, a faithful, modest, and sensible wife, and a tender, expressive, and caring mother," who had acted virtuously in all circumstances. The funeral took place in Mexico City, where numerous citizens expressed their devotion by placing poems near her remains at the cathedral. Santa Anna returned to his hacienda soon after her death to attend to family business. While gone, he arranged to marry fifteen-year-old María Dolores de Tosta on October 3, only six weeks after the death of his first wife. He did not return to the capital for the ceremony but married her by proxy. Despite his absence, the guests celebrated the wedding in style, attending a banquet after the mass. Far from changing the opinions of most Mexicans, the wedding celebrations angered many, who noted that Santa Anna had refused to observe the traditional mourning period after the death of Doña Inés.[29]

Complaints about daily life in Mexico City only increased residents' ire toward their president, as well as toward the ayuntamiento. Some inhabitants wrote letters to *El siglo XIX* bemoaning the lack of potable water in municipal fountains. Others argued that unpaved and poorly paved roads and plazas exacerbated flooding problems, creating unhealthy and uncomfortable conditions. One group of inhabitants even lodged a complaint with the ayuntamiento regarding the inferior condition of pavement in their neighborhood, which turned into impassable mud during the annual rains. Still others objected to the ever-present garbage that littered the streets. They suggested that effective city cleanup occurred only in areas where prominent people lived and worked.[30]

Grievances of citizens throughout the country continued to mount in November and December 1844, when an unusually unified movement rallied against Santa Anna. The uprising represented a rare alliance of distinct social and political groups comprised of rich and poor, traditionalists and moderates. Although the various participants later disagreed regarding Mexico's future, they all concurred that Santa Anna had to go. Many prominent people, including congressmen and the editors of *El siglo XIX*, had already expressed dissatisfaction with his plan to reconquer Texas, arguing that the government did not have the funds to mount such an ambitious campaign. Offended by the exorbitance of his regime, angered by his near-autocratic rule, and outraged at the ever-increasing taxes, the opponents united to remove Santa Anna from office.[31]

Traditionalist general Mariano Paredes y Arrillaga, who had allied with Santa Anna in 1841, rebelled against him on November 2, thereby initiating a series of events that forced the caudillo into exile. Paredes y Arrillaga proclaimed that he would empower Congress with its full constitutional liberties and that Santa Anna must account for the sixty million pesos spent in the last two years. The rebellious general quickly gained the support of other military officers, increasing the pressure on Santa Anna, who led his still loyal troops to Querétaro, where he hoped to win a military victory over his enemy. When interim president Valentín Canalizo tried to close the Congress, many of its members reacted in defiance and claimed that the acting president did not have the authority to dismiss it. They continued to meet despite the decree. Finally, on December 6, soldiers in Mexico City declared themselves against the government, forcing Canalizo to surrender to their commander, José Joaquín de Herrera, who promised to restore the health of the nation.[32]

Citizens rioted in the streets of Mexico City during the aftermath of the December coup, destroying monuments and challenging the notion expressed in Sierra y Rosso's 1842 eulogy that Santa Anna had achieved immortality. An agitated group stormed the cemetery where the caudillo's leg was enshrined. The citizens destroyed the memorial and seized the decayed leg, carrying it through the streets, shouting in their excitement. Unable to lay hands on Santa Anna, they vented their outrage on his lost limb, symbolically inflicting physical injury on the leader himself. Although a soldier eventually stopped the enraged mob and rescued the limb from further disgrace, he could not prevent the crowd from continuing its rampage. It proceeded to the Plaza de Volador, where one of the most hated Santa Anna statues was located. The sculptor had depicted the president pointing north to emphasize his quest to reconquer Texas, but opponents had implied that he was pointing at the national mint, signifying his objective to abscond with government funds. The irate throng attacked the monument to protest the policies that had enriched the president while they suffered. A similar fate befell his statue at the Teatro de Santa Anna. One person even took a fragment of the bust home in an attempt to possess a small part of the wealth to which so few had access. Sierra y Rosso had referred to the temporality of monuments and the immortality of Santa Anna in his funeral oration. He had noted that although statues were always destroyed over time, the honored legacy of the heroic caudillo would persist in Mexico for eternity. But only two years later, in December 1844, an impassioned mob hoped to abolish the memory of the president by demolishing the monuments erected in his honor.[33]

Mexicans explained the coup in pamphlets that circulated throughout the city. One such leaflet noted a significant irony regarding the December 6 rebellion. On the same day in 1822, Santa Anna had proclaimed against the imperial government of Iturbide. The pamphleteer reprinted the president's 1822 call for the emperor's removal from power, as well as his assertions that Iturbide had offended honor and justice. The leaflet's author criticized Santa Anna for similar abuses of authority, concluding that on December 6, 1844, Mexicans had simply expressed his 1822 desire to remove an autocrat from office.[34]

Satirical poems, or *décimas*, commemorated the riots, affirming the triumph of the rebellion as well as Santa Anna's disgrace; members of Congress also scorned the president. The verses described the destruction of the statues, with the poets writing that the monuments had fallen as the caudillo had. They dubbed the then president a "louse" and a "cripple," denigrating his sacrifice for the nation instead of praising it and using his injury to portray him as weak instead of strong. Another poet referred to him as "the Antichrist," and yet another depicted him as crying, the antithesis of a macho. One décima portrayed Santa Anna as the speaker, forced to admit that he had fallen from power. Still another poem, beginning "The head of Santa Anna / Comes to replace its statue," suggested that the former president should meet a fate similar to the executed Iturbide. During a secret meeting on the night of the coup to discuss the destruction that had occurred throughout the city, congressmen quipped that if the caudillo were still president, he would have requested extraordinary powers in order to avenge the attacks on his character.[35]

The mob that destroyed his statues, as well as the poets and pamphleteers, aptly demonstrated that Mexicans would not blindly accept personalistic leadership. Ceremonies and statues lauding Santa Anna were not enough to maintain the loyalty of the populace. Indeed, such self-aggrandizing festivities and monuments only accentuated the citizenry's feelings that Santa Anna acted to benefit himself rather than the nation as a whole.

Criticisms of the funeral and monument appeared in books published even after the memorial had been destroyed, further emphasizing the event's failure to inspire the intended respect. Carlos María de Bustamante, a newspaper editor and author who had defended the Constitution of 1836 against the 1841 coup, censured the memorial in his book, *Apuntes para la historia*. He characterized Sierra y Rosso's emotional eulogy as ludicrous, and then proceeded to mock the concept of the monument. On the day of universal resurrection, he observed, Santa Anna's body would rush to the Santa Paula Cemetery to reunite with its leg because the president could not stand in judgment before God until he was joined with his limb. Although Santa Anna could attempt to increase his popularity with ceremonies and statues, ultimately only God would decide if the caudillo merited adulation.[36]

Foreign traveler Albert Gilliam described the monument as a strange display and chastised Santa Anna for his dubious influence on Mexico. He remarked that the "pride and pageantry" of the structure "diverted my respect from the consecrated place in a most considerable manner." He also noted that someone had torn down one of the monument's flagstaffs, restoring "the honor of his country's flag, and show[ing] his opposition to the highest authority [Santa Anna] upon earth." Gilliam then related an anecdote regarding the infamous U.S. traitor, Benedict Arnold, comparing him to the famous caudillo. He wrote that Arnold had once asked an American in London what people would do if he returned to the United

States. The man had defiantly retorted that Americans would cut off the leg that had been wounded defending liberty and bury it with full military honors, but they would hang the rest of his body as a traitor. Gilliam concluded that although Santa Anna had earned gratitude for his loss, "it must be hoped that he never may meet the fate of Arnold had he returned to the United States."[37]

Santa Anna did return to power on two occasions even after this humiliating coup. But in 1855 he was forced from power for the last time, never again to enjoy prominence as a national hero. The caudillo spent the years between 1855 and 1874 in exile in the Caribbean and Venezuela. During that time, he engaged in various failed attempts to reinsert himself into the Mexican political scene. The elderly caudillo was not allowed to return to Mexico until 1874, when the Liberals finally granted him amnesty following the death of President Benito Juárez. His property had been confiscated following his 1855 ouster, and Santa Anna lived his last two years modestly in Mexico City. When he died, in June 1876, friends organized his funeral and formed a procession from his house to his burial site at the cemetery next to the chapel of the Virgen de Guadalupe. No military troops or government officials participated to honor the former president who had left such an indelible mark on nineteenth-century Mexican history.[38]

In the years following Santa Anna's death, most Mexicans expressed derogatory opinions about the deceased caudillo. For example, textbooks published from the 1880s through the 1970s presented almost uniformly negative depictions of Santa Anna, whose leadership did not accomplish the positivistic goals of order and progress that many of the textbook authors themselves valued. The authors described the caudillo as an opportunist who took advantage of political instability and foreign invasions to regain popularity among the Mexican people. They also chastised him for his irresponsible use of government funds. They expressed the belief that the former president was a man who discouraged national unity and diminished national strength. These complaints implied that Santa Anna was more interested in his own success than in the well-being of the nation. The authors did not criticize Santa Anna for occasionally exhibiting dictatorial traits but for acting selfishly and incompetently. In contrast, despite the fact that he also emerged as a villain in the annals of Mexican history, many of the authors praised later dictator Porfirio Díaz (the subject of the following chapter) because, they contended, his strong leadership increased Mexico's political stability and encouraged national progress.[39]

History professor Luis Pérez Verdía wrote the *Compendio de la historia de México* in 1883; this book was updated and still in use as late as 1970. He argued that Santa Anna's 1834 actions against Gómez Farías demonstrated that the caudillo, who had been the "most staunch supporter of the Republic," had been "the first to destroy it" in order to satisfy his personal ambitions. Pérez Verdía further described Santa Anna's conduct during his 1841–1844 government as "immoral." But the author did commend the former president for his "glorious triumph" over the Spanish and his patriotism in the face of French aggression.[40]

Professor Rafael Aguirre Cinta wrote *Lecciones de historia general de México*, which was first published during the Porfiriato (1876–1911) and was still being used during the revolutionary era of the 1920s. Like Pérez Verdía, Aguirre Cinta credited Santa Anna for his "extraordinary activity" against the Spanish and his patriotism in 1838. Aguirre Cinta likewise criticized the caudillo for his record in domestic affairs. The author charged that Santa Anna had "killed" the federal republic in 1834. When describing the president's actions in the early 1840s, he depicted the caudillo as a leader who violated laws and whose behavior was "scandalous." Aguirre Cinta depicted his life at Manga de Clavo as a "continuous party," implying that Santa Anna was more concerned about having a good time than he was about the welfare of the nation.[41]

Justo Sierra, who served as the secretary of public instruction and fine arts during the final years of the Porfiriato, also criticized Santa Anna in his 1894 book, *Elementos de historia patria*. This book became one of the most commonly used and influential history texts in the 1920s. Sierra utilized the ideas of positivism to depict nineteenth-century Mexico, showing how the elite struggled to achieve order and progress following independence. He readily demonstrated that Santa Anna had interfered with the establishment of order during the early republic, although he did admit that the caudillo had exhibited "profound fondness" for Mexico. He believed that the president's actions in 1834 demonstrated his "insatiable ambition," and misrepresented the government that Santa Anna established after the departure of Gómez Farías as a dictatorship. Sierra depicted the general's actions against the French as an opportunity to regain his popularity among Mexicans. The author asserted that Santa Anna ruled as a despot and squandered the nation's financial resources when he returned to power in 1841. Besides mentioning Santa Anna at relevant points in his main narrative, Sierra included a fairly lengthy biography of the caudillo because he believed that Mexicans could learn about the weaknesses of their nation by understanding the man who best personified those deficiencies.[42]

Textbooks published in later years also characterized Santa Anna in negative terms. José Vasconcelos, who had served as secretary of education from 1921 until 1924, wrote *Breve historia de México* in 1937, which was updated into the 1970s. Vasconcelos utilized a biographical approach to history and

included an entire chapter about Santa Anna. He argued that the caudillo
was simply a product of his times; if Santa Anna had not risen to prominence from the ranks of the military, a similar character surely would have
emerged. He referred to Santa Anna's 1834 administration as "disorderly" and
accused the leader of misusing public funds. Rather than credit Santa Anna
for his role at Tampico, Vasconcelos asserted that, in the absence of heroic
activities, Santanistas invented reasons to praise the general in order to
increase his base of support. Vasconcelos wrote that the sacrifice of Santa
Anna's leg reinvigorated the image of the caudillo as a hero; in fact, according to Vasconcelos, Mexicans chose Santa Anna to be president in the 1843
election only because they loved his wound. In *Historia de México*, first published in 1951, Jorge Fernando Iturribarría depicted Santa Anna as an opportunist who imposed his caprice on the nation. He admitted that the general
had fought bravely against the French, but believed that he had done so to
"erase the difficult impression left" by his activities in Texas.[43]

The opinions of the textbook authors, as well as the reactions of
Mexicans during the early republic, indicated that personalistic policies and
ceremonies failed to win Santa Anna lasting acclaim or to accomplish the
goals of nation building. Yet Santanistas had created holidays and monuments to remind the public about his important contributions to the
national welfare; they thought that these ceremonies would augment
nationalism while simultaneously increasing Santa Anna's popularity.
Because Mexicans did not share a strong national identity in the years following independence, Santanistas believed that people from all economic
backgrounds related more easily to the caudillo's dramatic exploits than to
abstract notions of pride in the republic or liberty. The caudillo and his supporters maintained that personalistic ceremonies emphasizing his heroism
would increase national confidence and hoped that Mexicans would identify themselves with the brave actions of their leader.

Not all citizens agreed that personalism created national pride or contended that Santa Anna had earned a position in the pantheon of Mexican
heroes. Some politicians feared that too much focus on Santa Anna jeop-
ardized democracy because personalistic ceremonies often suggested that
the national welfare depended on the leadership of the caudillo. This discouraged the democratic selection of different men to govern and belied the
notion that Mexico existed on the basis of more enduring qualities, such as
the strength of its institutions, the abundance of its natural resources, or the
merits of its citizenry. Mexicans, furthermore, did not always trust Santa
Anna. They remembered his actions at Tampico and Veracruz fondly during national crises, when their fear and uncertainty made having a hero on
whom to depend reassuring. But they recalled his seeming ideological

inconsistencies, military blunders, and ceremonial extravagance when no internal or external threat loomed. At such times they regarded him as a villain who placed his own interests before those of the country rather than as a hero and patriarch who saw no distinction between his own needs and those of the nation. Personalistic ceremonies could not succeed when people believed that the man being venerated was selfish.

Pomp and statuary honoring Santa Anna therefore did not maintain the citizenry's loyalty or bring stability to Mexico. A decision of the Mexico City ayuntamiento regarding an infamous statue of Santa Anna demonstrated the strength of conviction both against the former president and his use of personalistic ritual. Late in 1855, the city council approved a plan to melt the metal that had gone into making this monument of "tyranny." From the material they endeavored to create a statue that represented a more enduring symbol of national pride: an eagle atop a nopal cactus. The ayuntamiento thus planned a monument that they believed would better promote nation building and ensured that the image of Santa Anna could never be resurrected.[44]

Notes

* The author would like to thank Pedro Santoni for his extensive comments, which improved this chapter.

1. Silvia Marina Arrom, *The Women of Mexico City, 1790–1857* (Stanford, Calif.: Stanford University Press, 1985), 5, 8–10; Barbara Tenenbaum, *The Politics of Penury: Debt and Taxes in Mexico, 1821–1856* (Albuquerque: University of New Mexico Press, 1986), xi, 13, 15; Michael P. Costeloe, *The Central Republic in Mexico, 1835–1846: Hombres de Bien in the Age of Santa Anna* (New York: Cambridge University Press, 1993), 2; Michael P. Costeloe, *La primera república federal de Mexico (1824–1835): Un estudio de los partidos políticos en el Mexico independiente*, 2nd ed. (Mexico City: Fondo de Cultura Económica, 1996), 12; Will Fowler, *Mexico in the Age of Proposals, 1821–1853* (Westport, Conn.: Greenwood Press, 1998), 265–266; Torcuato S. Di Tella, *National Popular Politics in Early Independent Mexico, 1820–1847* (Albuquerque: University of New Mexico Press, 1996), 1–4, 6; Richard A. Warren, *Vagrants and Citizens: Politics and the Masses in Mexico City from Colony to Republic* (Wilmington, Del.: SR Books, 2001), 6–7; Peter F. Guardino, *Peasants, Politics, and the Formation of Mexico's National State: Guerrero, 1800–1857* (Stanford, Calif.: Stanford University Press, 1996), 2, 4, 7; and Claudio Lomnitz-Adler, *Exits from the Labyrinth: Culture and Ideology in the Mexican National Space* (Berkeley and Los Angeles: University of California Press, 1992), 9. For more information on the role of the popular class and middle sector in early republican Mexico, see Di Tella, *National Popular Politics*, and Warren, *Vagrants and Citizens*.

2. Christon I. Archer, "The Young Antonio López de Santa Anna: Veracruz Counterinsurgent and Incipient Caudillo," in *The Human Tradition in Latin America: The Nineteenth Century*, ed. Judith Ewell and William H. Beezley (Wilmington, Del.: Scholarly Resources, 1989), 7, 15–16; John Lynch, *Caudillos in Spanish America, 1800–1850*

(Oxford: Clarendon Press, 1992), 456; Oakah Jones, *Santa Anna* (New York: Twayne, 1968), 36, 39, 47; Leonardo Pasquel, *Antonio López de Santa Anna* (Técamachalco, Mexico: Instituto de Mexicologia, 1990), 44; Enrique González Pedrero, *País de un solo hombre: El Mexico de Santa Anna,* vol. I, *La ronda de los contrarios* (Mexico City: Fondo de Cultura Económica, 1993), 389–390, 538; and Warren, *Vagrants and Citizens,* 5–6. For more information regarding Santa Anna's involvement in the election of 1828, see Chapter 7 of Costeloe, *La primera república.* During much of the early republic, the federalists divided into two main factions, the radicals and the moderates. Like the radicals, the moderates favored a federalist constitution, yet they did not believe in appealing to the masses, whom they regarded as a potential threat to public order. They also believed in a slower pace of reform. For more information on the political factions of the era, see Fowler, *Mexico in the Age of Proposals.*

3. Jones, *Santa Anna,* 92. For further information on Santa Anna's career, see biographies such as Wilfrid Hardy Callcott, *Santa Anna: The Story of an Enigma Who Once Was Mexico* (Norman: University of Oklahoma Press, 1936), and Agustín Yañez, *Santa Anna: Espectro de una sociedad,* with a prologue by Ernesto de la Torre Villar (Mexico City: Ediciones Oceano, 1982).

4. Lomnitz-Adler, *Exits,* 286–290; Lynch, *Caudillos,* 4, 133–134; Fernando Díaz Díaz, *Santa Anna y Juan Álvarez: Frente a frente* (Mexico City: SEP/Setentas, 1972), 10–11; Hugh M. Hamill, introduction to *Caudillos: Dictators in Spanish America,* ed. Hugh M. Hamill (Norman: University of Oklahoma Press, 1992), 6–8; Enrique Krauze, *Siglo de Caudillos: Biografía política de México (1810–1910)* (Barcelona: Tusquets Editores, 1994), 17; Peter Smith, "The Search for Legitimacy," in *Caudillos,* 87–96 ff.; Timothy E. Anna, *Forging Mexico 1821–1835* (Lincoln: University of Nebraska Press, 1998), 236–237; and Octavio Paz, *Labyrinth of Solitude: Life and Thought in Mexico,* trans. Lysander Kemp (New York: Grove Press, 1961), 81.

5. Carlos María de Bustamante, *Memorias para la historia de la invasión Española sobre la costa de Tampico de Tamaulipas, hecha en el año de 1829, y destruida por el valor y prudencia de los Generales D. Antonio López de Santa Anna, D. Manuel de Mier y Terán, en el corto espacio de un mes y quince dias* (Mexico City: Alejandro Valdés, 1831), 3, vol. 763, ex 8, CJML; Lucas Alamán, *Historia de Méjico desde los primeros movimientos que preparon su independencia en el año de 1808 hasta la época presente,* 2nd ed., vol. V (Mexico City: Editorial Jus, 1969), 531–532; Jones, *Santa Anna,* 49–51; Costeloe, *La primera república federal,* 224–226; Hubert Howe Bancroft, *The Works of Hubert Howe Bancroft,* vol. 13, *History of Mexico* (San Francisco: History Company, 1886), 73–75; and Callcott, *Santa Anna,* 71–74.

6. Bustamante, *Memorias para la historia,* 23–24; *El boletín oficial,* 12 de septiembre, 1829, n.; Jones, *Santa Anna,* 51; Callcott, *Santa Anna,* 76; Harold Dana Sims, *The Expulsion of Mexico's Spaniards 1821–1836* (Pittsburgh: University of Pittsburgh Press, 1990), 146; and González Pedrero, *País de un solo hombre,* I:535.

7. Bustamante, *Memorias para la historia,* 24–27; Will Fowler, *Tornel and Santa Anna: The Writer and the Caudillo, Mexico 1795–1853* (Westport, Conn.: Greenwood Press, 2000), 101; González Pedrero, *País de un solo hombre,* I:535–536; and Callcott, *Santa Anna,* 77. Fowler argues that Tornel played a crucial role as a "propagandist" in elevating Santa Anna to such a respected heroic status, *Tornel and Santa Anna,* 101. During the colonial period, New Spaniards paid homage to the monarchs in ceremonies such as the *jura del rey;* see Linda Curcio-Nagy, *The Great Festivals of Colonial Mexico City: Performing Power and Identity* (Albuquerque: University of New Mexico Press, 2004).

8. *Registro oficial*, 13 de julio, 1830, II, 306; 19 de [septiembre], 1830, III, 17 (Mexico City: Archivo General de la Nación); Agustín Guiol, *La patria hoy el grito apolla, y así, es fuerza que arda troya* (Mexico: Agustín Guiol, 1832), 1, LAC; Jones, *Santa Anna*, 51–52; Frank C. Hanighen, *Santa Anna: The Napoleon of the West* (New York: Coward-McCann, 1934), 60–61.

9. *Registro oficial*, 18 de septiembre, 1830, 16; 16, 18, 24 de septiembre, 1831, VI, 64, 71, 94 (Mexico City: Archivo General de la Nación). Santa Anna's victory at Tampico and the ensuing celebrations took place in the context of increasing political instability in Mexico, including the Acordada Revolt, the 1828 Parián riot, and the 1831 assassination of Vicente Guerrero. For more information on these events, see Fowler, *Mexico in the Age of Proposals*, and Warren, *Vagrants and Citizens*.

10. Jones, *Santa Anna*, 55–56; Costeloe, *La primera república federal*, 364–365; Callcott, *Santa Anna*, 96–101; Di Tella, *National Popular Politics*, 230; "Ignacio Martinez, General de Brigada, y Gobernador del Distrito Federal . . .," Mexico City, 29 de abril, 1833, num. de inv. 28351-C, pieza 9, CONDUMEX, Distrito Federal (hereafter cited as CONDUMEX); "Ignacio Martinez, General de Brigada, y Gobernador del Distrito Federal . . .," Mexico City, 27 de abril, 1833, num. de inv. 28349, pieza 7, CONDUMEX. Recent research asserts that Gómez Farías supported the type of legislation passed during his administration, but that Congress was responsible for the speed with which it was passed. The vice president would have preferred a more gradual approach. See Fowler, *Mexico in the Age of Proposals*. One of the medals distributed by the Mexican government to honor the soldiers at Tampico is on display in the museum at the San Jacinto historic site near Houston, Texas.

11. Callcott, *Santa Anna*, 101–103; Costeloe, *La primera república federal*, 385–390 ff.; *El telégrafo*, 14 de septiembre, 1833, 2. The name of the government newspaper changed frequently during the early republic, often reflecting transitions in power.

12. Warren, *Vagrants and Citizens*, 118–119, 126; Fowler, *Tornel and Santa Anna*, 136, 141–144; and Costeloe, *La primera república federal*, 428–429. See also Reynoldo Sordo Cedeño, *El congreso en la primera república centralista* (Mexico City: El Colegio de México, Instituto Tecnológica Autónoma de México, 1993), 61–67.

13. *El telégrafo*, 7 de septiembre, 1834, 4; Warren, *Vagrants and Citizens*, 128–129. Hidalgo issued the Grito de Dolores on September 16, 1810, initiating the Mexican wars for independence.

14. *El telégrafo*, 11 de septiembre, 1834, 3–4; 12 de septiembre, 1834, 4; 14 de septiembre, 1834, 3; *Diario del gobierno de los Estados Unidos Mexicanos*, 11 de septiembre, 1835, III, 42; Michael P. Costeloe, "The Junta Patriótica and the Celebration of Independence in Mexico City, 1825–1855," *Mexican Studies/Estudios Mexicanos* 13 (Winter 1997): 21–53 (25). Although traditionalists and *santanistas* favored strong leadership, most did not advocate for the creation of a military dictatorship at this time. See Fowler, *Tornel and Santa Anna*, 133–134, 141–145, and Costeloe, *Central Republic*, 214.

15. Jones, *Santa Anna*, 75–79, 84–85; Callcott, *Santa Anna*, 150, 155–157; Costeloe, *Central Republic in Mexico*, 144–146, 227; Michael Costeloe, "The Triangular Revolt in Mexico and the Fall of Anastasio Bustamante, August–October, 1841," *Journal of Latin America Studies* 20 (November 1988): 344–353 ff.; Fowler, *Tornel and Santa Anna*, 195.

16. Costeloe, "The Junta Patriótica," 24; Shannon L. Baker, "Santa Anna's Legacy: Caudillismo in Early Republican Mexico" (PhD diss., Texas Christian University, 1999), 107.

17. *El siglo XIX*, 11 de septiembre, 1842, 4; Rudolfo Anaya, "'I'm the King': The Macho

Image," in *Muy Macho: Latino Men Confront their Manhood*, ed. and with an introduction by Ray González (New York: Anchor Books, 1996), 66.

18. *El siglo XIX*, 11 de septiembre, 1842, 4; 12 de septiembre, 1842, 3; 13 de septiembre, 1842, 4; *Diario del gobierno*, 11, 12 de septiembre, 1842, XXIV, 165, 172; *El cosmopolita*, 14 de septiembre, 1842, 4; Costeloe, *Central Republic in Mexico*, 208–209, 223.

19. *Diario del gobierno*, 17 de septiembre, 1842, XXIV, 189; Manuel Gómez Pedraza, "Oración encomiástica que dijo Manuel Gómez Pedraza el 16 de septiembre de 1842," in *Conciencia nacional y su formación: Discursos cívicos septembrinos (1825–1871)*, ed. Ernesto de la Torre Villar and Ramiro Navarro (Mexico City: Universidad Nacional Autónoma de México, 1988), 199–208 ff.

20. *El siglo XIX*, 29 de septiembre, 1842, 4; *Diario del gobierno*, 3 de octubre, 1842, XXIV, 254–255; Rafael Espinosa, *Alocución que el ciudadano Rafael Espinosa dirijió el día 27 de septiembre de 1842, aniversario de la gloriosa entrada el ejército trigarante en México el año de 1821* (Mexico City: Vicente G. Torres, 1842), 4–15 ff., Box 3, Mexican Historical Pamphlets, 1820–1910, Hispanic Division, Library of Congress, Washington, D.C. (hereafter cited as MHP).

21. *El siglo XIX*, 29 de septiembre, 1842, 4; *Diario del gobierno*, 27 de septiembre, 1842, XXIV, 232; Carlos María de Bustamante, *Apuntes para la historia del gobierno del General D. Antonio López de Santa Anna, desde los princípios de octubre de 1841 hasta 6 de diciembre de 1844, en que fue dispuesto del mando por uniforme voluntud de la nación* (Mexico City: J. M. Lara, 1845), 84; Brantz Mayer, *Mexico As It Was and As It Is* (New York: J. Winchester, New World Press, 1844), 207.

22. Manuel Frances, *Los restos del Lic. Carlos María de Bustamante y el panteón de San Fernando* (Mexico City: Vida Gráfica, 1925), 10; Albert Gilliam, *Travels over the Tablelands and Cordilleras of Mexico: During the Years 1843 and 1844; Including a Description of California, the Principal Cities and Mining Districts of that Republic and the Biographies of Iturbide and Santa Anna* (Philadelphia: John W. Moore, 1846), 115–166, 119.

23. Bustamante, *Apuntes para la historia*, 84; *El siglo XIX*, 29 de septiembre, 1842, 4; Carlos María de Bustamante, *El gabinete mexicano durante el segundo período de la administración del Exmo. Señor Presidente Anastasio Bustamante, hasta la entrega de mando al Exmo. Señor Interino D. Antonio López de Santa Anna, y continuación del cuadro histórico de la revolución mexicana*, vol. I (Mexico City: José M. Lara, 1842), 144–145; Gilliam, *Travels over the Tablelands*, 119.

24. Ignacio Sierra y Rosso, *Discurso que por encargo de la Junta Patriótica pronunció de el panteón de Santa Paula el ciudadano Ignacio Sierra y Rosso, en la colocación del pie que perdió en Veracruz el Ecsmo. Sr. General de División, Benemérito de la Patria D. Antonio López de Santa Anna, en la gloriosa jornada del 5 de diciembre de 1838* (Mexico City: Antonio Díaz, 1842), 1–8.

25. Bustamante, *Apuntes para la historia*, 85; *El siglo XIX*, 29 de septiembre, 1842, 4.

26. Costeloe, *Central Republic in Mexico*, 204–205; Jones, *Santa Anna*, 86–87; Salvador Abascal, *La revolución de la reforma de 1833 á 1848. Gómez Farías—Santa [Anna]* (Mexico City: Tradición, 1983), 104; Fowler, *Mexico in the Age of Proposals*, 26–27.

27. Mayer, 207; Bustamante, *Apuntes para la historia*, 85–87.

28. *El siglo XIX*, 1 de octubre, 1842, 2. Reports of Junta Patriótica meetings that appeared in *Diario del gobierno* indicated that the organization did plan the September 16 and 27 independence celebrations. The reports provide no evidence that the Junta Patriótica planned either the September 11 holiday or the funeral. The vice president of the Junta, Tranquilino de la Vega, did attend the September 27 memorial.

29. *El siglo XIX*, 19 de abril, 1842, 4; 20 de abril, 1842, 4; *Diario del gobierno*, 24, 27 de agosto, 2, 10 de septiembre, 6 de octubre, 1844, XXX, 96, 108, 132, 162, 268; Actas de Cabildo, 26 de agosto, 1844, tomo 78, Archivo del Cabildo Metropolitano de la Catedral de México; "Sobre los de la Escma. Sra. Da. Inés García López de Santa Anna," Mexico City, 1844, Funebres y ceremonias funebres, vol. 1108, ex 12, AHDF; Costeloe, *Central Republic in Mexico*, 241–242; Callcott, *Santa Anna*, 200–201; Jones, *Santa Anna*, 90–91.

30. *El siglo XIX*, 11 de mayo, 1843, 3; 23 de mayo, 1843, 2; 25 de enero, 1844, 3; *Diario del · gobierno*, 6 de junio, 1844, XXIX, 128; "Los vecinos del Sapo y Ancho, piden se compongan, por estas inundadas," Mexico City, [1843], Obras públicas en general, vol. 1512-A, ex 213, AHDF.

31. Callcott, *Santa Anna*, 206–208; Costeloe, *Central Republic in Mexico*, 241–244, 251–255.

32. Costeloe, *Central Republic in Mexico*, 241–244, 251–255, 261; Jones, *Santa Anna*, 91–92; Guillermo Prieto, *Memorias de mis tiempos, 1828 a 1853* (Puebla: Editorial Jose M. Cajica Jr., 1970), 380–381; *El siglo XIX*, 6 de diciembre, 1844, 1. For more information regarding the political background to Santa Anna's 1844 fall from power, see Fowler, *Tornel and Santa Anna*, chap. 4.

33. Bustamante, *Apuntes para la historia*, 363–364; *El siglo XIX*, 7 de diciembre, 1844, 4; 13 de diciembre, 1844, 3; Jones, *Santa Anna*, 87; Di Tella, *National Popular Politics*, 242–243; Fowler, *Tornel and Santa Anna*, 231; Bancroft, V, 273; Sierra y Rosso, 8.

34. *Santa Anna por ambición* (Mexico City, 1844), n., vol. 797, ex 24, CJML.

35. *Décimas* (Mexico City, 1844) n., vol. 780, ex 32, CJML; Bustamante, *Apuntes para la historia*, 364.

36. Bustamante, *Apuntes para la historia*, 84–85.

37. Gilliam, *Travels over the Tablelands*, 119–120. Gilliam added that Santa Anna had sent his leg to Mexico City when Bustamante was still president. He stated that the people had accepted the gift enthusiastically, and had almost finished the monument when Santa Anna became provisional president. This suggested that Santa Anna had utilized the notoriety associated with his leg to become president, but waited until September 27 to hold the ceremony in order to identify himself better with Iturbide. This is the only source with information about the construction of the monument that I was able to locate.

38. Callcott, *Santa Anna*, 319–364 ff.

39. Mary Kay Vaughan, *The State, Education, and Social Class in Mexico, 1880–1928* (DeKalb: Northern Illinois University Press, 1982), 223–226. During the eras of the Reform and the Porfiriato, Mexican liberals espoused the ideas of positivism, a European philosophy that emphasized the necessity of establishing order as a means to achieving progress. According to this philosophy, the ideal society would be governed by scientific laws. See Colin M. Maclachlan and William H. Beezley, *El Gran Pueblo: A History of Greater Mexico* (Upper Saddle River, N.J.: Prentice Hall, 1999).

40. Luis Pérez Verdía, *Compendio de la historia de México desde sus primeros tiempos hasta la caida del segundo imperio* (Guadalajara, Jalisco: Author, 1883), 269, 274, 278, 280–281; reprinted, *Compendio de la historia de México desde sus primeros tiempos hasta los ultimos años*, 17th ed. (Guadalajara, Jalisco: Editores Libreria Font, 1970).

41. Rafael Aguirre Cinta, *Lecciones de historia general de México desde los tiempos primitivos hasta nuestos días*, 16th ed. (Mexico City: Sociedad de Edición y Librería Franco-Americana, 1926), 186, 191–192; Josefina Zoraida Vázquez, *Nacionalismo y educación en México* (Mexico City: El Colegio de México, 1970), 132, 190–191.

42. Vaughan, *The State, Education, and Social Class*, 21–22, 215, 223–224; Justo Sierra, *Historia patria* (Mexico City: Departamento Editorial de la Secretaría de Educación Pública, 1922), 103–104; Vazquez, *Nacionalismo y educación*, 125–126.

43. Jose Vasconcelos, *Breve historia de México* (Mexico City: Compañia Editorial Continental, 1976), 326–237, 341–342; Jorge Fernando Iturribarría, *Historia de México* (Mexico City: Secretaría de Educación Pública, 1951), 411, 415; Vazquez, *Nacionalismo y educación*, 186, 246.

44. "Sobre que se funda la estatua del Gral. Santa Anna que se halla en el mercado principal y que con el metal se fabrique una aguila con los trofeos de la nación colocandola en lugar de la estatua," Mexico City, 23 de noviembre, 1853, Historia—monumentos, 1790–1915, vol. 2276, ex 9, no doc. num., AHDF.

4

Presidential Ritual in Porfirian Mexico

Curtsying in the Shadow of Dictators

Víctor M. Macías-González

The scholarly approach known as new cultural history, which draws on anthropology, literary criticism, and gender studies, has allowed historians of the Porfiriato—General Porfirio Díaz's period of rule in Mexico from 1876 to 1911—to better understand how Díaz and his contemporaries constructed, contested, negotiated, and staged power and culture.[1] Cultural historians can thus explain Díaz's long rule and performance of power through exploration of quotidian Porfirian social practices.[2] Scholars have focused not only on public celebrations and rituals but also on mortuary practices, merchandising, criminology, leisure, architecture, gardens, love letters, and many other facets of everyday life to better understand the relationship of society to a regime intent on socially reengineering both the population and the spaces in which it lived, through secularization and modernization.[3] The research of Matthew D. Esposito, for example, underlines the importance of analyzing ceremonies to understand how Díaz used them to showcase his regime's material successes while constructing and enhancing his legitimacy with didactic funeral processions that helped the population to "imagine" the national—and the centrality of the dictatorship to society.[4] Mauricio Tenorio-Trillo's study of Mexico at the world's fairs explained these displays as self-representation exercises demonstrative of the country's faith in modernity and progress.[5]

This chapter explores how Díaz, aware of the political importance of self-fashioning and self-representation, used various heroic facets of his persona to construe and enhance his power through ceremony and ritual. We now know much about the mechanisms of power—compromise, tempting offers, threats, violence, encouragement of factionalism—but Díaz's fascinating use of what Daniel Cosío Villegas has dubbed "the cult of personality" merits further study, particularly in light of recent research on the self and modernity.[6] British social theorist Anthony Giddens argues that as societies transition from tradition to modernity, individuals cease fashioning an understanding of their social roles and expectations through institutions such as the church and family and increasingly work out their roles and identities for themselves, thus developing a deep sense of self and identity. As a modern individual, Díaz was engaged in continuous self-observation and reflection; the notebooks and diaries that he kept, first as a military officer and later as a statesman, not only allowed him to keep track of his actions and to evaluate his experiences, accomplishments, and mistakes, they also helped him craft his public image and lay out an agenda for the future. The image that Díaz and his collaborators fabricated was part of a "trajectory of development from the past to the anticipated future . . . self-actualisation."[7]

The Díaz myth and the propagation of his image as an indispensable, messianic *héroe de la paz*—"hero of peace"—sought to establish his indispensability to the nation. Díaz's feats against the fatherland's enemies and his development policies forged a modern country. Publicized in biographies, music, poems, texts, etiquette manuals, films, and sound recordings, the myth cultivated deference toward Díaz, establishing him as the fountain of political legitimacy and authority. Photographs, paintings, and other images placed Díaz at the center of the nation's struggle against internal and external enemies. Accordingly, Díaz and his entourage modified his image as necessary; he appeared in uniform when his military glory needed to be highlighted and dressed in civilian attire to underscore his government's stability.

Díaz and his collaborators creatively rendered ritual and representation into instances of the *bricolage* (or tinkering) that anthropologist Claude Lévi-Strauss presented in *The Savage Mind* in 1962. Lévi-Strauss characterized the *bricoleur* as a crafty individual who creatively and advantageously improvises solutions in situations where others would have failed to recognize the alternative applicability of structures, practices, and materials.[8] The bricoleur thus appropriates for his own purposes processes and meanings that may originally have been created with other intents. In the case of the Díaz myth, he and his entourage liberally improvised representations and rituals—primarily the elaborate ritual of the presidential audience—to Díaz's political advantage.

The inclusion of Díaz in this anthology devoted to heroes, as well as Antonio López de Santa Anna, may raise a few eyebrows. The official history of Mexico vilifies both: Díaz is derided as "father of foreigners, stepfather of Mexicans," and López de Santa Anna as a sellout. But, while the record of both caudillos is today judged after the fact, during their lifetime a significant portion of the population did support them, and as this chapter and Shannon Baker's Chapter 3 argue, ceremony and ritual legitimized and "heroized" these controversial figures. Posthumously pilloried, they were nevertheless heroes of their own time and, in the case of Díaz, at least, managed to maintain a significant cult following. Witness, for example, the campaign to repatriate Díaz's remains from their Parisian exile in the early 1990s, or how President Carlos Salinas de Gortari (1988–1994) compared his neoliberal economic policies to those of José Yves Limantour, the Porfirian "genius of finances." Díaz's policies—particularly his failure to institutionalize presidential succession—may very well have prompted the revolution, but his long dictatorship transformed Mexico from an unstable, bankrupt nation into Hispanic America's most prosperous and diversified economy, with significant achievements in the areas of public health, education, and culture. Díaz created the modern Mexican state.

Before discussing the heroic myth, it is useful to also consider the process and the crafters of the myth. This was primarily the work of two groups: the staff of various government ministries and the Círculo de Amigos del General Porfirio Díaz (Circle of Friends of General Porfirio Díaz). The first group, which included men such as Guillermo de Landa y Escandón, José de Algara y Cervantes, Luis Torres Rivas, and Colonel Pablo de Escandón y Barrón, was drawn from the country's upper crust; they handled public relations and coordinated social affairs for the Ministry of Foreign Affairs and the presidency.[9] Well traveled and versed in the ways of the world, these aristocrats placed their *savoir faire* at the disposal of the regime, profiting greatly from their proximity to power. The Círculo—which functioned as the regime's unofficial cheerleading squad—was a network of politicians, military brass, and businessmen who, beginning in the 1880s, had worked to reelect Díaz, believing his continuation in power would benefit the country—and their pocketbooks.[10] The Círculo—the name would change constantly—had Díaz's reelection as its mission. Accordingly, members wrote articles, published laudatory works, and organized festivals to influence public opinion. Alfredo Chavero y Cardona led the group that orchestrated Díaz's reelections, raised funds, drafted guest lists, and regaled the masses with fêtes celebrating don Porfirio.[11] Whether surrounded by his regally appointed guard corps or sitting under a velveteen, gold-fringed canopy, Díaz was the respectable statesman upon whom literati and artists heaped commissioned praise. He became a living hero, the indispensable savior and developer of Mexico.

The crafters of the Díaz myth created a series of ceremonies and rituals that established him as the uncontestable authority. The creation of the "routinized practices" of ceremony gave form and order to the myth; they provided the scenario for the fabricated Don Porfirio.[12] Díaz used a highly gendered strategy of representation that presented him as the embodiment of ideal manhood. Civics textbooks provided basic lessons drawn from heroic instances in the dictator's life that would serve as primers for ideal citizens based on his model of virtue.

Ephemera featuring the exemplary leader's portrait—pottery, busts, photographs, prints, fans, calendars—became as ubiquitous as the images of popular saints, and it was a rare courthouse, school, municipal palace, club, or place of business that lacked at least one image of the *héroe de la paz*. Mexican cinema of the 1940s, although grossly adherent to the anti-Díaz myth of the revolution, nevertheless recreated the widespread ephemeral adulation of the heroic Díaz most skillfully. This was particularly the case of the characters that Fernando Soler, the Porfirian stereotype actor par excellence, portrayed as pondering great moral dilemmas (such as how to deal with a troublesome, boy-crazy daughter), cognac snifter and cigar in hand, contemplating a portrait of Don Porfirio.[13]

The myth of the benevolent dictator was captured in the form of objects, such as photographs, that were used and displayed in everyday life. Such objects extended the mission of the mythified flesh-and-blood president into the private domain of the family home, bringing not only order but also progress, for in their gilded frames they formed part of an ensemble of sumptuary goods that demonstrated to visitors (and reassured the home's occupants of) the secure economic and social station of its residents. Sacralized in its objectification, the heroic Díaz myth clearly transcended our traditional understanding of heroic stature as the result of populist tactics. Whether most of the people viewed him as a charismatic hero or not became irrelevant, because the reality he created through the bricolage of ritual placed him at the center of the Mexican political and cultural universe. It is for this reason—namely, that Díaz and his collaborators used ritual to craft him as a charismatic, mythic hero—that this chapter focuses on ritual as the source of the myth.

The presidential audience proved particularly useful to the staging of the Díaz myth. To a large extent, its success was based on how it was used to humble the most powerful personages of the time, whose social status, prestige, and prerogatives would otherwise have outranked Díaz in Mexican or global hierarchies.[14] During these choreographed meetings, Díaz used light and sound, as well as temporal, spatial, and even emotional mechanisms, to symbolically and ceremonially position himself above powerful petitioners.

The Porfirian use of the presidential audience prompts a number of questions. How and why did Porfirians legitimize their purported republic from 1880 on with rituals that reeked of monarchy? What was the intent behind the complicated etiquettes and the redesign of interior spaces in government buildings? What payoff did the ruling circle perceive in the revival of courtly ways dangerously evocative of the ceremonial of the Church and the imperial regime? When and why did Díaz find it useful to capitalize on symbolic power?

Creating the Hero

BAPTIZED ON SEPTEMBER 15, 1830, as José de la Cruz Porfirio, Díaz spent most of his teen years studying Latin, mathematics, ethics, philosophy, and theology at the Colegio Seminario Conciliar of his native Oaxaca, where he was the protégé of future Bishop José Agustín Domínguez. Díaz abandoned his religious vocation during the turbulent late 1840s to join the ranks of the anticlerical Liberal Party, which Benito Juárez then headed in Oaxaca. The latter's role in national politics from 1858 to 1871 facilitated Díaz's rise to regional and subsequently national prominence, allowing him to play a leading role in the War of the French Intervention (1862–1867) as commander of the Army of the East. Following the Liberals' restoration of the republic in 1867, Díaz entered politics, becoming a congressman, and eventually contended for the presidency in 1870.[15] Unable to win, and claiming that the strengthened national executive endangered constitutional order, Díaz took up arms in 1871–1872. The revolt was eventually contained, and, in the spirit of reconciliation, President Sebastián Lerdo de Tejada amnestied Díaz and his supporters. Díaz did not waste time. Over the next four years he prepared a comeback that Lerdo de Tejada unwittingly facilitated through his attempt to reelect himself to the presidency in 1876. Claiming that Lerdo de Tejada's reelection was unconstitutional, Díaz deposed him, and held on to power until 1911. The brief interregnum of General Manuel González between 1880 and 1884 allowed Díaz to deal with unpopular policies from behind the scenes, solving, among other problems, the country's foreign debt.

From 1876 to 1890, Díaz imposed his authority over the country, creating a modern state at the expense of powerful regional, military, and political interests. He replaced the regional bosses, or *caciques*, in areas of economic and political relevance with *jefes políticos* (political bosses). He used these 300 local officials, whose portfolios included local judiciary, health, education, and defense matters, to counter the influence of governors, caudillos, and regional *camarillas* (political interest groups). Díaz also reformed, downsized, and professionalized the old republican army while increasing its mobility with the new railways. Díaz allied himself with a coalition of Liberal military and civilian interests, destroying the more radical Liberal factions.[16] Politics were neutralized as the Congress, which President Juárez had already weakened, became the rubber-stamping debating society it remained throughout the twentieth century. In essence, Díaz imposed the era of *"poca política y mucha administración"*—"little politics and much administration."[17]

In addition to consolidating his political power, Díaz mended relations with the oligarchy and the Church. After his marriage to Carmen Romero Rubio y Castelló—a youthful, pious, and savvy bourgeois woman who, despite bearing the honorific and belittling term of endearment Doña Carmelita, came to wield great power—Díaz obtained access to the oligarchy's inner circle. From the scions of the aristocracy he drew a number of close advisors, rewarding them with prestigious postings abroad as envoys. The urban middle classes solidified their alliance with the regime: the technocrat *Científico* faction, chief among them Finance Minister José Yves Limantour, began its rise to power. As his respectability rose, Don Porfirio secured the blessings of a Church with which he established cordial relations—thanks to his friend the Oaxacan archbishop Eulogio Gillow y Zavalza—turning a blind eye toward the anticlerical provisions of the Constitution in order to secure consensus from society.[18]

From 1890 to 1906, the political and economic consensus established earlier yielded its fruit. Foreign capital flowed into a now peaceful country whose improved relations with Europe had secured better terms for the debt.[19] The booming economy supported an expanded, increasingly more literate, and better paid population. Modernization swept across the country, bringing an interest in foreign ideas and goods to the most remote corners of the republic, creating the Mexican *belle époque*. Political opposition ceased as dissidents were repressed, and critical intellectuals were muffled with offers of employment at the state's flourishing cultural, educational, and scientific institutions.[20] Blue-ribbon commissions traveled abroad, increasing Mexico's prestige, and decorations from crowned heads of state began to eclipse the republican medals on Don Porfirio's chest. General Díaz increasingly resembled a European statesman, his whitening moustache lending him that aura of respectability to which he aspired when he visited—attired in frock coat and top hat—exclusive schools for young ladies, his dark Mixtec visage blanched with a dusting of alabastrine talcum. New theaters, libraries, palaces, and schools dotted the cities as hospitals and jails contained the country's social ills, and the statuary of the imagined community lined elegant avenues busy with carriages, bicycles, and automobiles.[21] In 1895 the treasury reported the first surplus in the nation's history.

From 1906 on, the Porfirian miracle stumbled as the worldwide economic depression of 1907–1908 coincided with climate change and the rising political activism of urban workers. Exports decreased and debts were called in; the haciendas suffered. Machinery purchases dropped, crop yields diminished, the peasantry went into debt crisis, tenant farmers' rent rose. The economy stopped growing and the ranks of the unemployed expanded. As government income shrank and salaries were frozen, bureaucrats became restless. The people scorned Limantour's policies, ineffectual during times of economic duress. Díaz, soon to turn 80, was believed to be too old, as was a cabinet the penny-press satirized as *la momiza*, or "living mummies." The system suffered from being too comfortable (static, some would argue) yet insecure in that Díaz never established a viable way to transmit power. In the midst of these challenges, Díaz struggled to remain in control, employing advances in technology and infrastructure to massacre striking miners and workers, unleashing ferocious warfare on the Yaquis and other recalcitrant *indios bárbaros*—nomadic, "barbarian" Indians.[22] But change, like old age, could not be kept at bay. Don Porfirio vacillated over whether he would step down from the presidency and introduce democracy. But just as the dark clouds gathered over the Porfirian age, there was one final hurrah, the centennial of Mexican independence in 1910. The world's great powers dispatched prominent statesmen and emissaries to feast in the Mexican Camelot whose pageantry celebrated an independence that magically coincided with the dictator's eightieth birthday and his final reelection.[23] Hardly had the bunting been put away and the last princeling departed when, from the north of the country, news of rebellion arrived. A revolution was beginning, and the *pax porfiriana* was at an end.

Porfirio, King of the Mexicans?

In order to build Mexican modernity, Díaz recast traditions that gave him access to coercive, nonviolent political tools inclusive of elegant etiquette, art, ceremony, and ritualized everyday practices and objects. To the contemporary observer it would have appeared that Díaz had become some sort of megalomaniac seduced by the trappings of monarchy. But nothing could be further from the truth: while a number of critics referred to him as the Aztec czar or the Mexican Caesar, a few keen observers recognized the usefulness of the rituals.

Porfirian use of *ancien régime* conceptions of power can best be understood in light of historians' arguments about the rise of absolutism in seventeenth-century France. Some scholars contend that early modern monarchs, rather than employ costly resources or violence, developed a rich repertoire of coercive, nonviolent political tools to accomplish their goals. In order to strengthen the authority of the French king, agents of the crown fined courtiers who, even in the absence of the royal person, failed to manifest their respect for the crown when they did not curtsey before the king's representatives or, even worse, everyday objects belonging to the monarch. Orest Ranum narrates how failure to make a reverence to the king's knife and fork was tantamount to committing the crime of *lèse majesté* (high treason).[24] Such practices enhanced monarchs' power and led to the development of court life. Accordingly, royal palaces functioned as theaters of power where symbolic exchanges (including bearing, speech, manner, and appearance) between the ruler and the ruled served as instruments of regal self-assertion and defense.[25] Emblems, allegories, courtesies, ornament, and especially their ostentation and performance according to established norms became the currency of choice. Ritual and spectacle allowed rulers to construct their claims to authority through the appropriation, redefinition, and manipulation of objects, traditions, and established rituals.[26]

Díaz's and particularly his collaborators' symbolic manipulation aimed to construct a new type of national leader who created consensus and had absolute authority. Díaz established the presidency as a post of unquestionable power and endowed it not only with his patriarchal-military authority, the legitimating mantle of the Liberal institutionalization of the state, and the technocratic efficiency of the *científicos*, but also with charisma. Weber (see the Introduction to this book) defines charisma as the third component of his tripartite explanation of why individuals concede authority to rulers.[27] For him, charismatic authority is distinct both from rational legal authority, a modern phenomenon based on institutionally sanctioned rules, and from traditional authority—a premodern phenomenon based on unwritten, long-established customs or practices. Opposed to rational legal and traditional authority, charisma is based on the widespread appeal or popularity of a leader's personality; it is revolutionary, transformative, and subversive of order. It releases one from all that is traditional, sacred, conventional, and ordinary.[28] In short, charisma creates new meaning. In the case of Díaz, it allowed him to be indifferent to extant social hierarchies and to use etiquette and ceremonies to give new meaning to himself and the office he held.

Nineteenth-century Mexican civilian, military, and ecclesiastic leaders had a rich repertoire of ritual to enhance their rule. Not only could they draw on Church ritual, Mesoamerican traditions, the viceregal past, and

European courtly ceremonials, they could also bring into play the rich material culture and social capital of the country's predominantly European-origin upper class, thanks to the regime's splendid working relationship with the aristocracy and the Church. Moreover, the brief imperial regimes of 1822–1823 (the First Empire) and 1863–1867 (the Second Empire), as well as the quasi-monarchical dictatorship of López de Santa Anna from 1852 to 1855, had featured ostentatious pageantry. Throughout this time, surviving members and descendents of the Spanish viceregal nobility and imperial courts kept their titles, coronets, uniforms, and coats-of-arms close at hand, ready for a comeback. José Manuel de Hidalgo y Esnaurrizar, together with members of the Iturbide family, intrigued against Díaz in Madrid, New York, Paris, and Rome well into the 1890s.[29] A few Mexicans continued to reauthorize their titles in Spain, and the allure of the aristocracy had such a hold on social climbers throughout the long nineteenth century that more than a few bore false titles or obtained obscure pontifical distinctions.[30] Nor were Liberals unfamiliar with monarchical trappings and aristocratic delusions. Liberal bureaucrats learned European etiquette through interaction with representatives of Maximilian's empire on numerous occasions, and, after the triumph of 1867, they found themselves working in buildings replete with symbolic references to the vanquished archduke. Penury forced the Liberal governments of Benito Juárez, Sebastián Lerdo de Tejada, and even Díaz to continue using buildings, equipment, furnishings, and other trappings of the overthrown Second Empire. Foreign visitors, for example, noted that the crystal, cutlery, dishes, and tablecloths used for state dinners still bore the gold-embossed initials of Maximilian well into the 1870s.[31] Díaz and his collaborators were clearly familiar with the uses and paraphernalia of ceremony and pageantry. They jockeyed to outshine each other's decorations and honors, competing viciously for medals, crosses, and plaques.

The best examples of Porfirian ceremonial magnificence were undoubtedly the president's audiences, which employed a strategy resembling that developed in the court of the medieval dukes of Burgundy, whereby petitioners were made to approach the monarch through a succession of magnificently appointed halls or antechambers. Under this system, the relatively weak rulers of the Grand Duchy of Burgundy displayed war trophies, costly furnishings, and the heraldic crests of vassals and clad their retinue in elegant garb to impress visitors with a grossly exaggerated sense of the ruler's economic and political power.[32] The Burgundian model, which the emperor Charles V had brought to his domains in Spain and the New World in the early 1500s, used spatial constructions of the private and the public to maintain a hierarchy of rank and to express the ruler's authority

and power by limiting or extending access to the ruler. In spatially restricting the public's proximity to the leader, the Burgundian model could arbi-
trarily impose or modulate rank above and beyond the social hierarchies in
use.[33] All classes found themselves humbled before the artificially magnif-
icent prince.

Thus, Porfirian observance of the Burgundian ceremonial model proved
useful because its ritual made the heroic Díaz the final arbiter of power.
Díaz and his collaborators paid increasing attention to ceremony and etiquette because it gave them a useful and relatively cheap political tool.
Accordingly, the Foreign Ministry regularly requested updates on changes
in etiquette, particularly from those diplomats posted to protocol-conscious
monarchical capitals such as Berlin, Brussels, London, Madrid, Saint
Petersburg, Tokyo, or Vienna.[34] In transmitting their observations of ceremony abroad, the diplomatic corps came to function as an important channel by which Porfirian officialdom assimilated the political uses of etiquette.[35] The minister to Japan, Carlos Américo Lera, for example, studied
the relative successes of the missions of foreign envoys or the careers of
Japanese bureaucrats based on detailed observations of seating arrangements at official functions of the Japanese imperial household.[36] Mexican
preoccupation with questions of etiquette also stemmed from earlier problems in the early 1880s, when members of the cabinet had unknowingly
committed a number of ceremonial *faux pas* that had created difficulties for
the country's diplomatic corps.[37] During the regime's final decade,
Mexicans had become so ceremonious that they adeptly employed etiquette
as a tool against the foreign policy of the United States. The imperial
Russian envoy, for example, noted that Díaz had effectively avoided meeting with Elihu Root during his visit in 1907—purportedly to obtain politically costly concessions from Díaz—by cramming the American secretary
of state's agenda full of wreath-laying ceremonies, state dinners, parades,
and military reviews.[38] Clearly, Porfirians had learned the political uses of
etiquette.

The regime remodeled and redecorated various edifices to provide the
president with spaces appropriate for the deployment of the Burgundian
model. Between the 1880s and 1900, officials modified the layout of major
public buildings. Although these reforms and modifications of government
office floor plans have often been interpreted as largely superficial
makeovers meant to "modernize" Mexico through the provision of faddish
European façades and novel amenities such as electric lighting, water clos-
ets, and telephones, we need to recognize the importance of these spatial
transformations to the articulation of an ambitious program of ritual and
ceremony in Mexican officialdom.[39] And most important, we need to real-

ize that the implementation of the Burgundian system was not limited to the presidency but was also gradually extended to the state and local level. State legislatures, for example, devoted much time to elaborating instructions regarding the décor, functional specificity, and order of precedence to be observed in the rooms, halls, and apartments of the legislative chambers and governors' palaces.[40] Regional oligarchies revamped ceremonial spaces, commissioning portraits and busts of prominent ancestors to decorate the remodeled halls and galleries.[41]

An excellent example of Porfirian reconfiguration of interior spaces was the costly reformation in the 1890s of the National Palace. This project created a series of ceremonial antechambers, waiting rooms, and hallways to impress visitors with Díaz's power. To do this, the government implemented an unparalleled purchasing and construction spree that relocated various ministries out of the crowded National Palace into more modern buildings suited to their specific needs. Wherever possible, existing structures were acquired and remodeled; the palatial residence of Don Francisco Espinosa was transformed from 1895 to 1900 to house the Foreign Ministry, freeing up a large suite of rooms in the National Palace.[42] Similarly, the Ministry of Justice and Public Instruction relocated to the grand neoclassical palace famed eighteenth-century architect Manuel Tolsá had built for the Marqués del Apartado, prior to extensive remodeling by Porfirio Díaz, Jr., in 1900 and 1901.[43]

The extensive remodeling of the ancient National Palace began in 1895, one year after Finance Minister Limantour had succeeded in presenting the first budget surplus in the nation's history. Workers replaced ornaments bearing the seal of the Second Empire with motifs emblematic of the republic. Two allegorical statues of the Liberals supplanted the parapets from which the empire's flags had hung.[44] In 1896, the bell Father Hidalgo had used to call for independence in 1810 was placed above the palace's central balcony.[45] Concrete and stucco transformed the colonial-style façade into a bad copy of the Élysée Palace, home of the French president.[46]

Once work on the exterior was completed, the interior of the National Palace became the focus of an extensive transformation.[47] Between 1900 and 1902, nearly 300,000 pesos were spent creating new offices for Díaz and his staff. Much of the work consisted of partitioning the vast old Hall of the Ambassadors, 110 yards long by 9 yards wide, into a new executive suite. The grand salon's earlier renovations in the 1870s and 1880s had failed to capitalize on its great dimensions beyond using its long walls to display portraits of the country's rulers.[48]

In 1900, architects carved a number of smaller departments out of the Hall of the Ambassadors to house Don Porfirio's offices, including a new presidential library, salon, audience room, waiting rooms, antechambers, and vestibules. The diplomatic corps welcomed the inclusion of comfortable seating areas in these new rooms. Hitherto they had been forced to stand before the president, who, in keeping with ceremonial forms in place since the time of the viceroys, had been the only person for whom a chair had been provided in the gargantuan hall.[49] But these changes did little to relax presidential etiquette. Although diplomats could now make themselves comfortable in the presence of the president and his party, the executive found himself vastly removed from the average mortal. Six doors separated the president from the public reception area, and, thanks to a new elevator installed in the palace's southern tower, Díaz could leave or enter the palace unseen by the waiting petitioners. A new presidential throne featuring two gilt spread eagles as legs and upholstered in red damask embroidered with the seal of the republic was placed under a red velvet canopy in the main reception room.

The president's personal secretary obtained a new suite of offices in the mezzanine (*entresuelo*) previously occupied by the Foreign Ministry, with a specially constructed private hallway and elevator that allowed Rafaelito (as President Díaz referred to Rafael Chousal) to enter and leave the palace, like Díaz, without the impediment of having to pass by waiting petitioners.[50] Given his high rank and proximity to power, a suite of four rooms separated the president's secretary from the public reception area: employees' office, vestibule, waiting room, and conference room.

By the time these modifications to the palace had been implemented, the Office of the President of the Republic sprawled across nearly twenty different rooms and salons, including the new blue and red parlors, the gentlemen's smoking room, a luxuriously appointed powder room for women visitors, and two elegant salons that served as audience waiting rooms, named "Paz" (a reference to the Liberal Peace) and "Hidalgo," after the allegorical and historical portraits that hung prominently on their walls.[51] An adjoining wing housed functionally differentiated rooms for eating, rest, and work: a cabinet meeting room, a parlor where the ministers could rest between meetings, dining rooms, a smoking parlor, a private parlor, a butler's pantry, kitchens, and bathrooms.

The modifications to the palace's layout required changes to regulations concerning the appearance and distribution of palace staff, as well as the redrafting of the executive ceremonial. The military garrison included more officers (a brigadier general, a cavalry major, and a cavalry captain), perhaps because their uniforms and medals lent an air of regal elegance. Noncommissioned officers replaced the civilians who had formerly worked as servants and doormen.[52] Newspaper ads announcing the need for additional staff at the palace reminded the reader that only individuals of a "pleasant appearance"—Porfirian lingo for middle-class whites and light-skinned, cultured mestizos—need apply.[53]

New legislation duly codified the new spaces and practices. The order of precedence, sumptuary regulations, and other dispositions for palace functions had been formulated over the years, building on precedent. Article 85 of the Constitution, as well as a law dating from 1891, granted the executive the right to codify a ceremonial, but it was not until 1908–1910, during planning for the centennial celebrations of independence, that officials finally drafted a presidential ceremonial. It codified thirty-nine ranks of precedence for private citizens, corporations, and federal, state, municipal, military, and foreign officials (art. 1). Visiting royals were accorded a higher rank than the representatives of republics (art. 5). Four types of presidential audiences—public, individual, private, and general—accommodated, with varying degrees of pomp, different ranks of visitors (art. 11). The type of carriage, clothing, uniform, and language employed to attend these ceremonies was also regulated (arts. 11 and 15). Separate dispositions were made for the first lady's audiences and receptions (arts. 31–34). Within the ministry of foreign affairs, a special department was founded to implement these procedures, the Servicio de Protocolo. This Office of Protocol worked closely with the Intendant of the Presidential Residences, the head of the palace guards, and the chief of staff to prepare seating charts, to arrange itineraries for distinguished visitors, and to elaborate appropriate menus, all in accordance with established precedences, ranks, and titles (arts. 93–108). In sum, by the end of the Porfiriato, the regime had delineated sophisticated measures regulating ceremony and ritual.[54]

The ceremonial function of the spaces created in the National Palace can best be understood in the context of the presidential audience. Executive etiquette effectively distanced Díaz from the common citizen because ceremonial usage and trappings rendered visible a heightened degree of hierarchy. Individuals who wished to appeal an unfavorable judicial hearing to Díaz or who sought employment, pensions, or dispensation from government regulations and tax contributions thus found it a daunting task to present their case before a Don Porfirio surrounded by the material trappings and symbolic allegories of his power, fame, and strength. Although officials liked to claim that it was relatively simple to secure an audience, the elaborate ceremonies of the executive audience probably discouraged supplicants.[55]

Petitioners proceeded through an elaborate set of motions before they accessed the president. Before a petitioner met Díaz, he or she had to prepare a number of supporting documents for his or her cause and had to secure letters of introduction from prominent acquaintances or community members who would not only attest to the validity of the request but also to the petitioner's honorability. This letter, along with a carefully worded narrative addressing the desired outcome, would often be dispatched to Mexico City weeks or months before the arrival of the petitioner, in the hope that the expense of traveling to the capital could be avoided by having the matter resolved through correspondence. In the average month, the Office of the President processed more than 100 such requests, usually rerouting them to the appropriate ministry or official with special instructions for their resolution; Díaz sent a separate letter to the petitioner, making him or her aware of the measures taken. Whenever the favor seeker did not receive a favorable reply, the next step was to appeal personally and directly to the president in Mexico City.

Díaz held public audiences on Monday, Wednesday, and Friday afternoons. Petitioners inscribed their names and the subject of their visit before noon on the day of the requested audience in the notebook kept for that purpose at the entrance of the National Palace. Some petitioners left their *carte de visite* with the ushers, perhaps giving a small tip to a member of the palace staff in the hope of having the card (with a message inscribed on the back) delivered to the president's secretary. They next proceeded into the building's largest patio and up the grand flight of stairs known as the "honor staircase" (*escalera de honor*) that led to the presidential suite. Here, in the first of three great antechambers before the executive audience room, they entered the first phase of a drawn-out process affecting the petitioner's career, life, family, and community.

The primary function of these three antechambers was to distance the supplicants from the president. The arrangement, color, size, light, and assorted other accouterments of each chamber created a favorable impression of Díaz's power in the anxious visitors. While each successive room was smaller the closer one approached the president's private offices, each successive antechamber was more luxurious, giving the impression that increased proximity to power translated into greater opulence, amenity, and sophistication. This phenomenon was not unique to Mexico but was in common use in the homes of European and American elites, as confirmed by the novelist Edith Wharton, who in her book of advice on interior décor suggested that a "carefully graduated scale of ornamentation culminate in the most important room of the house."[56]

The first reception room, often called either "hell" or "the hall of common mortals," initiated a drawn-out petitory process. This salon of grand proportions featured monumental leather-upholstered sofas and settees where peasants and workers waited in democratic comfort seated next to generals, senators, clerics, artists, bureaucrats, and businessmen.[57] Sunlight streamed through the many windows, brightly illuminating the hall. An allegorical painting of Peace as a lightly clad, cloud-enveloped angelical feminine figure hung on the wall, seemingly reminding the petitioners of the celestial quality of the all-powerful man whom they beseeched. Days to months could pass before hopefuls would hear the imposingly clad presidential aides utter their names with great ceremony, as the bells of the cathedral and the clock in the National Palace sounded at four o'clock in the afternoon. This signaled the possibility of an eventually successful, if protracted, wait during the rest of the afternoon and evening. Díaz and his private secretary had deemed the petitioner's case—and the signatures of the personages on the letters of introduction, posted in advance of the petitioner's arrival in Mexico City—worthy of attention from among the over 1,200 letters, reports, telegrams, and petitions received weekly.[58] A place on the audience list enabled them to pass through the stone lion–flanked double doors leading to the second antechamber. Those who had not been selected that day could then retire and return again the next audience day.[59]

Unmistakably, petitioners regarded a summons into this second chamber (and subsequent ones) as a clear marker of their status. Díaz had considered them more worthy than those he had turned away. Individuals with good political connections or high social standing may have regarded their inability to obtain an audience as an indicator of their changing political worth (or *crédit*, as scholars of the dynamics of early modern French political networks and clientelism have termed it).[60] In order to clarify the matter, they, their friends, or protectors wrote to the dictator, his wife, or his private secretary seeking an opinion on the matter.[61] Those who were able to do so visited briefly with these influential personages at a ball, opera performance, or charity bazaar; during these encounters the petitioner or his agent keenly observed body language, facial expressions, and the tone of the comments exchanged.[62] Díaz, famous for his self-control, had only one telltale sign of disagreement or anger, flared nostrils, and petitioners especially feared this sign. For all of their fear, however, few were so rash as to consider themselves ostracized by the denial of entrée during the limited time Don Porfirio had available for audiences. They knew he was a busy man.

Those who rejoiced at gaining entry into the second waiting room, however, were not guaranteed an audience that day. Weeks might pass before these optimists left the elegantly appointed antechamber many called "purgatory." The room's silk wallpaper and porcelain vases, embossed with the motto of Emperor Maximilian, "Equality Before Justice," offered hope to the favor seekers.[63] The reddish tones of the antechamber's color scheme psychologically communicated the omnipotence of the authority being approached.[64] Almost as if to offset the tone of Maximilian's ephemera, a great painting of independence leader Father Miguel Hidalgo y Costilla hung on the wall. The canvas was quite a conversation piece, owing to the celebrity that its painter, the Catalan master Antonio Fabrés, had acquired from the exorbitant sums his works commanded.[65] Those awaiting a summons into the third waiting room were significantly fewer in number than those waiting in the first room, but passage through a final filter still lay ahead. Invariably, a lengthy stay was in order. Important matters of state, personal illness, family affairs, travel to the provinces, or the arrival of foreign envoys or prospective investors cut into Díaz's audience time. Unless petitioners proved persistent and had the resources to spend days if not weeks waiting in the second antechamber, not to mention the influence and connections indispensable to secure entry into the third waiting room, they stood little chance of seeing the president.

The fortunate few summoned into the third waiting room (approximately ten individuals on any given day) found themselves in a regally appointed antechamber known as "limbo." Plush carpets and heavy curtains filtered out the noise of the fidgeting, coughing nervousness emanating from the first two waiting rooms. Wing chairs arranged in conversational groups gave the petitioners a reassuring feeling of security and intimacy. Artistically arranged marble and bronze statuary guarded the air of relaxed formality. Here they patiently waited to be summoned, one by one, into a final room, an antechamber to Díaz's audience hall, where a group of presidential aides-de-camp and palace staff congregated, ready to tend to the president's needs. Petitioners who for some reason had yet to realize their relative insignificance to the dictator finally got the message when they had to stand in this antechamber built expressly as a holding pen for staff for which the president had no use at the moment. Here they nervously reviewed their notes and quietly rehearsed the speeches they had prepared to convincingly present their causes to the regal Don Porfirio in the twenty minutes allotted each audience.[66]

It was then that the climactic moment happened: a palace guard announced Díaz was ready to see them. An usher opened the double doors of the executive audience room, revealing Díaz in one of two positions: standing, holding out a hand in welcome, if Díaz was receptive and amicable to the matter underlying the audience, or enthroned, cold, and distant if he considered the topic of the meeting to have specific political significance.

If he was receptive to the subject matter of the audience, Díaz would ask the petitioner about her or his health, her or his family, and motion for the petitioner to sit on the settee facing the comfortable chair that the executive occupied. The president sat quietly, listening to the visitor's comments, and took notes in a small notebook. On some occasions, the petitioners forgot their much-practiced speeches, and Díaz would have to encourage them and give them time to recompose themselves. In those cases he would just question the nervous guest about the object of her or his visit, or glance at the notes that the presidential staff had handed him regarding the petitioner's case.[67] In an instant of nervousness, this routine bureaucratic operation (preparing an executive brief that detailed the particulars of the matter at hand and provided additional background information) may have momentarily lent credence in the petitioner's mind to the myth of Díaz as a well-informed—if not omniscient—leader. Often, if the issue at hand could not be immediately resolved, Díaz would ask the supplicant to make an appointment with the appropriate cabinet minister to expedite the matter. Díaz would call in his secretary, give him verbal instructions in the case, and perhaps, after autographing a photograph to the petitioner, Díaz would hand him or her a small note with instructions on how to resolve the affair.

If, however, Díaz was not positively disposed toward the topic of the meeting, or if he wanted to use the occasion to reprimand the visitor, the dictator had a panoply of theatrics at his disposal. To begin with, Díaz would arrange himself so that the visitor would find him- or herself blinded by too much light. A great window behind the president's chair facilitated this operation, allowing the afternoon sun to flood the room, almost blinding the petitioner, who was forced to talk to Díaz without being able to see him clearly. If the visitor was a foreign dignitary whom the president wanted to impress, Díaz would receive him surrounded by his cabinet, the highest-ranking officers of the armed forces and navy, and by the bedazzling presidential guards. Alfred Dumaine, the French representative in Mexico, noted that during such imposing circumstances, Díaz hardly seemed to move: "he is rigid, his forehead high, his eyes fixed upon you, he rests in a theatrical immobility."[68]

The final moments of a presidential audience were often the most symbolically charged, particularly because it was often at this time that Díaz momentarily lapsed from his otherwise "theatrical immobility." Don Porfirio would approach the visitor for an embrace or clasp his or her hand while he gazed into the visitor's eyes and shared a few words of solace or affection, perhaps remembering old times or passing on his regards to family members or to some magnate residing in the visitor's home town. Foreign envoys often could not wait to get home from such interviews in order to write glowing reports to their governments of the "special distinctions" of which they had been the object in audiences where they had exchanged a few intimate words or had stood close to the president.[69]

On occasion, Díaz would perhaps become emotional, momentarily breaking with the "three-F—*Feo* (ugly), *Fuerte* (strong), *y Formal* (and for-mal)" traditional Mexican male mode of conduct. He apparently saved these displays of emotion—reportedly accompanied by the shedding of tears—to convey a special distinction to a visitor, particularly when he met with foreign dignitaries to express condolences for the death of a head of state. In the summer of 1894, the Vicomte de Petiteville reported to his superiors in Paris that Díaz had become teary-eyed during a brief audience following the assassination of French President Sadi Carnot.[70] The impor-tance of emotion and gesture was well understood and the frequent topic of dispatches home; the Vicomte de Benghem, Belgian minister to Mexico, remarked on the need for reserve in public functions because he recognized that Mexicans keenly read his body language.[71]

The interview ended after Díaz fell silent and looked at the door. At this signal the visitor would exit the executive office under the escort of a guard. If for some reason Díaz was unable to see all the individuals waiting in the third antechamber and one of them had an urgent matter that had to be resolved that day, a member of the presidential staff would ask him to visit Díaz's private residence at 9:30 that evening. One or two others could also be accommodated between Díaz's meetings and appointments the next morning.[72]

Conclusions

PORFIRIANS EXHIBITED A STRONG DESIRE to creatively interpret proto-colary and sumptuary practices to solemnize affairs of state and to arbitrar-ily introduce hierarchy and distinction. In one operation they demonstrat-ed Mexico's membership in "the Concert of Civilized Nations"; enhanced the power of the Porfirian regime vis-à-vis the Conservatives, the Church, and the army; and articulated the leader's charisma. The hero's charisma accomplished a number of things. First, it broke with established conven-tions and, through bricolage, created a new myth that gave meaning and place to a ruler whose authority was based on an extralegal operation (a coup) and whose ideology (liberalism) broke with the country's traditional forms of legitimacy (provided by Catholicism). Second, in establishing the hero as exceptional, it opened the way to an expanded exercise of power. What produced the charismatic moment, the opportunity for Díaz to assume the heroic posture? Fallaw and Brunk suggest that the hero takes the stage, or at least a new stage, in Mexico and Latin America in the nine-teenth century, the region's era of nation building. Díaz exemplified the nation in many ways, from his ethnic origins and early family history (the grandson of creoles, mestizos, and Mixtecs) to a job history (from cleric to lawyer to general) that mirrored the rise of the mestizo, the growth of secularism, and the victory of liberalism. More than any other nineteenth-century Mexican or Latin American hero, he personified the great transformations of the long nineteenth century. As a warrior and statesman, he embodied the nation and reinforced the Liberal party's vision of it—grounded on the pantheon of martyr-heroes like Hidalgo, Morelos, and Cuauhtémoc—in the newly remodeled and redecorated audience chambers of the country's public edifices. Díaz's use of ritual and ceremony thus bolstered, and to a certain degree also sacralized, the collective identity.

Since one of the primary characteristics of the nineteenth century in Mexico is the breakdown of social hierarchy and the vacuum of power or respect for institutionalized authorities, the use of ceremony and etiquette in the Porfiriato bears vital evidence of how agents of the nascent state employed civic ritual to awe society into respecting central authorities. Charisma helped elevate a heroic Díaz to a level of authority that no other Mexican leader had yet achieved. Officials codified the order of precedence in processions and public festivities to underline the importance of the executive; Díaz and a select coterie received greater symbolic importance than representatives of other branches of government, such as the president of the Congress or the chief justice of the Supreme Court. Contingents of elegantly clad officials such as firemen, policemen, *rurales*, and soldiers marched alongside floats presenting allegories of the president's accomplishments (commerce and peace were frequent subjects of representation) during civic celebrations marking the observance of national feast days. The presence of these representatives of public order, not to mention the great efforts at incorporating technological advances into state pageantry, such as the trimming of public buildings with decorative light bulbs, symbolically reinforced the regime's positivist motto: Peace, Order, Progress.

The creative adaptation of European courtly protocol to a republican milieu and the reorganization of interiors in public buildings were corollaries to propagandistic Porfirian pageantry. While Mexicans were not newcomers to the visual reinforcement of institutional strength through architecture, the adoption of the Burgundian construct of spatial hierarchy and ritual constituted an innovation that incorporated novel ideas of the private and the public developed in eighteenth-century Europe. These new practices also revealed the growing functional differentiation typical of affluent, developing industrial economies. Historians of furniture note the simple character of Mexican interior décor prior to the 1820s, which stood in sharp contrast to the profligate flamboyance of late nineteenth-century interiors, where ornately carved and luxuriously upholstered furnishings with specific, limited functions filled rooms dedicated to a particular activity.[73]

As my engagement of charisma and Lévi-Strauss's definition of bricolage already suggests, Porfirian ritual practices enabled Díaz to escape the
traditional social constraints, allowing him to subvert a caste structure that
would have doomed him, as a mestizo general, to an inferior position in the
country's social scale. It is important to note that Diaz's use of ceremony
was not simply an attempt to acculturate into the country's Europeanized
oligarchy but rather indicated a calculated effort to carve out his own social
niche. Combined with new notions of space and material culture, affluence,
and the observance of European etiquettes, the charismatic operation
allowed Porfirians to institute novel social ranks. This meant that government offices had to incorporate multiple rooms to better enable bureaucrats
to carry out their duties without the interference of the public or underlings. Waiting rooms with benches, with a balustrade marking the distance
between the waiting public, a minor functionary responsible for regulating
traffic into internal offices (usually exercising the powers of the panopticon
from an elevated workstation), and, most important, a portrait of Díaz
hanging on the most prominent wall, became widespread. Adjoining suites
of reception and meeting areas made it possible for higher officials to conduct affairs of state in greater privacy. New audience rooms, and the complicated ceremonial that accompanied the creation of these chambers, also
made it possible for officials to observe different protocols tailored to the
rank of the petitioner; the mayor of a minor provincial town need not be
received in the same style as the ambassador of a great power. The décor of
these new spaces allowed Porfirians to play powerful psychological games
on those anxiously waiting to conduct an interview with the officials inside;
comfortable furniture, color schemes, statuary, paintings, and even the
amount of light in a waiting room could begin to place the supplicant in a
submissive or more cordial mood.

Whether in the private office of President Díaz or in the grand reception halls of the National Palace, high-ranking Porfirians became adept
manipulators of highly sophisticated mechanisms designed to enhance
their status through the use of material culture. Portraits of influential
friends such as the German Kaiser, but also costly furnishings, or simply the
presence of uniformed guards and liveried servants, helped to theatricalize
the power and influence of the statesman. And, again, over the entire system of symbols, spaces, and rituals loomed the mythic figure of the heroic
president.

Why did Porfirians place so much emphasis on building social distance
between themselves and the population? Why did the state's pageantry, in
the words of cultural historian William H. Beezley, turn observers into
"spectators rather than celebrants, observers rather than participants"?[74]

The answer is relatively simple: the passivity of audiences of state spectacle mirrored the virtuous obedience that the Porfirian ideal of order and peace dictated as the citizens' proper participation in efforts to achieve progress. A receptive crowd was the only acceptable result of the regime's ideal of a centralized, authoritative, unquestioned state. Díaz, like most Liberal presidents after Juárez, struggled to submit a number of powerful centrifugal agents (the Church, the army, regional strongmen) to the strong central state that he believed to be the only force capable of uniting the country and ensuring its independence. The symbolically enhanced, charismatic figure of the president appeared as a new type of authority. The question remains, however, whether ceremony served to distance Díaz from the population or whether it provided society with a reformulated yet traditional way of approaching the leader. I suggest it was the latter.

It should not surprise us that Díaz did this recasting of old traditions and forms of etiquette; Don Porfirio and his supporters were merely engaging in an old game of "inventing" or tinkering with traditions. Eric Hobsbawm and Terence Ranger—and, earlier, Lévi-Strauss—thus defined "responses to novel situations which take the form of reference to old situations" and which establish "their own past" or novel meanings.[75] Díaz and other Liberals may have destroyed the Conservatives and the Church, but they kept alive and enhanced their enemies' ceremonies and rituals (duly desacralized and properly linked to the state) to give the country a sense of identity and to some degree of continuity at the same time that Porfirians ushered in modernization.

The pageantry of civic ritual and state ceremonial thus offered the Porfirian state a tool of governance. Among the capacities of ceremony that nation-builders most admired (and ably employed) was its "imaginative" function, used to create a unifying force through the display of icons and symbols that embodied shared values.[76] Rituals allowed the Porfirian elite to build a new national culture with Díaz at the center. The president thus benefited from spectacles of civic virtue that also made the state the sole arbiter of rank and the regulator of access to power.

If Porfirio Díaz was a hero, what kind of hero was he? Sources suggest that whether we view him as a public person or as a private individual, Díaz was a complex, savvy, and practical man. Neither completely rational nor traditional, he turned to the liberating pragmatism of charismatic leadership. This explains the longevity of his power and at the same time presents the problem that, as a modern, complex individual, there existed a Porfirio for every season. As such, it is not a necessarily productive historical exercise to speculate on whether Díaz was a hero or a villain. If he was a hero, he was a hero of his time and place. The heroic condition, as Brunk and

Fallaw contend, is one that arises from the relationship between exemplary persons and the communities where they exercise their extraordinary capacities. If we conclude that Díaz was a villain, what would this say about the society and the time in which he lived? Perhaps the answer is that Díaz, like the Machiavellian prince, was both. Díaz was a hero who was willing to do whatever was expedient and necessary—including acts that some would label as villainous—in order to accomplish the great feat of nation building.

Notes

* This chapter is made possible thanks to grants from the International Faculty Development Fund and the Faculty Research Fund of the University of Wisconsin–La Crosse. I would like to thank Sam Brunk and Ben Fallaw for their commentaries and suggestions.

1. For an overview of cultural history, see Joyce Appleby, Lynn Hunt, and Margaret Jacob, eds., *Telling the Truth about History* (New York: W. W. Norton, 1994).

2. Judith Butler, *Gender Trouble: Feminism and the Subversion of Identity* (New York: Routledge, 1990), 25.

3. The historiography of power in Porfirian Mexico includes Romana Falcón and Raymond Buve, eds., *Don Porfirio Presidente . . ., Nunca Omnipotente: Hallazgos, reflexiones, y debates, 1876–1911* (Mexico City: Universidad Iberoamericana, 1998), and Gilbert Joseph and Daniel Nugent, eds., *Everyday Forms of State Formation: Revolution and the Negotiation of Rule in Modern Mexico* (Durham, N.C.: Duke University Press, 1994). For an introduction to Porfirian cultural studies, see the work of William H. Beezley, especially *Judas at the Jockey Club and Other Episodes of Porfirian Mexico*, 2nd ed. (Lincoln: University of Nebraska Press, 2004).

4. Matthew D. Esposito, "Death and Disorder in Mexico City: The State Funeral of Manuel Romero Rubio," in *Latin American Popular Culture: An Introduction*, ed. William H. Beezley and Linda A. Curcio-Nagy (Wilmington, Del.: Scholarly Resources, 2000), 87–103.

5. Mauricio Tenorio-Trillo, *Mexico at the World's Fairs: Crafting a Modern Nation* (Berkeley and Los Angeles: University of California Press, 1996).

6. On mythmaking, see Daniel Cosío Villegas, "El barbero de Sevilla," in *Daniel Cosío Villegas, El historiador liberal*, ed. Enrique Krauze (Mexico City: Fondo de Cultura Económica, 1984), 232.

7. Anthony Giddens, *Modernity and Self-Identity: Self and Society in the Late Modern Age* (Stanford, Calif.: Stanford University Press, 1991), 70–77.

8. Claude Lévi-Strauss, *The Savage Mind* (Chicago: University of Chicago, 1966), 19–21.

9. For an overview of aristocrats' work for Díaz, see Víctor M. Macías-González, "The Mexican Aristocracy and Porfirio Díaz, 1876–1911" (PhD diss., Texas Christian University, 1999), chap. 7.

10. The Círculo went by many names: Junta Central Porfirista (1891), Comité Central Porfirista (1892), Club de Amigos del Presidente (1894), Círculo de Amigos del General Porfirio Díaz (1895), Junta Central del Círculo Nacional Porfirista (1896), and Círculo Nacional Porfirista (1900–1911).

11. Víctor M. Macías-González, "El ocaso de Júpiter: La crisis de representación simbólica de la dictadura porfiriana. México, 1890–1915," paper presented at the VIII International Colloquium of the Centre Interuniversitaire de Recherche sur l'Éducation et la Culture dans le Monde Ibérique et Ibéro-Américain, "Texte et Image dans le Monde Ibérique et Ibéroaméricain," Université François Rabelais, Tours, France, March 15–18, 2002.

12. Giddens, *Modernity and Self-Identity*, 80–83.

13. One of the best examples is the 1948 Azteca Films production, *Una familia de tantas*.

14. Vicomte de Petiteville, Mexico City, 16 April 1894, to Casimir Perier, Paris, in Affaires Politiques Diverses du Méxique Series, tome 78 (1893–1895), Archives of the Foreign Ministry of the French Republic, Quai d'Orsay, Paris. Hereafter cited as AMAE.

15. Paul Garner, *Porfirio Díaz* (Harlow, U.K.: Pearson, 2001), 21–54.

16. Hira de Gortari Rabiela, "La política de la formación del Estado nacional," *Revista Mexicana de Sociología* 44, no. 1 (1982): 263–284.

17. Enrique Krauze, *Místico de la autoridad: Porfirio Díaz* (Mexico City: Fondo de Cultura Económica, 1987), 31–53.

18. Jorge Fernando de Iturribarría, "La política de conciliación del general Díaz y el arzobispo Gillow," *Historia Mexicana* 14, no. 1 (1964).

19. Don M. Coerver, *The Porfirian Interregnum: The Presidency of Manuel González of Mexico, 1880–1884* (Fort Worth: Texas Christian University Press, 1979).

20. Krauze, *Místico de la autoridad*, 51.

21. Barbara A. Tenenbaum, "Streetwise History: The Paseo de la Reforma and the Porfirian State, 1876–1910," in *Rituals of Rule, Rituals of Resistance: Public Celebrations and Popular Culture in Mexico*, ed. William H. Beezley, Cheryl English Martin, and William E. French (Wilmington, Del.: Scholarly Resources Books, 1994), 127–150

22. Friedrich Katz, ed., *Porfirio Díaz frente al descontento popular regional (1891–1892): Antología documental* (Mexico City: Universidad Iberoamericana, 1986).

23. Genaro García, ed., *Crónica oficial de las fiestas del primer centenario de la Independencia de México* (Mexico City: Talleres del Museo Nacional, 1911).

24. Orest Ranum, "Courtesy, Absolutism, and the Rise of the French State, 1630–1660," *Journal of Modern History* 52, no. 3 (1980): 426–451.

25. Norbert Elias, *The Court Society* (New York: Pantheon Books, 1983), 56–60.

26. Sarah Hanley, *The Lit de Justice of the Kings of France: Constitutional Ideology in Legend, Ritual, and Discourse* (Princeton, N.J.: Princeton University Press, 1989), 288–291.

27. Max Weber, *Economy and Society: An Outline of Interpretive Sociology* (Berkeley and Los Angeles: University of California Press, 1978), 242. Shils and Geertz further define charisma in Edward Shils, "Charisma, Order, Status," *American Sociological Review* 30 (1965): 199–213, and Clifford Geertz, "Centers, Kings, and Charisma: Reflections on the Symbolics of Power," in *Local Knowledge: Further Essays in Interpretive Anthropology* (New York: Basic Books, 1983), 121–146.

28. Thomas E. Dow, Jr., "An analysis of Weber's work on charisma," *British Journal of Sociology* 29, no. 1 (1978): 83.

29. Sofía Verea de Bernal, ed., *Un hombre de mundo escribe sus impresiones: Cartas de José Manuel Hidalgo y Esnaurrízar, Ministro en París del Emperador Maximiliano*, 2nd ed. (Mexico City: Editorial Porrúa, 1978); and Matías Romero, New York City, to Foreign Minister, Mexico City, 16 April 1883, fojas 1–2, in "La Leg. Mex. en los E. U. de A. informa . . . 1883–1885," 22 fojas, Legajo 11-10-59 Archivo Histórico de la Secretaría de

Relaciones Exteriores, Tlaltelolco, Mexico City, Mexico. Hereafter cited as AHSRE.

30. Of the many interesting cases, see Claudia Canales, *El poeta, el marqués, y el asesino: Historia de un caso judicial* (Mexico City: Ediciones Era, 2001).

31. Refer to descriptions of diplomatic functions dispersed throughout José F. Verges, *Recuerdos de Méjico* (Barcelona: Imprenta de Henrich y Cía., 1903), and Albert S. Evans, *Our Sister Republic: A Gala Trip through Tropical Mexico in 1869–1870* (Hartford, Conn.: Columbian Book Company, 1873), 309–315.

32. José Manuel Nieto Soria, *Ceremonias de la realeza: Propaganda y legitimación en la Castilla Trastámara* (Madrid: Nerea, 1993); and Antonio Rodríguez Villa, *Etiquetas de la Casa de Austria* (Madrid: J. Ratés, 1913).

33. Samuel John Klingensmith, *The Utility of Splendor: Ceremony, Social Life, and Architecture at the Court of Bavaria, 1600–1800*, ed. Christian F. Otto and Mark Ashton (Chicago: University of Chicago Press, 1993), 10–14.

34. José Yves Limantour, Mexico City, to Jesús Zenil, Mexican Minister to Belgium, Brussels, 14 Oct. 1900, Roll 16, 2nd Series, Archivo José Yves Limantour, Centro de Estudios de Historia de México CONDUMEX, Mexico City, hereafter cited as JYL-CONDUMEX; Miguel Covarrubias, London, to Foreign Ministry, Mexico City, 14 Feb. 1909 and Francisco A. de Icaza, Berlin, to Foreign Ministry, Mexico City, 23 Dec. 1908, in unpaginated vol. 1 of *Ceremonial diplomático mexicano, 1908–1910*, 3 tomes, Legajo 19-5-28 (3 partes), AHSRE, hereafter cited as *Ceremonial diplomático mexicano*, AHSRE.

35. Pauline Raquillet-Bordry, "Le milieu diplomatique hispano-américain à Paris de 1880 à 1900," *Histoire et Sociétés de l'Amérique latine* 3 (1995): 81–106.

36. The observant envoy submitted copies of seating charts, menus, and society notes in his reports to the Foreign Ministry. These are contained in a thick file titled "Invitaciones del y al Ministro de México en Tokyo, Japón, 1899–1905," Legajo 15-8-68, AHSRE.

37. Guillermo Crespo, Mexico City, 15 Oct. 1884, to Foreign Ministry, Madrid, Legajo H1657, Méjico, Correspondencia 1880–1901, Archivo Histórico del Ministerio de Asuntos Exteriores, Palacio de Santa Cruz, Madrid. Hereafter cited as AHMAE.

38. Evgueni Dik, "La percepción que el gobierno imperial ruso tenía del México porfirista: 1890–1911," *Signos Históricos* 5 (2001), 195–212.

39. For this interpretation, refer to Beezley's *Judas at the Jockey Club*.

40. Mexico, Congreso del Estado Libre y Soberano de Chihuahua, "Reglamento Interior del Congreso," in *Nueva colección de leyes del Estado de Chihuahua* (Mexico City: Imprenta de Horcasitas Hermanos, 1880), 545–546.

41. Eduardo Merlo, *El Palacio Municipal de Puebla, una semblanza histórica* (Puebla: El Ayuntamiento Municipal Constitucional de Puebla de 1993–1996, 1994), 67–125.

42. Mexico, Secretaría de Relaciones Exteriores, *La Secretaría de Relaciones Exteriores: Edificios que ha ocupado, 1821–1966* (Mexico City: Imprenta de la Secretaría de Relaciones Exteriores, 1966), 17–27.

43. Israel Katzman, *Arquitectura del siglo XIX en México*, 2nd ed. (Mexico City: Editorial Trillas, 1993), 352; and Luis Ortíz Macedo, *Los palacios nobiliarios de la Nueva España* (Mexico City: Seminario de Cultura Mexicana, 1994), 203–207.

44. Manuel Rivera Cambas, *México pintoresco, artístico, y monumental*, 3 vols. (Mexico City: Imprenta de la Reforma, 1882), 1:15.

45. Michael Johns, *The City of Mexico in the Age of Díaz* (Austin: University of Texas Press, 1997), 10.

46. Consult photographs of the plaza dating from c. 1900 in Box 1, Folder 1, Gertrude

Fitzgerald Photograph Collection, Department of Special Collections, Library of the University of Texas at El Paso, El Paso, Texas.

47. Katzman, *Arquitectura del siglo XIX*, 352–353.

48. Rivera Cambas, *México pintoresco, artístico, y monumental*, 14.

49. Lambert de Sainte Croix, *Onze mois au Mexique et au Centre-Amérique* (Paris: Librairie Plon, 1897), 39–40; and Rivera Cambas, *México pintoresco, artístico, y monumental*, 13–14.

50. Tello Díaz, 196.

51. By 1903, 360,000 pesos had been spent. See Mexico, Secretaría de Comunicaciones y Obras Públicas, "Obras en Palacio Nacional y de Chapultepec," *Memoria presentada al Congreso de la Unión por el Secretario de Estado y del Despacho de Comunicaciones y Obras Públicas, General Francisco Z. Mena* (Mexico City: Tipografía de la Dirección General de Telégrafos, 1902), 57, and Secretaría de Comunicaciones y Obras Públicas, "Obras en Palacio Nacional y de Chapultepec," *Memoria presentada al Congreso de la Unión por el Secretario de Estado y del Despacho de Comunicaciones y Obras Públicas, General Francisco Z. Mena* (Mexico City: Tipografía de la Dirección General de Telégrafos, 1903), 150.

52. Título IV, Gobierno de los Palacios del Ejecutivo, articles 16 and 17, *Código Militar, Ley de organización del ejército y armada de la República Mexicana* (Mexico City: Tipografía de "El Siglo XIX," 1897), 3.

53. "Los Guardias de la Presidencia," *El Imparcial* 4, no. 1386 (6 July 1900): 1.

54. The parenthetical citations in this paragraph coincide with the sequential article numbers of the 18-page manuscript, Secretaría de Relaciones Exteriores, "Ceremonial para reglamentar las formalidades en cualquier acto oficial y solemne de la República, Palacio Nacional, 26 Agosto 1910," in unpaginated second volume of *Ceremonial diplomático mexicano*. AHSRE.

55. "Cómo emplea su tiempo el General Díaz: La audiencia," *El Mundo Ilustrado* 2, no. 2 (15 Sept. 1895): 81.

56. Edith Wharton and Ogden Codman, *The Decoration of Houses* (New York: Charles Scribner's Sons, 1902), 24.

57. "Cómo pasa su tiempo el Presidente de la República: Palacio Nacional," *El Mundo Ilustrado* 4, no. 206 (4 Dec. 1904): 788.

58. Carlos Tello Díaz, *El exilio. Un relato de familia*, 11th ed. (Mexico City: Editorial Cal y Arena, 1994), 196.

59. Federico Gamboa, *Mi diario. Vol. I* (Guadalajara, Mexico: Imprenta de "La Gaceta de Guadalajara," 1907), 213–217; Victoriano Salado Álvarez, *Memorias*, vol. II, *Tiempo Nuevo* (Mexico City: EDIAPSA, 1946), 72–75; and "La audiencia," *El Mundo Ilustrado* 4, no. 206 (4 Dec. 1904): 789–790. Subsequent description of the presidential suite is based on these sources.

60. Sharon Kettering, *Patrons, Brokers, and Clients in Seventeenth-Century France* (New York: Oxford University Press, 1986).

61. Carmen Romero Rubio y Castelló de Díaz, Mexico City, to Archbishop Próspero María Alarcón y Sánchez de la Barquera, Mexico City, 24 Feb. 1893, Box 7, Expediente 86, Fojas 15–16, Correspondencia de la señora doña Carmen Romero Rubio y Castelló de Díaz, Fondo Documental del Archivo de Rafael Chousal, 1860–1967, Centro de Estudios sobre la Universidad, Centro Cultural Universitario, UNAM, Mexico City, hereafter cited as CRRCD.

62. Salado Álvarez, *Memorias*, vol. II, *Tiempo Nuevo*, 75–76; and Vicente Luengas,

Mexico City, to José Yves Limantour, Paris, 29 May 1903, 2nd series, roll 18, JYL-CON-DUMEX.

63. Gamboa, *Diario* Vol. I, 188. The sources are unclear whether the imperial décor was replaced by republican finery after remodeling at the turn of the century. This description dates from the 1890s.

64. Red denotes "eccentric, active, offensive, aggressive, autonomous, competitive, expressing desire, domination, and [powerful] sexuality," according to Lüscher's psychological color scale. See John Gage, "Colour and Culture," in *Colour: Art and Science*, ed. Trevor Lamb and Janine Bourriau (Cambridge: Cambridge University Press, 1994), 195.

65. Salvador Moreno, *El pintor Antonio Fabrés* (Mexico City: Instituto de Investigaciones Estéticas-UNAM, 1981), 41.

66. Salado Álvarez, *Memorias*, vol. II, *Tiempo Nuevo*, 73.

67. "El General Díaz en las audiencias privadas," *El Mundo Ilustrado* 4, no. 206 (4 Dec. 1904): 797–798.

68. Alfred Dumaine, Mexico City, 24 Nov. 1907, to Stephen Pichon, Paris, Nouvelle Series 21, *Mexico, Politique Etrangère. Relations avec la France*, vol. 1, 1891–1912, AMAE.

69. Lorenzo de Castellanos, Mexico City, 24 Sept. 1889, to Ministry of State, Madrid, and *Idem.*, 18 Sept. 1890, to Ministry of State, Madrid, Legajo H1657, Méjico, Correspondencia 1880–1901, AHMAE.

70. Vicomte de Petiteville, Mexico City, 22 Aug. 1894, to Mr. Hanotaux, Paris, Nouvelle Series 21, Mexico, Politique Etrangère. *Relations avec la France*, vol. 1, 1891–1912, AMAE.

71. Vicomte F. de Benghem, Mexico City, 9 Apr. 1902, to Baron de Favereau, Ministry of Foreign Affairs, Brussels in "Relations avec Mexique, 1838–1916," Dossier P1712-1713, in Direction des Archives du Ministère des Affaires Étrangères, du Commerce Extérieur, et de la Coopération au Développement, Brussels, hereafter cited as AMAECECD.

72. Gamboa, *Diario,* Vol. II, 189.

73. Carmen Aguilera, Elena Vargas Lugo, Marita Martínez del Río de Redo, Jorge Loyzaga, Luis Ortiz Macedo, Teresa Castello Iturbide, Manuel Carballo, María Cecilia Martínez López, and Fernando Sánchez Martínez, *El mueble mexicano: Historia, evolución, e influencias* (Mexico City: Fomento Cultural Banamex, 1985).

74. William H. Beezley, "The Porfirian Smart Set Anticipates Thorstein Veblen in Guadalajara," in Beezley et al., eds., *Rituals of Rule*, 176.

75. Eric Hobsbawm, "Introduction: Inventing Tradition," in *The Invention of Tradition*, ed. Eric Hobsbawm and Terence Ranger (Cambridge: Cambridge University Press, 1983), 1–14.

76. Érika Pani, "El proyecto de estado de Maximiliano a través de la vida cortesana y del ceremonial público," *Historia Mexicana* 45, no. 2 (1995): 423–460.

5

The Eyes of
Emiliano Zapata

SAMUEL BRUNK

On December 4, 1914, Emiliano Zapata met Francisco "Pancho" Villa in a school building at Xochimilco, in Mexico's Federal District, to firm up an alliance against the revolutionary faction led by Venustiano Carranza. It was one of the pivotal moments of the Mexican Revolution's decade of fighting (1910–1920), and Zapata dressed for the occasion. Wearing a black jacket and tight black pants with large silver buttons along the outside of each leg, a loosely knotted, light blue silk tie, and a lavender shirt, Zapata as *charro* embodied country elegance as it was understood in his south-central Mexican world.[1] His dress reflected success, and it was meant to leave an impression. This it certainly did, combined as it was with his dark, penetrating gaze and his enormous moustache.

Zapata and Villa complained of Carranza and spoke of the challenge of running the country, something neither of these relatively unschooled men professed the ability to do. Villa had more to say than Zapata on most subjects, but when they came to the issue of land Zapata was less reserved: "They [the villagers of his region] have a great deal of love for the land. They still don't believe it when you tell them, 'This land is yours.' They think it's a dream." The two men talked of their individual struggles, Zapata tracing his rebellion back to his teenage years and promising to fight until death if necessary. Indeed, there was plenty of *machismo* in the air. "I fulfill a duty," Zapata bragged, "in killing traitors." They also spoke of hat styles, of Zapata's broad sombrero and Villa's pith helmet. Zapata indicated that "he wouldn't be found in a hat other than the kind he wore."[2]

Two days later, side by side, the two men, the people's revolutionaries, rode into Mexico City at the head of 50,000 troops to establish a national government. Spectators lined the streets and hung from the balconies, throwing confetti and streamers. When the procession reached the National Palace, Zapata and Villa posed for what is probably the revolution's most famous photograph: Villa in the president's chair, grinning broadly; Zapata beside him, staring into the camera, his sombrero on his knee. Zapata refused to sit in the chair that Villa occupied. Some say he suggested it be burned, "to put an end to ambitions."[3]

This was not high political theater on Zapata's part, but he was projecting an image—or perhaps two. In the triumphant ride into Mexico City and the photographs that were taken there he was symbolically placing himself, his movement, and his program on the national stage and making the claim that they belonged there. This was crucial, because the revolution had become a tangle of competing interests, and many of the key participants did not see the land reform and the local liberties that Zapata championed as priorities. That was particularly true of leaders from the upper and middle classes, men such as Francisco Madero and Carranza, who were more interested in such issues as democracy, deepening capitalist development, and increasing the power of the central government. Their programs would have to be challenged at the national level.

But Zapata always denied that he was a politician. He shared with most of the villagers of his home state of Morelos, which was just south of the capital, a distrust of politicians, from whom they had learned to expect little but the betrayal of their interests. It is not, therefore, surprising that the declaration of national power in which he was engaged was full of signs—the general reserve, the charro outfit, the discussion of land reform, the refusal to occupy the presidential seat—that this power would not bewitch him into forgetting his home constituency. The limits to the political theater, in other words, were politics themselves, and it was this balancing of the need to compete for national power and to hold local and regional support that was the biggest challenge of Zapata's revolutionary career. In fact, a counterpoint of local and national perspectives would continue to shape his image long after he was dead.

A War of Images

NATURALLY, ZAPATA'S IMAGE first encountered a local audience. Zapata was born in Anenecuilco, Morelos, in 1879 and raised during the dictatorship of Porfirio Díaz (1876–1880, 1884–1911). The Díaz regime provided a kind of political order after decades of instability and a measure of prosperity based on Mexico's greater integration into the world economy. But while the sugar planters who dominated the economy of Morelos participated in that prosperity, the same could not be said for the state's *campesinos* (peasants). For them, insecurity increased as the *hacendados* (hacienda owners) pursued higher profits by extending their control over land, water, and labor.[4]

In 1909, the aging president of Anenecuilco's village council resigned, in part because he felt helpless in the face of the loss of communal resources. Zapata was elected to replace him.[5] The citizens of Anenecuilco were looking for a younger man who could do whatever it took to help them survive Porfirian progress. They chose Zapata because—whether he had consciously cultivated his image or not—they had come to see him as both one of them and one of their best. He was one of them in his love of local culture—of the rodeos and fireworks and drinking that came with market days and fiestas, which were the best way the villagers knew to break up the monotonous cycle of country life. He was one of their best in his economic success as a small landowner and mule train operator, in his modest literacy, in his reputation as a macho who was not afraid to stand up to authority.[6] Zapata, in sum, had charisma.

As Zapata was entering local politics, on the national scene a diminutive landowner from Coahuila named Francisco Madero prepared a run against Díaz in the presidential election of 1910. At the center of Madero's campaign was the simple demand for democracy, but he managed to appeal to enough people of various classes, interests, and regions that Díaz eventually decided to arrest him while the vote was fixed. Freed from jail soon after the election, Madero fled to the United States and called for a revolution to begin on November 20, 1910.[7] Madero's uprising got off to a rocky start. Guerrilla warfare did, however, gradually develop, and Zapata and his co-conspirators eventually joined the larger movement, which would help confer legitimacy on their struggle. Zapata soon proved himself adept at guerrilla warfare, and success brought more and more people to his side. On May 12, 1911, he was able to lay siege to the important regional center of Cuautla, Morelos, at the head of 4,000 troops. Shortly thereafter Cuautla, and then the rest of the state, fell into rebel hands.

At the same time, representatives of the old regime and of Madero were nearing the agreement, codified in the Treaty of Ciudad Juárez, that would end the first stage of fighting. Unfortunately, this recipe for peace was largely devised by upper- and middle-class leaders on both sides. It paved the way for Madero to take power, but it did not settle the social and economic issues that motivated Zapata and many other revolutionaries.[8] Conflict was destined to continue.

Threatened by Zapata's drive for the return of village lands, the hacendados of Morelos now began to tell the Maderistas about the ravages of the Zapatista "hordes," in the hope of fashioning an image for Zapata that would destroy his cause.[9] They thought of themselves as "the class that thinks, feels, and loves," and felt menaced and bullied by the "unconscious masses."[10] At base, it was a conviction that many Mexicans of urban culture and upper- or middle-class standing had come to share with their counterparts in other Latin American nations, namely, that theirs was a society in which the forces of civilization and progress struggled against those of barbarism.[11] Given such preconceptions, it was easy for many Mexicans to accept that Zapata was just a blood-soaked bandit—especially since Mexico City newspapers supported that conclusion. On June 20, for instance, beneath the headline "Zapata Is the Modern Attila," *El Imparcial* attributed to him the saying, "the only government I recognize is my pistols."[12]

Zapata tried to defend himself against this libel, but he proved unable or unwilling to meet the insistence of the new regime that he disarm his followers before they received the land for which they had fought. In August 1911 the war started again in Morelos, this time with the forces of Zapata pitted against those of Madero. Zapata now had the responsibility of justifying his own revolution to a national audience. To do so, in November 1911 he produced the Plan of Ayala, which summarized fundamental Zapatista goals of land reform and political liberty. Still looking to Madero's revolution for legitimacy, the plan charged that Madero had betrayed his followers by labeling those who asked that promises be fulfilled "bandits and rebels." Zapata proposed to continue the revolution that Madero had abandoned.[13]

In rejecting charges of banditry, Zapata did not have the truth completely on his side. The rebellion that he now headed had bubbled up out of communities in Morelos and southwestern Puebla in a decentralized manner, and each Zapatista leader enjoyed broad powers within his own zone of operations. Some Zapatistas took advantage of the decentralization to engage in activities that can accurately be called banditry, and complaints about those activities did not come only from the elite. Campesino reports of forced loans, robbery, murder, rape, and the destruction of property arrived at Zapata's headquarters in a steady stream, serving notice that Zapatista misbehavior could damage Zapata's credibility at the local level as well as at the national one. The movement's decentralized origins also meant that while the revolutionary motives of campesinos from diverse villages often centered on land, different priorities created by differences in local experience were sometimes evident.[14]

Thus, Zapata faced the related tasks of providing his followers with a group identity that would draw them together and disciplining those who transgressed. The Plan of Ayala was critical both in its delineation of collective demands and in its reaffirmation of Zapata's leadership. Another means of forging Zapata's image at the center of a united Zapatismo was through folksongs called *corridos*. In a corrido that dealt with the break from Madero, Marciano Silva, who was at that time becoming the movement's official bard, emphasized Zapata's bravery by describing an engagement in which Zapata and a handful of Zapatistas fought off six hundred federal soldiers. This corrido also praised Zapata's lack of political ambition. "I don't desire the [presidential] chair," Silva had Zapata say as he called his people back into arms, "or a high office."[15]

In another corrido Silva explicitly rejected the account of a battle given in *El Imparcial*.[16] By using a medium for which the peasants of his region were the main audience to refute the claims of a national newspaper, Silva revealed the Zapatistas' awareness that campesinos could be influenced by the press—even those that had to depend on having someone else do their reading for them. There was, in other words, no hard line between the literate, urban, national culture and the largely illiterate rural, local, and regional cultures. Local and national positions on Zapata were already influencing one another.[17]

The campaign to form a Zapatista identity was a qualified success. Much of the population of Morelos and southwestern Puebla backed Zapata when he broke with Madero, and the region in which he could recruit expanded through 1914, until it included parts of the Federal District and the states of Guerrero and México. By that time a number of educated urbanites had drifted into the Zapatista camp, and Zapata put them to work organizing, centralizing, and disciplining.[18] But Zapatismo would centralize only so far, partly because Zapata tried to honor the grassroots democracy with which the movement began. This meant that Zapatista misbehavior would persist, as would the recriminations from both village and metropolis.[19]

As the size and strength of Zapata's rebellion crested, the enemy changed names. In February 1913 Conservative General Victoriano Huerta came to power in Mexico City after a coup against Madero. In July 1914 Huerta was driven out by the converging forces of Zapata, from the south, and the Constitutionalists, led by Venustiano Carranza, from the north. Zapata shared little with Carranza—who, like Madero, was a landowner from Coahuila—other than the struggle against Huerta. Rather than compromise with him, Zapata turned to Pancho Villa, whose class background and goals were closer to his own. Villa had fought in alliance with Carranza, but the two were now estranged, and, as we have seen, at the end of the year Zapata and Villa were able to establish a government—the Convention—in Mexico City. By then they were at war with the Constitutionalists.

With Zapatista troops in the capital, Zapata's national image improved overnight. In Morelos the acclaim was greater than ever before, but so were the expectations. It was time to fulfill the promise of land reform. As the villagers pursued their land claims, however, it became clear that neither oral tradition nor the maps and titles in their possession provided the data that was needed. The hacendados had fled the state, but tensions rose between neighboring communities competing for land.[20] Still, Zapata did his best to divide the land equitably and thus earned his lasting reputation as the only major revolutionary fully committed to land reform.

During the spring and summer of 1915 the Constitutionalists won the revolution by defeating Villa in battles at Celaya and León on the plain north of Mexico City. The Zapatistas were driven from the capital and Zapata again became, in both press and public pronouncement, the leader of ignorant bandit hordes. In 1916, Carranza's forces moved into Morelos, and the strain on resources intensified. The difficulties of war were not new, but the years of destruction were mounting up, and the wealth of the haciendas had already been appropriated. Internal conflict and defection would mark the rest of the decade for Zapatismo.

Image, however, remained important. Zapata reconstituted the Convention government in Morelos in an effort to demonstrate that the Zapatistas were capable of "establishing the Administration of the Revolution."[21] He also created the Center for Revolutionary Propaganda and Unification, charged with easing centrifugal tendencies by resolving conflicts among Zapatista generals and between Zapata's troops and villagers who were not involved in the fighting.[22] Finally, Zapata sought to turn the tide of the war by attracting new allies. His ambassadors scoured Mexico in search of other regional rebels, revolutionary politicos, and disgruntled Constitutionalists who might cooperate to drive Carranza from power.

This was how things stood when Zapata's search for allies led him to a Constitutionalist colonel, Jesús Guajardo, who was reputedly unhappy with Pablo González, the general in charge of pacifying Morelos. After some testing of the waters, Zapata met Guajardo for talks on April 10 at the hacienda Chinameca. According to Salvador Reyes Avilés, author of the official Zapatista report of Zapata's death, Zapata ordered ten men to follow him and rode toward the hacienda, where Guajardo waited. As he approached the gate, wrote Reyes Avilés, the guard appeared ready to do him the honors. The bugle sounded three times, the call of honor, and when the last note fell silent, as the General arrived at the threshold, in a manner most treacherous, most cowardly, most villainous, at point-blank range, without giving him time even to clutch his pistols, the soldiers who were presenting arms fired their rifles twice, and our general Zapata fell never to rise again.[23]

The Local Cult

MORE THAN FIFTY YEARS after this ambush, in the 1970s, researchers from the National Institute of Anthropology and History (Instituto Nacional de Antropología e Historia, INAH) undertook an oral history project to record the impressions of aging revolutionaries. Many Zapatistas used the opportunity to talk about what happened at Chinameca in 1919. One veteran, Agapito Pariente, claimed he had been told that Zapata's supposed corpse had all of its fingers, which was suspicious because Zapata had lost a finger in a roping accident. Zapata, Pariente continued, had clearly not died. Instead, "like the prophet Moses," he had retired to private life. He later reappeared as "a humble man," who cared for some cattle, had a woman, and sold wood in the district of Jonacatepec.[24]

Serafín Plasencia Gutiérrez, meanwhile, asserted that his sister, a spiritualist, knew that Zapata had not died at Chinameca. From her he gleaned that a Hungarian or Arab compadre had taken Zapata either to Hungary or to Arabia. There Zapata learned "certain languages and was doing well. They loved him like a god." Later, Zapata returned to Morelos and had a girlfriend in Cocoyoc; he dressed like a charro to call on her. Ultimately, though, "[t]he Arabs no longer let him come," Plasencia explained, "because he had many enemies." He had died twenty or thirty years prior to the interview, "in his bed, over there in Arabia."[25]

In contending that Zapata survived Guajardo's ploy and could therefore return, Pariente and Plasencia were making him into a man-god in the style of the Precolumbian figure Quetzalcóatl and, of course, Jesus Christ. Precisely why they did so is uncertain, but perhaps Pariente gives us a hint when he notes that Zapata lived because he did not enter the hacienda. He sent a compadre who looked like him, Joaquín Cortés of Tepoztlán, to die in his place. Zapata lived, in other words, because he was too smart and too strong—and, we might add, too symbolic of the Zapatista cause—to be fooled and killed by the Carrancistas. At any rate, for Pariente, Plasencia, and countless other Morelenses the relationship remained intact: Zapata maintained his charisma after what some believed was his death.[26]

In the immediate aftermath of Chinameca, many took pains to influence how Zapata would be remembered. "[M]ost treacherous, most cowardly, most villainous"—the body was not even cold, we might speculate, when Reyes Avilés started loading it with meaning. "Thus die the brave," he continued, "the men of dignity, when the enemy, to stand up to them, resorts to treason and crime."[27]

But the Constitutionalists had the advantage of having the corpse, which they took north to Cuautla. There Pablo González, who was in on the plot, waited with witnesses prepared to identify it before a judge. The body was then "injected" so that photographs could be taken. "[T]hose who desired to or might doubt" could thus see "that it was actual fact that the famous *jefe* of the southern region had died."[28] In the early hours of April 11, the injection finished, the body was presented to the public at the police station. It remained on display for nearly twenty-four hours, and thousands came to look.

Various newspapers suggested that the body also be taken to Mexico City to calm metropolitan fears of the southern Attila—this was not the first time there had been rumors of his demise. Carranza took the position, however, that to bring the corpse to the capital "would be to do honor to his [Zapata's] unhappy memory."[29] Instead, González sent the photographs to the papers. In the most striking of these pictures, excited young soldiers propped up the bloated head of the body so the camera might leave no doubt. On April 12, Zapata's remains were carried to Cuautla's cemetery. González ordered the gravediggers to bury the body deeply, so "Zapatista fanatics" would not try to move it.[30]

It quickly became clear that the issues of Zapata's remains, the remains of Zapatismo, and how Zapata's life should be summarized were interconnected. "With respect to Zapata's corpse," reported *Excélsior* on April 12, Zapatista captives of the Constitutionalists "said they did not remember having seen that man before." But then, "with terror painted on his face," one prisoner made the identification. This article added that as Zapata's body made its journey from Chinameca to Cuautla, "men, women, and children had emerged from the humble huts of the hot country" to watch the procession. "All of those that contemplated the cadaver agreed in asserting that it was that of Emiliano himself . . . and began to recall the outrages they had suffered at Zapata's orders."[31]

In describing the funeral, though, a different piece in the same edition noted that the locals were "dismayed and demoralized" by Zapata's death, adding that "[m]any, before viewing it [the body], doubted that the man they judged invincible had died." *Excélsior* also indicated that the Carrancistas in Cuautla had had similar doubts. On hearing that the body was on the way, they took precautions, "given the possibility that Guajardo had fallen into the hands of Zapata . . . and it was the rebel leader who approached Cuautla with his troops." But the author of this article was quick to point out that when Guajardo and his soldiers arrived, "all of the doubts were dispelled."[32] In general, the papers of the capital agreed that it was Zapata's body, that his death meant the end of Zapatismo, and that his life had been that of a "roving marauder."[33]

The inconsistencies concerning local reaction to the assassination were probably generated in part by the hope that Zapata's death meant the war against Zapatismo was over. Also significant, surely, was the desire of both the journalists and the Carrancista officials who informed them to do what they could to turn that hope into reality by convincing Zapata's followers that without him, the fight could not continue. This involved them in a contest over the meaning of his death. In a manifesto of April 15, the remaining leaders of Zapatismo argued that, far from discouraging the people of the region in which he operated, Zapata's death had "provoked virile indignation" among them. They added, "Zapata died when it was possible for him to do so, when his meritorious work of disseminating ideas was over." He could now "live his life of an immortal tranquilly."[34]

What was really happening in the minds of the residents of Zapata's home territory? Questions about peasant consciousness are difficult to answer because campesinos rarely leave much evidence of what they were thinking at a given moment. My guess, though, is that inconsistencies in the press about local reactions to Zapata's death also reflected the fact that feelings about him were in flux. Here the testimony of Luz Jiménez might help. Jiménez witnessed the revolution from Milpa Alta, in the Federal District, and told of her experiences many years later. Her specific memories of the Zapatistas concentrated on the murder, rape, and destruction that they perpetrated. "When the men of Zapata entered the town," she claimed, "they came to kill." Despite those sordid details, when she told of the arrival of Carrancista troops, Jiménez asserted that the villagers of Milpa Alta would "never forgive him [Zapata] for leaving us in the hands of the enemy." And yet—another twist—there appeared to be some forgiveness, for Jiménez named Zapata as one of her three heroes, as "the only man who fought for the poor." The fact that Jiménez had come to identify with Zapata despite exhibiting few concrete memories of Zapatismo that were positive suggests she may have finalized her opinions after Zapata's death.

When that might have occurred is anyone's guess, but it is noteworthy that in speaking of his death, she bestowed nobility upon him. "Though he knew he was going to lose," she observed, "his spirit did not fail him."[35]

Given the hardships of recent years, many of the villagers of Morelos and surrounding areas undoubtedly shared some of Jiménez's reservations about Zapata as 1919 began. But death changes things by requiring, suddenly, that a life be summarized in its entirety. Faced with the challenge of summarizing Zapata's life, it is likely that many recalled the promise and the successes of earlier years and the sincerity of the effort to implement land reform. And as that reevaluation was going on, if indeed it was, Pablo González was injecting, photographing, and displaying Zapata's body, while the newspapers expressed their doubts, however fleeting, about the reality of Zapata's demise. Was González reacting to rumors that some campesinos did not believe it was Zapata's body? Or did his actions create that disbelief? In any event, the myth that Zapata did not die at Chinameca did began to take shape, just as Agapito Pariente indicated so many years later, in the immediate aftermath of the ambush.

In 1930, anthropologist Robert Redfield published hard evidence of this train of thought based on fieldwork he had done in 1926 and 1927 in the village of Tepoztlán, Morelos. "It is not known whether Zapata still lives or whether he was really killed as reported," one of Redfield's informants told him. "Some say he is in Arabia, and will return when he is needed. For myself, I think he still lives." Redfield also reported that this argument was taken up in a corrido of the period. "The singers have circulated," the corrido asserted, "a phenomenal lie, / and everyone says that Zapata already / rests in peace in eternity." But this was not the case. Rather, "since Zapata is so experienced, / alert and intelligent / he had thought beforehand / to send another man in his place."[36] Periodic references to stories of Zapata's survival demonstrate that the tradition persisted over the following decades.[37] These accounts consistently included the notion that Zapata had survived either because he had a premonition or because he was warned. Over time, too, the display of the body was a key event. "I know he had a scar on his cheek," said Redfield's informant, "and the corpse that was brought back from Chinameca had no scar. I saw it myself." The post-Chinameca refuge in the Middle East was another consistent element.

One might also suggest continuity in the type of logic displayed in these stories. In 1938 one campesino argued that if Zapata did die, why did his son Nicolás not attend the ceremonies held annually on the anniversary of his death, and why had Zapata's sisters "never dressed in mourning"? In the 1970s, one of the INAH interviewees reasoned that Jesús Delgado must have died in Zapata's place because Delgado did not reappear when peace came. Finally, Zapata's daughter Ana María told me in 1997 that her father certainly had died, since he would not have abandoned his family. The logic in each of these cases reflects the village environment in which the local myth was generated, both in its expectations about individual behavior and in the sense that, in a small community, people are able to scrutinize the actions of others.

The position that Zapata did not die in 1919 illustrates the force and depth of his local cult. Perhaps it shows that some needed to hang on to him more than others, but even for those who believed he was dead, Zapata remained a charismatic presence and an important part of the experience and identity of communities within Morelos and of Morelos as a whole. Still, local concepts of Zapata did not develop in a vacuum. Stories about his survival were shaped by the Carrancista manipulation of the body. Moreover, most of the evidence for the belief's existence comes from the accounts of journalists and historians from the city. Surely they often romanticized the quaint peasant lore they found, and may even have prompted some of it. At a minimum, they filtered it through their urban lenses.

Zapata, State, and Nation

IN 1920, ALVARO OBREGÓN, Constitutionalism's most successful general, took power from Carranza—with some support from the remaining Zapatistas—in a brief uprising that ended the most violent stage of the revolution. As he looked for means to consolidate his power, he found it useful to remember Zapata in a different light than had Carranza. Obregón understood that Mexico had just experienced a revolution in which many country people had taken up arms to demand land. He realized that that demand would have to be addressed before political stability could be achieved. But Obregón believed too much in capitalism and the sanctity of private property to want a thorough land reform. Instead, he mostly handed out land in areas—such as Morelos—where it would help him gain support.[38] And, since it was Zapata who was most closely associated with the land issue, Obregón complimented this limited land reform by presiding over the beginning of the rehabilitation of Zapata's image at the national level. He and his successors would seek to make Zapata one element of a deeper, postrevolutionary national identity intended to unite Mexicans after the long civil conflict and thus make them more governable. Naturally, they hoped to tie this sense of nationalism closely to their new state.

There was, however, a major obstacle to the use of Zapata's image by the new government: both González and Guajardo were still around, having joined the insurrection against Carranza. Luckily, Guajardo rebelled against

the new regime in June 1920. According to Antonio I. Villarreal, then secretary of agriculture, Guajardo "rose up in arms because he was choked with
worry. He knew he was accused of a base betrayal that was repugnant to the
sentiment of nobility of the nation." Villarreal also hinted that Guajardo's
revolt solved the government's problem about what to do with him, which
suggests that his decision to rebel was related to complications that arose
for him from the new official attitude toward Zapata. In that case, Zapata
now had his revenge, for Guajardo was soon caught and executed. Pablo
González, meanwhile, was implicated in the revolt and faced a court martial, but after a few days of drama he was allowed to go into exile rather than
share Guajardo's fate.[39]

Though many members of Obregón's faction had fought against Zapata
and learned to hate him, the most obvious culprits in his death—together
filling the role of Judas—had been made scapegoats and removed from the
scene. The adoption of Zapata could now go forward rapidly. One of the
main ways in which that adoption was accomplished was by the participation of officials of the new state in the ceremonies of commemoration held
at Zapata's grave site in Cuautla on the anniversary of his assassination.
Already at the time of the 1921 anniversary, national officials had begun to
elevate Zapata, rhetorically, toward founding father status.[40] In 1924,
Plutarco Elías Calles, Obregon's hand-picked successor, made the commemoration part of his presidential campaign and ritually embraced
Zapata's program. Another significant commemoration was that of 1932,
when Zapata's remains were moved to the base of a new statue on one of
Cuautla's main squares. The statue, around which subsequent rituals would
revolve, portrayed Zapata on horseback, leaning down, paternalistically, to
confer with a peasant on foot beside him.[41]

These were highlights, but in a sense all of the ceremonies were equally
significant—or, rather, equally routine. Year after year the events were
attended by representatives of national, state, and local governments from
around the country; Zapatista veterans; representatives of peasant, worker,
and women's groups; schoolchildren being indoctrinated into the cult; and
such dignitaries without portfolio as Zapata's children and world-renowned
muralist Diego Rivera. Year after year wreathes were arranged around the
monument and politicians made speeches full of promises. After the
speeches, veterans, dignitaries, representatives, and schoolchildren paraded
through Cuautla's historic streets along with, increasingly, such evidence of
modernization as tractors or motorcycle clubs. Since 1940 every president
has made a point of going to Morelos at least once during his term for the
anniversary of Zapata's death.

The postrevolutionary government also identified itself with Zapata's image in other ways. Zapata became an official founding father in 1931 when his name, along with that of Carranza, was inscribed in letters of gold in the chambers of Congress.[42] As a founding father, he occupied a prominent place in the history textbooks used by the educational system that expanded dramatically—especially into the countryside—after 1920. In the 1920s and 1930s, Diego Rivera painted many images of him on the walls of government buildings. Finally, the inclusion of the Zapatistas under the umbrella of the triumphant revolution meant that the state benefited from the arguments that such urban Zapatistas as Octavio Paz Solórzano, Gildardo Magaña, and Antonio Díaz Soto y Gama—some of whom were awarded government posts—advanced on behalf of their fallen leader. Zapatista scribes published several books about their movement, and were quick to leap to Zapata's defense when others maligned him in print. In 1933, for instance, they joined in a debate in *El Universal* over whether Zapata was truly "intransigent."[43]

While the vision of Zapata as hero was being nationalized, his cult also began to be celebrated in Mexico City, and in the late 1940s an organization of Zapatista veterans called the Zapatista Front began to lobby for a monument to him in the capital. The result was an equestrian statue, located in the southern part of the city, which was unveiled in 1958.[44] The appearance of the cult of Zapata in Mexico City suggests a final and crucial part of its history. To make Zapata's image a useful ingredient of national identity, the new rulers would have to push it into the corners of Mexico—and particularly rural Mexico—that Zapata had never visited in life. The educational system, the arts, and the mass media all helped in this endeavor, as did the land reform to which Zapata's name was often rhetorically attached. In 1937, for example, President Lázaro Cárdenas (1934–1940) instructed the country's governors to circulate the first two volumes of Gildardo Magaña's government-subsidized history, *Emiliano Zapata y el agrarismo en México.* "I believe it would be suitable to promote the distribution of the publication in question," he indicated, "in the schools, libraries, *ejidos,* unions, and civic centers, and so I urge you to acquire sufficient copies."[45]

In 1951, the municipal committee of the Zapatista Front in Paracho, Michoacán, held a commemoration of Zapata on the central square. Schoolchildren from kindergarten on up took part, and speakers included a representative of the Zapatista Front's state committee, a young girl named Socorrito Moreno, and Rubén Estrada Moreno. Estrada Moreno praised both Zapata and the present government, which provided schools that would help the locals "get ready to conquer their rights."[46]

On the surface, this event was largely a patriotic echo of those that took place under the watchful eyes of national authorities in Cuautla. It was probably what Cárdenas had in mind as he disseminated Zapata's cult, and similar rituals took place at countless sites around the country from the 1930s to the 1960s. But this does not mean that the leaders of the institutionalizing revolution were able to control Zapata as he entered new locales. Even during these decades in which he was usually remembered in an orderly way, dissent sometimes lurked beneath apparently placid surfaces.[47]

In the early 1970s, April 10 became an occasion for what we might call ritual protest in the proliferating localities that Zapata had come to call home. Against a backdrop of growing economic and political instability, it has remained so ever since. This change is not surprising, given that, after 1940, the postrevolutionary regime had pursued rapid industrialization to the detriment of policies intended to help campesinos, who remained the poorest segment of Mexican society. Other, urban and middle-class participants in these commemorations were perhaps more motivated by the 1968 massacre of student protesters in the plaza of Tlatelolco in Mexico City, with its lessons in authoritarian rule. In any event, instances of local ritual protest have been legion since 1972, when hundreds of peasants from Tlaxcala and Puebla marched on Mexico City.[48] In 1983, the Coordinator of Popular Struggle "Emiliano Zapata" brought together seven hundred peasants, tenant farmers, and students to rally in Tapachula, Chiapas, against high prices, loss of land, and "the repression of all social sectors."[49] The next year peasants and other protestors marched on Mexico City from and through eighteen different states.[50] As the tide of opposition in Zapata's name rose and the marches became more synchronized, local and regional dissent threatened to steal the nationalized Zapata away from the state that had done so much to create it.

In 1994, when a new group of Zapatistas, the Zapatista Army of National Liberation (EZLN), took up arms in rebellion in Chiapas, that is exactly what seems to have happened. "The oldest among the old of the communities," wrote EZLN spokesman Subcomandante Marcos, "say that there was a man named Zapata who rose up for his people and that his voice sang, more than shouted, Land and Liberty! And these ancient ones say that he has not died, that Zapata must return."[51] In this passage the ancient ones of Chiapas echoed the stories told by campesinos in Morelos of Zapata's survival, thus demonstrating the geographical movement of the popular strand of Zapata's myth. Another way in which the Chiapan rebels adapted Zapata to their milieu was by linking him to the figure of Votán, according to Tzeltal Indian myth the first man to give land to indigenous peoples.[52] The EZLN placed Votán-Zapata at the center of the national community that it conceptualized. "All of us," read one missive, "are one in

Votán-Zapata and he is one in all of us."[53] Composed of Indians and, broadening from there, those who lived in "misery," the EZLN's nation continues to stand in opposition to the national government.

Conclusion

IN THE MORE THAN NINETY YEARS that have passed since Emiliano Zapata took up arms, much has ridden on his image. While Zapata lived, the viability of his movement—its recruiting, its coherence, its legitimacy—depended in part on that image, over which the Zapatistas and their enemies struggled. After 1919, some of his followers chose to believe that he had not died at Chinameca. National authorities did not borrow that position—they were presumably content to conclude that he was thoroughly dead—but they did adopt the positive local and regional assessment of Zapata as the raw material for their image of him as a founding father of the postrevolutionary state. In an effort to make him an element of national identity, they then spread memories of him around the country. But as the residents of the new localities that he came to inhabit became increasingly frustrated with the government's failure to promote the land reform and, more broadly, the social justice that he represented, they generated oppositional Zapatas that seem, in recent years, to have overpowered the state's founding father.

The consistent factor in this history is that Zapata has kept one foot on the national scene and the other planted in more intimate surroundings. This is precisely the balancing act he performed when he met with Villa in 1914, and it clearly separates him from many other "heroes." Zapata is most solidly present, of course, in and around Morelos, where he could lead because he convinced people that he was capable and that he was trustworthy—that his promises were not empty like those of other politicians. But his presence in other locales has become appreciable, too, and it is possible, ironically, that his deep roots in Morelos have served him well in other sites where trustworthiness and "intransigence" are valued. Zapata's national career has been less remarkable. Obregón and his heirs largely did what politicians do when trying to build legitimacy for a new system: they tried to please their constituencies with a combination of material rewards and effective symbolism. And since land reform was a key demand of the revolution and Zapata was its best-known proponent, they took Zapata seriously. The result has been a contest with local conceptions of Zapata—more over who could claim him than over what he meant—that has endowed Zapata's image with unusual vitality.

There is nothing in Zapata's story that suggests that Mexico is unique, in general terms, in the way that it relates to its heroes. Still, Zapata's image has helped give Mexican history its unique flavor. Returning again to the idea of charisma as a relationship between leaders and followers, we might think of the hero as someone through whom the history of the place in which he arises is refracted. Zapata was made a hero by what fed into him: the historically conditioned expectations and aspirations of those who became his followers. Something also emerged from him after his death to feed back into the culture, in terms of what he meant and how he could be used. But what came back was not precisely what went in, in part because of the life that lay between the creation of the hero and the posthumous image: Zapata's moustache, his eyes, his horse, what he said, how he died. Would land reform have played such a large role in Mexico's twentieth century without Zapata? Some have argued that it would not have, because his ideological influence on the Constitution of 1917 was great. Perhaps. What I am suggesting is that it might not have because Mexico would then have missed his moustache and the insistent icon that was built around it. In 1989, José Muñoz Cota waxed poetic about a painting by Fernando Alferez that portrayed only Zapata's eyes. "In the sad gaze of Emiliano Zapata," Muñoz Cota wrote, "the tragedy of our history comes to light."[54] Five years later ski-masked rebels in the state of Chiapas served notice that Zapatismo was somehow an ongoing phenomenon, not a historical relic. It was probably just coincidence that we saw only their eyes.

Notes

1. A *charro* is a horseman best identified by the manner of dress described here.

2. For the quotations, see the Pact of Xochimilco in Manuel González Ramírez, ed., *Planes políticos y otros documentos* (Mexico City: Fondo de Cultura Económica, 1954), 113–122. See also Leon Canova to the U.S. Secretary of State, Mexico City, December 8, 1914, Department of State, Records Relating to the Internal Affairs of Mexico, 1910–1929, 812.00/14048.

3. For the quotation, see Enrique Krauze, *El amor a la tierra: Emiliano Zapata*, Biografía del poder, no. 3 (Mexico City: Fondo de Cultura Económica, 1987), 81. See also the photographs in Alba C. de Rojo, Rafael López Castro, and José Luis Martínez, *Zapata: Iconografía* (Mexico City: Fondo de Cultura Económica, 1979), 62–68.

4. Roberto Melville, *Crecimiento y rebelión: El desarrollo económico de las haciendas azucareras en Morelos (1880–1910)* (Mexico City: Editorial Nueva Imagen, 1979), 22, 34–44; John Womack, Jr., *Zapata and the Mexican Revolution* (New York: Vintage Books, 1970), 42–50; and Alicia Hernández Chávez, *Anenecuilco: Memoria y vida de un pueblo* (Mexico City: El Colegio de México, 1991), 109–110, 252–257.

5. Jesús Sotelo Inclán, *Raíz y razón de Zapata*, 2nd ed. (Mexico City: Comisión Federal de Electricidad, 1970), 448–453, 466–469.

6. Womack, *Zapata*, 3–9; Sotelo Inclán, *Raíz y razón*, 493–499.

7. Charles C. Cumberland, *Mexican Revolution: Genesis Under Madero* (Austin: University of Texas Press, 1952), 101–126.

8. Alan Knight, *The Mexican Revolution*, 2 vols. (Cambridge: Cambridge University Press, 1986), 1:228–229.

9. *El Imparcial* (Mexico City), 17–20 June 1911; "Relación de los sucesos en el estado de Morelos," Centro de Estudios Sobre la Universidad, Mexico City, Archivo de Gildardo Magaña (hereafter cited as AGM), 12:1:119; Sergio Valverde, *Apuntes para la historia de la revolución y de la política en el estado de Morelos* (Mexico City: n.p., 1933), 43–44, 93–94.

10. Representatives of the Merchants, Professionals, and Agriculturists to Francisco León de la Barra, undated, AGM 12:7:140.

11. For the classic Latin American statement on this theme, see Domingo Faustino Sarmiento, *Life in the Argentine Republic in the Days of the Tyrants; or, Civilization and Barbarism* (New York: Collier Books, 1961).

12. *El Imparcial*, 20 June 1911.

13. For the Plan of Ayala, see Womack, *Zapata*, 400–404.

14. For a deeper exploration of this subject, see Samuel Brunk, "'The Sad Situation of Civilians and Soldiers': The Banditry of Zapatismo in the Mexican Revolution," *American Historical Review* 101 (1996): 331–353.

15. "Bola de la historia del pronunciamiento del general Emiliano Zapata o la traición de Federico Morales," in Catalina H. de Giménez, *Así cantaban la revolución* (Mexico City: Grijalbo, 1990), 289–294.

16. See Silva's "Bola de la toma de Cuautla por Zapata," in Giménez, *Así cantaban*, 275–282.

17. Giménez, *Así cantaban*, 49, calls this a culture of mixed oral and written tradition.

18. For more on the urbanites, see Samuel Brunk, "Zapata and the City Boys: In Search of a Piece of the Revolution," *Hispanic American Historical Review* 73 (1993): 33–65.

19. See, for instance, the citizens of San Andrés de la Cal to Zapata, October 14, 1913, Archivo General de la Nación, Mexico City, Archivo de Genovevo de la O (hereafter cited as AO) 13:9:33–34; and Timoteo Sánchez to Zapata, Tepoztlán, March 30, 1914, AO 14:4:28.

20. Jesús Blancas to Zapata, June 12, 1915, Archivo General de la Nación, Mexico City, Archivo de Emiliano Zapata (hereafter cited as AZ) 19:2:85; Modesto Rangel to Zapata, Xochitepec, Morelos, June 27, 1915, AZ 19:2:49; Benigno Veliz to Zapata, Acatlán, July 18, 1915, AZ 9:2:43; Zapata to Ricardo Reyes Márquez, Tlaltizapán, Morelos, August 25, 1915, AZ 9:6:36; and Adalberto Hernández to Zapata, Mexico City, May 28, 1915, AGM 28:23:1038.

21. Zapata to Antonio Díaz Soto y Gama, Tlaltizapán, Morelos, February 8, 1916, Archivo General de la Nación, Mexico City, Archivo del Cuartel General del Sur, 1:2:54–55.

22. Acts of the meetings creating the Centro Consultivo, Tlaltizapán, Morelos, January 3–5, 1917, AZ, box 26; and Díaz Soto y Gama, "Bases a que se sujetará el Centro Consultivo de Propaganda y Unificación Revolucionaria," Tlaltizapán, November 28, 1916, AGM 28:2:525.

23. Salvador Reyes Avilés to Gildardo Magaña, April 10, 1919, in Isidro Fabela and Josefina E. Fabela, eds., *Documentos históricos de la revolución mexicana* (Mexico City: Editorial Jus, 1970), 21: 313–16.

24. Interview with Agapito Pariente A., conducted by Alicia Olivera, Tepalcingo, Morelos, March 2, 1974, Instituto Nacional de Antropología e Historia and Instituto de Investigaciones Dr. José María Luis Mora, Mexico City, October 2, 4, 1973, Programa de Historia Oral (hereafter cited as PHO) Z/1/29, pp. 16–19. For a somewhat different approach to this subject, see Samuel Brunk, "The Mortal Remains of Emiliano Zapata," in *Death, Dismemberment, and Memory*, ed. Lyman Johnson (Albuquerque: University of New Mexico Press, 2004).

25. Interview with Serafín Plasencia Gutiérrez, conducted by Laura Espejel and Salvador Rueda, September 13, 20, 1974, Mexico City, PHO-Z/1/59, pp. 87–89.

26. The myth that Zapata survived was apparently confined to the state of Morelos. See Alicia Olivera de Bonfil, "¿Ha Muerto Emiliano Zapata? Mitos y leyendas en torno del caudillo," *Boletín INAH*, época II/Abril–Junio (1975): 44, 50.

27. Reyes Avilés to Magaña, in Fabela and Fabela, eds., *Documentos históricos*, 21:313–16.

28. Pablo González to Carranza, Cuautla, April 10, 1919, in Centro de Estudios Históricos del Agrarismo en México, *El ejército campesino del sur (ideología, organización y programa)* (Mexico City: Federación Editorial Mexicana, 1982), 218.

29. *El Demócrata* (Mexico City), 11 April 1919.

30. *Excélsior* (Mexico City), 13 April 1919.

31. *Excélsior*, 12 April 1919.

32. *Excélsior*, 12 April 1919.

33. *El Demócrata*, 11 April 1919.

34. Francisco Mendoza et al., "Al Pueblo Mexicano," April 15, 1919, in Laura Espejel, Alicia Olivera, and Salvador Rueda, eds., *Emiliano Zapata: Antología* (Mexico City: Instituto Nacional de Estudios Históricos de la Revolución Mexicana, 1988), 447–451.

35. Luz Jiménez, *Life and Death in Milpa Alta*, trans. and ed. Fernando Horcasitas (Norman: University of Oklahoma Press, 1972), xvii, 125–141, 173. See also Samuel Brunk, "Remembering Emiliano Zapata: Three Moments in the Posthumous Career of the Martyr of Chinameca," *Hispanic American Historical Review* 78 (1998): 467–468.

36. Robert Redfield, *Tepoztlán, A Mexican Village: A Study of Folk Life* (Chicago: University of Chicago Press, 1930), 201–204.

37. Juan Gualberto Aguila, "Zapata, héroe, no asesino," *Universal Gráfico* (Mexico City), 10 April 1934; Salvador Martínez Mancera, "Perdura en el sur la leyenda de que E. Zapata no ha muerto," *Universal Gráfico*, 13 April 1938; Alfredo Castillo, "Presencia de Zapata," *Novedades* (Mexico City), 20 October 1949, Mexico City, Hemeroteca Nacional, Fondo Silvino González (hereafter cited as FSG); Mario Gill, "Zapata: Su pueblo y sus hijos," *Historia Mexicana* 2(1952): 294–295; Ma. del Carmen Carreño A.,"¡Zapata no ha muerto!'" *Nosotros*, 25 January 1958; letter to the editor from Pablo B. Peña Ruiz of Chimalacatlán, Morelos, *Excélsior*, 6 February 1960.

38. Linda B. Hall, "Alvaro Obregón and the Politics of Mexican Land Reform," *Hispanic American Historical Review* 60 (1980): 213–238.

39. For the quotation, see *Excélsior*, 6 July 1920; see also *Excélsior*, 29 June 1920, and 15, 16, 17, 18, 19, 20, 21, 23 July 1920.

40. See Francisco Bulnes, "Juárez y Zapata," *El Universal*, 26 April 1921.

41. *Excélsior*, 11 April 1924, 11 April 1932.

42. Thomas Benjamin, La Revolución: *Mexico's Great Revolution as Memory, Myth, and History* (Austin: University of Texas Press, 2000), 126.

43. Octavio Paz Solórzano, *Hoguera que fue*, ed. Felipe Gálvez (Mexico City:

Universidad Autónoma Metropolitana, 1986) and *Zapata, Tres revolucionarios, tres testimonios*, vol. 2. (Mexico City: Editorial Offset, 1986); Gildardo Magaña and Carlos Pérez Guerrero, *Emiliano Zapata y el agrarismo en México*, 5 vols. (Mexico City: Editorial Ruta, 1951–1952); Antonio Díaz Soto y Gama, *La revolución agraria del sur y Emiliano Zapata, su caudillo* (Mexico City: Imprenta Policromia, 1960); Diego Arenas Guzmán, "Cuando Transigió Zapata," *El Universal*, 26 August 1933, FSG; Carlos Pérez Guerrero, "¿Cuando Transigió Zapata?" *El Universal*, 6 September 1933, FSG; Manuel Palafox, "Zapata Nunca Transigió con los Principios," *El Universal*, 23 September 1933, FSG; Octavio Paz, "Zapata no fue Intransigente," *El Universal*, 7 August 1933, FSG.

44. *El Campesino* (Mexico City), 1 September 1949 and 1 March 1956; Moisés González Navarro, *La Confederación Nacional Campesina (un grupo de presión en la reforma agraria mexicana)* (Mexico City: B. Costa-Amic, 1968), 200; and Carlos J. Sierra Brabatta, *Zapata: señor de la tierra, capitán de los labriegos* (Mexico City: Departamento del Distrito Federal, 1985), 111–112, 121.

45. Lázaro Cárdenas to Governor of Aguascalientes Juan G. Alvarado, Mexico City, December 1, 1937, Archivo General de la Nación, Mexico City, Fondo Presidentes, Lázaro Cárdenas, exped. 704/215. An *ejido* was the collectively owned land distributed in the revolutionary land reform program.

46. *El Campesino*, 1 May 1951.

47. See, for example, the account of the 1950 commemoration at San Pablo, Oxtotepec, D.F., in *El Campesino*, 1 May 1950.

48. Armando Bartra, *Los herederos de Zapata: Movimientos campesinos posrevolucionarios en México* (Mexico City: Ediciones Era, 1985), 106, 153.

49. *Excélsior*, 11 April 1983.

50. *Excélsior*, 11 April 1984.

51. Subcomandante Marcos, "Chiapas: El sureste en dos vientos, una tormenta y una profecía," in *EZLN: Documentos y comunicados* (Mexico City: Ediciones Era, 1994), 1:62.

52. Lynn Stephen, "Pro-Zapatista and Pro-PRI: Resolving the Contradictions of Zapatismo in Rural Oaxaca," *Latin American Research Review* 32, no. 2 (1997): 41–70 (quotation on 60).

53. The Comité Clandestino Revolucionario Indígena—Comandancia General del Ejército Zapatista de Liberación Nacional, "Votán-Zapata se levantó de nuevo," April 10, 1995, in *EZLN: Documentos y comunicados*, 2:306–309.

54. José Muñoz Cota, "Los ojos de Emiliano Zapata," *Novedades*, 30 May 1989, FSG.

6

Felipe Carrillo Puerto of Revolutionary-Era Yucatán, Mexico

Popular Leader, Caesar, or Martyr?

BEN FALLAW

Shortly before dawn on January 3, 1924, a firing squad of rebellious federal troops executed Felipe Carrillo Puerto, world-renowned Socialist leader and governor of the southeastern Mexican state of Yucatán. The execution took place during a failed coup supporting Adolfo de la Huerta against President Alvaro Obregón (1921–1924) and his chosen successor, Plutarco Elías Calles (president 1925–1928). Over the previous seven years, Carrillo Puerto had emerged as one of the most important radical leaders in Mexico and indeed all of Latin America, advocating land reform, mass education, democracy, prohibition, and women's rights. For years before his death, Carrillo Puerto was a hero to many sympathizers, from peasants to foreign journalists such as *The Nation* editor Ernest Gruening.[1] Detractors, however, accused him of using such authoritarian tactics as inciting violence, persecuting political opponents, tolerating corruption, and practicing nepotism.[2]

In death as in life, the figure of Felipe Carrillo Puerto has been surrounded by controversy. Yucatecan and national politicians proclaimed him a martyr of the Mexican Revolution. They blamed reactionary landowners and clergy for his death and claimed his sacrifice legitimized the postrevolutionary regime. For enemies of Carrillo Puerto, his death did little to alter their opinions. Conservative journalist (and former mentor) Carlos R. Menéndez called him a "Red Caesar," a Mexican Robespierre who sacrificed life and liberty on the altar of godless socialism.[3]

Contemporary critics and supporters alike recognized his abilities to mobilize mass support among the rural poor. In fact, Carrillo Puerto pio-

Figure 6.1. Felipe Carrillo Puerto, governor of Yucatán, 1922–1924. From Bartolomé García Correa, *Como se hizo su campaña política: Recopliación de informaciones, comentarios, editoriales y artículos publicados por la prensa de la capital en los meses de junio, julio, agosto, septiembre, octubre y principios de noviembre, de 1929, en torno a la campaña electoral y personalidad del Presidente del Partido Socialista del Sureste* (Mérida: Imprenta Gamboa Guzman, 1930).

neered many of the techniques of populism, a political style that amplified a leader's charismatic personality through the deployment of mass media and mass organizing. The first part of this chapter considers Carrillo Puerto as one of the first populist leaders in Latin America. We then turn to his hero cult as a revolutionary martyr and explore how it employed many of the same techniques as populism.

Felipe Carrillo Puerto: The Rise of a Leader

BORN IN 1874 to a middle-class family in the provincial town of Motul, Yucatán, Felipe Carrillo Puerto received only a few years of formal education. He was, however, an autodidact who read widely. Inspired by the progressive Spanish parish priest of Motul, Serafín García, he began to delve into radical writers, though probably not spending much time on the Marx he would later claim to have devoured. Like many Latin American self-taught intellectuals, he read English reformers such as Samuel Smiles, as well as French novelists such as Victor Hugo, soaking up a generic socialism tempered by Anglo-Saxon liberalism.[4]

As a youth and a young man, Carrillo Puerto's political formation came in the ranks of the conservative yet populist movement headed by journalist Delio Moreno Cantón, who unsuccessfully campaigned for governor against state-backed "official" candidates.[5] Politics led to journalism, one of the many trades that Carrillo Puerto pursued periodically, in addition to jobs as a carter and a railroad worker. As a member of the partisan press supporting Moreno Cantón's cause, he fell under the tutelage of Carlos R. Menéndez, who would be the most important publisher and conservative ideologue in Yucatán. Although the Morenista campaigns often took on a radical tinge—they even chose red as their color—their leadership was decidedly upper class and right of center. But a handful of Moreno Cantón's operators, above all the strapping young carter, Carrillo Puerto, began to move in a more radical direction.[6]

Early on, Carrillo Puerto excelled as a political organizer because of his command of Yucatec Maya and his years of hard manual labor, which gave him an understanding of the daily struggles of most peasants and rural workers. Many remarked on his *cariño*, or empathetic concern for the plight of the Mayan-speaking poor. He expressed his ideas through speeches in Yucatec Maya in a style that was simple and authentic; even his physical presence suggested honesty and a respect for those to whom he appealed.[7] Although the use of a homespun political style to reach common men and women would be widespread across Latin America during the great age of populist politicians such as Getúlio Vargas and Juan Perón in the 1930s and 1940s, Felipe Carrillo Puerto was among the first to master such an approach in Mexico during the armed phase of the revolution.[8]

Yet Felipe Carrillo Puerto built his formidable political base with more than just a new political style; ideas mattered. When getting his start in the early 1910s, he endorsed more radical solutions to the problems faced by Mayan campesinos than did other mainstream politicos. Though far from a Bolshevik, as his enemies charged, Carrillo Puerto might have been predisposed to radicalism because of his time working on the railroads, where he became the protégé of early labor leaders such as Carlos Castro Morales (governor 1918–1919), Anatolio B. y Buenfil, and Héctor Victoria. Not merely political mentors, these men exposed him to alternative belief systems such as freemasonry, anarcho-syndicalism, and homeopathic medicine.

Anarcho-syndicalism would also help shape the ideals of Augusto Sandino during his sojourn in the Mexican port of Tampico (see Chapter 7).

Personality also played a part. Carrillo Puerto emerged as an effective political organizer in the last years of the Porfiriato in no small part because of his unusual integrity. Unlike others, who would compromise their positions or even sell out their own followers for personal advantage, young Felipe was honest, unyielding, and even willing to use violence in self-defense in his confrontations with state officials and pro-government politicians. Because of his refusal to back down when faced with intimidation, he was known as *loco* (a little crazy).[9] In 1911, while publishing an opposition newspaper, Carrillo Puerto defended himself against a paid assassin. Although the murder of his assailant gave local landowners the chance to jail him again, the incident reinforced his charismatic aura as a popular leader who would not bend when challenged by the powerful.[10]

Although he had built up a following in several rural communities, Carrillo Puerto had to navigate the often treacherous politics in the state capital of Mérida in the waning years of the Porfiriato and dawn of the revolution. Carrillo Puerto's alignment with Delio Moreno Cantón's faction led to more problems. Although opposed to dictator Porfirio Díaz, most of Moreno Cantón's party were distanced from Francisco Madero, who in 1910 overthrew Díaz and went on to be elected president in 1911, because Madero chose José María Pino Suárez, head of a rival Yucatecan faction, to be his vice president. This left Carrillo Puerto stranded in jail until 1913, when complex national events dramatically changed his future. Madero fell to a counterrevolution headed by General Victoriano Huerta. Governor Venustiano Carranza of Coahuila refused to recognize the military regime, and was seconded by Francisco "Pancho" Villa of Chihuahua and Alvaro Obregón of Sonora. They joined southern agrarian rebel Emiliano Zapata in revolt. Loosely united, these warlords waged full-scale civil war against loyalists of Huerta. The pro-Huerta state authorities of Yucatán released Carrillo Puerto from jail on March 27, 1913, apparently in a bid to gain his support. After briefly working for his old patron, Carlos R. Menéndez—and perhaps even supporting the Huerta regime in Yucatán—Carrillo Puerto had to flee the state when supporters of Carranza took power.[11]

Drawn by a combination of idealism and a keen political survival instinct, Carrillo Puerto fled to central Mexico, where he joined the radical agrarian movement headed by Zapata. Commissioned as a colonel to serve on the Agrarian Commission headquartered in the Morelos town of Cuautla, he worked under the direct supervision of Fidel Velázquez, the man who would head organized labor in the postrevolutionary state for decades. While in central Mexico, he soaked up the Zapatistas' agrarian doctrine and realized the possibility of using legal reforms to address rural poverty.[12] But, as the previous chapter demonstrated, Zapata was hindered by infighting among his subordinates and suffered a series of defeats at the hands of the rival Constitutionalist faction; Carrillo Puerto found himself once again on the losing side in the latest phase of the revolution. As a result, he turned in his resignation and, apparently after working as a stevedore in New Orleans, went home to Yucatán.[13]

There he ran afoul of the military government of General Salvador Alvarado, which jailed him upon his return in March 1915. Alvarado, loyal to Carranza, suspected Carrillo Puerto of being an agent of Zapata, who at the time was allied with Villa against Carranza. However, the intercession of friends and family who were in the good graces of Alvarado earned his release. Carrillo Puerto went on to serve Alvarado as a Maya-language propagandist and as the head of Motul's agrarian commission, which was charged with restoring land from haciendas to villages. Wearing his trademark Australian hat with its ideologically significant upturned left brim, Carrillo Puerto emerged as the most effective emissary of Alvarado's regime by 1917. He combined Alvarado's legalistic approach to reforms and emphasis on state action with attention to the demands of the Maya-speaking poor majority. The Socialist Party founded by Alvarado (later known as the PSS, for Partido Socialista del Sureste, or Socialist Party of the Southeast) increasingly relied on his formidable talents and charismatic appeal.

This was especially apparent in the 1918 gubernatorial campaign of Carlos Castro Morales, Alvarado's candidate and an old friend of Carrillo Puerto. At the helm of the PSS, Carrillo Puerto used his office to institutionalize his own political power by organizing from the base. The poorer, previously marginalized Mayan communities such as Pisté, Muxupip, and Opichén became bulwarks of Yucatecan socialism. Unlike other political parties of the day, which served as electoral vehicles, under Carrillo Puerto the PSS was to be an instrument of permanent mobilization aimed at connecting popular demands with state power. The two keys to Carrillo Puerto's strategy were ceaseless visits to rural communities, where he met with grassroots leaders and the rank-and-file, and the careful cultivation of the party's local branches, or Leagues of Socialist Resistance. These organizations sprang up in villages, towns, and some haciendas, and they served both to channel popular grievances up to the party's Central League and to transmit directives from the party leadership down to the base.[14]

As a result of his rural barnstorming, between 1918 and 1921 Carrillo Puerto established himself as the unquestioned *jefe* (chief) of the Yucatecan Socialist Party. At the same time, as federal congressman he cultivated support in Mexico City. Powerful patrons included left-leaning national notables Alvaro Obregón (president 1921–1924) and Plutarco Elías Calles (secretary of the interior to Obregón, then president 1924–1928).[15] Support of national authorities proved crucial when Carrillo Puerto broke with President Venustiano Carranza (1917–1920) over the presidential election of 1920; Carranza attempted to use the federal army and antisocialist factions to dismantle Yucatecan socialism in 1919–1920, touching off a bloody civil war in much of the state. Yet Carrillo Puerto escaped and lived to fight another day.

In 1921, after Obregón's toppling of Carranza in the past year and with his regional power at its zenith, Carrillo Puerto declared his own candidacy for governor. In the most hotly contested electoral campaign since the revolution broke out in Yucatán, Carrillo Puerto's Socialist Party triumphed. His legislation as governor reflected a series of radical goals: agrarian reform, popular education, feminism, anticlericalism, debtors' relief, penal reform, and popular democracy. Before considering how Carrillo Puerto used state power to realize his ideals, we will turn to the countryside to see how he garnered such strong support among Yucatan's rural poor.

Carrillo Puerto in the Campo, Carrillo Puerto in Power

IN UNDERSTANDING who supported Carrillo Puerto and Yucatecan socialism and why they did so, the factors of geography, ethnicity, and economics explain much. To be sure, backing for Carrillo Puerto was strong in many rural communities, but it was neither universal nor unanimous. To begin with, Yucatecan rural communities were divided into two social strata, although the line between the two was far from impermeable. In villages and towns, local political and economic power had long been in the hands of a Spanish- and Maya-speaking, relatively educated elite of merchants, landowners, and a few professionals. A monolingual Maya-speaking majority of peasants, field hands, and petty artisans lacked access to schooling, the courts, and all but the lowest rung of political offices. The upper stratum of provincial Yucatecan society generally opposed socialist rule, although there were many exceptions. Similarly, the lower stratum in broad terms backed Carrillo Puerto, although patron-client ties with local notables and resentment of Socialist Party violence turned some among them against him.[16]

Though social factors such as class and ethnicity might have predisposed most campesinos to support Carrillo Puerto, alone they cannot explain his success. Carrillo Puerto appealed to the Mayan majority in direct, effective terms, invoking equality and justice to argue that Mexican society must be reordered to favor the poor peasants, and not the rich landowners and merchants privileged before the Mexican Revolution. While Carrillo Puerto claimed to have read Marx and anarchist ideologue Prince Kropotkin, he expressed his ideology to the masses in much simpler terms. Laureano Cardos Ruz, a teacher and Socialist propagandist, recounts how Carrillo Puerto, like Jesus, used parables to make his point. In one speech, he used the story of the tortoise (Yucatecanized into an iguana) and the hare to explain how, through persistence, the poor could win out over the rich. Mottoes like that of the mythical three musketeers of Dumas, "All for one and one for all," explained the importance of group solidarity against the wealthy.[17] Such folksy but politically potent messages, delivered in fluent Maya by the handsome six-footer, often erased decades of deference and roused the rural poor to action under the Socialist Party banner.[18]

In communities where the Mayan majority unified around the issues of local democracy, land reform, and access to education, Carrillo Puerto found bedrock support. In the poor village of Muxupip, only a few kilometers from his home in neighboring Motul, Carrillo Puerto had been cultivating a following since his days as an opposition politician before the revolution. On his visits to Muxupip, Carrillo Puerto promised land, political empowerment, and an end to abuse by the neighboring hacendados who had carved up the community's collective land (*ejido*). His ability to speak idiomatic Maya and identify with the plight of members of such small, overwhelmingly indigenous villages long ignored by city folk should not be underestimated. Carrillo Puerto addressed the injustices suffered by Muxupip's peasants, but he also listened to demands voiced by men and women. By the late 1910s, Carrillo Puerto was "an idol" in Muxupip.[19] Carrillo Puerto also visited and campaigned repeatedly in Kanasin, a heavily Mayan town just south of the state's capital of Mérida. Socialist zeal ran so high that the residents painted the town red.[20] But in other communities such as Hocaba, bitter and often violent divisions between supporters and opponents of Carrillo Puerto lingered for years.[21]

Once in power as governor in 1922, Carrillo Puerto had to seek the means to overcome divisions and suppress political violence; at the same time, he tried to execute his ambitious program of social reform in the face of a declining economy and an uncertain national situation. He governed in Mérida, the state capital, through a burgeoning bureaucracy of lawyers, teachers, and civil servants whose socialist convictions were at times questionable. And, like Emiliano Zapata, he at times relied on local petty bosses or *caciques* to control troublesome localities and check conservative opponents. In return for their support, Carrillo Puerto had to tolerate their petty tyrannies, violations of alcohol laws, and abuse of opponents.[22] Just as Zapatismo had faltered because of popular resentment of the excesses of

Zapata's deputies, so too did Carrillo Puerto suffer when his underlings ran rum, murdered opponents, and looted local treasuries with apparent impunity. At times Carrillo Puerto lashed out at abusive local officials.[23] But privately, he clearly realized that at times, political necessity forced him to impose unpopular, corrupt mayors in order to gain the support of powerful vested interests.[24] Critics claimed he was too soft on crime, but when his state police force used assassination to deal with outbursts of banditry, conservatives charged he was relying on brute force to silence opponents.[25]

As governor, Carrillo Puerto faced a host of other problems. When his relatives flocked to government service, opponents denounced nepotism.[26] His support of feminism and state distribution of a birth control pamphlet outraged pro-Church elements.[27] And his personal behavior stoked charges of immorality. The construction in his hometown of Motul of a lavish social center in a subterranean grotto, or *cenote*, complete with bathing stalls in the shape of the PSS's red triangle, led to accusations that he was staging orgies at state expense. The separation from his wife and his dalliances with several mistresses—including young North American journalist Alma Reed only a few months before his demise—were seized upon by his enemies as clear evidence that he was corrupted by power.[28]

While right-wing detractors spun narratives of a power-drunk Caesar, the changing political realities of regional and national politics help explain Carrillo Puerto's growing distance from his popular base. To maintain the support of his national patrons President Alvaro Obregón and his secretary of the interior, Plutarco Elías Calles, Carrillo Puerto had to moderate his policies and reach out to political opponents, above all landowners. On the local level, consequently, Carrillo Puerto and some his collaborators bonded with local ranchers and merchants.[29] The economic necessity of keeping henequen prices low by resisting demands of organized urban labor led to an ugly clash with striking stevedores and railroad workers in the summer of 1922.[30] To operate the state-run henequen-exporting cooperative, Carrillo Puerto invited some lawyers, accountants and bureaucrats from the old upper class into government.[31] Criticism of Carrillo Puerto's public and private life spoke less to any alleged moral decline than to the former reporter's toleration of a critical free press—a far from common political virtue in revolutionary-era Mexico. He reportedly went so far as to provide armed guards to protect editor Carlos R. Menéndez, who had once dubbed him "the Red Clown."[32]

While the old oligarchy and the conservative press focused on the alleged dictatorial tendencies of Carrillo Puerto, popular elements had other complaints. As we have seen, Carrillo Puerto broke with most of organized urban labor in the 1922 strike. And his program to transform deep-seated inequalities that held back Mayan peasants encountered serious operational problems. Although he carried out an ambitious land reform program that gave many peasants and peons access to land to farm corn in the traditional slash-and-burn, or *milpa*, method, national and international pressure blocked attempts to redistribute henequen land from plantations. Sadly, the land that was redistributed was frequently mismanaged and often environmentally degraded after a few years because it was not allowed to lie fallow.[33]

Education, an important means of transforming a colonial legacy of racism and classism, also encountered serious difficulties. Falling henequen revenues cut into governmental expenditures, forcing cutbacks in the vaunted program of free primary school education that had reached into remote rural villages.[34] At the same time, attempts to strengthen democracy at the local level ran up against problems of corruption, often linked to alcohol smuggling.[35] The Socialist Party's program to foster a new class consciousness clashed with deeply ingrained religious and cultural attitudes.

Similarly, limited but significant attempts to open up governmental jobs and education to women were frustrated because of entrenched patriarchal attitudes, and not just among the right-wing opposition but within Carrillo Puerto's own Socialist Party as well.[36] For instance, Buenaventura Lizama, a delegate to the party's first congress, feared that feminist legislation would cause women to lose their "reserve and prudence."[37]

In trying to make the difficult transition from popular organizer to administrator of a state beset by serious economic challenges, Carrillo Puerto experienced many of the problems subsequent populist leaders in Latin America such as Juan Perón would face decades later, above all the problem of how to address deep-seated socioeconomic inequalities without provoking conservative opposition or U.S. intervention. Carrillo Puerto did better than most. In spite of growing criticism in the press, from the pulpit, and from most of the old oligarchy, he maintained his popularity among his core constituency, the Mayan peasantry, and might well have weathered the difficult economic times of the early 1920s to reap the benefits of the moderate economic recovery of the late 1920s.

Yet national events associated with another revolutionary upheaval would once again reverse Carrillo Puerto's fortunes. In 1923, when incumbent president Alvaro Obregón decided to impose Calles as his successor, Carrillo Puerto eagerly supported him, his most important national patron. Several key generals and influential civilian politicians revolted in favor of Adolfo de la Huerta, once a key collaborator of Obregón and Calles. When the federal battalion garrisoning Yucatán defected to the de la Huerta rebellion, Carrillo Puerto knew they would come for his head.

What happened next is one of the great mysteries of Carrillo Puerto's life. With *federales* closing in, Carrillo Puerto refused his lieutenants' pleas either to organize a conventional defense of the capital or to fight a guerrilla war from the bush. Instead, he told his incredulous followers not to resist in order to save their own lives. He then headed for the coast, first by train, then by horse, hoping to sail to Cuba and then to the United States, in order to buy arms and then return to help his loyalists. Some speculated that he planned to continue west to San Francisco to reunite with his former lover, Alma Reed. Bad weather and worse luck kept him land-bound. Betrayed, he was turned over to the rebels and brought back to Mérida. Jailed and then sent before a hastily convened court martial, his fate was sealed. Some still argue that one or another faction of the old landholding oligarchy paid the rebel governor Juan Ricardez Broca to murder him. Others claim that Adolfo de la Huerta himself gave the orders. It seems most likely, but not certain, that the rebellious generals themselves decided to eliminate Carrillo Puerto to forestall potential popular uprisings.[38]

When Felipe Carrillo Puerto was executed, along with three of his brothers and eight others, he passed into history. But his status as a hero (or villain) and the controversy around his life were only just beginning.

Origins of the Carrillo Puerto Hero Cult

THE FAILED COUP that killed Carrillo Puerto created a gaping political vacuum in Yucatán. After the Socialist Party regained power with the triumph of the national regime of Obregón and Calles, surviving Yucatecan socialists began to fashion a hero cult around their fallen leader in order to bolster their own political legitimacy. A mere six months after his death, Carrillo Puerto's son-in-law, Javier M. Erosa, who was mayor of the state capital Mérida, proposed erecting a monument to him in a large traffic circle on a prominent avenue. This, he argued, would both commemorate Carrillo Puerto and also "better the laboring classes" by reminding them of Carrillo Puerto's ideals.[39]

What lay behind Erosa's proposal? Ilene O'Malley has argued that after the armed phase of the revolution, the emerging postrevolutionary national government, dominated by the middle class, used the hero cults of martyred machos Pancho Villa and Emiliano Zapata (see Chapter 5) instrumentally to justify their increasingly conservative, unpopular policies.[40] To some degree, the deployment of the Carrillo Puerto hero cult begun by Erosa and elaborated by a series of national and regional actors fulfilled a similar function. They used media, ceremony, and the testimony of the hero's family and trusted followers to closely identify themselves and the postrevolutionary regime with the memory of the "revolutionary martyr." Many Yucatecan Socialist leaders hoped it would remind the workers and peasants that Carrillo Puerto died for them, and that the postrevolutionary regime—represented in Yucatán by the Socialist Party of the Southeast— would paternalistically look after them. But there was more to the hero cult than that. No politician or intellectual could monopolize its meaning. Carrillo Puerto's heroic status could be called on by progressive revolutionary politicians and intellectuals to press for change within the system, or by peasants to demand that politicians comply with their promises. Or it could be invoked by Carrillo Puerto's family to demand respect for his legacy and a share of power.

Socialist authorities quickly moved to commemorate the anniversary of the death of Carrillo Puerto in marble and stone. They exhumed his mortal remains and those of three of his brothers executed with him and placed them in a "Socialist Rotunda." Joining him in his last resting place were other Socialist Party heroes and eventually a Yucatecan sailor who died when a German U-boat torpedoed his ship in the Gulf of Mexico in 1942.[41] The Socialist Party observed the anniversary of Carrillo Puerto's death through a long procession of delegations from dozens of Socialist leagues that laid wreaths and red flowers on his last resting place.[42]

National luminaries paid homage to his cult, too. While visiting Yucatan to campaign for reelection, Alvaro Obregón compared him with the other great Yucatecan benemérito (roughly equivalent to an official patriotic hero), Manuel Cepeda Peraza, credited with leading the war against the French occupation of the mid-nineteenth century.[43] This tribute brought a crowd of Yucatecan socialists to their feet in applause. A few federal schools and unions took his name elsewhere in the republic, and Diego Rivera adorned a mural in the federal education ministry in Mexico City with an image of him as a red angel, complete with halo and wings.[44] In the pantheon of national revolutionary deities, however, Carrillo Puerto never ranked high.

It was in regional politics that the hero cult of Felipe Carrillo Puerto shone. It came to play a central role in the success of the PSS in monopolizing regional politics for decades after his death. Party propaganda used the image of Carrillo Puerto aiding indigenous peasants and his alleged last words, "Do not abandon my Indians," to project a paternalistic facade. As a symbol, Carrillo Puerto stood for land reform, free schoolbooks, and infrastructure projects in return for the loyalty of campesinos.

The hero cult was much in evidence in the 1926 gubernatorial victory of Alvaro Torre Díaz, whom President Plutarco Elías Calles ordered the PSS to impose for the 1926–1930 term. To mobilize the peasantry, who were left uninspired by the virtually unknown Torre Díaz, the PSS repeatedly relied

on the memory and image of Carrillo Puerto. Party propaganda prominently displayed his picture and recited his Zapatista slogan, "Land and
Liberty," to capitalize on Carrillo Puerto's image as savior and protector of
the Indians. For good measure, the PSS printed up thousands of flyers in
which the figure of a bloodied Carrillo Puerto was embraced about the
knees by grateful, newly manumitted Mayan peasants. Ironically, one of the
main critics of the hero cult was none other than Javier M. Erosa, now on
the outs with the PSS leadership. He charged that Torre Díaz cynically
realized "the devotion that the Indians still felt for Carrillo Puerto's memory." Erosa alleged that Torre Díaz manipulated it to pose as a "raging
socialist, almost Bolshevik," even though he was at heart a conservative.[45]

Once in office, Torre Díaz devoted considerable state resources to further institutionalize the cult of Carrillo Puerto. The old party headquarters
of Carrillo Puerto's day was razed and a vast new home for the party, the
House of the People, or Casa del Pueblo, was built in its place. Constructed
in neoclassical style but adorned with Mayanesque features such as giant
plaster serpents, it was, in Torre Díaz's words, Yucatecan socialism's "cathedral." Its auditorium was eventually named after Carrillo Puerto, and a large
statue of him greeted visitors out front. The Casa, then, was a means by
which the PSS and the governor used architecture to try to claim the legitimacy of his hero cult for themselves. In case anyone missed the connection, one of Torre Díaz's favorite intellectuals, Dr. Gonzalo Pat y Valle,
claimed that the spirit of Felipe Carrillo Puerto visited him in the form of
a pink mist in the flower garden of the Casa del Pueblo. The poet-politi-
cian even went so far as to say that the lips of the statue of don Felipe
moved and spoke to him, saying that Torre Díaz was his worthy heir.[46]
Such mystical invocations of the spirit of Carrillo Puerto became a central
feature of PSS ritual.

The party's unopposed candidate for the 1930–1934 term, Bartolomé
García Correa, represented himself even more forthrightly as the heir of
Carrillo Puerto, whom he once served as personal secretary. The house
organ of the PSS, *Tierra* magazine, repeatedly identified García Correa
with Carrillo Puerto, going so far as to hint that he was virtually a reincarnation of don Felipe: "The spirit of Felipe Carrillo Puerto is alive today in
a modest and strong man like him."[47]

After the PSS's decline in popular support under Torre Díaz, García
Correa went to great lengths to make the hero cult the focus of renewed
devotion. In January 1932, several spectacular observations of his martyrdom
took place across the state that showcased the use of multiple media. The
"wake" featured a full orchestra playing the commemorative song,
"Passionate Pilgrim," numerous speeches (including one in Maya for visit-

ing campesinos), and a film of the exhumation and transferral of his earthly remains to the Socialist Rotunda. And the Socialist League of Professors that year gave out a special prize for the student with the best oration in memory of Felipe Carrillo, and decreed that the winning entry would be recited with "respect and veneration" by every Yucatecan schoolchild.[48] Pupils that year sang "a song consecrated to the memory of Felipe Carrillo Puerto, Martyr of the Nation's Proletariat" during a school festival.[49]

For adults, the newly created official Socialist Party newspaper, *Diario del Sureste*, featured a special supplemental section on January 3, 1932, lavishly illustrated and adorned with red ink. Numerous house intellectuals in the party, such as Edmundo Bolio and Luis Rosado Vega, contributed flowery poetry in his honor. Interestingly, the latter claimed that the avowedly anticlerical Carrillo Puerto was "a redeemer in the strictly Christian sense" because he had spared a priest's house from demolition for the state museum. Such a selective reinterpretation of Carrillo Puerto, however ahistorical, served party interest in reassuring the Church of its good intentions a few months before an upcoming gubernatorial election. A poem by Julio Canché, a Mayan socialist leader of humble origins from Carrillo Puerto's hometown of Motul, shared space with poems by those distinguished men of letters. His contribution, "Mi ofrenda al Maestro" (My Offering to the Master), described the by then traditional offering of red flowers on the grave of Carrillo Puerto in a way that emphasized the almost Christlike reverence that good party members were to emulate. Most readers—and, perhaps more important, illiterate viewers—would have appreciated a selection of eye-catching photographs of Carrillo Puerto captioned "Felipe Intimo" (Family Life) and "Felipe Amigo de los Pobres"(Felipe, Friend of the Poor).[50] The familial portrait countered lingering rumors of Carrillo's infidelities, while the second reinforced his status as advocate of the downtrodden before the revolutionary state.

In constructing the official cult of Carrillo Puerto, governors and party leaders trotted out speakers from a stable of poets and orators, generally professional men of letters, for florid speeches that were featured at formal commemorations in the House of the People or the Socialist Rotunda. But to reach a broader audience, the party relied on mass rituals and modern media. This was largely the work of Socialist Party intellectual and politico, Manuel Cirerol Sansores.

A scion of one of the most powerful and wealthy landowning families in Yucatán, Cirerol threw his lot in with the Mexican Revolution early on. He eventually became one of Carrillo Puerto's closest advisors. Felipe Carrillo Puerto undoubtedly valued Cirerol's various skills: he coproduced and directed the first motion picture filmed in Yucatan, was a pilot, and, as a self-described "entertainment entrepreneur," helped popularize vaudeville in the theater he owned.[51]

Cirerol soon put his theatrical talents to work in the service of the hero cult of his late friend. More than most, he fully grasped the importance of new media in reaching a wide audience. For instance, he commissioned Teodoro Zapata to paint a dramatic depiction of Carrillo Puerto's death at the hands of a firing squad entitled *Baax Ma Tu Tuusbal* (That Which Is Not Forgotten). It was later reprinted in the widely distributed official biography of Carrillo Puerto penned by Edmundo Bolio, *De la cuna al paredón* (From the Cradle to the Firing Squad Wall).[52] Cirerol's theater (called Virginia Fábregas) staged the first commemorations of his death in 1925.[53]

In 1930, Cirerol convinced the new governor Bartolomé García Correa to support the most grandiose monument to Felipe Carrillo Puerto ever conceived. Assisted by architect Miguel Angel Cervera, he drafted plans for a gargantuan three-level Mayanesque pyramid to cover four entire city blocks. The massive building was to have served as the new final resting place of Carrillo Puerto.[54] Governor García Correa announced his plans to build the mausoleum with great fanfare. He pledged to raise 300,000 pesos and encouraged every party member to bring three stones to realize the project (the opposition press snidely remarked that poor socialists robbed their quotas of stones from the walls of the well-to-do around the construction site). When completed, it would have covered some 7,000 square meters—twice the size of its only spiritual rival, Mérida's cathedral. However, infighting over choice construction contracts and Depression-era economic realities stalled it. Construction on the pyramid terminated after completion of the hulking first level—no easy feat, considering it was ten meters high. Under new governor César Alayola Barrera (February 1934–June 1935), Cirerol managed to wrest control of it back from the "well-known bandits" who had hijacked the pyramid, but the monument was not to be. Further funding never materialized, and structural problems blocked further construction. Undeterred, Cirerol moved on to pioneer archaeological tourism, today a mainstay of Yucatán's economy. In 1938, the state demolished the aborted monument, and the site eventually became the Park of the Americas, devoted to Latin American solidarity. The change underscored the new ideological priorities of the postrevolutionary regime in Mexico, which valued identification with the rest of Latin America more than the celebration of local (and quite radical) revolutionaries.[55]

The ill-fated project marked the beginning of the end for Carrillo Puerto's cult. In the mid-1930s the PSS, which had long monopolized control of regional politics, began to lose influence owing to the rise of the

Communist Party on its left and new groups linked to landowners on the right.[56] A new generation that barely remembered Carrillo Puerto came of age. The hero cult consequently lost much of its appeal, although the PSS hierarchy and a dwindling number of party stalwarts kept the faith. On the eleventh anniversary of his death, for instance, José Castillo Torre quoted Rosa Luxembourg and compared Carrillo Puerto to Lenin.[57]

The official cult of Carrillo Puerto suffered as the PSS crumbled, a trend evident in the declining observance of his death. In the mid-1920s, the largest religious celebration in Yucatán, the Three Kings Fiesta, held on the Feast of the Epiphany in the Catholic Church liturgical calendar (January 6), was rescheduled to avoid conflicts with the anniversary of Carrillo Puerto's assassination, and stores had to close on January 3. By the 1930s such legal observances were a thing of the past.[58] At the same time, the PSS leadership was challenged by a man who could make a potent claim to be the heir of Carrillo Puerto, his brother Gualberto.

Gualberto Carrillo Puerto: The Family and the Legacy

AFTER THE ASSASSINATION OF CARRILLO PUERTO and three of his brothers, the surviving family had enjoyed a special place in Yucatecan public life.[59] The previously apolitical Gualberto founded the Socialist League "Felipe Carrillo Puerto" to help elect Alvaro Torre Díaz governor in 1925. The league was the first use by Don Gualberto of a very successful political formula. He called on the name, image, and memory of Carrillo to appeal to the rural poor. The league's leadership, however, came from party operatives and the upper class, whose wealth and social connections were put at the service of Don Gualberto. In recognition of his political usefulness, a series of governors granted him a string of elected and administrative posts, some of which were quite lucrative financially.[60]

Gualberto Carrillo Puerto not only fully exploited the hero cult of his brother, his effectiveness as a politician derived from many of the same superficial factors that had made his brother Felipe a legend. Both, after all, were tall, fair-skinned, and green-eyed, which physically marked them as "superior" persons of Spanish descent, yet both spoke fluent Maya and knew the folkways of the Yucatecan countryside, which gave them a familiarity with the rural poor and the ability to communicate with peasants on their own terms. But brother Gualberto's political opportunism drew charges of exploitation and betrayal of his brother's legacy. Many believed he was on the take. Such charges, however, must be examined in the context of his family's background.

Gualberto and the other surviving brothers, Eraclio, Aurelio, and Acrelio, considered themselves good socialists, yet they prided themselves on their entrepreneurial pursuits and had good relations with the wealthy *hacendados*, who had married two of their sisters. The surviving brothers of Felipe all honored their slain brother's radical legacy (Acrelio wrote two books embellishing it), but they continued to enjoy land, wealth, and political office because of the privilege their last name gave them.[61]

Like the rest of the surviving family, Gualberto's life before the revolution exemplified the precarious, hard-scrabble life of the provincial lower middle class who sought to make the most of family ties to get ahead. After finishing elementary school he was apprenticed to a silversmith, then tried his hand at ranching and marketing meat. The lure of the big city drew him to Mérida, where he worked in a general store and a liquor store before moving on to a shop that sold musical instruments. His employer there was also the orchestra director of the prestigious social club La Unión, which gave Gualberto Carrillo a social entree with the Mérida oligarchy. With his savings—and perhaps with some help from his rich in-laws and other family connections—Gualberto Carrillo managed to open a string of general stores, but his last business was in the end wiped out by fire. He had been reduced to selling chocolates when his brother's election to the governorship opened up a career in public service for the previously apolitical Gualberto.[62]

During his brother's term as governor, Gualberto served on the administrative council of the state-run railroads, an organization notorious for financial misconduct.[63] His actions during the De la Huerta coup that killed Felipe and two other brothers raised even more eyebrows. When Felipe decided to flee Mérida in hopes of escaping capture by rebellious federal troops, he ordered brother Gualberto to clear out the railroad treasury, presumably to fund a future counterattack. But the 75,000 pesos were loaded on the wrong caboose and remained in Mérida while Felipe fled on another train. When Gualberto Carrillo returned the money to the state government, which was by then controlled by the federal troops hunting down his brother, his actions struck many as a cowardly betrayal.[64]

Nevertheless, from the restoration of Socialist Party rule in mid-1924 until 1932, Gualberto Carrillo Puerto served as high priest of the hero cult of his brother, while he and other surviving members of the family were allowed to keep some of the sinecures and offices that they had acquired during Felipe Carrillo Puerto's life.[65] In 1933, however, Gualberto Carrillo broke with party chief Governor Bartolomé García Correa to launch his own candidacy for governor against the official candidate. Though thwarted, he would go on to run for senate in 1934 (unsuccessfully) and 1936 (successfully), and for governor again in 1937. Gualberto Carrillo's appropriation of his brother's legacy put the powers that be in the awkward position of trying to undermine the veneration of Felipe Carrillo Puerto that they had helped build up. In 1936, Gualberto's foe, Governor Fernando López Cárdenas, cancelled the January 3 commemoration of Felipe Carrillo's martyrdom, the high holy day of the hero cult, to deny Gualberto Carrillo Puerto yet another chance to capitalize on his brother's symbolic importance.[66] The increasingly mercenary usage of his brother's hero cult by Don Gualberto tarnished the family's reputation in the eyes of many, even as the Socialist Party lost its hold on the Yucatecan rural poor.

A Hero Cult Fades Away

FROM THE 1940S ONWARD, the national party-state, the PRI (Partido de la Revolución Institucionalizado, or Party of the Institutionalized Revolution), slowly absorbed regional affiliates like the PSS. Homegrown hero Felipe Carrillo Puerto gradually lost adherents among party apparatchiks to such national idols as Emiliano Zapata. True, a few old Socialists continued to attempt to bank on the diminishing political capital of the Carrillo Puerto myth, but Gualberto Carrillo Puerto's cynical and protracted use of his brother's memory and changing times took their toll.[67] To be sure, the anniversary of his death was celebrated in Mexico City until the early 1960s by the Felipe Carrillo Puerto Civil Association.[68] But in Yucatán, Mexicanization and urbanization sapped vitality from the Carrillo Puerto cult.

The decline of this cult, however, meant that Carrillo Puerto's memory was not associated with the PRI, whose popularity waned after the 1968 massacre in Mexico City's Tlatelolco Plaza, and further slipped due to the declining economy and political scandals in the 1970s and 1980s. Although the official cult lost its luster, his popular memory escaped such a precipitous decline. Candles are still burned and *ofrendas* (offerings) are still made to Carrillo Puerto in the old socialist stronghold of Muxupip.[69] If the PRI is to reinvent itself after its devastating defeat in the presidential election of July 2000, the enduring legacy of Felipe Carrillo Puerto might provide a means of reconnecting with the common folk of Mexico. Of course, such a change would require rediscovering the precocious populism and egalitarianism that made Carrillo Puerto such a significant politician in life and helped inspire an elaborate hero cult in death.

Notes

1. Ernest Gruening, "A Maya Idyl: A Study of Felipe Carrillo, Late Governor of Yucatan." *The Century Magazine*, April 1924, 832–836.

2. Hugo Sol (Anastasio Manzanilla), *Bolchevismo criminal de Yucatán: Documentos y apuntes para la historia trágica del estado* (Mexico City: n.p., 1921).

3. Manuel Escoffie Z., *Bajo el sol de mi tierra* (Mérida: El Porvenir, 1950), 212.

4. Acrelio Carrillo Puerto, *La familia Carrillo Puerto de Motul, con la Revolución Mexicana* (Mérida: n.p. 1959), 12; Renan Irigoyen, *Felipe Carrillo Puerto: Primer gobernante socialista en México (semblanza interpretativa)* (Mérida: Ediciones de la Universidad de Yucatán, 1974), 7.

5. Beatriz González Padilla, *Yucatán: Política y poder (1897–1929)* (Mérida: Maldonado, 1985), 88.

6. On Carrillo Puerto and Carlos R. Menéndez, see Antonio Betancourt Pérez, *Carta peninsular confidencial: Episodios históricos. Carlos R. Menéndez y Felipe Carrillo Puerto: La destrucción de los talleres de la Revista de Yucatán en 1924* (Mérida: Maldonado Editores, 1981).

7. José Castillo Torre, *A la luz de relámpago: Ensayo de biografía subjetiva de Felipe Carrillo Puerto* (Mexico City: Ediciones Botas, 1934), 49–50. See also Edmundo Bolio, *De la cuña al parredón: Anecdotario histórico de la vida, muerte y gloria de Felipe Carrillo Puerto* (Mérida: Basso/Talleres de la Compañía Periodistica del Sureste, n.d.).

8. See Michael Conniff, ed., *Latin American Populism in Comparative Perspective* (Albuquerque: University of New Mexico Press, 1982).

9. Castillo Torre, *A la luz de relámpago*, 44.

10. Guillermo Sandoval Viramontes and Jorge Mantilla Gutiérrez, *Felipe Carrillo Puerto: Ensayo biográfico (vida y obra)* (Mérida: Universidad Autónoma de Yucatán, 1994), 64–70.

11. David Arthur Franz, "Bullets and Bolshevists: A History of the Mexican Revolution and Reform in Yucatan, 1910–1924" (PhD diss., University of New Mexico, 1973), 298.

12. Castillo Torre, *A la luz de relámpago*, 52; and Marte R. Gómez, *Las Comisiones Agrarias del Sur* (Mexico City: Porrua, 1961), 80.

13. Samuel Brunk, *Emiliano Zapata: Revolution and Betrayal in Mexico* (Albuquerque: University of New Mexico Press, 1995), 182. According to Zapatista archives, Felipe Carrillo Puerto was sent to Yucatán in November 1914 to raise the Mayan Indians in revolt. See Laureano Cardoz Ruz, *El drama de los Mayas: Una reforma social traicionada* (Mexico City: Editorial Libros de Mexico, n.d.), 181–82.

14. Castillo Torre, *A la luz de relámpago*, 80–90.

15. Gilbert Joseph, *Revolution from Without: Yucatán, Mexico, and the United States, 1880–1924*, 2nd ed. (Durham, N.C.: Duke University Press, 1988), 205–206.

16. Robert Redfield, *The Folk Culture of Yucatan* (Chicago: University of Chicago Press, 1941), 39–40, 66–75.

17. Cardoz Ruz, *El Drama de los Mayas*, 283–285.

18. Bolio, *De la cuña al paredón*.

19. *La Opinion*, 5 August 1921; Santos Domínguez Ake, *La vida de Felipe Carrillo Puerto y su memoria en Muxupip* (Mérida: Maldonado, Consejo Nacional para la Cultura y las Artes, Culturas Populares, 1992); Santos Dominguez Aké, *La historia de la sociedad ejidal de Muxupip* (Tlahuapan, Puebla, Mexico: Instituto Nacional Indigenista Sedesol,

1994); *El asesinato de Carrillo Puerto (discursos y articulos en elogio del ilustre Mártir, y protestas contra sus infames asesinos)* (Mexico City: n.p., 1924); and José Castillo Torre et al., "Advertencia Preliminar," 6.

20. Franz, "Bullets and Bolshevists," 235.

21. Barbara Ellen Holmes, "Women and Yucatec Kinship" (PhD diss., Tulane University, 1978), 30–33.

22. Joseph, *Revolution from Without*; Gilbert M. Joseph, "Caciquismo and the Revolution: Carrillo Puerto in Yucatán," in *Caudillo and Peasant in the Mexican Revolution*, ed. David A. Bradling (Cambridge: Cambridge University Press, 1980), 193–221.

23. See, for instance, Carrillo Puerto's message in *La Revista de Yucatán*, 2 July 1919.

24. Felipe Carrillo Puerto to Governor Carlos Castro Morales, 11 July 1919, Mérida, Archivo General del Estado de Yucatán, Poder ejecutivo (hereafter cited as AGEY PE), 689.

25. Alvaro Gamboa Ricalde, *Yucatan desde 1910* (Veracruz: Imprente Standard, 1943), III:270–272.

26. Franz, "Bullets and Bolshevists," 275.

27. Felipe Carrillo Puerto to Alvaro Obregón, 13 March 1922, AGN Fondo Presidentes, Obregón y Calles (hereafter OyC), 243-Y1-N-1.

28. "Reuniones de Carrillo Puerto. El cenote Sambulá, un lugar con valor histórico," *Diario de Yucatán* on-line, http://www.yucatan.com.mx/especiales/motul/cenote2.asp; Gamboa Ricalde, *Yucatan Desde 1910*, III:258–259; [Luis] Amendolla, *La revolución comienza a los cuarenta* (Mexico: n.p., n.d.), 217, 220.

29. William Brito Sansores, *Tizimín en la historia* (Mérida: Ediciones Salettianas, 1995), 113.

30. Daniela Spenser, "Workers Against Socialism? Reassessing the Role of Urban Labor in Yucatecan Revolutionary Politics," in *Land, Labor and Capital in Modern Yucatan: Essays in Regional History and Political Economy*, ed. Gilbert M. Joseph and Jeffrey T. Brannon (Tuscaloosa: University of Alabama, 1991), 220–242.

31. This observation was gleaned from biographical analyses of government appointments listed in *Diario Oficial* from 1918 to 1925. As early as 1918, Felipe Carrillo Puerto had recognized the necessity of bourgeois collaboration in administering the government- and state-run henequen cooperative. See *Primer Congreso Obrero Socialista celebrado en Motul, Estado de Yucatán. Bases que se discutieron y aprobaron*, 2nd ed. (Mexico City: Centro de Estudios Históricos del Movimiento Obrero Mexicano, 1977), 59.

32. Escoffie Z., *Bajo el sol de mi tierra*, 211–213; and Manuel Sarkisyanz, *Felipe Carrillo Puerto: Actuacion y muerte del apostol "rojo" de los Mayas. Con un ensayo sobre hagiografía secular en la Revolución Méxicana* (Mérida: Congreso del Estado de Yucatán, 1995), 148.

33. Luis Aboites, *La Revolución Mexicana en Espita, Yucatán (1910–1940): Microhistoria de la formación del estado de la revolución* (Mérida: Maldonado Editores, INAH and SEP, 1985), 134–135.

34. Joseph, *Revolution from Without*, 228.

35. Ben Fallaw, "Dry Law, Wet Politics: Drinking and Prohibition in Revolutionary-era Yucatán, 1915–1935," *Latin American Research Review* 37, no. 3 (Summer 2002): 37–64.

36. Margarita Sanger, *La regulación de la natalidad: La brújula del hogar* (Mérida: Mayab, 1922).

37. *Primer Congreso Obrero Socialista*, 18–19.

38. Joseph, *Revolution from Without*, 264–274; Roque Armando Sosa Ferreyro, *El*

crimen del miedo: Reportaje histórico como y por que fue asesinado Felipe Carrillo Puerto (Mexico City: B. Costa-Amic, 1969); Cardoz Ruz, *El Drama de los Mayas*, 212–222; and Sarkisyanz, *Felipe Carrillo Puerto*.

39. Javier M. Erosa to governor, 11 July 1924, AGEY PE 796 SG.

40. Ilene V. O'Malley, *The Myth of the Revolution: Hero Cults and the Institutionalization of the Mexican State, 1920–1940* (New York: Greenwood Press, 1986).

41. Gabriel Ferrer de M., *Nuestra Ciudad: Mérida de Yucatán (1542–1938)* (Merida: Basso, 1938), 139; and Antonio Bustillos Carrillo, *Yucatán al servicio de la patria y de la revolución* (Mexico City: Casa Ramírez, 1959), 370.

42. *Diario del Sureste*, 4 January 1932.

43. *Tierra*, 30 April 1928. In fact, Terry Rugeley demonstrated that Buenaventura Martínez, not Cepeda, began the anti-imperialist struggle in the state. See Terry Rugeley, "The Forgotten Liberator: Buenaventura Martinez and Yucatan's Republican Restoration," *Mexican Studies/Estudios Mexicanos* 19, no. 2 (December 2003).

44. *Tierra*, 29 March 1928; David Craven, *Diego Rivera as Epic Modernist* (New York: G. K. Hall, 1997), 68–69, 81–82.

45. Javier Erosa to Calles, 26 March 1927, Mexico City, AGN OyC, 307-Y-2.

46. Alvaro Torre Diaz, *Cuatro años en el gobierno de Yucatán, 1926–1930* (Mérida: n.p., 1930), 198–199.

47. *Tierra*, 30 April 1928.

48. *Diario del Sureste*, 29, 30 December 1931, 3 January 1932.

49. Victor Echeverría Pérez to governor, 28 March 1932, AGEY PE 943.

50. *Diario del Sureste*, 3 January 1932.

51. Anacleto Cetina Aguilar, *Breves datos históricos y culturales del municipio de Hunucmá* (Mérida: n.p., 1990), 56; Joanne Hershfield, *Mexican Cinema/Mexican Woman, 1940–1950* (Tucson: University of Arizona Press, 1996), 36; Gabriel Ramírez, *El cine yucateco* (Mexico City: Filmoteca UNAM, 1980), 10, 25, 71; Fernando Muñoz Castillo, *El teatro regional de Yucatán* (Mexico City: Universidad Autónoma Metropolitana, 1987), 213; *Diccionario histórico y biográfico de la Revolución Mexicana*, tomo VII (Mexico City: Instituto Nacional de Estudios Históricos de la Revolución Mexicana and Secretaría de Gobernación, 1990), Mauricio Bretón González, coordinador for Yucatán; Bonifacio Frias Conor, *Divorcios celebres y amores fugaces: Historia auténtica de un famoso abogado especialista en divorcios* (Mexico City: Botas, 1939), 282; Sosa Ferreyro, *El Crimen del Miedo*, 20–21); and Sarkisyanz, *Felipe Carrillo Puerto*, 197–198.

52. Bolio, *De la cuña al paredón*, 81; *Diario del Sureste*, 3 January 1932.

53. Carlos Escoffie, "Resumen Cronologico de 1930," *Diario de Yucatán*, 1 January 1931; *Diario del Sureste*, 3 January 1932.

54. Photograph of construction found in AGEY PE 952 SG 2; J. Adonay Cetina Sierra, *Mérida de Yucatán, 1542–1984: Historia Gráfica* (Mérida: Secretaria de Educación Pública, 1984), 233.

55. Manuel Cirerol to Bartolomé García Correa, 2 September 1932; Manuel Cirerol to Bartolomé García Correa, 9 February 1933; Antonio Ramayo to Bartolomé García Correa, 28 November 1932, Contrato de Obras dated 5 April 1933, (1934); Manuel Cirerol to César Alayola Barrera, AGEY PE 952 S62; *El Yucatanista*, 19, 26 November 1932; *Diario del Sureste*, 24 June 1938.

56. See Ben Fallaw, *Cárdenas Compromised: The Failure of Reform in Postrevolutionary Yucatán* (Durham, N.C.: Duke University Press, 2001).

57. *Diario del Sureste*, 3 January 1935.

58. Brito Sansores, *Tizimín en la historia*, 187; Escoffie, "Resumen Cronologico de 1930."

59. Sol, *El Comunismo en México*, 157.

60. Aurelio Velázquez, "Memorandum: Política Electoral en Yucatán," 17 June 1937, AGEY PE 1022 SG 2; Acrelio Carrillo Puerto, *Familia*, 81.

61. On the brothers' histories, see Acrelio Carrillo Puerto, *Familia*, especially 96–105. The landholdings of Acrelio and Eraclio are listed in "Fincas Mayores de 300-00-00 Hectáres," 1936, Secretaría de la Reforma Agraria Archive. I would like to thank Paul Eiss for sharing this document with me. See also Gamboa Ricalde, *Yucatan desde 1910*, 3:248–249.

62. Acrelio Carrillo Puerto, *Familia*, 81–83; Aurelio Velázquez, Confidential Memorandum 17, June 1937, AGEY PE 1022 SG 2.

63. *Diario Oficial*, 27 April 1922.

64. Gardener Hunting, "A Despot Has No Luck Nowadays: The Firing Squad Spoiled Carrillo's Dream," *Collier's*, April 26, 1924, 15–16, 37–38.

65. Sol, *El Comunismo en México*, 157.

66. Miguel Civeira Taboada, *Felipe Carrillo Puerto: Mártir del proletariado nacional* (Mexico City: Comisión Editorial de la Liga de Economistas Revolucionarios de la República Mexicana, A.C., 1986), 10. The succeeding interim governor, Florencio Palomo Valencia, also failed to hold an official wake in 1937, leaving Gualberto Carrillos's Revolutionary Center of Yucatán to station its own honor guards at brother Felipe's grave. *Diario de Yucatán*, 30 December 1936.

67. Comite Socialista Yucateco "Felipe Carrillo Puerto" to Secretary of Government, Mexico City, 19 August 1957, AGN DGG 2.311G 2 II, Caja 338, tomo V. On Gualberto Carrillo Puerto's use of the hero cult of his brother, see Fallaw, *Cárdenas Compromised*, 61–69.

68. Civeira Taboada, *Felipe Carrillo Puerto*, 11.

69. Santiago Dominguez Ake, *La Vida de Felipe Carrillo Puerto y su memoria en Muxupip* (Mérida: Maldonado Consejo Nacional para la Cultura y las Artes, and Dirección General de Culturas, 1992), 59–62.

7

Augusto Sandino of Nicaragua

The Hero Never Dies

For when a hero dies
he doesn't die:
for that hero is reborn
in a Nation.

Ernesto Cardenal, *Zero Hour*

RICHARD GROSSMAN

On July 1, 1927, a young, relatively unknown Nicaraguan issued a political manifesto in which he declared,

> The man who doesn't ask his country for even a handful of earth for his grave deserves to be heard, and not only heard, but also to be believed. I am a Nicaraguan and I am proud because in my veins flows above all the blood of the Indian race, which by some atavism encompasses the mystery of being patriotic, loyal, and sincere. . . .

He added, "I accept the challenge of the dastardly invader and the nation's traitors. Our breasts will be the ramparts against which their hordes will shatter themselves. . . ."[1]

With these stirring words, Augusto Sandino announced his opposition to the intervention of the U.S. Marines in Nicaragua and his intention to fight the Marines and those Nicaraguans allied with them. In one of his first public pronouncements, Sandino presented himself to Nicaragua and the world as a hero who would defy the odds, defend and protect Nicaragua, and defeat the giant of the North. He was also already projecting potential martyrdom.

At the moment of this proclamation, Sandino was a minor Liberal leader based in the northern Nicaragua area known as the Segovias. A civil war (another in a series of conflicts that had started with independence from Spain) between the Liberal and Conservative factions had just been brought to an end by another intervention of Marines from the United States. Through the efforts of the special envoy, Henry L. Stimson, a deal had been worked out between the leaders of the two factions in which the Conservatives would continue to control the presidency but the Liberals would receive the governorship of half of the departments into which the country was divided. The deal also called for new national elections to be held, under U.S. supervision, in 1928. Though nominally a Liberal, Sandino rejected the deal and called for a new national war against both the U.S. occupiers and those Nicaraguans who had accepted what Sandino felt was a pact imposed by the United States.

With the exception of a small following in the Segovias, Sandino was an unknown in Nicaragua and the world. However, with his decision to defy and fight the U.S. Marines, he would be transformed into both a national and international hero whose cultlike status continues to this day. In both words and actions, Sandino consciously contributed to this development. For example, he was born Augusto Calderón Sandino but signed his manifesto Augusto César Sandino.[2] At the same time, he changed the name of the small town El Jícaro to Ciudad Sandino.

During Sandino's lifetime there were several distinct images of him as hero. To his non-Nicaraguan admirers, Sandino was a nationalist and anti-imperialist who was defending his country and defying the United States. Many throughout Latin America, the United States, and Europe rallied to his support. Within Nicaragua, especially in his base area, Sandino had a different image. Here his focus was on developing the concept of the nation among his peasant supporters. In this region he was perceived by his followers as the patriarch, or founding father figure, of a new national family that had to be defended against foreign aggression.

Nationalism as a political concept was just beginning to develop in Nicaragua. Most Nicaraguans identified first with either the Liberal or Conservative faction and with their home city or region, and only then with Nicaragua as a whole. However, since the beginning of the twentieth century, when the United States started to assert its hegemony over the Caribbean basin region, U.S. troops had intervened in Nicaragua several times. The major U.S. concern was that Nicaragua was a site for a potential interoceanic canal. Therefore, Nicaraguan nationalism was anti-imperialist, since it began to develop in opposition to the interventions and influence, both direct and indirect, of the United States. Still, in 1927, most Nicaraguans remained primarily partisan followers of either the Liberals or the Conservatives and saw U.S. intervention through the lens of how such intervention affected their party's opportunities, not how it affected the country. Sandino had a difficult job in trying to create a new, nonpartisan nationalist vision, especially for his peasant adherents.

Although many saw Sandino as a hero, a countering vision was projected by the United States and its Nicaraguan allies. In this vision he was an apolitical bandit concerned only with criminal gains. Almost all U.S. documents, both military and civilian, described him as a bandit. Most of the Nicaraguan elite, both Liberal and Conservative, initially accepted this definition of Sandino.

The debates over Sandino's image would continue after his death, especially within Nicaragua. As a new generation became politically active his image was resurrected and expanded, and a new hero cult developed. This generation of revolutionaries named their organization after him—the Frente Sandinista de Liberación Nacional (FSLN; Sandinista National Liberation Front). After the 1979 revolution, Sandino became the founding father symbol for a new nation.

Enter Sandino

AUGUSTO SANDINO was born in 1895 in the village of Niquinohomo, near Masaya. His father, Gregorio Sandino, was the owner of a midsized estate; his mother, Margarita Calderón, was a poor peasant woman who worked on Don Gregorio's coffee plantation.[3] Augusto was illegitimate, and his father did not recognize him until he was eleven.

In 1921, while still a young man, Sandino fled the country after a fight. He first worked on a sugar plantation in Honduras, then on a United Fruit banana plantation in Guatemala, and finally in the Mexican oil fields as a skilled worker for the U.S.-owned Huasteca Petroleum Company. He arrived in Mexico just after the end of the great Mexican Revolution and was working in the port city of Tampico, which had a large and radical working-class movement, when the Nicaraguan civil war broke out in 1925.

In 1926 Sandino returned to Nicaragua and started working in the U.S.-owned San Albino gold mine. As Sandino described it, "I heard that a revolutionary movement had broken out in Nicaragua. . . . I heard what was going on . . . and got into active political life."[4] In the mines, Sandino began to organize. His first "army" consisted of twenty-nine men, mainly mine workers. By April he had 800 followers fighting the Conservatives in power. Sandino was now the leader of the largest Liberal force in the Segovias.[5]

In December 1926 the U.S. Marines landed, and by May 1927 negotiations organized by the U.S. representative Stimson had led to the ceasefire and demobilization of the various forces. The Liberal commander, José

Maria Moncada, accepted that the Conservatives would temporarily retain the presidency and that a new election would take place the following year.

During the civil war, Sandino had nominally been a Liberal general. Although he started fighting on his own initiative, he did go to the Liberal army headquarters, where he received official orders naming him "Expeditionary Chief in Nueva Segovia."[6] Even during the civil war, however, he stood apart from the other Liberal leaders, and there were clear tensions with the Liberal commander, Moncada. Sandino's time in postrevolutionary Mexico had influenced his personal political development. He had his own identifying symbols, such as a Sandinista flag based on the Mexican revolutionary anarcho-syndicalist strike colors of red and black (versus the Liberal party color of only red).[7]

When the pact was signed, most of Sandino's soldiers returned to their homes. One historian described this as "the most difficult and hard moment of his political and military career."[8] Sandino had to regroup, reorganize, and redefine himself. In this moment he issued the manifesto quoted at the head of this chapter. In this document Sandino, while still defining himself as a Liberal, clearly distinguishes himself from the national leadership of Nicaragua, both Liberal and Conservative, which he claimed had sold and abandoned the country to the United States.

On July 16, 1927, Sandino followed up with an attack against the Marine base in the northern city of Ocotal. Although the attack failed, the war was now on, and Sandino was being transformed from a local Liberal leader into a patriotic hero who was resisting the U.S. occupation.[9] In September 1927, Sandino called together his small band of followers and formally created a new army, the Ejército Defensor de la Soberanía Nacional de Nicaragua (EDSNN, Army in Defense of the National Sovereignty of Nicaragua).

What made Sandino the supreme leader? Sandino had projected himself as the only Nicaraguan leader ready to defend the nation and the national honor, and in fact this was true. He was also clearly becoming a charismatic figure whose force of personality and ideas held together his small army. Finally, as he became the patriarch figure to his followers, loyalty to Sandino became as important as loyalty to the nation. No difference was seen between the two, since Sandino was also the father of this new nation.

Despite Sandino's rousing words and actions, almost all Nicaraguans initially rejected him. Most of the elites of Nicaragua, both Liberal and Conservative, were now making their peace with the United States. Almost no Nicaraguans from outside the Segovias would join Sandino's struggle. Thus, despite his claim to be defending Nicaragua, he would end up fighting both the U.S. and the Nicaraguan governments. Those Nicaraguans who opposed him were defined by Sandino as traitors and *vendepatrias* (country-sellers, or sellouts) who accepted U.S. domination in return for personal gain.

Sandino's political development can be divided into two periods. In the first phase, from 1927 until 1929, he presented himself as a nationalist and anti-imperialist. Influenced by the Mexican Revolution, he had a broad but not clearly defined vision of social reform and transformation. He also believed in a united-front concept of trying to build a broad political alliance to oppose the U.S. intervention. To help achieve that last goal, Sandino left Nicaragua in 1929 and traveled to Mexico. He was hoping to unify the international support that had already developed and to obtain aid from the government of Mexico. Although he was in Mexico for nearly a year, he failed to achieve either of these goals. When he returned to Nicaragua in 1930, he was almost totally isolated from his earlier support networks. However, he returned more personally radicalized, now a committed social revolutionary. Beyond defeating the Yankees, his internal communications to his followers now spoke of "Divine Justice" having chosen them to lead the "'Proletarian Explosion' against the imperialists of the earth."[10] By the end of the war, in 1933, the Sandinista movement had become a movement of the mountain peasants of northern Nicaragua. Sandino himself now accepted the logic of peasant utopianism. He had redefined himself. In his first manifesto he had called himself a "mechanic." However, by 1933, he was describing himself as "nothing but a peasant."[11]

One can see the fusion of Sandino's postcapitalist vision with the peasants' views. During his second sojourn in Mexico, Sandino had become a member of the Magnetic-Spiritual School of the Universal Commune, which was a small anarcho-communal and spiritualist organization based in Buenos Aires, Argentina, but with a number of adherents in Mexico. He had not renounced his original political positions, but his views had evolved. He now defined himself as a "rationalistic communist" and a "theosophist," as well as a patriot.[12] At the end of the war, he did not move into the capital city of Managua, or even into one of the Segovian towns. Taking the position that his task of transforming Nicaragua had just started, he retired to the wilderness of the Segovias to create a new world.

For six years the EDSNN engaged the U.S. Marines and the Guardia Nacional de Nicaragua (National Guard of Nicaragua) in a bitter guerrilla war. The guard was a creation of the United States in which Nicaraguan soldiers were commanded by U.S. Marines in the fight against Sandino. The rules of war did not apply to confrontations with Sandino and his followers because they were considered bandits. The Marines and the Guardia

Nacional also made few distinctions between the Sandinistas and the civilian population of the Segovias. As Marine General Dion Williams noted, "a large portion of the inhabitants of the mountain regions of the north were *potential* bandits."[13] Thousands of Nicaraguans died, and many others saw their homes and farms destroyed. The brutality of the Marines and the guard contributed to the support that developed for Sandino. Many joined the EDSNN out of anger at the atrocities, and also in the hope that they and their families would then be protected from further attacks.

Finally, in November 1932, the Liberal Party leader whom Sandino had backed during the 1926–1927 civil war, Juan Sacasa, was elected president. The U.S. Marines withdrew from Nicaragua on January 2, 1933. Command of the Guardia Nacional was turned over to Nicaraguans, and Anastasio Somoza García became the Guardia's new director. In February 1933, Sandino signed a ceasefire agreement with the Nicaraguan government. In some senses he had won the war, since most of his original goals had been achieved.

Sandino had slowly become a hero to a broader sector of Nicaraguan society. As the U.S. occupation continued year after year, more and more Nicaraguans had grown tired of U.S. influence and accepted Sandino as a nationalist hero. By 1932, pro-Sandino leaflets were being circulated in the cities. One, dated May 1932 and signed by a "group of Workers and Students," spoke of Sandino and "his valor, his heroism" in defending the country.[14] Also, various politicians, particularly Conservatives, who now saw the United States as propping up the Liberals, tried to use Sandino as a counterweight to create a path for their resumption of power.[15]

At the war's end, Sandino seriously underestimated the guard. There were no provisions in the peace accords discussing the future role of the National Guard. Thus, the EDSNN was officially disarmed, while the guard functioned as the sole military force within the country. Despite the signing of the peace accord, the guard continued to harass the Sandinistas. Sandino quickly realized his mistake and began to call for the dismantling of the guard as an unconstitutional force. President Sacasa wavered in his opinion of the guard. Beyond the question of its constitutionality, the guard was also a heavy economic burden on the Nicaraguan government. Disbanding the guard, however, would have opened up the possibility of a total Sandinista victory in Nicaragua, since no other military force existed.

Its institutional existence at stake, the guard leadership decided to act. On February 21, 1934, Sandino went to Managua for another negotiating session. After dining with President Sacasa, Sandino, his half-brother Socrates, and two aides were arrested by the guard and murdered. Almost simultaneously the guard attacked and destroyed Sandinista camps.

Hundreds, possibly thousands, of Sandinistas were killed or fled into exile in the repression that followed. With Sandino dead, Somoza García quickly consolidated power. By 1937 he was president of the country as well as director of the guard.

Sandino, buried in an unmarked grave, had achieved the martyr's status he had anticipated in his opening manifesto. He had received his handful of dirt, but the new government tried hard to make sure he would never be heard of again.

Perceptions of the Hero

WHEN THE WAR STARTED IN 1927, two images of Sandino as hero began to develop. Both were encouraged by Sandino. The first was the image that Sandino projected to both the nation and the world, a David defying the Goliath of the North. The other image was the internal face that Sandino showed his soldiers and followers inside Nicaragua. Here Sandino combined the first expression with a second role, that of the patriarch of a new, extended family. There is no evidence that this dual imagery was a conscious strategy. However, it did meet the various requirements of the war in which he was engaged.

In his first manifesto, Sandino presented himself to the world as a brave patriot willing to risk everything, including his life, to defend his country. Thus, throughout Latin America and much of the world, he was almost immediately perceived as the new hero resisting U.S. intervention. A large number of articles and pamphlets praising Sandino were published. Gabriela Mistral, the Chilean poet, noted that Sandino carried "upon his vigorous shoulders" the honor of all of Latin America. Jose Vasconcelos, the Mexican author, called Sandino a hero and "one of the grandest figures" in Latin American history.[16]

Even within the United States there were a number of favorable articles about Sandino. At the very start of the war, *The Nation* editorialized that "Latin American hearts from Cape Horn to the Rio Grande beat in sympathy with any Latin who fights the Yankee invasion of a Latin country."[17] The magazine then sent reporter Carleton Beals to Nicaragua. His articles would help build Sandino's fame.

Sandino's name and struggle thus became known worldwide. In 1928 a Sandinista delegation attended the International Anti-Imperialist Congress in Frankfurt, Germany. Among those present were Jawaharlal Nehru and Madame Sun Yat-sen. Henri Barbusse, the French author and one of the leaders of the Congress, wrote a glowing letter to Sandino:

At the vanguard of the struggle and your challenged continent you,
Sandino, general of free men, are performing a historic, indelible
role, by your luminous example and splendid sacrifices. The hearts of
all of us are with you.[18]

As the war continued, a number of distinct political factions vied for
Sandino's support, hoping to use him to advance their own visions. Initially,
Sandino's key foreign representative was the Honduran intellectual Froylán
Turcios, who published the influential journal *Ariel*. This journal was read
throughout the region and represented the liberal anti-imperialist view that
Latin Americans had to defend themselves from the corrupting influences
of the Yankees, and from Anglo-Saxons in general. Sandino was in communication with Turcios by September 1927, and a number of his letters were
published in *Ariel*. In his first letter to Turcios, Sandino emphasized his
patriotism and declared that his actions were "intended to defend my country's honor faithfully and without personal ambition."[19] Turcios accepted
and promoted Sandino's self-description as a selfless patriot and thus
helped define this initial image of Sandino as a continental hero.

Other political tendencies also proclaimed their support and admiration
for Sandino. These included followers of both Peru's American Popular
Revolutionary Alliance (APRA) and communist movements. Communist
activities were coordinated throughout the Western hemisphere by the
Antimperialist League of the Americas and the Hands Off Nicaragua
Committee. The leaders included the Cuban Julio Antonio Mella, the
Venezuelan Gustavo Machado, and the Mexican artist Diego Rivera. The
Salvadoran communist Agustín Farabundo Martí was the official represen-
tative of the Antimperialist League to Sandino, serving for a while as
Sandino's personal secretary.[20] The communists organized a number of
events in support of Sandino. There were rallies and demonstrations, as well
as attempts to raise material support.

Although APRA contributed less material aid to Sandino, the Apristas
also offered their support. APRA's founder, Victor Raúl Haya de la Torre
(see Chapter 9), wrote, "The people of Nicaragua and Sandino, their revolutionary leader, are the actual champions of our threatened twenty peoples."[21] He added that APRA offered its services and blood unconditional-
ly to Sandino's struggle.

A small number of international volunteers representing these different
tendencies arrived at Sandino's headquarters. Although they played a minor
role in actual combat, the ensuing debates within this group of supporters
clearly helped in Sandino's personal political developments. For a while,

these non-Nicaraguan intellectuals were Sandino's brain trust.[22] They also were key contacts with the outside world.

Sandino was aware of the solidarity movements taking shape around the world. In one letter to a wavering supporter, he stated, "I am sending you some magazines so that you will see that our cause has numerous friends in the world. . . ." With this letter Sandino included several copies of the magazine *La Sierra* from Peru, which was supportive of APRA, and articles from the *Daily Worker*, the newspaper of the Communist Party of the United States. *La Sierra* included an ode entitled "Canto a Sandino" (Song to Sandino), which included the lines, "Sandino . . . you have opened the dawn . . . shaking the continent toward the future."[23]

Despite this glowing praise, Sandino would have continual problems with his international supporters. All were trying to define him through their own lenses. Turcios would be the first to break with Sandino over policy issues. Turcios thought the war was only to expel the United States and return the Liberals to power. In 1928 the Liberals, now under U.S. tutelage, won the Nicaraguan elections, but Sandino decided to continue the war.[24]

The communists would be the next to desert Sandino. By 1929 the international communist movement, led by the Communist International (Comintern), made a dramatic shift to an ultraleft position with the claim that the world communist revolution was imminent. The communists then claimed that all "true" revolutionaries had to join the Communist Party or they would be considered traitors. Sandino, who was not a Marxist-Leninist communist, believed in the concept of building a strong, broad "united front" (as had the communists up until 1929) and refused to follow this ultraleft position imposed by Moscow.[25] The various communist parties denounced Sandino and ceased all their solidarity activities. They falsely suggested that Sandino had stolen the money they had raised and donated.[26]

Thus, by 1930, Sandino's star on the international scene was fading. Beyond the political disputes with some of his international supporters, another factor that lessened support was the start of the Great Depression in October 1929. The concerns of most, including those who were politically active in the anti-imperialist movement, shifted to domestic economic issues. Sandino's international support network dwindled to a few Nicaraguan exiles and the Magnetic-Spiritual School. Still, many in Latin America continued to see Sandino as a hero. In an article dated July 11, 1932, the Mexican newspaper *La Prensa* discussed "the recent victories of the army of the Nicaraguan patriots headed by General Augusto Cesar Sandino. . . ."[27]

Sandino: The Father as Hero

SANDINO PROJECTED A DIFFERENT IMAGE of himself for his soldiers. The various debates over and visions of Sandino, which had defined and then destroyed his international support, had almost no echo within the rank and file of his Nicaraguan followers. The Segovias were a remote and rugged section of Nicaragua. Much of the region was isolated, politically and economically, from the rest of the country. This was an agricultural frontier zone where there were still large sections of virgin forest and a low population density. Much of the vacant land, however, was in the isolated mountainous regions and hence not easily accessible. The vast majority of Segovians lived in poorly defined communities or scattered houses.[28] Largely illiterate, many barely realized that a Nicaragua existed. Patriotism, anti-imperialism, and communism were all obscure concepts to these individuals (as they were to most Nicaraguans) and certainly no reason to fight and possibly die. Sandino's opening manifesto would have made little sense to the Segovian peasants.

In order to defend the nation, Sandino had first to create a conception that there was one. The problem was how to describe this new idea to his peasant followers. Resorting to more familiar speech, his nationalist discourse became both patriarchal and familial, with the nation depicted as an extended family. The members of his army were all described as brothers. Their mother was the homeland. Implicitly, the father (or patriarch) became Sandino himself.

Sandino developed this idea of the national family in various writings. In one letter Sandino described his vision of the nation:

> "Beloved brother in the Homeland," is the salutation in correspondence among members of our Army. With this our intention has been to keep present in our people the concept that the Homeland is our Mother, that since we are brothers in her, it is our duty to go to the forefront of her defense, because in defending her, we defend ourselves.[29]

Although most of the original Sandinistas were illiterate and so left few written documents, a number of those who survived the war and the following years of repression were interviewed after 1979.[30] According to these survivors, Sandino treated the soldiers fairly and with respect; therefore, they followed him and loved him like a father. For example, one Jerónimo Zelaya Hernández stated that Sandino was their leader because he "dominated, like a father of the family."[31] Another stated, "He was my father, yes that man was loved by us." He added, "We were 'brothers' and to him we said 'the old man.'"[32] Sandino was fairly young, only in his thirties, but he became the patriarch to his followers.

As the good father, Sandino wanted nothing for himself and everything for his "family" and Nicaragua. Thus, Calixto Tercero González remembered him as someone who embraced everyone he met, and if they were poor he would give them a little money to buy some food.[33] Although Sandino did not have much to give during the war, many of the survivors had similar stories of him giving out "good" cigarettes and other presents to his soldiers. These little gifts were an important part of the public expression of a beneficent patriarch and helped personalize and cement the relationship between Sandino and his followers.[34]

Sandino was successful in explaining the idea of the nation and the need to defend the country by extending the concept of a patriarchal family. Because of the war, this new national family was under attack. According to this patriarchal vision, it was the duty of men to defend their homes and families and, by extension, their homeland. Many Sandinistas clearly felt they had to fight to defend themselves, their families, and their country from the Marines and members of the Guardia Nacional.

How did Sandino convey these concepts to his scattered and illiterate followers? He was not in direct personal contact with most of the members of the EDSNN, but he did address a number of letters and communiqués to his soldiers, usually to be read aloud. The language of these was different from that in the letters to his international supporters. One letter from May 1931 serves as an example. This letter was almost a sermon, with Sandino discussing his vision of heaven and hell. He urged his followers to "[p]rocure to be Angels, not demons." The letter was addressed to two officers, but ended with these instructions: "Please give my personal regards to all the brothers who are with you. . . . Also please read it in public when they are not too worried about the enemies."[35]

Sandino also relied on songs. Songs are an important method of transmitting ideas in illiterate societies. Most of the songs he used were originally written by only a few people, particularly Pedro Cabrera and Tranquilino Jarquín. Both of these men were assistants to Sandino and were in effect his "official" songwriters. Therefore the lyrics were not those of the average soldier but more closely resembled Sandino's own language. They became popular with the troops and were sung throughout the Segovias. While a number of themes were raised, these songs clearly helped develop the image of Sandino as hero. For example, one titled "Hymn to Sandino" included the words, "Oh! Sandino your name is sublime!"[36] Another song had the following lyrics:

It is the valiant Sandino
Example of dignity
That against the assassin yankee
fights for liberty.[37]

By the war's end, the EDSNN had become a brotherhood and Sandino
its charismatic, heroic patriarch. The goal was not only to defeat the United
States but to transform Nicaragua, and Sandino's personal spiritualism and
communalism gave the movement an almost millenarian aspect.[38]

Black Legend of Sandino

IN THE EYES OF U.S. POLICY MAKERS and their Nicaraguan allies,
Sandino was neither a patriot nor a hero but, like Zapata before him, a bandit. The choice of the word *bandit* to describe Sandino was made for clear
political reasons.[39] By using this word, U.S. policy makers, the Marines, and
the Nicaraguan National Guard were able to deny the political and social
nature of the war or that there was any legitimacy to Sandino's cause, making him a criminal instead.

At the very start of the war, U.S. Secretary of State Frank Kellogg stated that Sandino's "activities cannot be considered to have any political significance whatsoever." He added that the Sandinistas "are in effect nothing
more than common criminals."[40] Admiral Julian Latimer, commander of
the U.S. forces in Nicaragua for the first half of 1927, gave a similar description of Sandino. Latimer called him "merely a bandit," with no more support or following than the "Jesse James gang in the United States."[41]

Occasionally, U.S. officials admitted that Sandino had some political
motives. In an interesting article in the November 1930 issue of *Marine
Corps Gazette* (the semi-official magazine of the Marines), Brigadier
General Dion Williams, commander of the Marines in Nicaragua, again
emphasized the criminal nature of Sandino. He noted,

> Sandino soon collected around him a force of professional bandits
> augmented by malcontents from both sides in the late civil war and
> by a number of fugitives from Justice in Nicaragua and other Central
> American countries.

However, General Williams also noted that Sandino was a "symbol of
hope." He added that Sandino had distributed pamphlets that were against
"'foreign intervention and the exploitation of the country by the money
powers of Nicaragua and Wall Street'" and that these pamphlets had "all the

hackneyed phrases of the communism [*sic*]. . . ." Williams did not explore the contradictions in his statements that Sandino was both a common criminal and a communist hero to the common Nicaraguans, perhaps because to Williams and many Americans, communism was roughly equivalent to banditry.[42] Although use of the term bandit was somewhat controversial within the United States, it came to dominate the debates over the war.[43] U.S. policy makers, both civilian and military, never varied much from this initial official characterization of the Sandino movement.

In 1927 most of the Nicaraguan elite, both Liberal and Conservative, repeated the claim that Sandino was a mere bandit. The Liberal Party leader and later president, José Maria Moncada, called Sandino "a bandit and a fanatic."[44] Conservative leader Carlos Cuadra Pasos said, "Sandino is a bandit, and his principal business is now robbery, murder and assassination. . . ."[45] While there is some debate about who used the word bandit first, the Nicaraguan elite, whatever they truly felt, clearly were parroting the U.S. position in an attempt to curry favor with the United States. In one internal memo, State Department officials debated whether to emphasize that General Moncada used the term or to leave his name out, since "it could well be said that he was simply following our lead to gain our favor."[46]

Sandino's struggle did not resonate with most Nicaraguans during the war. The war was not visible outside the Segovias, and what news the other Nicaraguans received was through the press, which was controlled by the elites. For example, in the November 26, 1930, issue, *Diario Moderno*, a Liberal paper, published an article under the heading, "Urges the Extermination of Banditry; the Terrible Situation of the Segovias."[47] Catholic Church officials, generally aligned with the Conservatives, also denounced Sandino.

As some Conservatives began to perceive him as someone they could use to pressure the United States to leave Nicaragua, they sometimes described him differently. By the end of the war, a Conservative deputy proclaimed during the legislative debates over the peace treaty that "General Sandino because of his very high status does not need the official rank of general for history to recognize him as the continent's leading figure. . . . Sandino is a hero!"[48]

Sandino: In Death Larger Than Life

By 1933 the war had ended and Sandino was seen as a hero by a large number of Nicaraguans, since he had apparently driven the United States from the country. Still, to many, especially urban Nicaraguans, he was an unknown entity, and there was uncertainty over his future plans. He did enter discussions, which failed, for the formation of a new political party. For a period, some Conservatives hoped to use him to create a dictatorship, a concept that he rejected. Many potential supporters were confused by his political declarations in support of "rational communism." Especially after the failed 1932 communist-inspired uprising in El Salvador, the elites of Nicaragua became more concerned with his radicalism. Thus, by 1934, Sandino, remaining true to his own revolutionary ideology, was politically isolated from almost all Nicaraguans except his peasant base in the Segovias. When Somoza García ordered his assassination, there was almost no reaction inside Nicaragua.

The image of Sandino, however, continued to be used and debated. Although Sandino's name, and the entire war, almost disappeared in the United States, he never vanished from the consciousness of Latin Americans.[49] By the 1950s, a new generation of Latin Americans was portraying him as an anti-imperialist symbol of resistance to U.S. domination. The Chilean poet Pablo Neruda would write several poems that paid homage to him. For example, his *Canción de Gesta* (Lyric Romance) noted that

> Sandino was the night that fell
> and the light from the sea that killed
> Sandino was a tower with flags,
> Sandino was a rifle with hopes.[50]

Alberto Bayo, an exiled Spanish Civil War veteran, wrote a manual for guerrilla warfare, *150 Questions for a Guerrilla*. He dedicated his book to the "glorious guerrillas of the immortal school of Sandino, hero of the world . . . ."[51] Bayo played an important role in transmitting the memory of Sandino to a new generation of Latin American revolutionaries. In the 1940s he was a military advisor to the Caribbean Legion, a group of democratic reformers organized to overthrow the dictatorships of Central America and the Caribbean. One section was called the Sandino Battalion. Bayo met Nicaraguan exiles and used their experiences to help define his study of guerrilla warfare. By the 1950s Bayo was living in Mexico, where he helped train the young Cuban exile Fidel Castro and the other members of the 26th of July Movement. Owing to Bayo's encouragement, Sandino became a hero and inspiration for these Cuban revolutionaries.

A more influential work was *Sandino: General de hombres libres*, by the Argentine writer Gregorio Selser. First published in 1955, Selser's book helped revive the image of Sandino as an anti-imperialist hero for a Latin American audience. Selser later described how his "moral and political indignation at the overthrow of Jacobo Arbenz Guzmán" in Guatemala led him to study the history of Central America until he "came upon the figure of Augusto Calderón Sandino, who moved, captured, and held me."[52]

Within Nicaragua, however, there was no glorification of Sandino after his assassination. Instead, the black legend would be emphasized and expanded by the regime of Somoza García and his sons. The new "official" history was a book entitled *El verdadero Sandino, o el Calvario de las Segovias* (The True Sandino, or the Calvary of the Segovias). Although Somoza García was credited as the author, the book was actually ghostwritten, and relied heavily on U.S. Marine and Guardia Nacional archives. Sandino was called a bandit, and a number of alleged Sandinista atrocities were described in detail in the book. Of course, the war was brutal, and both sides did commit atrocities. The book also suggested that Sandino had wild communistic ideas and thus was a threat to Nicaraguan civilization. One of the ironies of this book is that many of Sandino's letters were published to show how crazy he was. Thus, new generations of Nicaraguans had ready access to Sandino's thoughts and, reading between the lines, could form their own opinions about him.

While some Nicaraguan exiles continued to write about Sandino, within the country the only legal view of Sandino was that he had been a bandit. When Carlos Fonseca's personal library was confiscated by the Guardia Nacional in 1956, not one of those books mentioned Sandino.[53] Fonseca, who would become the founder of the FSLN, was then a student activist and a member of the small Nicaraguan Communist Party and had not yet begun his study of Sandino.

Nevertheless, Sandino remained a powerful countering image to Somoza. Almost all those opposed to the dictatorship, including members of both the Conservative and Independent Liberal parties, referred to Sandino as an inspiration.[54] Sandino was now generally described by the opposition as a patriot and a martyr with whose assassination the tyranny of the Somozas began. During the 1944 demonstrations against Somoza, the student newspaper *El Universitario* published prohibited photographs of Sandino.[55] In April 1956, Nicaraguan exiles forming the Nicaraguan Democratic Union Party issued a manifesto praising him and traced the modern political problems of Nicaragua to his assassination. Among those who signed were several surviving officers of Sandino's army.[56]

In September 1956, Rigoberto López Pérez, a young student, assassinated Anastasio Somoza García. Although López Pérez acted alone, Sandino was one of his inspirations. Shortly before the assassination he wrote poems about Sandino:

The seed of Sandino's blood
lashes the murderous rooftops
multiplied, in torrents
it will cover exposed rooftops
will exterminate all the murders.
and each and every one
of the murderers' seed.[57]

At the very same moment, another young poet, Ernesto Cardenal, was writing his epic poem *Zero Hour*, with Sandino again the heroic character.

With the assassination of Somoza García and the succession to power by his sons Luis and Anastasio Somoza Debayle (and, coincidentally, the initiation of Castro's guerrilla war in Cuba), many Nicaraguans again considered guerrilla warfare as the best method to finally overthrow the Somoza regime. A number of small guerrilla groups were formed in the late 1950s. While these groups came from many political orientations, including some from both the old Conservative and Liberal parties, all referred to Sandino as an inspiration.[58] All of these movements were dismal failures.

Influenced by the Cuban Revolution and the Cubans' admiration for Sandino, however, several young Nicaraguans began to study Sandino seriously. With both the Cuban Revolution and Sandino as inspirations, they created the Frente Sandinista de Liberación Nacional. Who were these founders of the FSLN? They came from different backgrounds. All had entered the university and had become student activists against the dictatorship. Several, like Fonseca, the leader of the group, had been members of the pro-Soviet Nicaraguan communist party. But the communist movement earlier had defined Sandino as a traitor, and it remained committed to this position.[59] It had also opposed Castro when he launched the guerrilla war in Cuba. For those reasons, these individuals had left to form a new organization.[60]

The image of Sandino, then, remained at the center of the vision of opposition to the Somozas. But how did the FSLN define him? The founders' knowledge of the real Sandino was limited. Although several survivors of the EDSNN, such as Santos López, did join the FSLN, Fonseca and the others had to reconstruct Sandino from the small number of available books, redefining him through the lens of the 1960s.[61] Their vision of Sandino, based on their readings, was of the patriot hero, the courageous individual who had fought the U.S. invaders and their Nicaraguan allies and thus redeemed the national honor. This was similar to the image projected by the international supporters of Sandino during the war. The vision of Sandino's peasant followers was lost to this new generation.

With their twin inspirations, Sandino and Cuba, the FSLN saw guerrilla warfare as a way to defeat the Somozas. Despite their claim to be followers of Sandino, the FSLN did not understand the concerns of the peasants or the conditions in the countryside. As a result, the first FSLN guerrilla forces were quickly defeated. Still, the FSLN was able to survive the years of repression.

In one of their first leaflets, dated November 27, 1963, the FSLN proclaimed, "To the Yankee military advisors we say: remember that in the veins of the Nicaraguan people circulates the blood of Augusto Cesar Sandino!"[62] Fonseca would also revive the idea that Sandino was a social revolutionary as well as a patriot, and that the task of the FSLN was to complete all of Sandino's work. In his pamphlet entitled *Sandino: Proletarian Guerrilla*, Fonseca noted that

> the conditions that the nascent character of the people's anti-imperialist modern movement imposed, did not allow Sandino's correct military strategy to coincide with a correct political strategy that guaranteed the continuation of the revolutionary process. . . . Throughout the years of his struggle one can see in Sandino an idealist who wants social transformation. . . .[63]

It was this image of Sandino as the revolutionary patriot that the FSLN would continue to project throughout the years of struggle against the Somoza dictatorship. The FSLN was clearly using Sandino as a symbol of national resistance to oppression. Sandino as a man with his own complex political ideology was harder for them to understand. Many aspects of his views, especially his membership in the anarchist Magnetic-Spiritual School and his spiritualism, they downplayed or ignored.

By the time of the insurrection of 1978 and 1979, the image of Sandino was a unifying factor for all those who opposed the Somoza regime. With the triumph of the revolution in July 1979, Sandino became almost a demigod to many Nicaraguans. His image was everywhere, from posters to T-shirts to wall graffiti. Just a simple graffito drawing of a cowboy hat (Sandino was usually photographed wearing a ten-gallon cowboy hat) reflected support for Sandino and the FSLN.[64] When in 1980 the new government organized the national literacy crusade in a successful effort to end adult illiteracy, the first image in the text was a picture of Sandino, and the first sentence students were to learn was "Sandino, guide of the Revolution."

After the 1979 revolution, the debate over Sandino's legacy continued. Many political forces that opposed the FSLN also tried to claim Sandino as their inspiration and suggested that the FSLN had misused the image of Sandino. The Independent Liberal Party, which had opposed Somoza and by the 1984 elections was running candidates in opposition to the FSLN, had a poster of Sandino that proclaimed, "Sandino was a Liberal." Eden Pastora was an FSLN leader who moved into the opposition and formed his own armed resistance organization called the Sandinista Revolutionary Front.[65] However, none of these organizations was successful in instituting a different image of Sandino among the Nicaraguan population.

Although the FSLN lost national elections in 1990, Sandino remains a national hero. The vision of Sandino as the revolutionary patriot, recreated by Carlos Fonseca, is now the image accepted by most Nicaraguans, whether they agree with the FSLN or not. The real Sandino, a complex man and political thinker, has long been lost in the image.

Conclusion

DURING HIS LIFE, Sandino clearly tried to cultivate his image as a hero. He presented himself as the only one capable of resisting the Marines and saving the nation. As his own political ideas developed, Sandino expanded his vision and the description of his goals. Thus, to his intellectual supporters, both within Nicaragua and around the world, he was seen as a nationalist, an anti-imperialist, and perhaps a social revolutionary. However, to the actual soldiers and followers in the Segovias, Sandino had first to create the concept of a nation that needed to be saved. Here his image was that of the patriarch, the founding father, as well as the revolutionary patriot. Thus, even during his lifetime, several distinct images of Sandino were projected.

After his death others recreated a new, heroic mystique for Sandino. To many opponents of the Somoza regime, Sandino's assassination made him the first martyr of the dictatorship, and this made him a hero. It was Carlos Fonseca and the other leaders of the FSLN who revitalized the perception of Sandino as a revolutionary as well as a patriot and martyr. While the FSLN clearly filtered his ideas, they did resurrect the social transformational aspects of Sandino.

As the poet Ernesto Cardenal, who became the FSLN's minister of culture, had predicted in 1956, the hero had indeed been reborn in the nation. Writing years later, after the FSLN had lost the 1990 elections, Cardenal noted that "Sandino is a unique historical case: an assassinated hero who fifty years later rises again incarnated in an entire people and defeats those who had assassinated him. And thus he continues to live."[66] Cardenal, who is also a Catholic priest, described a popular image of Sandino as a martyr whose resurrection leads to a new Nicaragua. Whereas the FSLN had projected Sandino as the revolutionary patriotic hero, he had become even more. Ironically, he had in the end become the founding father, or patriarch, of the nation. As Cardenal concluded in *Zero Hour,*

> But the hero is born when he dies
> and the green grass is reborn from the ashes.[67]

Notes

* This chapter's epigraph is from Ernesto Cardenal, *Zero Hour* (New York: New Directions Books, 1980), 12.

1. Manifesto, July 1, 1927, in Robert Edgar Conrad, ed., *Sandino: The Testimony of A Nicaraguan Patriot* (Princeton, N.J.: Princeton University Press, 1990), 74–75.

2. For more on this name change, see Marco Aurelio Navarro-Génie, *Augusto "Cesar" Sandino: Messiah of Light and Truth* (Syracuse, N.Y.: Syracuse University Press, 2002), 42–43.

3. For more on Sandino's life and ideas, see Alejandro Bendaña, *La Mística de Sandino* (Managua: Centro de Estudios Internacionales, 1994); Michelle Dospital, *Siempre mas allá . . . reseña del movimiento Sandinista Nicaragua, 1927–1934* (Managua: Editorial Nueva Nicaragua, 1996); Donald C. Hodges, *Intellectual Foundations of the Nicaragua Revolution* (Austin: University of Texas Press, 1986); Donald C. Hodges, *Sandino's Communism: Spiritual Politics for the Twenty-First Century* (Austin: University of Texas Press, 1992); Sergio Ramírez, ed., *Augusto C. Sandino: El pensamiento vivo*, 2 vols. (Managua: Editorial Nueva Nicaragua, 1984); Gregorio Selser, *Sandino* (New York: Monthly Review Press, 1981); Oscar-René Vargas, *Sandino: Floreció al filo de la espada* (Managua: Centro de Estudios de la Realidad Nacional, 1995); and Volker Wünderich, *Sandino: Una Biografía Política* (Managua: Editorial Nueva Nicaragua, 1995).

4. Selser, *Sandino*, 65.

5. Selser, *Sandino*, 65–70.

6. Wünderich, *Sandino*, 68.

7. The Liberal leader General Moncada would later claim that when he first met Sandino he distrusted him, since he heard Sandino speak of "the necessity for the workers to struggle against the rich and other things that are the principles of communism." Quoted in Neill Macaulay, *The Sandino Affair* (Durham, N.C.: Duke University Press, 1986), 55.

8. Wünderich, *Sandino*, 74.

9. The best book on the war remains Macaulay's. See also Richard Grossman, "'Hermanos en la Patria', Nationalism, Honor and Rebellion: Augusto Sandino and the Army in Defense of the National Sovereignty of Nicaragua, 1927–1934" (PhD diss., University of Chicago, 1996); Richard Millet, *Guardians of the Dynasty* (Maryknoll: Orbis Press, 1977); and Michael Jay Schroeder, "'To Defend Our Nation's Honor': Toward a Social and Cultural History of the Sandino Rebellion in Nicaragua, 1927–1934" (PhD diss., University of Michigan, 1993).

10. "Light and Truth: Manifesto to the Members of Our Army, . . ." in Conrad, *Sandino*, 362.

11. Conrad, *Sandino*, 74, 469.

12. Letter to Humberto Barahona, May 27, 1933, in Conrad, *Sandino*, 474–475. Hodges, *Intellectual Foundations*, 42, estimated that in 1935 the Magnetic-Spiritual School had a total membership of some 5,000 throughout Latin America. For more on the school and Sandino's rational communism, see Bendaña, *La Mística*; Hodges, *The Intellectual Foundations*; and Navarro-Génie, *Augusto "Cesar" Sandino*.

13. Dion Williams, "The Nicaragua Situation," *Marine Corps Gazette* 15, no. 3 (November 1930): 19–20.

14. National Archives and Records Administration (NARA), Records of the United States Marine Corps, Record Group 127, Entry 200, Box 2, Folder Flyers (hereafter referred to as NARA, RG 127, E no., followed by the Folder and Document).

15. For more on the convoluted attempts of the Conservatives to use Sandino, see Michel Gobat, "Revisiting Revolutionary Nationalism: Sandinismo, Elite Conservatives and U.S. Military Intervention in Nicaragua, 1927–1933" (paper presented at the XXIII International Congress of the Latin American Studies Association, Washington, D.C., September 6–8, 2001). From 1909 to 1928, U.S. policies generally favored the Conservatives. The United States' first major military intervention in 1909 helped the Conservatives overthrow a Liberal president. However, the Liberals were the largest faction, and during the civil war the Liberal military leader General Moncada reached an accommodation with the United States that led to Moncada becoming president in 1928. From that moment on, U.S. policies generally favored the Liberals, and some Conservatives then proclaimed themselves to be nationalists.

16. Instituto de Estudio del Sandinismo, *El Sandinismo: Documentos básicos* (Managua: Editorial Nueva Nicaragua, 1983), 38, 213.

17. *The Nation*, August 3, 1927.

18. Quoted in Selser, *Sandino*, 110.

19. Letter to Froylán Turcios, September 8, 1927, in Conrad, *Sandino*, 100.

20. See Hodges, *Intellectual Foundations*, 96–100; and Macaulay, *The Sandino Affair*, 112–113.

21. Selser, *El pequeño ejército*, 303.

22. Nicaraguan intellectuals were not really involved in the EDSNN. Although some would come to sympathize with Sandino, and a few became active supporters and correspondents, almost none joined with Sandino in the mountains. Although few Nicaraguan intellectuals fought with Sandino, particularly during the first phase of the war from 1927 to 1929, there was a core of intellectuals surrounding Sandino. These men, whom Donald Hodges described as a "general staff" (1992, 64), were mainly the foreign-born representatives of various Latin American political currents.

23. Letter to Tomás Guatemala, January 7, 1929, NARA, R G 127, E 192, Box 4, Folder Case File G. *La Sierra*, Abril–Mayo 1928, 42. Sandino's letter was dated January 7, 1929, while one of the *Daily Worker* articles was dated October 24, 1928, which means that Sandino, isolated in the mountains of Nicaragua, was clearly in regular contact with the outside world.

24. On the break with Turcios, see Hodges, *Intellectual Foundations*, 88–92.

25. Sandino wrote, "Neither extreme right nor extreme left, but rather 'united front' is our slogan." Letter to Gustavo Alemán Bolaños, September 9, 1929, in Conrad, *Sandino*, 273.

26. For more on the break between Sandino and the communists, see Hodges, *Intellectual Foundations*, 98–106; Macaulay, *The Sandino Affair*, 160; and Navarro-Génie, *Augusto "Cesar" Sandino*, 65–80.

27. NARA, Department of State (DOS) microfilm no. 817.00/7487.

28. During the war against Sandino, the U.S. Marine Corps Intelligence Section wrote a "Monograph of Nicaragua." In this monograph, the Marines described many of the towns and communities of Nicaragua. One example serves to highlight the scattered nature of these Segovia communities: "Los Robles. Consists of 2 houses, 1 at the foot of Mt . . ." (NARA, DOS no. 817.00/7294 1/2).

29. Letter to Enoc Aguado, October 26, 1930; and Ramírez, *Augusto C. Sandino*, 2:152.

30. These interviews, many carried out during the Nicaraguan literacy campaign and its follow-up and others I obtained in 1990, are all located at El Instituto de Historia de Nicaragua y Centroamérica (IHCA)—Universidad Centroamericana. The majority of the interviews were conducted during the 1980s. They vary greatly in length, quality, and the questions asked. I conducted an additional twenty interviews in July, August, and September of 1990. Altogether, 118 people were interviewed.

31. Personal interview with Jerónimo Zelaya Hernández, August 14, 1990.

32. Francisco Centeno Fonseca, IHCA cassette no. 066, pp. 5, 13.

33. IHCA cassette no. 097-2-2.

34. See Ana Maria Alonso, "Gender, Ethnicity, and the Constitution of Subjects: Accommodation, Resistance, and Revolution on the Chihuahuan Frontier" (PhD diss., University of Chicago, 1988), 324–325.

35. Sandino to Col. Inez Hernández and Sergeant Major Ladislao Palacios, May 20, 1931—USMC/GN translation. NARA, R G 127, E 202, Folder 35. For a discussion of this letter see Grossman, "'Hermanos en la Patria'," 1996.

36. Luis Boedeker González, IHCA cassette no. 055-1.

37. 3 May 1930, USMC/GN Memo 1 July, 1930.

38. See Navarro-Génie, *Augusto "Cesar" Sandino*, 2002.

39. The term bandit was commonly used to describe members of the various rural resistance movements that developed in opposition to the U.S. interventions (or to European colonial occupations). Edward Herman and Gerry O'Sullivan suggest that the use of the term was "part of an ideological (and strongly racist) apologia for imperialist aggression and domination." See *The 'Terrorism' Industry* (New York: Pantheon Books, 1989), 6.

40. *New York Times*, July 19, 1927.

41. *New York Times*, July 21, 1927. In the same issue of the *Times*, in the column next to the Latimer article, was a statement of Sandino in which he explained his political motives and denied he was a bandit. Latimer's reference to Jesse James is interesting since James has also been portrayed as a social bandit.

42. Williams, "The Nicaragua Situation."

43. Even the *New York Times*, which was generally supportive of U.S. policies, gave an editorial comment on Secretary Kellogg's statement: "These epithets are applied apparently only because General Sandino and his men follow the customary practice of guerrillas in Latin America by looting as they go and living off the country. The same might be said of some of the leaders of armed forces in China. But they are not for that reason declared by our Government to be beyond the pale of the law." *New York Times*, July 20, 1927.

44. *New York Times*, October 26, 1927.

45. *New York Times*, January 6, 1928.

46. NARA, DOS no. 817.00/5118.

47. NARA, DOS no. 817.00/6912.

48. Quoted in Gobat, "Revisiting Revolutionary Nationalism," 11.

49. By the 1950s, a minuscule number of U.S. scholars had begun to reexamine Sandino. Several scholarly articles were published. Despite these few articles, Sandino's legacy was generally ignored in the United States. The major U.S. academic study of Sandino could not find a U.S. publisher. Lejeune Cummins's *Quijote on a Burro: Sandino and the Marines* was self-published in Mexico in 1958.

50. Bridget Aldaraca et al., *Nicaragua in Revolution: The Poets Speak* (Minneapolis, Minn.: Marxist Educational Press, 1980), 43.

51. Alberto Bayo, *150 Questions for a Guerrilla* (Denver, Colo.: Panther Publication, 1963), 15.

52. Selser, *Sandino*, 205. Arbenz was the elected president of Guatemala who was overthrown by a CIA covert operation in 1954. Selser's book was one of the first published in Cuba after the revolution.

53. Matide Zimmermann, *Sandinista: Carlos Fonseca and the Nicaraguan Revolution* (Durham, N.C.: Duke University Press, 2000), 60.

54. Somoza García was a Liberal and created the Nationalist Liberal Party. Many of his opponents within the liberal movement created their own party in 1944, the Independent Liberal Party.

55. Carlos Pérez Bermudez and Onofre Guevara, *El Movimiento Obrero en Nicaragua. Primera y Segunda Parte* (Managua: Editorial El Amanecer, 1985), 116.

56. Instituto de Estudio del Sandinismo, *El Sandinismo: Documentos Básicos* (Managua: Editorial Nueva Nicaragua, 1983), 248–250.

57. Aldaraca, 111.

58. For more on these groups, see Jesus M. Blandón, *Entre Sandino y Fonseca* (Managua: Departamento de Propaganda y Educación Política de FSLN, 1982), and Enrique Camacho Navarro, *Los Usos de Sandino* (Mexico City: Universidad Nacional Autónoma de México, 1991).

59. Of all the opponents to Somoza, only the Communist Party rejected Sandino and did not use his image.

60. For the founding of the FSLN, see Zimmermann, *Sandinista*. Also see Hodges, *Intellectual Foundations*.

61. The most important sources were Selser's and Somoza García's books.

62. Copy of leaflet in the possession of the author, courtesy of Richard Millett.

63. Carlos Fonseca, "Sandino: Proletarian Guerrilla," *Tricontinental* 24 (1971): 15.

64. Joel E. Sheesley et al., *Sandino in the Streets* (Bloomington: Indiana University Press, 1991).

65. John A. Booth, *The End and the Beginning: The Nicaraguan Revolution* (Boulder, Colo.: Westview Press, 1985), 209.

66. Booth, *The End and the Beginning*, x.

67. *Zero Hour*, 15.

Frida Kahlo

Heroism of Private Life

NANCY DEFFEBACH

The reason people need to invent or imagine heroes and gods is unmitigated FEAR. Fear of life and fear of death.

Frida Kahlo, "Hablando de un cuadro mío"

Because Frida Kahlo's posthumous fame is vastly greater than her reputation during her lifetime and because she did not believe in heroes, it is ironic that she should occupy a chapter in a book about heroes. It is even more ironic considering that during her lifetime, Mexican national identity was being forged largely through the creation and artistic portrayal of great public heroes, while her own art and concerns were insistently private and personal. Kahlo and her now great fame stand as a foil to the heroes and heroic myths of her day.

Frida Kahlo (1907–1954) became an artist during the height of the Mexican Muralist movement, which completely dominated the visual arts in Mexico from the early 1920s until at least the end of the 1950s. The muralists' aesthetic philosophy demanded that art be monumental, heroic, and public. Kahlo is best known for intimate self-portraits. Her paintings deviate from the muralists' prescriptions for art: they are small—sometimes remarkably so—and her themes are intensely personal. Kahlo and the muralists made major artistic innovations, but, although there is some overlap in their concerns, their innovations are of an entirely different nature. The difference between her vision and theirs was profoundly affected by gender issues. The very qualities that made her seem slightly out of place in the artistic climate of the postrevolutionary period are the same qualities that command attention now.

For Frida Kahlo and other Mexican women artists and writers of the postrevolutionary period, the construction of national identity as masculine and the ubiquitous presence of male heroes presented serious problems.[1] How could a woman be female, Mexican, modern, and powerful? To a large degree Kahlo's work is a response to this challenge. She met this challenge by repeatedly using her own image to create a strong female protagonist. She introduced new themes in art that added a female viewpoint to artistic discourses, and she expropriated and transformed religious imagery as a way to legitimate and empower her own image. Through an astute combination of *mexicanidad*, traditional iconography, vanguard style, masquerade, and irony, she invented herself as a subject who was female, Mexican, modern, and powerful. One of the principal aims of this chapter is to explore her strategies for achieving interpretive power and inserting her ideas into the visual culture of Mexico.

Much has been written about how Kahlo addressed personal issues such as physical and emotional pain in her art; relatively little has been said about how she worked within a social context that actively discouraged the exploration of these themes and how she turned artistic conventions on their head in order to create a distinct artistic voice. To understand how she converted the challenges of her artistic milieu into opportunities for innovative art, it is necessary to explore the remarkable historical and theoretical artistic developments that began in Mexico in the early 1920s.

After the military phase of the Mexican Revolution (1910–1920) subsided and a stable government was established, Mexico embarked on a period of cultural renewal in which artists and state patronage of the arts played a central role. In the early 1920s, José Vasconcelos, the secretary of public education, commissioned young Mexican artists to paint murals on the walls of prestigious government buildings. Vasconcelos believed strongly in artistic freedom and never imposed aesthetic or ideological dogmas on the artists. The artists themselves, however, soon decided to use their art to promote a political agenda. The painter David Alfaro Siqueiros wrote a manifesto on behalf of the Union of Technical Workers, Painters, and Sculptors that was signed by Diego Rivera, José Clemente Orozco, and other committee members and published in the magazine *El Machete* in 1924.[2] The manifesto repudiated easel painting, embraced all forms of art that were monumental and public, and declared that art should valorize Indian traditions and destroy bourgeois individualism. While society was in a transitional phase between the destruction of the old order and the establishment of a new order, artists should "turn their work into clear ideological propaganda for the people."[3] Realizing that many of the peasants and workers with whom they wished to communicate were illiterate, the muralists presented Mexican history in a visual form on public walls. Many of the murals created in the 1920s address the theme of the Mexican Revolution.

In the postrevolutionary period the Mexican Revolution was publicly proclaimed as—and in fact was—a major social transformation.[4] However, although women participated directly in the revolution as *soldaderas* and acquired additional legal rights, after the war their position was largely ignored.[5] In postrevolutionary Mexico national identity was constructed as essentially masculine. The literary critic Jean Franco has observed, "The Revolution with its promise of social transformation encouraged a Messianic spirit that transformed mere human beings into supermen and constituted a discourse that associated virility with social transformation in a way that marginalized women at the very moment when they were, supposedly, liberated."[6] Franco concludes that "the very construction of national identity was posited on male domination."[7]

One of the central ways that the muralists contributed to the formation of this masculinist national identity was through their representations of heroes. While the gender of the heroes was always male, in other ways the images demonstrated considerable diversity. At the end of his life Rivera proudly recalled that for the first time in the history of monumental painting, "muralism ceased to employ as its central heroes the gods, kings, chiefs of state, heroic generals, etc. For the first time in art history . . . Mexican mural painting made the masses the hero of monumental art, that is, the man from the country, from the factories, from the cities to the towns. When the hero appears among them, he is part of them and the result is clear and direct."[8] Rivera depicted sweeping masses of people and cast average workers, peasants, and soldiers in key roles.

In addition to his glorification of the masses and individual nonelite leaders, Rivera and other muralists produced numerous idealized images of heroic figures that follow traditional precedents. In *The Ancient Indian World* (1929) at the National Palace, Rivera depicted daily life in ancient Mexico with Quetzalcóatl—a Mesoamerican god, Toltec ruler, and culture hero—at the center of the composition. Rivera also created several images of the agrarian leader Emiliano Zapata (see Chapter 5) as a romantic horseman or a revolutionary martyr. Orozco painted dramatic images of Quetzalcóatl to symbolize the achievements of a lost golden age, and he repeatedly portrayed the Greek god Prometheus, whom he considered a great benefactor of mankind, rising boldly from conflagrations. Siqueiros extolled Cuauhtémoc, the last Aztec ruler who defended the nation's integrity against foreign invaders, and he immortalized himself as the *coronelazo* (big hard-hitting colonel), whose foreshortened fist thrusts aggressively toward the viewer. But, whether the muralists portrayed peasants or rulers in heroic roles, they inevitably used them to associate virility with social transformation.

Two decades after writing the manifesto of the Union of Technical Workers, Painters, and Sculptors and after most of the great murals had already been painted, Siqueiros wrote *No hay más ruta que la nuestra* (There Is No Other Route But Ours) (1945), in which he prescribed the goals of modern Mexican art at length. Siqueiros insisted that art must be monumental, heroic, public, ideological, social, realistic, and polemical. He repeatedly denigrated easel painting, which he damned as chic and domestic. While Siqueiros did not overtly address gender issues, he clearly associated a muscular avant-garde with masculinity. By the time *No hay más ruta que nuestra* was published, Kahlo had already invented her own artistic route, which deviated in significant ways from the path that Siqueiros claimed was the only legitimate way to make art.

Frida Kahlo was born on July 6, 1907, in Coyoacán, then a town on the outskirts of Mexico City (it has long since been engulfed by the vast metropolis). Her father, Guillermo Kahlo, was an educated, atheist, German-Jewish immigrant, who had come to Mexico as a young man and become an accomplished photographer, specializing in architectural photography. Her mother, Matilde Calderón, was Mexican, *mestiza*, and Catholic. Frida attended secondary school at the prestigious National Preparatory School, located in the heart of Mexico City, where she was one of only thirty-five girls in a student body of about 2,000.[9] She had originally intended to become a medical doctor, but began painting after a near-fatal traffic accident left her bedridden for nine months and permanently destroyed her health. She married Diego Rivera on August 21, 1929: she was twenty-two years old, he was forty-two and the most famous artist in Mexico. In 1943 she began teaching at the Escuela de Pintura y Escultura (School for Painting and Sculpture).

Kahlo's artistic production consists of approximately 200 paintings and drawings. About eighty of these are self-portraits, more than forty are portraits, and at least twenty-five are still-life paintings. Her earliest paintings are rendered in a naïve style, and she has often been called a self-taught artist. Because she never attended art school the "self-taught" label is technically correct but somewhat misleading, since she lived with Rivera and surely acquired extensive information about artistic techniques and issues. By 1937 she painted with consummate skill.

Like many of the artists of her day, she greatly admired Mexican folk art and traditional popular customs, which she incorporated into her daily life and art in significant ways. As an affirmation of *mexicanidad* she wore traditional Mexican clothing: *rebozos*, or shawls; *huipiles*, or sleeveless blouses; and flowing skirts. She owned embroidered and handwoven garments from different regions of Mexico, but preferred the clothing from the Isthmus of Tehuantepec (Oaxaca, Mexico), and often represented herself wearing this costume in self-portraits. The everyday attire of the Tehuana (woman from Tehuantepec) consists of a short, loose huipil, usually in red or purple muslin with a yellow band decorated with chain stitching; the huipil is worn with a long, floral print skirt with a wide white ruffle at the hem.[10]

Kahlo's preference for wearing the clothing of Tehuantepec has often been dismissed as a way to hide a weak right leg (damaged first by childhood polio, then by the traffic accident), and as a way to please her husband, who viewed indigenous attire as a political statement. Rivera once proclaimed that "[t]he classic Mexican dress has been created by people for people. The Mexican women who do not wear it do not belong to the people, but are mentally and emotionally dependent on a foreign class to which they wish to belong, *i.e.* the great American and French bureaucracy."[11] While Rivera's opinion and her desire to camouflage physical problems undoubtedly influenced her choice, the clothing had explicit feminist connotations. Kahlo, who did not have relatives in Tehuantepec and never visited the region, was not alone in her adoption of this costume. In the 1930s and 1940s the Tehuana dress was worn by a small group of women artists and intellectuals who associated with vanguard circles. By the standards of residents of Mexico City, Tehuantepec was an exotic location, and, as the artist Miguel Covarrubias observed, a Tehuana was "as romantic and attractive a subject as a South Sea maiden to an adolescent American."[12] The Tehuanas, who were Zapotecs, were reputed to be independent, strong, beautiful, and proud. The women controlled the local market and thus the economy. In the 1940s Covarrubias wrote, "The frankness of Zapotec women, their rather loose use of strong language, and their social and economic independence give them a position of equality with men, and a self-reliance that is unique in Mexico."[13] When women artists and intellectuals adopted the dress of the Tehuana, they not only assumed some of the Tehuanas' independent, proud, and exotic aura, they also scandalized the *gente decente* (decent people) of the middle and upper classes.[14] When Kahlo depicted herself dressed as a Tehuana, her attire connotes ethnicity, class, gender, sexuality, and power.

Kahlo also incorporated traditional Mexican popular arts into her paintings by using the media and format of *retablos* or ex-voto paintings. Retablos are tiny paintings on tin that offer thanks to the Virgin or a saint for help escaping misfortune. They depict the danger, often an illness or accident, and the holy being who intervened, who is frequently shown floating in a cloud above the scene. An inscription, which usually appears on a scroll at the base, records the name of the person who was saved, the nature of the miracle, the name of the Virgin or saint, and the date. In 1932 Kahlo began painting her own versions of retablos. She adopted the oil on tin media, the small size, and the banner for inscriptions, which she occasionally left mysteriously blank. She sometimes used the format to represent grave danger, as in her portrayal of her miscarriage in *Henry Ford Hospital* (1932), but she dispensed with the saints or, in the case of *Childbirth* (1932), included the Virgin of Sorrows, but no miracle.

Kahlo is best known for her self-portraits. Although some are highly unconventional in content and composition, many use the traditional bust-length format. In these works she portrays herself looking out at the viewer with a remarkably direct gaze. She represents herself without flattery, emphasizing her faint mustache and exaggerating her heavy eyebrows until they converge in a single calligraphic line that resembles an ideogram of a bird in flight. (Photographs of the young Kahlo invariably show a prettier woman, at least by conventional standards, than the paintings do.) Yet she also depicts herself wearing deep red lipstick, elaborately braided coiffeurs with bright ribbons, and spectacular Mexican jewelry.

Throughout her career Kahlo introduced new themes in art that challenged assumptions about what topics art can deal with, and she assiduously inserted a female viewpoint into artistic and national discourses. These acts are her most significant contribution and her greatest legacy. Kahlo's lifelong predilection for self-portraiture has often been dismissed as narcissistic or explained away as a convenient subject for an invalid, but a more insightful explanation has been offered by Jean Franco, who sees it as "a long and never-completed struggle to understand female identity."[15] Many of Kahlo's paintings deal with topics that had not been addressed in art or had only been portrayed from a male point of view. Some of her themes were taboo or heretofore unimaginable. *Henry Ford Hospital* (1932), *The Miscarriage* (1932), and *Childbirth* (also known as *My Birth*) (1932) record her miscarriage in Detroit in 1932. The latter painting also envisions her own birth. *A Few Small Nips* (1935) protests violence against women. *Remembrance of an Open Wound* (1938) and *Self-Portrait with Cropped Hair* (1940) are usually interpreted as protests against Rivera's sexual infidelities; the former may also allude to masturbation, and the latter raises questions of gender identity.[16] *Two Nudes in a Forest* (1939) and the detail of two nude women floating on a sponge in *What the Water Has Given Me* (1939) probably suggest a lesbian relationship. *Self-Portrait as a Tehuana* (1943) and *Diego and I* (1949) visualize the way that thoughts of her husband fill her mind. *The Two Fridas* (1940) explores her feelings about her divorce and asserts her mestizo heritage. In addition to the issues raised in her self-portraits, Kahlo declares her unabashed fascination with sexuality in several paintings that defy categories but roughly approximate still lifes. In *Xochitl* (1938), *Flower of Life* (1944), and *Sun and Life* (1947) she uses anthropomorphized plant forms to invent a new type of erotic art that does not depend on the display of the nude female body. By painting these subjects and exhibiting the works in important group and solo exhibitions, she legitimized women's issues as themes.

Although Kahlo repeatedly addressed women's issues through self-portraiture, she never allowed her image to become that of a generic woman. By emphasizing the idiosyncrasies of her appearance (penetrating gaze, heavy eyebrows, faint mustache) and the specifics of her life (wife of Rivera, childless woman, invalid, artist) she insisted on her singularity. Her choice of self-portraiture as her genre of preference and her predilection for depicting herself "warts and all" fight against the possibility of her image being construed as an embodiment of "Woman with the capital letter, the *representation* of an essence inherent in all women."[17] The extreme individuality of her face works against her becoming a symbolic figure that could be reduced to the dichotomies of virgin/whore or good mother/*mala mujer* (bad woman), categories that function "to displace women as historical subjects and replace them with symbolic figures."[18] Particularly remarkable is Kahlo's insistence on stressing her individuality at the same time that Siqueiros was vociferously attacking bourgeois individualism.

One of Kahlo's principal strategies for gaining interpretive power was to create a strong female personage—herself—whose repeated image helped to counterbalance the ubiquitous images of male heroes. She empowered this female personage by appropriating and transforming the visual languages of various religions. And she did this despite her fierce objections to institutionalized religion and her belief that gods were something "man invented in his delirium."[19]

As an adult, Kahlo advocated Marxism and eschewed religion. Unlike many of her compatriots who strongly opposed the Church but did not necessarily object to private devotion, she gave no indication of believing in a god of any kind. Her views about religion, dialectical materialism, and the need for a classless society were inspired by Marx and other communist theoreticians. Yet her diary shows that her political convictions were mixed with ideas and attitudes from other sources. She implies a belief in reincarnation when she professes, "we are headed toward *ourselves*, through millions of stone beings—of bird beings—of star beings—of fountain beings toward ourselves." She also allies herself with the ancient Mesoamerican world view in which all forms of life are interconnected. In her diary she

writes, "we are hatred—love—mother—child—plant—earth—light—ray
—as usual—world bringer of worlds—universes and cell universes—
Enough!"[20] Kahlo was a Marxist, but she was not an orthodox one. She
incorporated ancient ideas from Asia and Mesoamerica into her Marxism,
and created a personal philosophy that defies labels.

Despite her objections to organized religion, Kahlo consistently
addressed spiritual issues in her work. Her paintings speak of birth, life,
death, and renewal. Her art is notable for what it contains and does not
contain in the way of religious references, and it is even more remarkable
for the ways in which these references are employed. With the exception
of one painting, *Moses* (1945), a commission that will be discussed later in
this chapter, her oeuvre lacks direct, unmitigated representation of deities
and heroes.

In her self-portraits Kahlo presents herself as a goddess or saint. Her
images of herself are frontal, immobile, hieratic, and identifiable through
symbols. One characteristic of most visual representations of deities,
whether Precolumbian, Hindu, Egyptian, or Greek, is that they can be
identified by their attributes. For example, the Aztec earth goddess
Coatlicue always wears a skirt of entwined serpents and usually sports a
necklace of severed hands, hearts, and a skull. Visually, Catholic saints function in the same way. The Virgin of Guadalupe is instantly recognizable to
all Mexicans by her dusky complexion, blue mantle, and spiky mandorla.
Catholic saints can be identified by the symbols of their martyrdom: Saint
Lucy holds a platter with her extracted eyes, and Saint Catherine kneels
beside a spiked wheel and a sword.

Kahlo created images of herself that are structurally equivalent to god-
desses, madonnas, and saints. Her consistent features are her single eye-
brow, her braided and beribboned hair, and her Tehuana dress. She also
endowed herself with supplementary symbols that include monkeys,
iztcuintli dogs, birds, jade necklaces, Precolumbian sculptures, wounds,
thorns, the sun and the moon, and a wide variety of Mexican plants. The
animals, plants, and objects function as secondary attributes with which she
communicates her current aspect and the themes of individual paintings. In
Mexican and Central American Mythology, Irene Nicholson observes that the
mytholology of ancient Mexico is filled with images of flowers, shells, jade,
birds, hearts, arrows, maize, and cactus thorns. The myths "create a world
compact of jewels and flowers and birds, bright as a kaleidoscope and as
everchanging. . . . The symbols are few and concentrated, manipulated
with such economy that each is made to serve a wide range of philosophi-
cal and religious ideas."[21] She notes that "the images used as symbols are
limited and may even seem monotonous until we begin to search for their

Figure 8.1. Frida Kahlo, *My Nurse and I*, 1937. Oil on sheet metal. 11¾ × 13¾ inches. 30.5 × 34.7 cm. Collection of the Dolores Olmedo Foundation, Mexico City. © 2006 Banco de México Diego Rivera and Frida Kahlo Museums Trust. Av. Cinco de Mayo No. 2, Col. Centro, Del. Cuauhtémoc 06059, México, D.F. Reproduction authorized by the Instituto Nacional de Bellas Artes y Literatura 2006.

deeper meanings," and she concludes that the recurring elements are skillfully handled to express all the concepts needed for a complete philosophy and cosmology.[22]

The images that Nicholson lists as having symbolic meaning in ancient Mexico—flowers, shells, jade, birds, hearts, arrows, and thorns—are precisely those that Kahlo chose for herself. When these elements appear in Kahlo's art, they retain some of their ancient symbolism, which she transformed and adapted to express aspects of her own life and philosophy. By drawing on Precolumbian symbolism she imbued her work with a sense of myth.[23]

Kahlo's venture into mythic thought and Precolumbian symbolism began with the creation of *My Nurse and I* in 1937 (Figure 8.1). In this narrative self-portrait she portrays herself as an infant suckled by an earth-brown indigenous woman, who cradles her in strong arms. Although Kahlo represents herself with a baby's body, she possesses a fully adult head. The wet nurse's face is concealed by a Precolumbian mask, suggesting that she is not an individual but a symbolic being. Although the woman's face is not visible and the child's skin is noticeably lighter, a sense of kinship unites the two figures. Both have almost straight black shoulder-length hair, and the eyebrows of the Precolumbian mask join in the middle the way that Kahlo's do.

Like most of Kahlo's self-portraits, *My Nurse and I* is loosely related to biographical fact and intimately related to her personal beliefs. Kahlo actually had an indigenous wet nurse when she was a baby. However, the significance of *My Nurse and I* is not that she was breast-fed by a woman other than her mother, but that she was nourished culturally by the Precolumbian heritage of Mexico. Of all her paintings, Kahlo's favorite was *My Nurse and I*, perhaps because it vividly expresses her belief that the Mesoamerican heritage continued to nurture modern Mexican artists and because it was a pivotal work in her career. After painting *My Nurse and I* she regularly incorporated Precolumbian symbolism into her work for the rest of her life.

The same year that Kahlo painted *My Nurse and I* she initiated a series of self-portraits in which a monkey appears as her companion. Between 1937 and 1945 she painted at least eight self-portraits in which she is accompanied by one or more monkeys. The monkeys were pets that lived in the garden of the blue house in Coyoacán and in the Riveras' studio in San Angel, but they were also beings laden with symbolism in ancient Mexico. In Mesoamerica monkeys were associated with the arts and the deities of fertility and dance. The archaeologist Alfonso Caso wrote that for ancient Mexicans, the monkey was "a happy and playful animal, companion and sometimes symbol of the gods of Dance, Flowers, Sports, and Love."[24] *Ozomatli*, or monkey, was a day sign in the Aztec calendar. It implied cleverness, craftsmanship, and instability. The day was associated with Xochipilli, the god of flowers, dance, song, and games, and it was considered an auspicious day for marriage.[25] Those born on the day of the monkey were believed to be skilled in all the arts and were regarded as expert artists, singers, and dancers. Women born on this day were believed to have a cheerful disposition, but were not considered very respectable.[26] Among the Maya the monkey's strongest association was with the visual arts.[27]

For Kahlo, the monkey was a Precolumbian symbol that she could apply to herself in a flexible manner. It was simultaneously an emblem of her status as an artist, an expression of her desire for fertility and freedom of movement, and an assertion of sexuality and joy. The meaning of the monkeys in Kahlo's art shifts slightly with each painting and is communicated by the context and other elements in the painting. For example, in *Self-Portrait with Monkeys* (1943) she surrounds herself with four pet spider

Figure 8.2. Frida Kahlo, *Self-Portrait with Monkeys*, 1943. Oil on canvas. 32⅛ × 24¾ inches. 81.5 × 63 cm. Jacques and Natasha Gelman Collection. © 2006 Banco de México Diego Rivera and Frida Kahlo Museums Trust. Av. Cinco de Mayo No. 2, Col. Centro, Del. Cuauhtémoc 06059, México, D.F. Reproduction authorized by the Instituto Nacional de Bellas Artes y Literatura 2006.

Figure 8.3. Aztec glyph
signifying *olin*, or movement. (After Sahagún,
Florentine Codex, Paso y
Troncoso's facsimile
copy, Book 4, plate 35.)

monkeys, two of which embrace her while two others peer from behind the
lush tropical foliage in the background (Figure 8.2). The monkey in the
foreground stretches one dark paw across her white huipil and points to an
Aztec glyph embroidered on her huipil. The glyph is *olin*, or movement
(Figure 8.3).[28]

Kahlo was one of many modern Mexican artists who incorporated
Precolumbian elements into her work, but her manner of incorporating
ancient Mexican art and culture into her art is strikingly different from that
of other Mexican artists. The use of Precolumbian imagery in Mexican art
began in the nineteenth century. After Mexico achieved independence from
Spain in 1821, liberal politicians chose to make ancient indigenous culture
their politically legitimizing cultural heritage. With the execution of
Maximilian and the restoration of the republic in 1867, indigenous people
and culture became increasingly central to a discourse about national identity, and Mexican artists began representing Precolumbian subjects.[29]

The next big wave of interest in Precolumbian subjects and ancient
Mexican art occurred during the next period of intense nationalism, which
was the postrevolutionary period. During these years the most vocal advocate of Precolumbian art was Diego Rivera, whose name is inextricably

linked with the revitalization of interest in indigenous culture and the use of Mesoamerican subjects and sources in twentieth-century art. In his murals he often portrayed idealized scenes of ancient Mexico that mix history and mythology. In an early example, *The Ancient Indian World* (1929), he established the format that he frequently used in subsequent depictions of ancient Mexican culture: a panoramic view in which many different activities take place, careful attention to detail, especially in the clothing, and a strong tendency to idealize Mesoamerican culture. Despite his meticulous attention to historical detail, he often combined elements from different times and cultures.[30]

In contrast to Rivera's utopian illustrations of Mesoamerican civilizations, the semi-abstract artist Rufino Tamayo (1899–1991) honored ancient Mexican culture exclusively through the use of design elements such as color and proportion. According to Tamayo, the Precolumbian arts of Mexico have a sense of proportion and coloring that is native to the country, and for him these formal elements are the real roots of a Mexican school.

Kahlo's use of Precolumbian symbolism is distinct from the literal depictions created by Rivera and other artists and from the purely formal approach of Tamayo. She repeatedly depicted herself accompanied by elements that played a profound role in Mesoamerican symbolism and used these elements in ways that retain some of their ancient meaning, which she transformed into personal symbols. She resolved her opposition to religion and her fascination with spiritual issues by selectively evoking the Precolumbian past: she banished the gods and resurrected ancient themes. By incorporating ancient symbols and themes into modern images, she implied that Mesoamerican culture continued to be vital and relevant. As she told her students, Precolumbian art is the "root of our modern art."[31]

Kahlo also used Christian iconography as a means of self-definition and empowerment. Her biographer, Hayden Herrera, identifies several instances in which Kahlo portrays herself as Christ or Saint Sebastian. Referring to the crown of thorns that encircles Kahlo's neck in *Self-Portrait* (1940), Herrera notes that the "baroque opulence and the predominance of an opalescent pink contrasts in the strongest way with the painful image of Frida's bleeding neck. One is reminded of the lacerated Christ figures in Mexican churches, where gruesome wounds are surrounded by pretty flowers, luxurious laces, velvets, and gold."[32] In an analysis of *The Broken Column* (1944), Herrera observes, "With her hips wrapped in a cloth suggestive of Christ's winding sheet, Frida displays her wounds like a Christian martyr; a Mexican Saint Sebastian, she uses physical pain, nakedness, and sexuality to bring home the message of her spiritual suffering."[33]

Less obvious but equally important are Kahlo's allusions to the Virgin

Mary. In *Fulang-Chang and I* (1937) she portrays herself happier than usual, with her pet monkey Fulang-Chang sitting in the place where Kahlo, if she had been a mother, would have proudly displayed her baby. The size and placement of the monkey and the physical relationship between the monkey and Kahlo evoke Renaissance and Baroque paintings of the Madonna and Child. Her subsequent self-portraits with monkeys also hint at a mother-child relationship.[34] While *Fulang-Chang and I* is one of Kahlo's most contented self-portraits, other self-portraits allude to the Virgin in her sorrowful aspect, a quality of Kahlo's work that has been independently and briefly noted by Sarah Lowe and Eduardo de Jesús Douglas. Lowe mentions Kahlo's "identification with the Madonna of Sorrows (the image of the Virgin Mary who has lost her Son)," and Douglas states that Kahlo equates herself with *La Dolorosa* (The Sorrowful One).[35] These observations are undoubtedly based on several self-portraits in which tears flow from her eyes and on the retablo-style painting entitled *Childbirth* or *My Birth,* in which a picture of the Virgin of Sorrows hangs above the bed in which Kahlo gives birth to herself.

When Kahlo portrayed herself in ways that combine sacred and profane imagery, a long tradition already existed in Mexico of drawing on the visual language of religion for secular purposes. In the nineteenth century the state began to expropriate Catholic symbology to glorify the heroes of the independence movement. Ironically, one of the pioneers of this appropriation was the Emperor Maximilian, who favored the civil beatification of heroes of the independence movement.[36] After the Liberals regained power, idealized images of national heroes were created and "distributed, like the saints, as educational prints for children."[37] Discussing the Porfiriato (1876–1911), Mexican historian Enrique Krauze observes that while the heroes never replaced the saints in Mexican popular culture, they became the subjects of innumerable songs, anthems, novels, and poems. "The religion of the *patria* never supplanted Catholicism, but the fact remains that hero worship in Mexico assumed the peculiar form of beatification. In the collective imagination, the heroes of the fatherland would become lay saints."[38] The tradition of appropriating religious imagery for patriotic purposes continued after the Revolution and is exemplified by Diego Rivera's individual portraits of Cuauhtémoc, Felipe Carrillo Puerto, Emiliano Zapata, and Otilio Montaño at the Ministry of Education, where each of the historic figures appears as a heroic martyr surrounded by a full body halo. When Kahlo portrayed herself as a secular saint, she knowingly drew on the immense power of Catholic symbolism to communicate with the Mexican people; and at the same time she undermined the authority of the Church with irony.

While many modern Mexican artists used spiritual imagery in secular

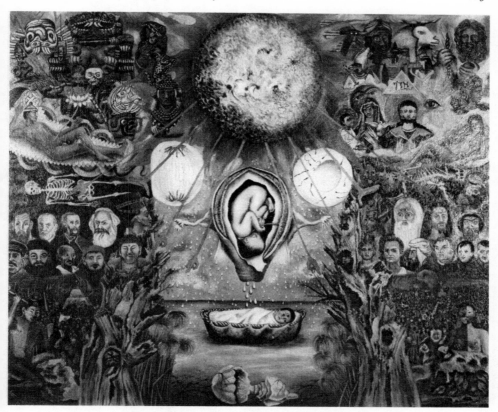

Figure 8.4. Frida Kahlo. *Moses* (also known as *Nuclear Sun*), 1945. Oil on masonite. 37 × 20 inches. 75.6 × 61 cm. Private collection. © 2006 Banco de México Diego Rivera and Frida Kahlo Museums Trust. Av. Cinco de Mayo No. 2, Col. Centro, Del. Cuauhtémoc 06059, México, D.F. Reproduction authorized by the Instituto Nacional de Bellas Artes y Literatura 2006.

ways, Kahlo employed it to negotiate her way through the special problems facing women artists in Mexico. Her self-portraits as secular saint or profane goddess were a way of creating an alternative to the countless images of male heroes. Since spiritual power was one of the few types of power commonly attributed to women, she expropriated and transformed religious imagery as a way of legitimating and empowering a female protagonist. By combining Precolumbian symbolism, Catholic iconography, Mexican folk art, and a vanguard style, she invented a female personage who was powerful, modern, and irrefutably Mexican.

Kahlo produced only one painting that directly addresses the theme of the male hero: *Moses* (also known as *Nuclear Sun*) (1945) (Figure 8.4). Unlike the

rest of her work, it embraces a vast sweep of history, and although it is only
20 × 37 inches, the composition resembles that of a mural.[39] The painting's
unusual characteristics can be attributed to its origin as a commission.
Around 1943, José Domingo Lavin asked Kahlo to read Sigmund Freud's
Moses and Monotheism and paint a work based on it.[40] In *Moses and
Monotheism* Freud posits that Moses was not a Jew but an Egyptian follower of the pharaoh Akhenaten, who advocated monotheistic worship of the
sun god Aten. Freud argues that the religion Moses gave to the Jews was
the monotheistic religion of Aten, a god who, in stark contrast to earlier
practice, was not represented in animal or human form but as a sun disk
emitting life-giving rays. As part of his argument Freud cited Otto Rank's
theory of the archetypal nature of the birth of major cultural heroes, in
which the hero is usually found and adopted as an infant after being
exposed to grave danger; often the future hero is put in a casket or basket
and set adrift in water.

The central section of *Moses* is rendered with greater simplicity and in
significantly larger scale than the sides. At the top an adaptation of the
ancient Egyptian sun disk of Aten appears as an enormous fiery sun emitting long, thin rays that end in hands. According to Kahlo, the sun signifies the "center of all religion," "the First GOD," and "creator and reproduc-
er of LIFE."[41] Directly below the sun, at the exact center of the composition, is a fully developed human fetus in the placenta, an image that is rendered with the accuracy and detail of a medical illustration. From the sides
of the placenta, fallopian tubes extend like two outstretched arms. To the
left is a greatly magnified image of a dividing cell; to the right is an equally enlarged ovum in which healthy sperm dart about. Below the fetus, the
infant Moses floats in a basket on the waters of the Nile. A light rain echoes
the drops that fall from the placenta. At the base of the composition, a
conch squirts fluid into an open seashell. The waters of the Nile are bor-
dered by papyrus and framed by ancient, gnarled tree trunks that sprout
new buds.

Flanking the central section of *Moses* is a multitude of tiny figures
arranged hierarchically: gods at the top, leaders in the middle, and masses
of anonymous people at the bottom. Occupying the lower corners are, on
the left, a Stone Age man at work, and on the right, a Stone Age woman
with a baby in her arms; each of these figures is rendered in four colors to
represent the four races. Monkeys positioned directly behind the man,
woman, and child mimic their roles and postures, creating juxtapositions
with Darwinian connotations.

In a talk Kahlo gave about *Moses* at the time of its unveiling, she spoke
about Freud's book and expressed her own ideas about heroes, gods, and

religion. She began with a disclaimer, saying she had only read the book once and based the painting on her first impressions. After completing the painting she reread the book and realized the painting was quite different from Freud's analyses. "But now," she said, "there's nothing to be done, neither to take away from it or add to it. . . . Of course, the theme is especially about MOSES or the birth of the HERO."[42]

Kahlo could not find a way to represent Moses as either Jewish or Egyptian, so she just painted "a kid, who in general would not only represent Moses, but all those who according to legend had the same beginning, later becoming important personages, leaders of their people, that is to say HEROES."[43] She painted him as cultural heroes have been described in many legends, abandoned and floating in a basket in the water. She explained that she tried to make the basket resemble a womb, "because, according to Freud, the basket is the exposed womb and the water signifies the maternal fount when giving birth to a baby."[44]

Kahlo portrayed the baby with tenderness and empowered him with a third eye on his forehead. (She said that since heroes are keener than others, she gave him the *ojo avisor*, or "all-seeing eye.") But despite the infant's innocent appearance, Kahlo was highly critical of heroes. At the beginning of her presentation she warned her audience, "What I wished to express most intensely and clearly was that the reason that people need to invent or imagine *heroes* and *gods* is unmitigated FEAR. Fear of life and fear of death." Later she noted, "Like Moses, there have been and there will be a great number of 'higher ups,' transformers of religions and of human societies. It may be said that they are a type of *messenger* between the people who they manage and the 'gods' invented by them [the managers] in order to manage them [the people]."[45]

Kahlo was genuinely intrigued by the ideas Freud presented in *Moses and Monotheism*, and elements in her painting refer to his concepts, but the painting is an odd collage of his ideas and hers. And ultimately her ideas triumph. The real protagonist of the painting is not a human hero but the life cycle. The painting pays homage to the life-giving sun, the maternal womb, sexual union, conception, birth, old age, and renewal. Major elements in the painting encompass both genders; this is explicitly true in the case of the womb and the male infant, and metaphorically apparent in the case of the conch spurting liquid into the open scallop shell.

Kahlo's depiction of Moses as an infant stands in stark contrast to the muralists' portrayals of heroes as powerful adult men. Her thematic and formal emphasis on nature and the life cycle and her relegation of gods, heroes, and the masses to the periphery defy the established practices of muralism, even though the composition seems to suggest that the painting was

Figure 8.5. Details of the central section of Diego Rivera's *Man at the Crossroads*, as recreated at the Palace of Fine Arts, Mexico City, in 1934. Fresco. Museo del Palacio de Bellas Artes, Mexico City. © 2006 Banco de México Diego Rivera and Frida Kahlo Museums Trust. Av. Cinco de Mayo No. 2, Col. Centro, Del. Cuauhtémoc 06059, México, D.F. Reproduction authorized by the Instituto Nacional de Bellas Artes y Literatura 2006.

designed as a miniature mural. The degree to which Kahlo rejected the visual rhetoric of the muralists is revealed by a comparison of Kahlo's *Moses* with Rivera's *Man at the Crossroads* (1933) (Figure 8.5). In Rivera's fresco the main figure is a monumental adult worker who controls a large machine and stands before two enormous intersecting ellipses that represent the world as viewed through a microscope and a telescope. The worker's ability to control the machine and his placement at the intersection of the microcosm and the macrocosm imply a mastery of technology and science that permits him to control the world. In contrast, Kahlo's Moses is a helpless infant adrift on the water.

Kahlo sincerely admired the work of the muralists and the *escuela mexicana*, and she held the work of her husband in highest esteem. Yet her words about heroes and the scale and themes of her paintings demonstrate resistance to some of the dominant cultural codes. Her imagery can be understood as a bid for interpretive power and an attempt to insert a female protagonist into the visual language of a nation that preferred to exalt male heroes.[46] In order to write her own personal history she incorporated the ideas of the *escuela mexicana* that she appreciated—the valorization of indigenous culture and the affirmation of *mexicanidad*—and rejected what she did not—the glorification of male heroes and the relegation of women to supporting roles.

Kahlo's reputation as an artist and her degree of public recognition have changed dramatically over time. Throughout their lives, Rivera's artistic reputation overshadowed hers. From the time of their marriage, she was known as the nearly beautiful, exotically dressed, invalid wife of Rivera; by the late 1930s she had established a reputation as a talented painter in her own right. In addition to the international acclaim that Rivera's work attracted, he habitually provoked controversies about art and politics that generated enormous publicity. Besides the political controversies, Rivera and Kahlo were celebrities whose personal lives were fodder for the press. Mexican newspapers and magazines referred to them familiarly as "Diego" and "Frida" and gossiped about their private lives.

Kahlo was not the only woman artist active in Mexico from the late 1920s to the mid-1950s, nor was she irrefutably the most famous.[47] In the years immediately after her death in 1954, Kahlo became a largely forgotten artist. Few people other than connoisseurs of Mexican art would have recognized her name. The Frida Kahlo Museum opened in Coyoacán in 1958, and although it eventually had a significant impact on her reputation, during its first decades it attracted relatively few visitors. In the 1960s information about Kahlo in English was limited almost exclusively to material contained in books about Rivera.[48] By the late 1970s, however, feminist artists and art historians in the United States had rediscovered Kahlo and were resurrecting her as a prime example of a woman artist whose work deserved greater recognition. Chicano artists and intellectuals chose Kahlo as a figure of affirmation and resistance. In Mexico art historian Teresa del Conde published a short book titled *Vida de Frida Kahlo* (Life of Frida Kahlo) in 1976; the following year Raquel Tibol, who had met and interviewed Kahlo in the early 1950s, published *Frida Kahlo: Crónica, testimonios y aproximaciones* (Frida Kahlo: Chronicles, Testimonies and Approximations). Major retrospectives of Kahlo's work were held in Mexico and the United States, and numerous articles appeared in both countries.[49] On the Day of the Dead in 1978 the Galería de la Raza in San Francisco opened an exhibition of art inspired by her, including a traditional *ofrenda*, or altar-like offering, in her honor.[50] By the time Hayden Herrera published *Frida: A Biography of Frida Kahlo* in 1983, the artist had become an underground heroine, and her reputation was growing rapidly.

Since the early 1980s, Kahlo's reputation has soared. In 1982 the Whitechapel Gallery in London mounted a major exhibition of work by Frida Kahlo and Tina Modotti, which traveled to Berlin, Hamburg, Hannover, Stockholm, New York City, Mexico City, and Monterrey. The Mexican feature film *Frida: Naturaleza Viva*, directed by Paul Leduc, was released in 1984. That same year the Mexican government decreed her art to be national patrimony. From the mid-1980s to the early 1990s, solo exhibitions of Kahlo's work were hosted in Spain, Australia, Japan, the United States, and Mexico. In addition to the catalogues that accompanied each of these exhibitions, dozens of books about her were published. By the 1990s she had entered the art history canon, appearing in general art history textbooks.

As Kahlo's fame increased, auction prices of her work skyrocketed. In May 1990 Sotheby's sold *Diego and I* for $1,430,000, making it the first painting by a Latin American artist to sell for over a million dollars. A decade later her *Self-Portrait* (1929) sold for over $5 million, the highest price ever paid for a work created by a woman as well as the highest price ever paid for a work by a Latin American.

In 1991 the National Fine Arts Institute in Mexico presented the exhibition *Pasión por Frida* (Passion for Frida), which documented Kahlo's prodigious rise in popularity. Examples of Fridamania were selected without regard to quality, in the same way that anthropological exhibitions strive for representative objects (as opposed to fine arts exhibitions, which aim for aesthetic quality). The exhibition displayed scholarly publications that featured articles on Kahlo, images of Kahlo created by other artists, commercial products that used her name or picture, and fashions inspired by her style of dress and adornment. The Kahlo artifacts ranged from thought-provoking and beautifully executed paintings to "Frida" brand shoes and a shade of deep red nail polish dubbed "Frida." Scholarly journals coexisted with fashion spreads and newspaper clippings about Frida Kahlo look-alike contests. Frida T-shirts, posters, and jewelry abounded. The exhibition, which opened in Mexico, traveled in the United States and was documented in a catalogue that provided a visual record and a dozen short essays about the phenomenon.[51]

Among the most interesting objects in the show were paintings created by contemporary artists who portrayed Kahlo in ways that commented on her religious sources and her posthumous role as a secular saint. The works included Cristina Cárdenas's *Santa Frida, Fourteenth Century* (1991), Alfredo De Batuc's *Our Lady of Perversion* (1984), Luis Fernando Enríquez's *In Style* (1985) (Figure 8.6), and Adolfo Patiño's *Virginal Apparition* (1990).[52] In different ways, and with varying degrees of admiration for her

Figure 8.6. Luis Fernando Enríquez, *In Style* (1985). Ink on paper. 5⅞ × 9½ inches (15 × 24 cm). © 2006 Luis Fernando Enríquez. Courtesy of the artist. Photograph: Nancy Deffebach.

work or criticism of the way she has become idolized, these works mime her use of Marian imagery.

Kahlo's posthumous reputation rose at the same time and in similar ways in the United States and Mexico, but some significant differences exist in the ways she is perceived in her own country and abroad. The most important is that while Kahlo and her work are sometimes cited by artists in the United States, her work has not had a major impact on later art. (The possible exception to this statement is within the Chicano art movement.) In Mexico her work profoundly influenced the generation of painters that matured as artists and began to receive recognition in the 1980s. These artists, who include Monica Castillo, Julio Galán, Rocío Maldonado, Dulce

María Nuñez, and Nahum B. Zenil, rejected the abstract and concrete tendencies of their immediate predecessors and returned to figurative art. They do not form a tightly knit group, but they share a predilection for personal imagery and tend to work in a small to moderately large scale. Such qualities also reject the agenda of the Mexican muralists, whose reputations loomed over the Mexican art world for decades after their death. Many of the younger artists find inspiration in the personal, private themes of Kahlo (Figure 8.7). This generation has been called Neomexicanists and Postmodernists, but the most significant trait that links these painters is their exploration of gender issues and sexual themes, often from viewpoints previously underrepresented in Mexican art.

For many of Kahlo's admirers she personifies resistance to gender prescriptions; for many others she embodies the strengths of her Mexican heritage; for some she epitomizes a stoic response to physical and emotional pain; and for others it is the way she combines ethnicity, gender, art, and politics that makes her a figure of intense personal identification. Art historian Edward Sullivan believes that Kahlo has achieved such celebrity because she is "a role model for many people—feminists, lesbians, gay men and others who were searching for a hero—someone to validate their struggle to find their own voice and their own public personalities. Frida, as a woman of personal and aesthetic strength and courage, met that need."[53] One contestant in a Kahlo look-alike contest in San Francisco revealed that she admired Kahlo because she gave people courage: "I am forty years old," she explained, "and I don't have any children and I'm Mexican. . . . That's almost criminal for a Mexican woman. . . . She allowed me to be what I am."[54] The winner of the contest said she was flattered that the judges thought she resembled the artist physically, but hoped she emulated some of her inner qualities: "She persevered and made the most of what she had. . . . It really heartens me that she's caught on as a popular figure."[55] For many Chicano artists, Kahlo is a cultural icon, so much so that her name is listed in the glossary of the catalogue of the exhibition *Chicano Art: Resistance and Affirmation* (CARA). In the catalogue Kahlo is identified as an important Mexican artist who has "inspired Chicano artists, and especially Chicanas, to pursue an artistic identity without denying their indigenous heritage, severing their familial ties, or restricting their political activism."[56]

With some frequency the words "hero" or "heroine" are used by Kahlo's admirers to describe her, but it could be argued that the terms "role model," "saint," "martyr," "celebrity," or "icon" would more accurately reflect how they regard her. Kahlo fits the definition of hero written by the editors of this book, who intentionally constructed an inclusive definition (see the

Figure 8.7. Nahum B. Zenil, *With All Respect*, 1983. Serigraph. 17⅞ × 23⅝ inches. 44.5 × 60 cm. Courtesy Galería de Arte Mexicano, Mexico City.

introduction). More traditional assumptions about heroes—that they are brave warriors or successful political leaders or have rescued someone from danger—describe roles that until recent decades were primarily male prerogatives or that partly depend on physical strength. Such traditional assumptions tend to prioritize men and reduce the number of women who might be considered heroic. Kahlo does not fit the more traditional concept of a hero, and, paradoxically, that is probably part of her appeal. If she is a hero, it is precisely because she fills a need and a niche that could not have been occupied by a soldier or a politician.

Kahlo's popularity extends well beyond the art world and is manifest in a variety of ways. Her face and name appear in Mexican graffiti. The most interesting example is painted on a hill in Guanajuato, where a young Kahlo is portrayed as a girl-astronaut floating in space. She wears a space suit, and her long braids extend beyond the space helmet and function like "antennas to communicate with other worlds."[57] One hand holds a crescent moon, the other points to the stars; her glass helmet forms a white halo around her head. The painting is located on the Hill of San Miguel where an enormous statue of El Pípila, a local hero of the war of independence, was constructed in 1939.[58]

Kahlo, who once drew on the folk and popular arts of Mexico to invent her personal style, has now become a source of imagery for contemporary popular culture in Mexico. Shops in the crowded and lively Ciudadela artisan market in Mexico City offer small altar-like boxes that enshrine her photograph. The boxes are almost identical to others featuring the Virgin of Guadalupe. Both versions have an intense blue exterior (blue is the color of the Virgin's mantle and of Kahlo's home, which is often referred to as the *casa azul*, or the blue house). The interiors of the boxes contain a collaged reproduction of the artist's or the Virgin's face above a crescent of pink ribbon rosettes; sequins star the background.

"Frida" has become a highly commercial property. One of the clearest examples of her marketability is her presence on the Internet. On any given day eBay offers for auction approximately 300 objects related to Kahlo. The items comprise the predictable T-shirts, posters, books, photographs, and jewelry, but they also include a bizarre smattering of religious objects: Frida Kahlo votive candles, rosaries, folk art crosses, and handmade minishrines.[59] Are the vendors of the religious items oblivious to Kahlo's lack of religious beliefs? Do they know that she was an atheist, but cynically use her name to sell merchandize? Has she become a symbol for all Latino culture in which everything from Mexican art to Catholicism is conflated? Or is this the first manifestation of a nascent cult in which a secular, Marxist painter becomes Saint Frida?

From the point of view of 1970s-style feminism, Kahlo's rise to fame in recent decades is the realization of a dream. From the point of view of contemporary feminist scholarship, many of the publications and much of the media coverage that have encouraged this fame are problematic. Hayden Herrera's *Frida: A Biography of Frida Kahlo* provides the most extensive information on Kahlo to date in any language, and this book has been a major factor in Kahlo's escalating popularity. However, Herrera's biography offers a rather cause-and-effect interpretation of Kahlo's life and art in which the paintings are seen as merely or primarily autobiographical. Most subsequent writers have repeated and extended this biographical methodology to such an extent that it has become nearly monolithic. Interpretations of Kahlo's work are filtered through what is known, conjectured, or fantasized about her personal life and mental states. In 1990 Joan Borsa published a brilliant critique of the reception of Kahlo's work in which she argued that the "exploration of subjectivity and personal history has all too frequently denied or de-emphasized the politics involved in examining one's own location, inheritance and social condition."[60] Borsa noted that even though the motto "the personal is political" has been widely accepted by feminists since the 1960s or 1970s, most writings about Kahlo's work continue to gloss over her complex reworking of the personal and ignore or minimize her interrogation of cultural identity, gender, sexuality, marginality, politics, and power. Borsa concluded that by the time a reader has finished reading Herrera's 500-page biography of Kahlo, it has been established that her "life revolved around love, marriage, and pain; in short a rather traditional feminine sphere has been presented. . . . What is missing is a more critical reading of the *gaps* between the author and the text."[61]

Two years later art historian Janice Bergman-Carton expressed similar concerns about the simplification and depolitization of Kahlo's work when she observed that despite the artist's resistance to fixed identity boundaries, she is "repeatedly contained by the normalizing narratives of the media."[62] While journalistic treatments of Kahlo recognize her defiance and "otherness," they do so less as a challenge to social norms than as a way of noting her marketability. Bergman-Carton concluded, "In the same breath that her difference is acknowledged, it is often reinserted into the narrative of artistic fashion in a way that defuses its cultural critique."[63]

In the first book to depart from the biographical model, *Devouring Frida*, Margaret Lindauer undertakes a semiotic,[64] feminist analysis of the construction of the "Frida myth" and proposes alternative interpretations of Kahlo's work. Lindauer repeatedly chips away at the artist = art paradigm that relegates visual art to an ahistorical and apolitical realm.[65] Of particular interest are the author's citations of Griselda Pollock, who in the context of the essay "Artists, Mythologies and Media," which centers on Vincent van Gogh—an artist whose popular image is in many ways analogous to Kahlo's—argues that artists and art have been "'evacuated from history . . . [and] history from art history.'"[66] Lindauer concludes, "at the same time that a product (painting) becomes synonymous with the producer (painter), the artist is reduced to personal, psychological, and biological histories constructed parallel to, but separate from, social histories."[67]

At the beginning of the twenty-first century a small but growing part of the scholarship on Kahlo is becoming more insightful, relevant, and diverse, although it is still a minor trend among the deluge of conventional biographical and psychological interpretations that have been published in recent years.

During the last decade something of a backlash has developed among some specialists in Latin American art as a reaction to the phenomenal fame of Kahlo. Some of these scholars do not like Kahlo's work, which is not surprising, since her imagery is confrontational, provocative, painful, and personal. Her paintings never have been and never will be to everyone's tastes. Other scholars may admire her work but object to the level of attention she receives, when so many innovative Latin American artists remain

Figure 8.8. Cover of the Latin American edition of *Time*, October 18, 2001, showing Salma Hayek costumed as Frida Kahlo. The cover appeared shortly before the release of the film *Frida*, directed by Julie Taymor and starring Hayek, © 2001 Time, Inc. Reprinted by permission.

relatively unknown outside their own countries. Art historian Florencia Bazzano-Nelson likes Kahlo's art, "especially her rather revolutionary exploration of gender-based topics and the compelling combination of intellectual, cultural, and emotional factors she achieves in her paintings." Yet Bazzano-Nelson is troubled by how Kahlo's art and life "have been misused in the United States to represent Latin American visual culture as a whole, a role that in previous decades was imposed on three other Mexicans: Orozco, Rivera, and Siqueiros." Bazzano-Nelson adds, "We need to consider Kahlo in context: she was one among many interesting artists—both female and male—active in Mexico during her lifetime, and one among hundreds of artists of importance in Latin America."[68]

While some art historians deplore what they consider the disproportional fame of one artist, Kahlo's reputation continues to grow among the general public and her image shows up with increasing frequency in popular media in the United States, Mexico, and elsewhere. In 2001 in a coordinated effort the Mexican and the U.S. postal services issued similar postage stamps bearing Frida Kahlo's name and a reproduction of one of her blandest paintings. In 2002 Julie Taymor's feature film *Frida*, which boasted an international cast including Salma Hayek, Alfred Molina, Ashley Judd, and Antonio Banderas, introduced Kahlo and Rivera to an even wider audience (Figure 8.8).[69] More than half a century after her death, Kahlo is significantly more famous than she ever was during her life. According to Kahlo's first boyfriend and lifelong friend, Alejandro Gómez Arias, one of the reasons she painted herself was as "a last resort to survive, to endure, to overcome death."[70] Kahlo, who disapproved of people inventing heroes and gods but wanted to be remembered, has become a heroine and a media goddess.

Notes

This chapter is dedicated to Kathleen Connell Rohr.

I have talked about Kahlo's work with many friends, colleagues, former professors, and artists. I especially wish to thank Kim T. Grant for reading and critiquing this manuscript. I have benefited greatly from conversations with Jacqueline Barnitz, Florencia Bazzano-Nelson, Eduardo de Jesús Douglas, Ana Garduño, Salvador Mendiola, Debra Nagao, Daniel E. Nelson, Judy Rohr, Daniel J. Sherman, Susan V. Webster, and Mariana Yampolsky. Candy Marcela e-mailed me a digital photograph of the Frida Kahlo graffito in Guanajuato. Although only one of my interviews with a friend of Kahlo is cited (Antonio Rodríguez, 1986), my analysis of Kahlo's work developed after conducting numerous interviews in Mexico. I revised the manuscript while I was a Mellon Postdoctoral Fellow at Rice University. A Center for Latin American and Latino/a Studies at Georgia State University grant paid for the cost of making black-and-white prints of the photographs that illustrate this chapter. A grant from the Center for Latin American Studies at San Diego State University contributed to the cost of obtaining permission to reproduce the cover of *Time*.

* Epigraph is from Frida Kahlo, "Hablando de un cuadro mío," *Así* (18 Aug. 1945): 71.

1. In Mexico, women artists confronted substantial difficulties in addition to those faced by male artists. It is important to note, however, that despite the country's reputa-

tion for machismo, women artists did not suffer from more discrimination in Mexico than in the United States. Writing in 1975, Jacqueline Barnitz observed that in the preceding six decades, "more Latin American than North American women have become well-known artists." Jacqueline Barnitz, "Five Women Artists," *Review: Latin American Literature and Arts* 75 (Spring 1975): 38.

2. The Manifesto of the Union of Technical Workers, Painters, and Sculptors (Manifesto del Sindicato de Obreros Técnicos, Pintores y Escultores) was published in the June 1924 issues of *El Machete*. Alicia Azuela, "*El Machete* and *Frente a Frente*: Art Committed to Social Justice in Mexico," *Art Journal* 52, no. 1 (Spring 1993): 82.

3. David Alfaro Siqueiros, "Manifesto of the Union of Mexican Workers, Technicians, Painters and Sculptors," cited in Dawn Ades, *Art in Latin America: The Modern Era, 1820–1980*, exhibition catalogue (New Haven, Yale University Press, 1989), 324.

4. Jean Franco, *Plotting Women: Gender and Representation in Mexico* (New York: Columbia University Press, 1989), 102.

5. During the Mexican Revolution, women known as *soldaderas* followed their husbands, lovers, and sons to war. The *soldaderas* cooked, nursed the wounded, fought, gave birth, and performed a multitude of services not provided by the military.

6. Franco, *Plotting Women*, 102.

7. Franco, *Plotting Women*, 101.

8. Diego Rivera, quoted by Raquel Tibol in the prologue to *Arte y política*, by Diego Rivera (Mexico City: Grijalbo, 1979), 27.

9. Hayden Herrera, *Frida: A Biography of Frida Kahlo* (New York: Harper and Row, 1983), 25.

10. Other styles were worn to attend church, fiestas, and weddings, and by older women and previous generations. One of the most spectacular garments was a white lace headdress that was donned for festive events and arranged in various ways according to the occasion. In Kahlo's *Self-Portrait as a Tehuana* (1943) and *Self-Portrait* (1948), she shows herself wearing the headdress in the way it was worn to attend church. For information about the traditional clothing of Tehuantepec, see Miguel Covarrubias, *Mexico South: The Isthmus of Tehuantepec* (New York: Alfred A. Knopf, 1947), 246–266, 350.

11. Diego Rivera as cited in "Mexico: Fashion Notes," *Time*, 3 May 1946, 34.

12. Covarrubias, *Mexico South*, 246.

13. Ibid., 339.

14. Mariana Yampolsky, conversation with the author, fall 1994, Mexico.

15. Franco, *Plotting Women*, 128.

16. Herrera concludes her analysis of *Remembrance of an Open Wound* with the information that Kahlo "candidly told a male friend that the way she placed her right hand beneath her skirt and near her sex in the painting was meant to show that she was masturbating." It is, however, possible that Kahlo was putting her friend on. Herrera, *Frida: A Biography of Frida Kahlo*, 191.

17. Teresa de Lauretis, *Technologies of Gender* (Bloomington: Indiana University Press, 1987), 9.

18. Elissa J. Rashkin, *Women Filmmakers in Mexico: The Country of Which We Dream* (Austin: University of Texas Press, 2001), 2.

19. Frida Kahlo, "Portrait of Diego," trans. Nancy Deffebach (Breslow) and Amy Weiss Narea, *Calyx*, 5 (October 1980): 95.

20. Frida Kahlo, *The Diary of Frida Kahlo: An Intimate Self-Portrait* (New York: Harry N. Abrams/La Vaca Independente, 1995), 249–250.

21. Irene Nicholson, *Mexican and Central American Mythology* (London: Paul Hamlyn, 1967), 10.

22. Nicholson, *Mexican and Central American Mythology*, 10.

23. For more information on Kahlo's use of Precolumbian symbolism, see Nancy Deffebach, "Pre-Columbian Symbolism in the Art of Frida Kahlo" (master's thesis, University of Texas at Austin, 1991).

24. Alfonso Caso, *Thirteen Masterpieces of Mexican Archaeology*, trans. Edith Mackie and Jorge R. Acosta (Mexico City: Editoriales Cultura y Polis, 1938), 41.

25. Thomas A. Joyce, *Mexican Archaeology* (New York: G. P. Putnam's Sons, 1914), 61.

26. Eduard Seler, "Collected Works," vol. 1, 103. Unpublished English translation made under the supervision of Charles P. Bowditch of *Gesammelte Abhandlungen zur Amerikanischen Sprach- und Alterthumskunde*, in the collection of the Newberry Library, Chicago.

27. Linda Schele, conversation with the author, spring 1991, Austin.

28. *Olin* was also one of the twenty days of the Aztec calendar.

29. For information about representations of indigenous people in nineteenth-century Mexican art, see Stacie G. Widdifield, *The Embodiment of the National in Late Nineteenth-Century Mexican Painting* (Tucson: University of Arizona Press, 1996).

30. Betty Ann Brown, "The Past Idealized: Diego Rivera's Use of Pre-Columbian Imagery," in *Diego Rivera: A Retrospective* (New York: Founders Society of Detroit Institute of Arts/W. W. Norton, 1986), 139–155.

31. Arturo Estrada, who was one of Kahlo's students, as cited by Herrera in *Frida: A Biography of Frida Kahlo*, 334.

32. Herrera, *Frida: A Biography of Frida Kahlo*, 284.

33. Ibid., 77.

34. Deffebach, "Pre-Columbian Symbolism in the Art of Frida Kahlo," 75, 229.

35. Sarah M. Lowe, in *The Diary of Frida Kahlo*, 253; Eduardo de Jesús Douglas, "The Colonial Self: Homosexuality and Mestizaje in the Art of Nahum B. Zenil," *Art Journal* 57, no. 3 (Fall 1998): 20.

36. Enrique Krauze, *Mexico: Biography of Power*, trans. Hank Heifetz (New York: HarperCollins, 1997), 229.

37. Krauze, *Mexico: Biography of Power*, 229.

38. Ibid., 230.

39. The architect and artist Juan O'Gorman was the first person to have noted publicly that the composition of *Moses* was suitable for a mural. Juan O'Gorman speaking in the documentary film *The Life and Death of Frida Kahlo* (1965), directed by Karen Crommie and David Crommie.

40. Frido Kahlo, "Hablando de un cuadro mío," *Así* (18 August 1945): 71.

41. Ibid.

42. Ibid.

43. Ibid.

44. Ibid.

45. Ibid.

46. The work of the Mexican muralists contains a wide variety of images of women, including both positive and demeaning images. The most negative images of women are Orozco's countless depictions of prostitutes; in his mature work he uses the female prostitute as a metaphor for social and political corruption, as he did, for example, in *Catharsis* (1934) at the Palace of Fine Arts in Mexico City.

Among the many positive images of women are Rivera's portrayals of schoolteachers, such as *The Rural Schoolteacher* (1923) at the Ministry of Education in Mexico City. Yet Rivera also created problematic images of women. In his mural program in the former chapel at the Universidad Autónoma de Chapingo he associated women with nature and men with culture and social transformation. In the mid-1920s, when Rivera painted the murals, these stereotypes were common in Mexico, Europe, and the United States; such assumptions have since been questioned and rejected by intellectuals.

To find an image of a heroine that conforms to traditional notions of heroism it is necessary to look outside the work of *los tres grandes* (the big three, that is, Orozco, Rivera, and Siqueiros), outside the time of the postrevolutionary period (1920–1940), and beyond Mexico City. In 1942, Juan O'Gorman portrayed Gertrudis Bocanegra and Margarita Neri next to José María Morelos and Emiliano Zapata in *The History of Michoacán* in the Gertrudis Bocanegra Library in Pátzcuaro, Michoacán. Bocanegra, who was from Pátzcuaro, was executed by a Spanish firing squad in 1818 for supporting the independence movement. Neri was a *soldadera* who led troops to war during the Mexican Revolution.

Jean Franco, *Plotting Women*, 101–102; Elizabeth Salas, *Soldaderas in the Mexican Military: Myth and History* (Austin: University of Texas Press, 1990), 42; and Nancy Deffebach, "Human-Plant Hybrids in the Art of Frida Kahlo and Leonora Carrington: Sources, Contexts, and Issues." *Curare* 11 (Summer 1997): 99–100. I wish to thank an anonymous reviewer of this manuscript for drawing my attention to the images of Bocanegra and Neri in the mural by Juan O'Gorman.

47. Other women artists working in Mexico included Lola Alvarez Bravo, Rosario Cabrera, Olga Costa, Dolores Cueto, María Izquierdo, Tina Modotti, Nahui Olín, and Isabel Villaseñor. Between 1939 and 1943 the European Surrealists Alice Rahon, Remedios Varo, and Leonora Carrington immigrated to Mexico. In the 1940s Mariana Yampolsky came from the United States to work with the Taller de Gráfica Popular (Graphic Arts Workshop). Of all the women artists active in Mexico, the two who enjoyed the greatest professional reputations during the postrevolutionary period were Kahlo and Izquierdo. From the late 1930s to the mid-1950s, important survey exhibitions of Mexican art invariably included Kahlo and Izquierdo, who were often the only women represented in the shows. During their lives Kahlo and Izquierdo had comparable professional reputations. The careers of Leonora Carrington and Remedios Varo flourished later than those of Kahlo and Izquierdo.

48. Diego Rivera with Gladys March, *My Art, My Life* (New York: Citadel Press, 1960); and Wolfe, *The Fabulous Life of Diego Rivera*.

49. Two important group exhibitions contributed to the reevaluation of Kahlo's work: *Frida Kahlo acompañada de siete pintoras*, at the Museo de Arte Moderno in Mexico City in 1967, and *La mujer como creadora y tema del arte*, at the Museo de Arte Moderno in Mexico City in 1975. The key retrospectives were *Frida Kahlo: Exposición Nacional de Homenaje*, at the Palacio de Bellas Artes in Mexico City in 1977, and *Frida Kahlo*, at the Museum of Contemporary Art in Chicago in 1978. The Chicago show traveled to five venues in the United States. Teresa del Conde, *Vida de Frida Kahlo* (Mexico City: Secretaría de la Presidencia, Departamento Editorial, 1976); Raquel Tibol, *Frida Kahlo: crónica, testimonios y aproximaciones* (Mexico City: Ediciones de Cultura Popular, 1977).

50. *Homenaje a Frida Kahlo*, which opened on the evening of November 2, 1978, included fifty-two works created by Chicano/Latino artists and memorabilia provided by Kahlo's friends. Ramón Favela, "The Image of Frida Kahlo in Chicano Art," in

Pasión por Frida, ed. Blanca Garduño and José Antonio Rodríguez, exhibition catalogue (Mexico City: Museo Estudio Diego Rivera-INBA, 1992), 185–189.

51. Garduño and Rodríguez, eds., *Pasión por Frida*.

52. Garduño and Rodríguez, eds., *Pasión por Frida*, 47, 79, 153.

53. Edward Sullivan, "Frida Kahlo in New York," in Garduño and Rodríguez, eds., *Pasión por Frida*, 184.

54. Rosa Chavez cited by Jane Meredith Adams, "In Death, Mexican Artist a Cult Figure," *Chicago Tribune*, 8 November 1992.

55. Karen Armstead cited by Adams, "In Death, Mexican Artist a Cult Figure."

56. From the entry on Frida Kahlo in the "Chicano Glossary of Terms," in *Chicano Art: Resistance and Affirmation, 1965–1985* (CARA), ed. Richard Griswold del Castillo, Teresa McKenna, and Yvonne Yarbro-Bejarano, exhibition catalogue (Los Angeles: Wight Art Gallery /University of California, Los Angeles, 1991), 363.

57. Salvador Mendiola, conversation with the author, 13 October 2001, Buenos Aires.

58. Pípila, whose real name was Juan José Martínez (1782-1863), led the insurgents in an assault on the Alhóndiga de Granaditas on September 28, 1810 (*Diccionario Porrúa: Historia, biografía y geografía de México*, 6th ed. [Mexico City: Editorial Porrúa, 1995], s.v. "Martínez, Juan José"). The appearance of the Kahlo graffito at this site provokes several questions. Did the graffiti artist choose this site exclusively because it offered a good wall in a prominent place, or was he or she commenting on the need to update the national heroes? Did the graffiti artist add the image of Kahlo to create a more equitable balance in the gender of the nation's heroes? Does Kahlo's space age occupation and pronounced youth argue that Mexico should look to the future, not just to the past?

59. Between May 1 and June 30, 2003, all of these religious objects were offered for auction on eBay under the name of Frida Kahlo, but they were not all available simultaneously.

60. Joan Borsa, "Frida Kahlo: Marginalization and the Critical Female Subject," *Third Text* 12 (Autumn 1990): 26.

61. Borsa, "Frida Kahlo," 26–27.

62. Janice Bergman-Carton, "Like an Artist," *Art in America* 81 (January 1993), 37.

63. Bergman-Carton, "Like an Artist," 37.

64. Semiotics refers to the analysis of signs and their use.

65. Margaret A. Lindauer, *Devouring Frida: The Art History and Popular Celebrity of Frida Kahlo* (Hanover, N.H.: Wesleyan University Press, 1999), 152, passim.

66. Griselda Pollock, cited by Lindauer, in *Devouring Frida*, 151.

67. Lindauer, *Devouring Frida*, 151.

68. Florencia Bazzano-Nelson, personal correspondence, 21 March 2004.

69. *Time*, Latin American edition, 15 October 2001.

70. Alejandro Gómez Arias, cited by Martha Zamora, "Por qué se pintaba Frida Kahlo," *Imagine*, 2, no. 1 (Summer 1985): 2.

Haya de la Torre and APRA

DAVID NUGENT

In the early morning hours of August 15, 1931, people from all across the city of Lima, Peru, began to take to the streets for what they considered to be a momentous occasion. After eight years of exile, Víctor Raúl Haya de la Torre, leader of APRA (the Alianza Popular Revolucionaria Americana, or Popular American Revolutionary Alliance), was finally returning to Lima. His innumerable followers fully intended to give him the impassioned welcome they felt a man of his enormous stature deserved. Some Apristas congregated at local party offices scattered about the city, where they received instructions about the procession route they were to follow. Their destination was the Plaza de San Martín, in the center of Lima, where they were to arrive by the middle of the afternoon, when Haya de la Torre was to address his followers en masse. Other party members congregated at APRA's central headquarters, where they received similar instructions about the procession. Still others took to the streets with little more to guide them than what they had read in the party newspaper, *La Tribuna*. Regardless, by early afternoon long processions of Apristas were winding their way from all points of the city toward the plaza, in anticipation of the afternoon's mass rally. As they marched, a great many Apristas carried party flags, which had been made in large numbers by special planning committees. They sang songs and yelled cheers they had learned through repeated practice in party meetings. They were also very careful to maintain order as they proceeded through the streets—to march in precise rows, with a predetermined number of people in each—a special party committee (the disciplinary committee) having schooled them in how to do so. The Apristas were equally diligent about behaving with the utmost decorum, neither responding to provocations from onlookers nor offering any of

Figure 9.1.
Haya de la Torre

Figure 9.2. Haya de la Torre greeting the masses.

Figure 9.3. Haya de la Torre conferring with Albert Einstein.

Figure 9.4. Haya de la Torre preparing the next generation of Apristas.

their own. The order and discipline exhibited by the demonstrators left a powerful impression on APRA supporters and detractors alike.

As the cars of Haya de la Torre and other party notables slowly made their way toward the Plaza de San Martín, they were greeted by constant accolades, cheers, and shouts from the party faithful. So many admirers thronged the streets that it was difficult for the cars to make much forward progress. From the balconies of buildings located all along Haya de la Torre's route, party members (most of them women) showered their leader with flowers. Haya de la Torre's car was constantly being stopped by people who rushed up to greet him.

When the Aprista leader finally reached the Plaza de San Martín in midafternoon, something on the order of 60,000 people were awaiting him—an exceptionally large rally by the standards of the time.[1] When his car first appeared in the Plaza, Haya was greated by a sea of waving white handkerchiefs, an Aprista gesture signifying loyalty and allegiance. As he made his way toward the speaker's platform the crowd repeatedly chanted in unison, "A-PRA, A-PRA" and "Víctor Raúl, Víctor Raúl." They sang the national anthem and the "Marcellesa Aprista," the official party hymn. After other APRA leaders had made preliminary speeches, the moment everyone had been waiting for finally arrived, and Haya de la Torre took the stage. As he did so he was again greeted by a sea of white handkerchiefs. His speech was nothing less than mesmerizing, calling for the birth of a new Peru based on genuine democracy and social justice for the masses. After several closing songs and cheers, the rally came to an end.[2]

Víctor Raúl Haya de la Torre was the founder and leader of APRA, the most influential political party in twentieth-century Peru. From the moment of its inception in Peru in 1930, APRA was a major force to be reckoned with by ruling political and military elites, representing as it did the aspirations of countless poor and middle-class Peruvians who felt excluded from the avenues of wealth and power. So dangerous did the governing classes consider APRA to be, and such was the popular support enjoyed by the party and its leader, that the central government felt compelled to declare it illegal, while Peru's military would not even allow Haya de la Torre to run for president. Although it faced brutal and relentless repression, however, APRA survived and even thrived. The party's ability to do so is testimony to the enormous appeal it exercised with the general population.[3]

APRA was born of an alliance between the radical student movement that swept through Latin America beginning in 1918 and Peru's burgeoning working class, which was coming into its own at the same time.[4] Haya de la Torre, then a student at the national university, played an indispensable role in forging links between these two constituencies, and in the process he

helped give birth to a form of populist politics that presented a serious challenge to Peru's traditional ruling elite.[5] So central a role did Haya play in
this process that he emerged as the single most important leader linking the
two groups.

Who was Víctor Raúl Haya de la Torre, and how did he come to preside over Peru's most influential twentieth-century political party? What
was the source of his overwhelmingly broad popular appeal? How did he
and his followers succeed in translating his charisma into a stable political
force that could endure the long periods of persecution to which APRA was
subject?

Haya de la Torre was born in 1895 in Trujillo, a city on the north coast,
to a family of solid middle-class means and many connections to Peru's
elite.[6] Early in life Haya de la Torre revealed a fascination with politics.
While still a boy he would sneak out of his family's house in the evenings
and go to a nearby Workers Library, where he would hear speeches made
by members of the working class. The radical interpretations he heard of
the problems facing Peru differed profoundly from the conventional views
espoused by his family and led to considerable inner turmoil.[7]

At a time when most of his peers were still playing with toys, Haya
demonstrated a keen interest in problems of political organization. In his
own words:[8]

> We had some very spacious rooms to play in, and we created a repub-
> lic there. We had a president, we had cabinet ministers, deputies. We
> had politics. And there we practiced. And we were twelve-year-old
> kids. And we practiced at reproducing the life of the country with
> spools of thread. All of my brothers, I got them to play the game. I
> used to receive very nice toys: locomotives, trains. But I was not
> interested in these things. What interested me was to have an organ-
> ized setup, like a country. . . . When I recall this, you can see how
> early I had a political imagination. It was quite noteworthy, because
> we imitated life, but we assumed a life of order. Now I tell myself,
> how I've always had this thing about organizing. We directed polit-
> ical campaigns.

Haya's father was the editor of one of Trujillo's most important newspapers and was sufficiently well off to be able to send his son to the Colegio
San Carlos, the high school attended by Trujillo's elite. In 1917, having completed secondary school, the future leader of APRA traveled to Lima, where
he began to study law at the University of San Marcos, Peru's prestigious
national university. Haya described himself during this period in rather

unflattering terms as a somewhat spoiled, middle-class youth who was in awe of the elite and who wanted little more than to enter the privileged ranks of elite power.[9] Haya attributed his own transformation from a would-be member of the upper class to a committed organizer for the laboring masses to a trip he made in 1917 to Cuzco, the former capital of the Inca Empire.[10] In Cuzco Haya saw poverty and suffering of a kind he had not imagined possible, and what he witnessed had a profound effect on him.[11]

As disturbing and eye-opening as this trip undoubtedly was, it seems likely that more was involved in shaking the future APRA leader free of his dreams of joining the elite. Haya's own writings suggest that the broader intellectual milieu of which he was a part as a student in Lima also contributed in important ways to his transformation. In this regard, Haya singled out as especially important the writings of Manuel González Prada, a prominent Peruvian anarchist whose ideas were widely discussed in student circles (anarchism was also an early influence on Felipe Carrillo Puerto and Augusto Sandino, as discussed in Chapters 6 and 7).[12] González Prada was but one of the many figures Haya had first been exposed to as a boy, in his nighttime sojourns to the Workers Library.

It seems clear that social and political conditions in Lima were also important in directing Haya de la Torre's gaze toward the laboring poor. When the young Haya arrived in the capital to begin his university studies, Lima was in the throes of profound economic, social, and political change, owing to the rapid industrialization and urbanization that was taking place at the time. These processes were accompanied by increasingly widespread and vocal labor unrest and by the proliferation of radical ideologies that challenged the status quo.

The degree to which Haya de la Torre was affected by these several influences may be gauged by the following events. The year after his return from Cuzco he began writing newspaper articles calling for the establishment of a "popular university." University students like him would teach in this school, he proposed. However, these teachers would have a somewhat unusual student clientele. They would teach members of the urban proletariat.[13] Classes in the university would also be unconventional. While the popular education envisioned (and later implemented) by the future leader of APRA would not neglect traditional academic topics, it would emphasize practical, useful knowledge that working people could employ in their everyday lives. The popular universities were also to address moral and ethical issues, and to provide services to the urban poor that would otherwise not be available to them. In this way, Haya reasoned, forward-looking youth could help ameliorate the condition of the working class and put their country firmly on the road to prosperity.

In terms of Haya de la Torre's future as a political leader, the timing of his articles on the popular university was fortunate indeed. By early 1919, living and working conditions for Lima's working class had deteriorated considerably, and labor unions all across the city called for a general strike to win an eight-hour working day and also increases in pay. Faced with severe repression from the governing elite, several labor leaders reasoned that the government might be less intransigent regarding their demands if the workers had the support of university students—virtually all of whom came from privileged social sectors. Haya had already expressed sympathy for the working class in his newspaper articles about the popular university, and on this basis several labor leaders decided to approach him. Thus was born the coalition between middle-class intellectuals and working-class laborers out of which APRA would later emerge.[14]

Haya was very receptive to the workers' request for help and threw himself into the task of winning support for them among his fellow students at the University of San Marcos and also with government officials. After overcoming conservative student resistance to convince the Peruvian University Student Association to endorse the workers' cause, the future APRA leader further demonstrated his remarkable oratorical skills and his enormous powers of persuasion by succeeding in having himself named by workers as a strike negotiator in discussions with the government. After days of virtually nonstop negotiating, Haya finally triumphed. Not only did the government do a complete turnabout by acceding to the workers' demands (which Haya had drafted), but Haya himself brought the workers the good news.[15] In this way, Haya de la Torre established his position at the head of organized labor. Indeed, the day after the strike was settled, Haya presided over the creation of the Federación de Trabajadores de Textiles del Perú (Federation of Peruvian Textile Workers), an umbrella organization that united all of Lima's formerly independent textile unions in a single organization.[16] This federation was the single most important force in organized labor for the following decade.

From this point on, Haya de la Torre continued to strengthen his ties with organized labor and to defend the interests of the proletariat. He worked tirelessly to organize and promote his popular university. As university rector, he was brought into constant contact with workers, which gave him repeated opportunities to take full advantage of his extraordinary personal charm and his remarkable oratorical skills to expand his following.[17] On several occasions he publicly defied the police when they sought to break up demonstrations and protests, risking his own life in the process of defending workers.

Haya de la Torre came to exercise enormous influence over organized labor as a result of these activities. So influential did he become, and so dangerous did the government consider him, that Peru's dictator, Augusto Leguía, first had him jailed and then deported, in October 1923. By this time, however, he was already regarded in working-class circles not only as the champion of urban labor but also as a martyr to the proletarian cause. Haya's forced exile only reinforced this image. Within months of the fall of Leguía in August 1930, when APRA's leader was able to return to Peru, he reassumed control over the labor movement, and in 1931 he ran for the presidency as the APRA candidate. It was during his campaign that Haya delivered his electrifying speech and helped orchestrate the theatrical, stirring mass rally with which this chapter opened.

Haya de la Torre was the undisputed leader of APRA until his death in 1979 and thus remained a central figure in Peruvian politics for many decades after the emergence of the party he founded.[18] In trying to make sense of Haya's appeal to the general public, scholars often point to his charismatic, dynamic personality and his remarkable leadership qualities.[19] Virtually everyone with whom he came in contact, friend and foe alike, was struck by his enormous personal warmth, his infectious personality, and his ability to make each person with whom he spoke feel singled out, special.[20] In addition to Haya's personal qualities, he also benefited from the hero cult that developed around him and from the party's penchant for representing its leader as a martyr for the cause of the oppressed. Haya developed a unique and highly successful political style that emphasized the enormous sacrifices he made for the working class, his heroic struggles on their behalf, and his role as the father of the movement that defended their interests. APRA also lent a religious aura to its activities, drawing heavily on language and symbolism from the Bible to characterize the party's mission, depicting Aprismo as a new religion and Haya as the savior of the people and the nation.[21]

Haya's charisma, his cultivation of the air of the martyr, and the party's depiction of Aprismo as a form of popular religion all played a central role in solidifying APRA's broad appeal to the general populace. As important as these forces were, however, much more than Haya's personal qualities and the party's use of symbolism was involved in making Haya and APRA such a potent force in twentieth-century Peruvian politics, a party capable of surviving long periods of illegality and government persecution. The legacy that APRA's charismatic leader left was not only personal but also institutional. An important part of Haya's genius lay in his ability to create a party structure that was unique in the history of Peru: a nationwide party of unprecedented scope and complexity led by a highly disciplined group of cadres who were deeply committed to the party's program of social transformation.

In May 1931, the leader of APRA drafted a document that codified the party's structure.[22] The document outlined a party consisting of a nested hierarchy of cells made up of functionally specific ministries or secretariats, each of which was to cater to particular needs of the general population. The responsibilities of each secretariat vis-à-vis the populace and the party cells above and below it were carefully spelled out at every level of the party hierarchy. The secretaries who occupied these positions were expected to carry out their duties with the utmost diligence and care and to respect the rigid party chain of command at all times. Such strict attention to organization, discipline, and obedience, Haya believed, was essential if APRA was to survive.[23]

Haya's preoccupation with structure, order, and discipline was not limited to the party apparatus itself but extended beyond it to include the behavior and even the aspirations of individual Apristas, especially those who occupied positions of responsibility within the party apparatus. Haya conceived of these individuals as an elite vanguard that was to perform indispensable functions for the party. On the one hand, the Apristas were responsible for employing their party apparatus to effect structural change—to protect people from exploitation, oppression and abuse. On the other hand, they were to commit themselves body and soul to effecting personal change among the general populace. They were to contribute to the noble work of forming new kinds of subjects—autonomous and self-sufficient individuals who would be sufficiently disciplined in thought and behavior that they would be capable of helping to solve what APRA considered the most pressing problem of all, the backwardness and corruption that plagued the country.

Members of APRA's vanguard would be successful in their efforts to bring about structural and personal change, however, only if they first underwent a series of profound personal transformations. As they faced the challenges of doing so, Haya de la Torre was held out to them as the figure they should emulate. Only people who were willing to cultivate and then respect the rigorous disciplines of the mind and body that Haya required of them and that he himself religiously followed could act as living embodiments of the remade women and men the party sought to form. Only individuals who were willing to place the needs of the collective ahead of their own self-interest, as Haya did, could be trusted to direct the party ministries that were to moralize and democratize Peruvian society. Only individuals such as these, capable of extreme self-sacrifice on behalf of party and nation, were worthy to be called "priests of democracy" (*sacerdotes de la democracia*), a term of deep respect that truly committed Apristas used to refer to one another.[24] In other words, if Haya was the savior of Peru, those who made up his party vanguard were his political apostles. It was they who were to spread the good word, leading by example, proselytizing among the population as a whole.

It was these priests of democracy, formed in Haya's image, and the party structure they oversaw that provided the general populace with its most direct, concrete experience and understanding of APRA on a day-to-day basis. The rest of this chapter explores the nature of this mundane, concrete experience and in the process investigates what might be thought of as the institutionalization of Haya's charismatic vision.[25] That is, the discussion considers APRA's impact on the general populace not during those brief, dramatic, and relatively rare moments when Haya was able to cast his spell-binding magic but in the sphere of the quotidian. APRA's impact on the day-to-day life of the populace was mediated by the activities and attitudes of the party's priests of democracy, who directed a centrally organized but geographically dispersed and locally grounded party structure.

We focus in particular on the highland region of Chachapoyas, located on the eastern slope of the northern Peruvian Andes. Chachapoyas is isolated from the large urban centers (especially Lima) that were the foci of Haya's activities and so is an appropriate setting in which to examine the institutional rather than strictly personalistic or charismatic basis of APRA's appeal. In 1930, the year of APRA's founding, it took a full month in good weather to travel from Lima to Chachapoyas. This insularity meant that in the Chachapoyas region, as in many other parts of Peru, APRA had to sustain itself in the absence of Haya's personalistic appeal.

The time period to be discussed, 1930 to 1956, is also well-suited to analyzing the role of institutionalized charisma in Haya's and APRA's hold on the general population. With the exception of a brief period of legality from 1945 to 1948, throughout these decades APRA was the object of intense government persecution. In the face of this repression, Haya de la Torre had extremely limited ability to work his charismatic magic to hold the party together. Although locally based party cells and committees drew heavily on Haya's message of social justice (as conveyed in official party documents, which had to be smuggled into the region), they had to devise ways of transforming Haya's lofty pronouncements into concrete, tangible policies that made a difference in people's everyday lives. Furthermore, APRA had to devise strategies for appealing to the general populace that were sufficiently strong that people would be willing to accept the very real dangers posed by party membership. These ranged from arrest to losing one's job, deportation, torture, and even death.

The emergence of APRA in Chachapoyas, and the party's ability to maintain a loyal and committed following despite government repression, can only be understood by examining the organization of political power in this remote Andean region. This in turn entails considering how political power was structured at the national level and the peculiar nature of the Peruvian state.

The Compromised Nation-State

AT THE TURN OF THE TWENTIETH CENTURY, the polity that was Peru bore little relation to the classic model of the nation-state derived from the analysis of Western Europe. The Peruvian state did not enjoy a monopoly on the use of force, had limited ability to tax or conscript the general population, and exercised little effective control over the national territory. The bureaucracy was very small, and the vast majority of government functionaries received neither training for their posts nor salary for the work they performed. There was little pretense that these individuals served the public good. Rather, government workers generally used their positions as a means of accumulating wealth and establishing position by extorting goods and labor from those under their jurisdictions.[26] Nor could it be said that the Peruvian state exerted significant control over ideological processes, which would have allowed it to define a coherent national culture. The state's inability to do so was in part a function of the underdeveloped nature of its bureaucracy and the limited range of social activities it could effectively monitor. In addition, peculiarities of Peru's postcolonial history further contributed to the difficulties the state had in attempting to develop a truly national citizenry or culture. Particularly important in this regard was the relationship between the actual practice of class and racially based domination in the many regional domains that dotted the Peruvian landscape and the egalitarian discourse of a Peruvian nation-state that was still more imagined than real.

Although Peru had been founded as an independent state in the 1820s on the liberal principles of democracy, citizenship, private property, and individual rights and protections, the central government was not remotely able to make good on these pledges even 100 years later. Such principles were uniformly invoked in all political ritual and discourse, but everyday life in much of the country was organized according to principles that were directly opposed to these precepts of popular sovereignty. Chachapoyas, in the northern sierra, was one such region. Dominating the social and political landscape of this region was a group of white, aristocratic families of putatively Spanish descent who saw it as their birthright to rule over the region's multitudinous mestizo and Indian peasant population.

The practical problems of governing meant that the central regime in Lima was forced to ally with such aristocratic families if it was to maintain even a semblance of control in the national territory as a whole. It was they who wielded armed force, controlled appointments to the government bureaucracy, and ruled in the name of the central government. At any given time, select elements of the landed class in Chachapoyas enjoyed the backing of the central government, but this class was far from unified. Rather, all members of the elite saw themselves as having the inherited right to rule that *no one*, neither the central government nor other members of the elite, could legitimately deny them. Furthermore, the elite did not hesitate to use violence in exercising these rights. In a sense, elite men regarded themselves as having no true peers, and certainly no masters. Rather, each believed he had the right to use power in defense of prerogatives that were legitimately his because of the elite station in life that he enjoyed by right of birth.

As a result of this state of affairs, in the opening decades of the twentieth century the operation of the state apparatus and the imagined community of the nation were compromised. The region's landed elite used its control over public institutions to subvert the very forms of egalitarian personhood and homogeneous public imagined in national discourse. National discourse emphasized equality before the law, citizenship, and constitutional rights as the only legitimate basis for national life. These principles, however, were in blatant contradiction of the racial hierarchy and inherited privilege of the elite and were belied by the violent struggles for power that occurred as different factions of the elite, each with its own extensive clientele of mestizo artisans and "Indian" peasants, battled for regional control.

To address the threat posed by the discourse of popular sovereignty, the ruling *casta* (that is, the ruling faction of the elite) in the Department of Amazonas, within which Chachapoyas lay, repeatedly and publicly demonstrated its ability to ridicule national injunctions about proper behavior. The ruling casta took great care to violate the constitutional protections of those belonging to the opposing casta and to do great harm to their person and property. But just as important as the actual violation of these rights was the ruling faction's demonstration that it could do so with complete impunity. In other words, the ruling faction went to great lengths to compromise state institutions and national discourse, using both to further the aims of social groupings (their own privileged faction), status (superordinate racial categories), and forms of interaction (violence and domination) that were unthinkable within the discourse of the nation-state.

The Emergence of APRA

OPPOSITION TO CHACHAPOYAS'S elite-dominated aristocratic order began to emerge in the mid-1920s. It was led by youth from marginalized poor and middle sectors of urban society who had few avenues of upward mobility and who were denigrated by the racial logic of regional society. Although these disaffected youth drew on an eclectic mix of radical ideas to make sense of the predicament of their country, they identified themselves as communists. So strongly did they feel about the need for change that, at great risk to themselves, they organized an underground communist cell in Chachapoyas. Throughout the late 1920s, at nighttime meetings conducted in secret to avoid detection by the police, they read and discussed a range of radical materials that had been smuggled into the region.[27]

A turning point in the political evolution of Chachapoyas's communist youth came when they read and discussed *Por la emancipación de América Latina*, a work written by Haya de la Torre.[28] They found that Haya addressed the problems of their region and their nation in a way that communist doctrine, important though it was, could not. The members of the cell found particularly persuasive the author's argument about the historical particularity of Latin America. Haya de la Torre argued that the historical trajectories of Europe and Latin America were different, and therefore that Marxist theory, which was based on the historical development of Europe, could not be applied to Latin America without significant modification. True to their radical inclinations, cell members applauded Haya de la Torre's call for a socialism that was suited to the peculiarities of history and land tenure in Latin America.

In the early months of 1930 these young people sent a message to APRA's Central Committee in Lima asking for more information about APRA. The party leadership was quick to respond, shortly thereafter sending Manuel Chávez Vargas, a skilled organizer, to bring Haya's message to Chachapoyas. It was he who transformed the town's youth into "priests of democracy"—a disciplined, committed group of party cadres who exemplified the remade men and women the party sought to form and who were capable of conveying Haya's doctrine to the general population.[29]

Chávez Vargas arrived in Chachapoyas in the latter part of 1930, made contact with the local Apristas, and immediately began to organize. In addition to establishing the organizational structure of the party (which consisted of a series of ministries, or secretariats, for the department as a whole, as well as provincial commands and district-level cells), Chávez Vargas began training the group of twenty or so young radicals in the town who had already shown the most interest in Aprismo.

Chávez Vargas's efforts to form the party were made considerably more difficult by the fact that he was forced to carry out all organizing activities in secret. From the moment of its inception APRA had been viewed as dangerously radical by the central government, and with the exception of brief periods of quasi-legality, during the first twenty-five years of its existence the party was subject to brutal and relentless persecution by successive central regimes in Lima. Symptomatic of the repressive environment in which APRA was forced to carry out its activities was the situation of Chávez Vargas himself. When he arrived in Chachapoyas, Chávez Vargas was already a fugitive from justice. The central government had issued a general order for his arrest and had circulated this order to all prefects in the country. As a result, Chávez Vargas had to live under an assumed name and was forced to change residences on a regular basis to avoid detection by the authorities. Were it not for the fact that a number of police were themselves Apristas, even these precautions would not have been adequate to protect him. With the tacit assistance of at least some of the forces of order, however, Chávez Vargas was able to go about his organizing activities, but only as long as these did not become visible to the public or an embarrassment to the authorities.

It was not only Chávez Vargas who put himself at great risk by being involved in the organizing activities of the party. So, too, did the twenty-odd young radicals who became the core of the movement in Chachapoyas. The authorities were at pains to maintain a public sphere in which APRA had no presence, and those who sought to bring the party out into the open did so at their peril. Indeed, individuals who did not respect the authorities' insistence that APRA remain invisible, and who were apprehended in the course of seeking to provide the party with public exposure, could face anything from a lengthy prison term to deportation to a remote penal colony in the jungle (where many people died), arrest and torture, a long stretch in solitary confinement, and various forms of physical abuse. Only to the extent that APRA remained entirely underground was the party able to develop its alternative moral vision. Even then, however, the Apristas remained at risk. The police constantly sought to infiltrate the movement, and their informers became a regular part of the social environment with which party members had to deal. In a very real sense, then, APRA was forced to carry out its organizing activities in a context of extreme danger and insecurity. In these circumstances many of the qualities that Haya called upon his followers to adopt—not only discipline, self-sacrifice, obedience, trust, and group cooperation but also secrecy and subterfuge—were necessary for survival.

One of Chávez Vargas's primary goals in training the young Apristas was to produce a party vanguard, to form leaders who could take over the operation of the party apparatus in the Chachapoyas region and shoulder the responsibility of indoctrinating the local population over the long term. To produce such a vanguard, Chávez Vargas began by steeping the young radicals of Chachapoyas in Aprista philosophy and social policy. That is, he provided the apprentice Apristas with a comprehensive and in-depth analysis of the party's plan to reform Peru's social structure so as to make the country a more just place to live for the laboring poor and middle classes. In conveying to his students how APRA intended to remake Peru, Chávez Vargas stressed the party's plan to nationalize land and industry (especially mining) and to diffuse cooperative organizations throughout all branches of the economy. He also stressed APRA's plan to cleanse the state apparatus of elite influence and to reorganize the state in such a way as to ensure extensive input from the cooperative organizations of which the economy was to be composed. Finally, Chávez Vargas explained the party's plan to establish direct, participatory democracy and mass citizenship in which poor and marginalized groups (especially Indian peasants and women) that had long been excluded from membership in the political community would be granted an active role in political life for the first time. These reforms appealed powerfully to the young communists-turned-Apristas of Chachapoyas.

If they were to become party leaders, Chávez Vargas told his followers, they would have to do far more than simply learn party doctrine, important though that was. They would also have to endure great self-sacrifice. They would have to undergo a series of profound personal transformations before they could become true priests of democracy. Only then could they be entrusted with the all-important task of leading Peru toward a more just and equitable future. To prepare his apprentices for this task, Chávez Vargas immersed them in an intense program of training, indoctrination, and moralization. Over a period of five to six years they met in secret nighttime sessions several times a week. At these meetings Chávez Vargas explained to his followers that the success of the party depended on them. APRA could succeed in its mission, he said, only if its members stood out as shining examples of the remade men and women the party sought to form throughout the country. It was therefore essential that they conduct themselves at all times with the utmost rectitude, so that the general population could not fail to see the difference between Apristas and people involved in the degenerate ways of the aristocratic order. He warned them that the path would not be easy. "Many are called but few are chosen," he told them.

The Culture of Aprismo in Chachapoyas

To HELP GUIDE THEM on the path to becoming priests of democracy, Chávez Vargas taught his charges essential new disciplines of the mind and body—disciplines whose importance had been underscored by Haya de la Torre himself. To train the mind, Chávez Vargas had them read, discuss, and critique major works of political and economic theory that had bearing on the problems of Latin America. He was careful to place special emphasis on the ability to explain the strengths and weaknesses of different doctrines to simple, untutored folk, and constantly tested and assessed the abilities of his followers to do so. To assist his apprentices in developing new disciplines of the body, Chávez Vargas taught them to avoid the excesses considered typical of youth, sex and alcohol in particular. He encouraged good hygiene, regular sleeping habits, and moderation in alcohol consumption. He taught the young Apristas to do calisthenics daily upon waking, helped them organize soccer and volleyball teams, and insisted that they practice and compete on a regular basis. He also carefully monitored their conduct in these areas and had them monitor one another's conduct as well.

Chávez Vargas sought to make his novices as "cultured" as possible. There were two dimensions to this. On the one hand, aspiring party leaders had to acquire the knowledge and master the skills needed to defend their rights. For example, they had to master self-defense techniques, become proficient in the use of firearms, and learn how to evade the police. They also had to have a thorough grasp of the works of Marx, Proudhon, and Gandhi and be able to explain them succinctly and spontaneously to a variety of audiences. On the other hand, these future leaders had to develop the courage and integrity necessary to face the dangers involved in challenging injustice. To help them do so, Chávez Vargas involved his apprentices in "missions" in which they performed important tasks for the party, from delivering secret messages to Apristas in other towns to spreading party propaganda in the dead of night, gathering intelligence from the police and other government functionaries, and organizing new party cells. The missions were graded by level of difficulty, and Chávez Vargas was careful to expose his fledgling party leaders to progressively more risk. In this way he was able to gauge the degree to which they were developing the courage necessary to assume positions of party leadership.

As their training continued, Chávez Vargas carefully evaluated his novices' progress toward becoming priests of democracy, paying special attention to each person's strengths and weaknesses. He did so with an eye to who would be best suited to fill each of the fifteen secretariats of which the party was composed. After training his apprentices for half a decade and observing their behavior in increasingly trying circumstances, Chávez Vargas decided that they had matured to the point that they could assume direct control over the party apparatus. After assigning each novice his own secretariat, Chávez Vargas stepped down from his position of leadership in the party.

Throughout the entire period that Chávez Vargas trained his followers, he encouraged them to see themselves as martyrs to a greater cause: that of bringing justice, prosperity and democracy to the masses of Peru. The image of Haya de la Torre played an essential role throughout this entire process. If Chávez Vargas asked his leaders-in-training to forsake life's ordinary pleasures and aspirations, to discipline their minds and bodies, to regard their own interests as secondary to those of their party and nation, the model he constantly held out before them was Haya. The leader of APRA, he taught them, was a man who had sacrificed everything for the good of his country and his fellow citizens, and who called upon them to assist him in his efforts to bring into being a more just social order. To repeat, if Haya was the savior of Peru, APRA's cadres were his political apostles. They were to spread the good word, lead by example, and seize every opportunity to proselytize among the population as a whole.

APRA's Shadow State

THE ENORMOUS INFLUENCE that Haya exercised over the general population was not strictly a function of his charismatic personality, nor did the party's prominent place in Peruvian politics result only from APRA's ability to train a group of highly disciplined cadres, formed in Haya's image, who were deeply committed to APRA's vision of social transformation. Equally important to Haya's prominence and to APRA's success were the uses to which the priests of democracy put the party apparatus and the way they employed Haya's image in the process.

The complex organizational structure that Haya de la Torre designed served the party very well in its efforts to survive government repression. In some respects, this party structure reproduced the territorial grid of the Peruvian state. Thus, there were (in theory) APRA cells or committees for each district, province, and department in Peru, and a national committee for the country as a whole. The actual makeup of these cells, however, their manner of operation, and the powers and responsibilities allotted to the members of each reflected a degree of specialization and differentiation that went far beyond that of the formal state apparatus. APRA organized itself into a series of departments, or ministries. Throughout Peru there were ministries of the interior, organization, propaganda, discipline, culture, popular education, higher education, economy, social welfare, unions, labor, cooperatives, municipal government, indigenous and peasant affairs, and youth.[30] As the names suggest, each ministry was responsible for attending to the affairs of particular subgroups or activities. Furthermore, the prerogatives and responsibilities of each department were carefully spelled out. This meant that party secretaries were on hand to provide people with key services that they otherwise lacked, such as medical care, legal help, occasional financial assistance, advice about how to deal with abusive political officials, and even counseling about marital problems and spousal abuse.

By drawing on this party structure, APRA was able to involve itself directly in the everyday lives of the population, even though the party was forced to operate in secret, beyond the gaze of the legally constituted authorities. APRA attempted to have secretaries for as many of its ministries as possible in every cell or committee, whether it was the cell of a remote rural district or a large urban center. This meant that the bureaucracy that the party generated was considerably thicker than that of the formal state apparatus, whose representatives were sparsely scattered about the national territory.[31]

APRA was also careful to ensure that the behavior of its secretaries was in stark contrast to that of Peruvian government functionaries, who were infamous for extorting sexual favors, labor, and goods from the people under their jurisdiction (practices encouraged by the fact that they received no salary). State functionaries were equally well-known for imposing jail terms and corporal punishment on those who resisted their demands, and for ruling in the most arbitrary and personalistic of manners. The members of APRA took a very different attitude toward the population at large. APRA understood its mission in quite daunting terms. Haya and his priests of democracy hoped to effect what they characterized as a wholesale transformation of Peruvian society so as to make it democratic, inclusive, and just. APRA sought to transform Peru by eliminating the material and cultural markers of difference that segregated the country into separate groups (based on race, class, and gender). It was these distinctions, the party argued, that had long been used to justify excluding the majority from positions of socioeconomic, political, or cultural importance. In seeking to do away with such distinctions, APRA's sacerdotes represented themselves as seeking to establish an egalitarian society in which the great mass of the population would enjoy what they had been denied—constitutional rights and protections, safeguards ensuring their material well-being, the freedom to develop their abilities to the fullest, and the right to help determine the conditions in which they lived and worked. APRA saw one of its functions as providing those who did not yet benefit from them the rights, protections, and guarantees that the party hoped to make the basis of its more just and inclusive society of the future.

Party priests were able to extend some rights and protections to those who lacked them by adopting a novel strategy vis-à-vis the state apparatus. This strategy did not consist of a frontal assault on state institutions. Instead, APRA was able to transform the operation of these institutions by offering its own party apparatus as an alternative to state institutions at the latter's key point of contact with the general populace (especially within the rural districts), and to supplement or fill in for state institutions where the underdeveloped nature of the state apparatus had left gaps or openings into which the party might insert itself.

Quotidian Practices of Shadow Governance

HAYA'S CAREFULLY CONSTRUCTED STRUCTURE of governance did more, however, than simply offer institutional alternatives to the existing state of affairs. APRA's institutions and procedures also helped crystallize, actualize, and normalize a new vision of state, nation, society, and individual. To see how the party reworked the institutions of state, and how it articulated a new image of state and society in the process, we can compare the activities of Peru's formal state apparatus and the activities of APRA's party structure with respect to a problem that was endemic to the region, one that generated ongoing contact between the rural poor and the state. The problem in question had to do with the theft of livestock. The contrast in how it was dealt with sheds light on the APRA party's ability to generate intense loyalty on the part of the populace despite the repression to which APRA was subject at the hands of the state.

As elsewhere in the Peruvian Andes, the theft of livestock was among the most common problems faced by peasants in the Chachapoyas region.[32] A peasant whose livestock had been stolen could in theory appeal to the *personero*, the legal representative of the peasant community. The personero was then to inform the justice of the peace and the governor of the district in question. The justice was then responsible for carrying out an investigation in order to determine who the guilty party was. He was to interview witnesses, suspects, the injured party, and anyone else deemed relevant to the case. He was also to visit the scene of the crime, and collect whatever evidence was considered important.

Once the justice had determined who he believed was at fault, he would inform the governor, who was to order the person detained. The governor did not have a trained police force at his disposal and thus would be forced to deputize several ordinary people to apprehend the person in question. With the assistance of the personero, the deputies would then take the person prisoner and would place him at the disposition of the justice and the governor. As punishment, in addition to returning the stolen animals to their owner, the justice would often order the thief to work for the injured party, the number of days depending on the value of the livestock.

These legal procedures were in theory available to all peasants. Actual practice, however, was quite different. The ruling *casta* appointed all governors, justices of the peace, and personeros, and these individuals were responsible for using their positions in order to make public statements about the potency of their casta vis-à-vis the opposition, which mounted challenges to the ruling casta whenever possible. One way that functionaries like the governor and the justice of the peace could make such statements was by demonstrating the ability of their casta to disregard or even violate the rights of the opposition without suffering any reprisals. As a result, the governor and the justice went out of their way to ignore the claims of opposing casta members concerning stolen livestock, just as these functionaries went out of their way to extort labor and wealth from the opposition. The governor and the justice were equally scrupulous about showing that they could protect the rights of their own clients. To do otherwise would be to reveal ruling casta weakness, which would in turn invite armed challenge from the opposition.

One important consequence of the fact that the ruling casta controlled the administration of justice was that large numbers of people, especially poor ones, were unable to protect their belongings (or even themselves) from the predations of those in power. However, this system of justice did far more than reproduce casta conflict and class inequality. Embedded in the procedures followed by state representatives at their ongoing point of contact with the populace was a vision of sovereignty that conveyed clear and unambiguous messages about the nature of state rule and the national community. This vision of sovereignty was in direct contradiction to the egalitarian discourse of the nation-state.

Everyday judicial practice invoked a deeply stratified and hierarchical community in which race, class, gender and lineage defined a range of social categories, each with distinct and unequal rights and obligations. Those who were born to positions of rule (white, elite men) would care for their dependents (women of their own class, men and women of inferior classes) as long as the latter knew their place and adopted the appropriate behaviors of deference and respect. But there was no sense in which all individuals were considered equally endowed with rights, powers, and protections, nor was there any sense in which the administration of justice helped actualize or defend the equality asserted by the nation-state's egalitarian discourse, nor was there any sense in which people who occupied nonelite categories were seen by those who controlled the state apparatus as entitled to legal recourse simply by virtue of the fact that their rights had been violated. To the contrary: in the eyes of the elite, "justice" was something they could dispense as they saw fit, to be bestowed on the fortunate few who had curried elite favor.

The day-to-day operation of the state apparatus at its ongoing point of contact with the general population thus blatantly demonstrated the absence of a disinterested state apparatus that operated according to the principles of popular sovereignty. The administration of justice also revealed the authorities' utter disregard for impartial principles of justice, and showed that private interest ruled over the public good. It was this void of constitutional rights for poor and marginalized individuals that APRA attempted to fill.

As mentioned earlier, the party structure designed by Haya de la Torre consisted of a nested hierarchy of cells, from district to department, each of which was made up of secretaries who represented the various ministries of which APRA was composed. Among these individuals was a secretary of justice. A peasant whose livestock had been stolen and who had a connection to the party had an important option not available to other peasants. He or she could explain the problem to the district-level secretary of justice. Should the secretary conclude that the peasant had just cause (which was anything but a foregone conclusion), he would set the party apparatus in motion to defend the person in question. The secretary did so by referring the matter to the departmental secretary of justice. This individual would inform the departmental secretary general, who would generally call a special session of the departmental command, which was made up of the departmental secretaries for all party ministries. These individuals would then collectively work out a strategy for helping the peasant. Most commonly, the command would devise a plan for approaching someone who worked in the Superior Court of Amazonas. This was less difficult than it might seem. Among the lawyers, judges, and clerks who worked in the Superior Court there were almost always some party members. If there were none, however, then the departmental command would attempt to approach some other high-ranking government official, who could in turn speak to a Superior Court representative. This was a viable strategy, for two reasons. First, all the departmental secretaries were responsible for cultivating good relations with the departmental authorities—the prefect, the police chief, and so on. Maintaining close personal ties with these individuals was an obligation for departmental secretaries, who had to be individuals who were widely admired and respected. It was not uncommon, for example, for members of the departmental command to be the drinking partners of high-ranking public officials. Second, many of these secretaries had formerly held positions of greater or lesser importance in the state bureaucracy.[33] During their tenures as state officials they had controlled resources and had directed decision-making processes that allowed them to dispense a large number of favors, and in the process they had established strong and lasting interdependencies with considerable numbers of people. When Apristas in the party's departmental command sought to influence a public official on behalf of one of their fellows, the Aprista leaders were therefore doing more than just asking. They were activating long-standing interdependencies of kinship, friendship, and alliance.

By drawing on networks they had established when they had been political officials and by exploiting the fact that some state authorities were themselves secretly Apristas, APRA members were often able to intercede on behalf of the aggrieved peasant. The peasant was then able to prevail despite the wishes of the governor and the justice of the peace, and despite the wishes of the ruling casta as a whole.

APRA was thus able to link its subterranean party structure with select elements of the Peruvian state to effect a shift in how state power was articulated among poor and marginalized groups. As a result, individuals who would otherwise have had no legal recourse found themselves with new options. By offering an alternative to local state institutions at their ongoing point of contact with the populace, by using the party apparatus in the defense of principles that were blatantly disregarded by the state, and by adopting procedures that seemed neutral and impartial, APRA provided people with a very different view of what the state could look like, of what the state could do, and of what their relationship to the state might be. Although this state was still more absent than present, APRA's ability to subvert the normal operation of the state, and to do so in ways that produced tangible results for marginalized groups, provided glimpses or flashes of the APRA state-to-be. Brief though these flashes were, they left a powerful impression on the imaginations of many people, who felt drawn to the alternative moral and political universe the party appeared to represent.

The sense that APRA represented a moral alternative to the existing state of affairs was reinforced by the "disinterested" nature of its activities. The party was always very careful not to charge for the services it made available to the general populace, and Apristas who tried to use their positions to enrich themselves were expelled from the party (after a trial by their peers).[34] And finally, even if the momentary flashes of the future state were more virtual than real—even if aggrieved individuals did not prevail as a result of appealing to APRA's alternative judicial apparatus—people were still left with the impression that there was something "out there" that was struggling to defend their rights, a structure of governance that sought to make present the (legitimate) state that was absent.

APRA's state-in-the-making did not limit its activities to providing protections and safeguarding the rights of those who otherwise lacked them. The party's priests of democracy also invested a great deal of energy in forming new social institutions that operated according to principles that had previously been of limited importance in public culture: egalitarian involvement, democratic decision making, and generalized participation. A great many people joined these organizations, which varied widely in form and function. They included sports clubs (soccer and volleyball), neighborhood associations, social clubs, reading groups, discussion circles, and debating societies—organizations with a predominantly social or cultural orientation. They included, as well, cooperatives of various kinds (especially for savings, credit, and consumption), labor unions, and mutual aid societies—organizations that were more economic and political in nature. Party priests also put major emphasis on strengthening and expanding the institutions in peasant communities that involved cooperative exchanges of labor and the communal ownership of land. Furthermore, the party sought to generalize these organizations as widely as possible, so that an egalitarian, cooperative ethos replaced the hierarchical and authoritarian public culture of the past.

In the course of overseeing all these party activities—from protecting peasants from abusive governors to forming soccer teams to setting up rotating credit associations—APRA's priests of democracy were always careful to make one point abundantly clear to the rank-and-file. While they, as APRA secretaries, had been entrusted with coordinating party affairs on a day-to-day basis, it was Haya de la Torre who had created the party itself. It was through Haya's influence that they had come to see the importance of devoting their lives to the creation of a more just, democratic Peru. It was through Haya's example that they had come to understand how they must change their lives if they were to do so. Haya had taken it upon himself to challenge the old elite and to lead the fight to transform the country's backward, oppressive power structure. He was now calling on all Peruvians to assist him in this noble struggle. Party priests explained that they were doing little more than passing Haya's message on to the masses— that they were seeking to provide the common man and woman with the same guidance that Haya had provided them.

Conclusion

Víctor Raúl Haya de la Torre, founder and leader of the Alianza Popular Revolucionaria Americana, established a political party whose importance to twentieth-century Peruvian politics would be difficult to exaggerate. Haya articulated a message of social justice that had enormous appeal to huge numbers of his fellow citizens, especially those who felt excluded from the country's elite-dominated structures of power. Haya also showed consummate skill in delivering his message in a way that could captivate a broad, national public, just as APRA proved itself unusually capable of building a hero cult around its leader and of drawing on religious symbolism in order to represent Aprismo as a form of secular, political Catholicism. Despite the importance of Haya as a charismatic leader, however, and of the quasi-religious nature of the hero cult that grew up around him and his movement, additional factors were involved in making Haya such an influential figure and in making APRA the most important political party in the history of republican Peru. Particularly important in this regard was the party's ability to institutionalize Haya's charismatic appeal. The party did so by means of its "priests of democracy"—a vanguard of highly trained and disciplined young men and women, formed in Haya's image, who had committed themselves body and soul to the task of social transformation. It was these remade men and women who were put in charge of a novel, underground party structure established throughout much of the country that made a difference in people's daily lives. It was the everyday relationships that APRA's priests of democracy established with the general population that sustained the party and its founder through long periods of illegality and persecution and that gave substance to the image of Haya as a heroic, self-sacrificing figure. These relationships represent an important key to understanding Haya's (and APRA's) broad, long-lasting appeal and his ability to weather multiple changes in constituency and national political climate.

Postscript: By the late 1950s, the first generation of party priests had begun to retire in Chachapoyas, after having seen APRA through almost three decades of dark and difficult days. At the same time, the party, having achieved more public legitimacy on a national scale, was able to climb out of the shadows and became a normal, institutionalized part of the Peruvian political scene. Although his priests in Chachapoyas stepped down from their positions of party leadership, Haya de la Torre continued to direct APRA from Lima. But as the party became increasingly mainstream, it lost more and more of its critical edge—a tendency apparent even prior to the 1950s. Despite APRA's increasingly compromised position nationally, however, the sacerdotes who had founded the party in Chachapoyas remained deeply committed to APRA's original, radical vision. They remained equally committed to Haya, the heroic figure who had steered them down the difficult and demanding path toward personal and national regeneration.

Notes

* An earlier version of this chapter was delivered as a talk at the Colloquium Series of the School of American Research, Santa Fe, in the spring of 2002. I would like to thank colloquium participants for their suggestions regarding the paper. I also owe a debt of gratitude to Tom Biolsi, Samuel Brunk, and Ben Fallaw for their insightful reading of the article. I gratefully acknowledge the generous financial support of the National Endowment for the Humanities, the Colby College Social Science Grants Committee, and the School of American Research.

1. It is difficult to know with any certainty the number of people who crowded into the Plaza de San Martín to see Haya de la Torre on August 15, 1931. *La Tribuna*, the APRA paper, claims 80,000. Other sources are not so optimistic. I have opted for a more conservative number.

2. This reconstruction of the rally of August 15, 1931, is based on *La Tribuna*, 15 August 1931, *Edición extraordinaria*, and 16 August 1931.

3. According to Geoffrey Bertram "Peru, 1930–1960," in *Cambridge History of Latin America*, vol. 8 (Cambridge: Cambridge University Press, 1991) chap. 7, between 1930 and 1960 APRA controlled approximately one-third of the electorate. While this figure is undoubtedly accurate, it is important to remember that neither women nor peasants (if they were illiterate) could vote during this period. In the north of Peru APRA was quite popular with both groups.

4. See Peter Blanchard, *The Origins of the Peruvian Labor Movement, 1883–1919* (Pittsburgh: University of Pittsburgh Press, 1982), and Denis Sulmont, *El movimiento obrero peruano, 1890–1980: Reseña histórica*, 2nd ed. (Lima: Tarea, 1980).

5. See Manuel Burga and Alberto Flores Galindo, *Apogeo y Crisis de la República Aristocrática* (Lima: Instituto de Estudios Peruanos [IEP], 1979); Baltazar Caravedo, "Poder central y decentralización: Peru, 1931," *Apuntes* 5, no. 9 (1977): 111–129; and José Deustua, *Intelectuales, indigenismo, y descentralismo en el Perú, 1897–1931* (Cusco: Centro de Estudios Rurales Andinos "Bartolome de las Casas," 1984).

6. The general outlines of Haya's life are well known. In the section that follows, I have relied on Felipe Cossío del Pomar, *Víctor Raúl*, 2 vols. (Mexico City: Editorial Cultura, 1969); Víctor Raúl Haya de la Torre, *Obras Completas*, 7 vols. (Lima: Juan Mejía Baca, 1977); Peter F. Klaren, "Modernization, Dislocation and Aprismo," Latin American Monographs no. 32 (Austin: Institute of Latin American Studies and University of Texas Press, 1973); Frederick Pike, *The Politics of the Miraculous: Haya de la Torre and the Spiritualist Tradition* (Lincoln: University of Nebraska Press, 1986); Pedro Planas Silva, *Los orígenes del APRA: El joven Haya (mito y realidad de Haya de la Torre)*, 2nd ed. (Lima: Okura Editores, 1986); Luís Alberto Sánchez, *Haya de la Torre o el políti-*

co: *Crónica de una vida sin tregua* (Santiago: Editorial Ercilla, 1934), and *Haya de la Torre y el Apra: Crónica de un hombre y un partido* (Santiago de Chile: Editorial del Pacífico, 1955); and Steve Stein, *Populism in Peru: The Emergence of the Masses and the Politics of Social Control* (Madison: University of Wisconsin Press, 1980).

7. See Sánchez, *Haya de la Torre y el APRA*, 37.

8. See Stein, *Populism in Peru*, 134.

9. Victor Raúl Haya de la Torre, "Mis Recuerdos de González Prada," *Repertorio americano* (San José, Costa Rica), 15, no. 6, 1927.

10. See Steve Stein's authoritative study of the origins of APRA in Lima, *Populism in Peru*, and also his "Populism in Peru: APRA, The Formative Years," in *Latin American Populism in Comparative Perspective*, ed. Michael L. Conniff (Albuquerque: University of New Mexico Press, 1982), 113–134. I have drawn heavily on Stein's account.

11. See Stein, *Populism in Peru*, 133.

12. See Haya de la Torre, "Mis Recuerdos de González Prada."

13. For discussions of the popular universities, see Jeffrey L. Klaiber, "The Popular Universities and the Origins of Aprismo, 1921–1924," *Hispanic American Historical Review* 55, no. 4 (1975): 693–715, and Klaiber's *Religion and Revolution in Peru* (South Bend, Ind.: University of Notre Dame Press, 1977); Lisa North, *Orígenes y crecimiento del Partido Aprista y el cambio socio-económico en el Perú* (Lima: Pontificia Universidad Católica del Peru, 1975); Stein, *Populism in Peru*; and David Nugent, *Modernity at the Edge of Empire: State, Individual and Nation in the Northern Peruvian Andes, 1885–1935* (Stanford, Calif.: Stanford University Press, 1997).

14. See Stein, *Populism in Peru*, 129–130.

15. See Stein, *Populism in Peru*, 131.

16. Textile mills employed more workers and were better organized than other factories in Lima.

17. Haya took up the post of rector of his Popular Universities upon founding them in 1921 and continued in this role until his exile from Peru in 1923.

18. No hero cult has emerged surrounding Haya de la Torre in the brief interim since his death in 1979. The absence of such a cult is an important topic for future research.

19. See Klaren, "Modernization, Dislocation and Aprismo," and Stein, *Populism in Peru*.

20. See Cossío del Pomar, *Víctor Raúl*, and Eudocio Ravines, *The Yenan Way* (New York: Charles Scribner's Sons, 1951).

21. Klaiber, *Religion and Revolution*; Stein, *Populism in Peru*; and Imelda Vega-Centeno B., *Aprismo popular: Cultura, religion y política* (Lima: CISEPA y Tarea, 1991).

22. See Stein, *Populism in Peru*, 154, 259–260.

23. It is nonetheless true that the process by which party dictates were arrived at could be considerably more democratic. This was especially the case in the early years of the party in major urban centers such as Lima. In remote provincial towns such as Chachapoyas, on the other hand, democratic decision making continued far longer.

24. "Priests of democracy" is a term that the Apristas of the Chachapoyas region of northern Peru used to refer to one another. The activities of APRA in Chachapoyas are discussed later in the chapter.

25. See Max Weber, *Economy and Society*, ed. Guenther Roth and Claus Wittich, 2 vols. (Berkeley and Los Angeles: University of California Press, 1968).

26. In addition to government posts themselves being sources of enrichment, the ability to name people to positions in the bureaucracy was very lucrative. Those who

exercised this power charged a fee to those who were so appointed, who were in turn left to recoup their investment (and more) in their day-to-day interactions with the populace under their jurisdiction.

27. The main source of these ideas was upper-class youth from Chachapoyas who were able to pursue university training in Lima. A number of these individuals returned from Lima to discuss the radical ideologies that were circulating through the national capital during this era.

28. See Victor Raúl Haya de la Torre, *Por la emancipación de América Latina: Artículos, mensajes, discursos 1923–1927* (Buenos Aires: Gleizer, 1927).

29. While APRA's gender politics were unusually progressive for the era in question, it is nonetheless true that women occupied few positions of leadership in the party. A more detailed discussion of this point is beyond the scope of this chapter.

30. As a number of authors have noted, Haya de la Torre was heavily influenced by the discipline and order of fascist and communist parties he observed during his trip to Europe in the 1920s.

31. Every district in Peru was administered by a governor, justice of the peace, and mayor. Every province was managed by a subprefect (and small supporting cast), a provincial judge, and a mayor. Every department was administered by a prefect (and his subalterns) and a superior court.

32. See Carlos Aguirre and Charles Walker, eds., *Bandoleros, abigeos, y montoneros: Criminalidad y violencia en el Perú, siglos XVIII–XX* (Lima: Instituto de Apoyo Agrario, 1990).

33. Party members had to obtain special permission from the departmental command to occupy a position in the state bureaucracy. During the period the Aprista worked for the state he generally stepped down from his position as a party leader, but resumed his post when he stopped working for the government.

34. There were some exceptions to this rule. For example, when the secretary of welfare interceded with a physician in order to make medical care available to someone who would not otherwise have had access to it, the physician was not expected to subsidize the cost of medicine (although he usually provided his services without charge).

Evita Perón

Beauty, Resonance, and Heroism

LINDA B. HALL

Because Eva, with all her ignorance as a bastard child, as a woman who suffered during her childhood and everything, had something very great, very noble, that only the great ones have. She loved the poor; she used to enter the shacks without having them disinfected first. That is very important. She would go up to the bed itself.

Doña María Roldán, in Daniel James, *Doña María's Story*

In the other world, in the other memory, she hasn't forgotten us. We will dress her in her finest raiments, and once more, in her presence, we will repeat the oath to obey her unto death, and beyond death, too. . . . If she has deigned to return among us, it must be to bring us the peace that we need so badly. Hail to the Dead Woman! Hail to the Virgin! Hail!"

Luisa Valenzuela, *The Lizard's Tail*

After all this, only in death is it possible to be, as Evita, immortal.

Tomás Eloy Martínez, *Santa Evita*

What qualities and actions make a woman heroic? Heroism is largely associated with success in battle, with great courage, with overcoming dangerous obstacles, with leadership. While Eva Perón—better known to all as Evita—was no battlefield hero, she established her heroism during her own lifetime. Her image as heroic in behalf of the weak against the powerful has been both reinforced and attacked by the governments that have followed the first presidency of her husband, Juan Perón. But that image has proved resistant to promiscuous political use, either positive or negative. Peronist attempts to appropriate her appeal after her death largely failed to help their political cause, while her memory continued to have its own special power and resonance with the Argentine people. Attempts by various anti-Peronist governments to prevent the continuance of her popularity by restricting public observances of her memory and even hiding her body for a period of time also failed to erase her image in the public mind. A powerful woman outside the institutional structure of power, a living remembrance in the minds of Argentines, hated as well as loved, she was arguably the most important female political figure in the history of the country. She was deeply involved with the labor movement as her husband's representative, she undertook extensive and highly visible charitable activity, and she organized and led the Peronist Women's Party. The quotation from Doña María Roldán that introduces this essay speaks to her courage—a willingness to risk her life and health to help the poor. The other two quotations, from fictional accounts, reflect her continuing iconic status. Whether one admires her or not, Eva Perón was deeply connected to and identified with working-class Argentines, her "*descamisados,*" or "shirtless ones," during her life and revered by them after her death. She was strong in the face of terminal illness and was willing to contemplate and prepare for violence in the face of political challenges. All of these activities were involved with and sometimes challenging to the state while remaining relatively untainted by state bureaucracy. As Julie Taylor has observed, "To many Peronists, Eva, the woman herself, was the revolutionary element within their movement: Eva Perón as a person acted in a way that no one else dared act."[1] So she was perceived by the left in 1971, approximately at the time that the Peronist party was again legalized by the Argentine state. As one observer stated, "She exemplified personal force at the service of the Revolution. . . . In all this she is like el Che Guevara. For us Evita is the spirit of the guerrilla."[2] At the same time, she was beautiful and successful, a public figure before she was a political one, and she had a great story. As Cinderella, she ascended from the ashes to the height of political power and fame and from deprivation to material abundance. The combinations of actions and story, courage and image, led to an unprecedented resonance between a female political leader and the Argentine working classes who took her as their champion. It is the development of this resonance that I explore in this essay.

Argentina has been desperately troubled politically in the half-century since Evita's death. The kinds of unifying symbols and myths constructed in Mexico in the wake of its revolution, 1910–1920 (see especially Chapters 5 and 6), proved impossible to sustain in a nation riven by political polarization, military governments, violence from left and right, repression, and exile. Evita has been among the most polarizing of Argentine political figures, one that raises the raw edges of class, poverty, and privilege, one that Argentine governments since the end of the military repression of the Proceso, 1975–1983, have been reluctant to invoke. Still, she has remained in the memory of many and is still used by the Peronist party and by elements of the labor movement as an inspiration and touchstone of loyalty. Were she to be selected by the state in the ways that Mexican and Cuban revolutionary heroes have been for honor and commemoration, it is unclear just what image might be projected. Probably she would be remembered as a liberator for women, a champion of the working class, a woman who sacrificed her own health for that of her countrymen and -women. In order to understand these images, which exist within Argentina whether or not the state has chosen to emphasize them, it is important to look both at what she actually did and how her activities were presented to the Argentine public during her lifetime. Further, we must look to the way in which she was almost deified during the process of her dying, and then both remembered and deliberately obscured. When Perón was overthrown, three years after her death, her body was considered so potentially powerful that it was hidden for decades, and the desire to recuperate it was so strong on the part of the left that it led to the political murder of a former president.

Her story is full of contradictions. She was a leader; her battleground was the intersection of the poor and the rich in Argentina, her course was always precarious, her position was full of peril. The working classes of Argentina recognized that she had not chosen the easy path, and they rallied to support her, both the living woman and the dead but not forgotten one, as they felt she had supported them. Even when her actions might seem to be self-serving, her supporters stayed with her. Perhaps she maintained her backing because she framed her political projects in a traditional way—supporting her man—but more likely because her followers identified her well-being and her story with their own. When Juan Perón returned from exile in 1973, he brought with him another wife who he hoped would reestablish the feminine political presence and resonance that Evita had created with Argentines. That hope was futile, and, after his death, the short presidency of Isabel Perón was a failure and led to one of Latin America's most repressive military governments. Who was Eva Perón, this effective, powerful woman, and what was the milieu in which she was able to thrive?

Doña María Roldán's recollection at the beginning of this chapter gives us several clues. The example she uses of Evita's courage is her entrance into the shacks of the poor "without having them disinfected first." She follows with the indication, "That is very important." It is, indeed. Her willingness physically to embrace the poor and the suffering is well and extensively documented. Not only was she courageous, she was one of them—"a bastard child, a woman who suffered during her childhood and everything. . . ."[3] She empathized; she approached and touched. The disadvantaged were significant to her; as Doña María points out, "She loved the poor." Many of Evita's critics have doubted the sincerity of her claims of love, which served her so well in her own political power and that of her husband. I would maintain, however, that it was precisely the sincerity of that love and her sense of herself as the advocate of those in need against those who had much that actually made her effective. Her own background, as a woman who had suffered both poverty and social slights during her own childhood, led her to understand the people to whom she appealed, and this understanding resonated with them. It also made her intransigent in the face of those with wealth, those who had made her suffer before and sometimes after she became powerful. Her empathy, on the one hand, and her obvious and vital anger on the other were factors in the connection that her followers would feel to her.

Her message and her empathy would have failed, however, had they not reached a receptive audience. In the early decades of the twentieth century, hundreds of thousands of immigrants arrived in Argentina, particularly from Spain and Italy. These immigrants settled in Buenos Aires or made their way into the interior. Many of the newcomers thrived, creating an expanded middle class as well as providing skilled labor, but leading to a defensive reaction among nationalistic upper-class Argentines. After 1930 this emigration slowed significantly, although in 1947, 26 percent of the Argentine population was still foreign-born. World War II led to a significant growth in industrial production and a huge increase in the numbers of industrial workers in the country. Most of this increase in industrial capacity was located in and around the capital city, and much of it, especially the meat-packing plants where Doña María, among others, worked, was foreign-owned. The majority of the new industrial workers of the war years were internal migrants from the countryside. Between 1935 and 1946, the number of industrial workers increased from fewer than 500,000 to more than one million. By 1947, almost 1,400,000 migrants had arrived in Buenos Aires from the countryside. However, before the military government of which Juan Perón was a part took power in 1943, the armed forces repressed rather than cooperated with organized labor. Given heavy employer and state repression, it was very difficult for the working class to do anything to improve their situation, and, in general, real wages declined from an already low level. In 1937, for example, 60 percent of working-class families in Buenos Aires occupied only one room, and conditions became more crowded in the following years. The large numbers of foreign-born workers and their children were, moreover, scarcely considered Argentine because of the heavily nationalistic ideologies of the upper class.

It was Juan Perón's genius that led him to support the labor movement and eventually to bring it under his own control, first as secretary of labor under the military government and then as president of the country. His rhetorical attacks on foreign-owned business and the oligarchy, messages echoed by his wife, along with his definitions of workers as citizens of his "New Argentina," whether they were foreign-born or not, tapped powerful emotional currents. As filmmaker Maria Luisa Bemberg, whose wealthy family was targeted by the Peróns, has noted, "in Argentina, the dominant class lived apart, either unaware of or refusing to acknowledge the different historical winds that were blowing, thus allowing the political void to be filled by Peronism, a movement that knew very well how to attract the more disadvantaged classes—people without voice or vote, faceless and completely ignored by the oligarchy. . . ." The political repression and voting fraud perpetrated by the employers and the upper classes, she said, "contributed to the explosion of Peronism. . . ."[4] After Juan Perón's marriage to Eva Duarte, an internal migrant herself with strong feelings of injustice, she became his most important collaborator in stirring these feelings in the masses and enlisting them in their shared political project.

The vividness of her rage was something that her future husband noticed on first meeting her in 1944. As the secretary of labor in the military government, he was organizing relief efforts for the victims of an earthquake in the town of San Juan. A group of individuals from the entertainment industry had agreed to collect funds at a benefit for the victims. Evita came with others to the Secretariat to pick up the boxes for the donations, and, as Juan Perón reported, her intensity was stunning: "I was quite subdued by the force of her voice and her look. Eva was pale but when she spoke her face seemed to catch fire. Her hands were reddened with tension, her fingers knit tightly together, she was a mass of nerves."[5]

Evita's background and story were crucial to her attraction to and for the Argentine masses. Her birth was illegitimate. A major biography sets the date of her birth as May 7, 1919, in the tiny town of Los Toldos, and indicates that she was baptized in November of the same year.[6] Her mother's surname, Ibarguren, was used, rather than her father's, Duarte. Very shortly thereafter, Juan Duarte returned to his legal wife, despite a liaison of several years with Evita's mother. He left her with five children and no resources to speak of. Doña Juana apparently felt this fall from security and reasonable comfort bitterly. Evita, the youngest child, must scarcely have known her father. The townspeople were apparently unkind; references to Doña Juana's attempts to replace Juan Duarte were repeated secretly and sometimes openly to her children. The older daughters suffered as well from negative comments on their honor, despite the lack of evidence of lovers.

References to Evita's own easy virtue accompanied her rise to fame. A particularly agonizing memory for her must have been the events surrounding the death of her father. She was six years old when he died, and Doña Juana decided to take the children to the funeral, a strong and surprising assertion of her emotional and familial rights and those of her children. Unsurprisingly, they were denied entrance, and heated words resulted. Finally, after the intervention of Duarte's wife's brother, they were permitted to view the body briefly and later to follow the hearse—but not, of course, in front with the legal family—to the graveyard. Evita's own autobiography leaves out mention of her childhood, a childhood economically precarious and full of a shame not of her making.

A move to Junín provided the family with some respectability. Doña Juana (now representing herself as Duarte's widow) opened a boarding house catering to unmarried men. Two of them married Evita's sisters, but the youngest daughter was looking for something more. A quiet child, she spent much time at the cinema and loved movie magazines. Somehow, in her early teens, she managed to make her way to Buenos Aires, first appearing in traveling plays and reviews, then on the radio—especially soap operas—and even in films. Later rumors had it that she left Junín with a famous tango singer who happened to pass through, but there seems to be no evidence of that. However it happened, it does seem that she was not without male company, and that these men were often in a position to help her with her career. Later accounts by her enemies claimed that she had been a prostitute; while this charge was untrue, it certainly seems that she used her attractiveness and sexuality to help her climb the ladder of success. Yet Argentines, with the exception of the oligarchy, seemed inclined to forgive her early transgressions. Perhaps they understood the compromises her own struggles had required, as, perhaps, they had made some of their own. During her life, an adoring cult grew up around her in which she developed a charismatic and saintly image, her personal accessibility and involvement in acts of giving turning into epiphanies—appearances and miracles, it seemed, supernatural and superhuman in nature, to use Max Weber's terms.[7]

Despite initial struggles, she was already very successful by the end of 1939, and rumors about her date from the preceding several years when she needed help. Gossip connected her with the editor of a magazine that gave her some publicity, a manufacturer of household products, and a poet, Hector Blomberg, who wrote radio scripts for a living. When a new radio series featuring his work began, Evita had a leading part. Meanwhile, her sexual attractiveness was the focus of what publicity she got.[8]

The Argentine radio network was at this point the second-largest commercial system in the world, and soap operas were of enormous importance. The scripts, written in just a couple of hours before broadcast, focused on love frustrated and finally love fulfilled. The heroines were usually poor and the male objects of their affection well above them in status and wealth, leading to many opportunities for emotive female suffering. Evita was good at these roles, and her own life had an eerily similar scenario. Meanwhile, she had kept in close touch with her family, although she had not returned regularly to Junín. Her brother Juan, however, was working in the soap business in Buenos Aires, and he arranged for the Guerreno Company, the manufacturer of Radical Soap, to sponsor all of his sister's programs. Although she was not paid directly by the soap manufacturer, the huge amount of advertising revenue that her presence guaranteed made her an attractive option for those deciding what would be broadcast. By this time she had her own production company, which by 1943 had successfully moved its programs to the most important station in the country. She was about twenty-four years old. She had already appeared in a couple of not very successful movies, but she was becoming well known and well paid. She was, in fact, a long way from Los Toldos.[9]

When a military coup overthrew the civilian government in 1943, she was able to take advantage of the situation. The radio stations were taken over by the new government, with the allocation of radio time in the hands of Oscar Nicolini. He liked Evita and saw to it that she got her share of airtime. What she proposed to him was a series about powerful women, often married to or associated with powerful men. The series gave her an opportunity to portray the kind of women she would like to emulate, making her a kind of heroine, albeit a constructed one, for the military government. Her programs were announced, three times a week, as offering "the voice of a woman of the people—she herself of the anonymous masses—in whose voice has been revealed day by day the nature . . . of this saving revolution." Evita identified herself as "a woman like you, mothers, wives, sweethearts, sisters. . . ." The series was written by Francisco Muñoz Aspiri, who would later become the director of propaganda (that is, public relations) in the Secretariat of Information, a connection that continued to serve her well. She was establishing strong ties to the governing powers, and through her work in soap operas and in the portrayal of heroic women she was learning both a style and a rhetoric that would later suit her own political purposes. She seems to have had a hand in choosing the subjects for her "heroines," and they were formidable—Elizabeth I of England, Sara Bernhardt, Catherine of Russia, Madame Chang Kai-shek, Isadora Duncan, and the wife of the late tsar. Though Peronist circles avoided acknowledging the importance of these parts as either a training ground or an indication of her own political ambition, preferring to see her as born directly from her association with Juan Perón, it seems likely that these roles appealed to her in both their political and artistic aspects.[10] After all, all of these women were powerful and famous, and their stories were first of all excellent vehicles for an actress and secondarily a significant training ground for her political future.

From the day of their first meeting, she and Juan Perón were together. She remembered it as her "marvelous day," while Perón called it his "destiny."[11] The association, however, was not particularly well received, either by the public or by Perón's fellow military officers. As they quickly rented adjoining apartments, the association became an open scandal. Nevertheless, she actively maintained her own pursuits, and her connection with the military continued to serve her well professionally. When in 1944 performers in the broadcast industry formed a union, she became its president. She also took up a new radio program that was even more overtly political in nature than the one on heroines and was closely tied to the military regime. Announced with a military march, one of the first half-hour presentations was called "The Soldier's Revolution Will Be the Revolution of the Argentine People." The program attacked the wealthy and underlined social problems such as illness, illiteracy, and undernourishment among the poor. Significantly, Evita herself, speaking at the end of the program, opened up a theme she would pursue until her death. "The Revolution," she said, speaking of the government of which Juan Perón was a part, "was made for exploited workers." The program went on to distinguish Juan Perón, then secretary of labor, specifically as the savior of the workers, a message that probably came as an unpleasant surprise to some other members of the military government. No doubt it was seen by them as a deliberate attempt on Perón's part to build an independent political base. Evita went on, "There was a man who could bring dignity to the notion of work, a soldier of the people who can feel the flame of social justice. . . . It was he who decisively helped the people's Revolution." Just in case there was any doubt about who that man might be, the body of the program was followed by a recorded speech by Juan Perón himself.[12]

Perón later said that he had trained her to "create . . . a second I" and that "she had followed me like a shadow." Even Perón's own supporters, however, found the liaison difficult to accept as it stood; in the spring of

1945, demonstrators outside his apartment shouted, "Get married, get married."[13] The marriage that would give Evita the platform and legitimacy that she needed, however, would require more dramatic circumstances. The opportunity was not long in coming, and was characterized by precipitate changes in Perón's political position and the nature and strength of his support by the Argentine masses.

Juan Perón had continued to increase his popularity with the working classes and especially the unions during 1944 and the early months of 1945. As early as June 1945, he was addressing popular rallies that the unions organized in the industrial suburbs of Buenos Aires. At the same time, antigovernment rallies, which included student demonstrators, began to accelerate, and Perón became suspect in the eyes of his military collaborators. Meanwhile, Evita's friend Oscar Nicolini was appointed secretary of communications, when the expectation had been that a military man from the powerful Campo de Mayo delegation would get the post. As one of the officers stated, "We were convinced that it was our duty to stop the nation from falling into the hands of that woman. . . ."[14] Events, however, were carrying power directly in Juan Perón's direction, and when it arrived, he would share it with the woman in his life.

Power for Perón was not an outcome that had seemed inevitable during the first few days of October. On October 9, the day after his fiftieth birthday, he was forced to resign from all his government posts at the president's request. Speaking before a crowd of followers the next day, using as his pretext a good-bye speech to employees of the Secretariat of Labor, he took an important step toward firming up his own support. He announced a wage increase and a system of indexing to make wages and salaries immune to inflation. He was enthusiastically applauded, and the speech was broadcast nationally; of course, workers were delighted and the military officers who wanted him out of politics were angered. Threats to his life began to circulate within the military, and some officers called for his arrest. As the dangers grew, he and Evita decided to leave the city for a refuge on a small, private island in the delta of the Paraná River a few miles from Buenos Aires. While he was deciding whether or not to flee the country, police began to pick up his supporters, and to search for him as well. Evita and Juan were soon found, strolling arm in arm near the island's dock; the chief of police, who had come with the searchers personally, informed them that the president had ordered Juan Perón's arrest and detention on the island of Martín García. After the entire party returned to Buenos Aires, he was forced to leave the struggling and distraught Evita by the elevator of their apartment building.

Despite attempts by Evita and his other supporters to gain his release, even his whereabouts were unknown for several days and his safety was in doubt. The most effective help came from his staff at the Secretariat of Labor and from the unions. Strikes began with the sugar workers of Tucumán on October 15 and soon spread around the capital as well, frightening the military. On October 16, a friendly doctor was permitted to see the prisoner on the island and was successful in persuading the authorities that Perón was quite ill and must be sent to the military hospital in Buenos Aires. The former secretary of labor was finally returned to the city in the early hours of the following day.

The events of October 17, 1945, changed the landscape of politics in the country and dramatically ensured Perón's power. The mobilized working class moved more quickly than their leaders, who had called for a strike on October 18, and marched immediately into the Plaza de Mayo, the political center of the city. They had come to demand Perón's immediate release. Taking possession of this important public space, they settled down to wait, dancing and drinking in the streets. Meanwhile, labor leaders had been negotiating on Perón's behalf. Perón himself demanded the immediate resignation of the cabinet and its replacement with his own choices; that evening, after his demands had been accepted, he came to the Plaza de Mayo to try to calm the situation. "Calming" was not quite what occurred.[15]

The event became, both spatially and politically, an announcement of the arrival of the working class at the center of Argentine public life and of Perón's unquestioned leadership at the head of that movement. The crowd had arrived across the iron bridge connecting the workers' neighborhoods, known as the *cinturón obrero*, or "belt of workers," with the center of Buenos Aires, until the police closed it; then they had begun to cross the river crowded into small boats or improvised rafts. Buses were commandeered, along with streetcars. Some of the police joined the marchers, usually after changing into civilian clothes. Even before Juan Perón's arrival, the crowd had taken over the city and had begun to feel its power.[16] Though Evita had little to do with the event, she was not forgotten: one of the chants of the crowd emphasized both the class antagonisms at work in the demonstration and the strong masculinity of her lover, "*Oligarcas a otra parte / Viva el macho de Eva Duarte*," that is, "Oligarchs stay away / Long live Eva Duarte's man."[17] This chant already indicated that the masses identified her as one of them in their opposition to the rich, and rejected the significance of the unsanctified nature of her liaison with the political leader. In fact, the couple's sexual relationship emphasized Juan Perón's masculinity and toughness.

Estimates of the crowd awaiting Perón's appearance were in the range of 200,000, small when compared with later Peronist gatherings but strikingly large at that time. Newspapers had been rolled up and set aflame to combat the darkness. When Perón appeared, the roar of the crowd and the lights of the improvised torches gave the event a sense of epiphany. An emotional and almost spiritual contract was forged between those in attendance and Juan Perón, with Evita an element that "proved Perón's manliness."[18]

Evita was not present, though she dined with Perón that evening. Her own political epiphanies would come later. The whole set of events, however, had made a huge difference to the remaining course of her life. While imprisoned, Perón had decided to marry her, despite her questionable reputation. In a letter to her from Martín García Island, he called her "my adored treasure" and admitted that he could not live without her. In a telling sentence, he announced his intention to marry her immediately if his retirement from the army was approved, and if that not did not occur, he would arrange something "one way or another; but either way we'll put an end to your vulnerable situation."[19] In so saying, he acknowledged the difficulties of her uncertain and less than honorable status. She would soon be a real wife at last, an honorable woman and, as she later continually restated, reborn. Not only would she be honorable, she would also be powerful as the consort of the man soon to be president of the country. It was legitimation from a lover who was also, possibly, a substitute for and a better father than her own, a powerful man more than twenty years her senior. Her gratitude to Perón for changing her status and her near-total identification with him were reflected poignantly in a letter she wrote him as she was leaving for Europe in 1947. She insisted, "you have purified me, your wife with all her faults, because I live in you, feel for you and think through you. . . ."[20]

Eva Perón's self-reinvention would extend to a great deal more than just her name and her birth date. She had already begun altering her appearance for her career as an actress. Photographs in 1936 and 1937 show her with a significantly different nose than the one she boasted in 1939.[21] A later physical alteration was simpler and more successful: she became a blond. She made this change for a starring role in the cinema, and it suited her so well that she kept the color and the hairstylist, Pedro Alcaraz, for the remainder of her life. She had always had pale and luminescent skin; her new golden hair, "a gold that imitated the effect of the golden halos and backgrounds of the religious paintings of the Middle Ages," harmonized with her beautiful skin and gave her a kind of permanent glow. Further, it gave her an air of innocence, useful in dispelling her less than honorable past. Interestingly, she was reported to have often referred to herself as a "repentant brunette." Such a designation resonates, of course, with allusion to Mary Magdalene.[22] But the Magdalene was not the religious figure with whom

Evita would become most publicly and closely associated. That figure, as we will see below, was the Virgin Mary, who was also of such importance to Frida Kahlo (see Chapter 8).

Not only would Evita change her physical attributes, she would also change her way of dressing as she moved into her public political role. She was acutely conscious of appearance, but unlike Zapata, Bolívar, and other figures discussed in this book, she moved away from glitter and medals in her daily garb in favor of dark and simple suits. For formal occasions she continued to dress lavishly, and she always loved jewelry, but more and more, her normal dress was tailored. This way of dressing was well received by her public: the dark suits emphasized the angelic nature of her extreme fairness and were appropriate to the tasks she began to perform.

Marysa Navarro has spoken of a kind of shared charisma between Juan and Evita, and I agree that was what developed. At least initially, however, Evita hovered in the background in public appearances.[23] A turning point in the confidence of her self-presentation seems to have been her good-will trip to Europe without her husband in mid-1947. Welcomed by enthusiastic crowds in Spain, received by the Pope in Rome, visiting the Cathedral of Notre Dame in Paris, she was covered widely by the international press and proved an excellent public relations ambassador for the Perón regime. Europeans were less nasty than Argentine elites; her audience with the Pope seems to have touched her deeply and certainly must have given her a sense of legitimacy and exoneration. Throughout the trip, she visited sanctuaries of the Virgin Mary, perhaps seeking reassurance, as she was reported to feel extremely insecure moving among royalty, Church leaders, and heads of state. When he observed her kneeling at the altar of the Our Lady in Notre Dame Cathedral in Paris, the papal nuncio to France, Monsignor Angelo Roncalli, is reported to have said in Italian, "The Empress Eugenie has returned." The monsignor later became Pope John XXIII. After the ceremony, Roncalli and Evita had a short conversation; both from humble origins, they apparently understood each other quite readily, discussing charity projects and the foundation she was already thinking of establishing in Argentina. Roncalli advised her to avoid extensive red tape in such an organization and to commit herself completely to the project. It was advice that she took very much to heart.[24] It seems that this emotionally and spiritually satisfying experience stayed with Evita and helped strengthen her resolve to make a difference, in a direct and personal way, to the poor in Argentina.

Though Evita was reported to have agonized nervously throughout the European trip—keeping her companion Liliane Guardo up at night talking anxiously about what had transpired during the day, about her sense of her work and her husband's, about the enemies from whom her husband needed her protection—she nevertheless acquired a new confidence and energy. She became an international personality, covered widely by the world press, and the reaction to her beauty and style (so rancorously criticized in Argentina) was largely positive. Evita's sense of inadequacy surfaced from time to time, however, and on one occasion after receiving communion from her confessor, Father Hernán Benítez, she collapsed in distress. Revealing to him the strain of the protocols and public events, she questioned why she, an illegitimate and shamed child, should deserve the status and attention she was receiving. Just before her departure from Argentina, news about her illegitimacy had surfaced in the international press, specifically in *Time* magazine in a cover story on June 23. Perhaps this sudden revelation about her past heightened her anxiety and precipitated her collapse a few weeks later in the presence of her confessor.[25]

Yet she was developing a personal presence and style that would serve her well on her return to Argentina. During her stay in Paris, not only was she honored by receiving the Légion d'Honneur from Georges Bidault, the French foreign minister, she also had time to visit the major fashion houses, leaving her measurements at Christian Dior and Marcel Rochas. Later, she would order much of her clothing from Paris, staying at the forefront of tasteful fashion.[26] No longer was she the naive girl from the country, at least in public presentation.

Hence the beginning of Evita's own epiphanies. Only one month after her return, she spoke from the balcony of the Casa Rosada—the Argentine White House—to acknowledge publicly her reception of the bill granting Argentine women the right to vote. Dramatically, Juan Perón signed it and handed it to her, symbolically investing her with not only the victory but also with the leadership of his female supporters. She also immediately threw herself into her charity work, founding the Eva Perón Foundation in 1948. Although she had a huge staff, she herself attended personally to many of the interactions with clients. The fact that she herself appeared to petitioners, day after day, providing desperately needed material things ranging from food to money to houses or access to jobs or medical care, must have seemed miraculous, and contributed still further to her saintly aura. More extraordinarily, she often gave the petitioners more than they asked for, and even thought to provide them with the bus fare to return home. Certainly, for most of those who came to ask, there was no other way to meet these needs. Her confessor Father Benítez recounted that she kissed the leprous, the tubercular, the cancer-ridden, reinforcing Doña María Roldán's testimony of Evita's giving herself to the poor. There were many other witnesses to her direct approach to the physically suffering, as well; when she was discouraged from touching the ill, she protested that such acceptance meant a great deal to the suffering and insisted that she would not be stopped.[27]

Evita began early to serve as Juan Perón's emissary to Argentina's workers, the major constituency that had brought him to the presidency. In 1946, she was named First Worker of Argentina and, shortly thereafter, Queen of Labor, and soon she began to receive delegations of workers on her own. In 1947 she was receiving as many as twenty-six labor groups daily. Later in Perón's presidency she took a more active role in labor issues, intervening directly in strikes and conflicts. Her first public intervention in 1948 had to do with a problem concerning bank employees, but the press did not say much about her role. Nevertheless, from this time forward, she was often mentioned as having been involved in settlements of one kind or another. One of the most famous had to do with a strike by railway workers that began in November 1950. Perón sent Evita to mediate the conflict, one that threatened the country's economic situation, as it would close the ports and shut down the nation's railroad network. Though already showing the signs of the illness that would kill her less than two years later, she not only went in person to railway terminals in Buenos Aires to protest to the pickets that they were helping the opposition, she also went from station to station on a hand-cranked cart, delivering her message. Still, she was unsuccessful, and Perón himself cracked down by issuing a decree that would permit him to draft the strikers into the army in case of an emergency. In effect, of course, this action did away with their right to strike.[28] Evita had failed, and the alliance between her husband and the labor movement was beginning to fail as well.

Still, she continued to be seen as labor's champion. Interestingly, though her efforts were unavailing with the railroad workers, the union's official newspaper stressed her significance in the supposed solution of the strike.[29] In another, more successful case in 1951, when news vendors struck against *La Prensa*, an important opposition newspaper, the government supported them. Later, when the newspaper passed to the ownership of the major government-aligned labor federation, the General Confederation of Labor (CGT), Evita herself, through her Eva Perón Foundation, paid the vendors' lost salaries.[30] In August 1952, after her death, the Newspaper Vendors Union put her forward as a candidate for canonization and circulated a painting of her with her hands crossed on her chest, wearing a Mary-like shawl around her face. Forty-six years later, in December 1998, they again printed the image.[31] One author believes that it is possible that at this time, Evita had come to control all government agencies involved with labor and was exercising considerable responsibility for collective bargaining, disputes, pensions, contracts, and other labor matters.[32]

She had also taken up the cause of women's suffrage, though she was certainly not the first to do so, and the fact that she took credit for getting such a law passed did not sit particularly well with all women, particularly the Socialists, who had been attempting to push it forward for some time. Nevertheless, it was she who formed and headed the Women's Suffrage Association and began to give weekly speeches about Peronist feminism. She also created women's civic centers throughout the country. When suffrage was granted to women in September 1947, she presented the law to the Argentine people, saying, "The nation's government has just handed to me the bill that grants us our civil rights. . . . I am accepting this on behalf of all Argentine women, and I can feel my hands tremble with joy as they grasp the laurel proclaiming victory."[33] Changes within the Peronist party made it possible to establish a separate women's branch in mid-1949, and she was quickly made its president. In later elections this party provided female congresspersons, as well as the first female congressional president in the world.[34] It is hard to argue with these achievements, and while they certainly added to Evita's own power, they simultaneously empowered Argentine women. The post as head of the Peronist Women's Party was her first specifically political one, and she was hugely successful, recruiting 500,000 members with 3,600 headquarters across the country within the next five years. Yet it was an organization separate from the government, and she still had no official post. Though the Peronist women were organized in a profoundly hierarchical and rigid organization, somehow it seemed to be outside official institutions and almost working against them. She completely controlled the organization, urging women into nontraditional roles, organizing them and sending them out around the country, giving "their lives" to the Peronist cause and not to their families. At the same time, she positioned herself and them as traditionally feminine, devoting their activities to the cause of Juan Perón. As she put it, "Our movement is inspired theoretically and doctrinally by Perón's words. . . . To be a Peronist is, for a woman, to be loyal and to have blind confidence in Perón."[35] In 1951, in a series of lectures written for classes at the Escuela Superior Peronista, she was much more emotional as she connected that loyalty directly with the Argentine nation and a love for Perón, saying "we must teach them [the Argentines] in the cradle and in the home that they must love Perón as they love Mother and Fatherland."[36]

She also began to take a more intense role in the developing Peronist rituals. As these became more institutionalized and less spontaneous, her own

appearances tended to make this process less obvious. Her increased participation went along with a propaganda effort to provide her with a fictitious
but significant role in the original October 17 events in 1945. An example was
an article that took up an entire page in the labor newspaper, *El Laborista*,
on October 16, 1947. It was entitled, "María Eva Duarte de Perón: Symbol
of the Lineage of the Argentine Woman." This article positioned Evita as
one of the major organizers of the mobilization that had saved Perón. At the
same time, other Peronist newspapers failed to mention the significance of
labor leaders in stimulating the first October 17 demonstration.[37]

The celebration in 1947, just two years after the original event, was taking on the characteristics of a national holiday. Perón received civil and military authorities through the afternoon; on the same day, 24,200 employees
received promotions. Meanwhile, Evita joined the festivities as a major
player. Many of the placards carried by those in attendance bore her picture.
However, in spite of the crowd's urging, she declined to speak.[38] In 1948 it
was a different story. This time Evita herself was featured, and in her honor
new lyrics had been created to a stirring march previously known as "The
Peronist Boys": "The Peronist girls, with Evita we will triumph and with
her we will offer our lives for Perón." By this time she had acquired many
titles within the movement—"the Lady of Hope," "the Mother of the
Innocents," and "the Workers' Plenipotentiary." On this occasion, however,
she emphasized the three-way relationship in which she was so significant:
Juan Perón, on the one hand, the workers—los descamisados—on the
other, and herself as the intermediary between them. She urged the workers to struggle constantly in behalf of Juan Perón's "grand project," defined
as social justice based on workers' rights that were to be guaranteed consti-
tutionally. She spoke as Perón's voice to the workers, and then as the voice
of the workers to her husband. She was beginning to convey intense emotion and connection with her listeners but constantly reinforced her role as
intermediary rather than as primary actor. Further, she was one with the
descamisados and not with her husband, identifying herself as his most
humble follower.[39] Emphasizing the significance of her husband rather
than herself, she spoke elsewhere adoringly and admiringly of Juan Perón,
calling him the "only man here in our movement with his own source of
light. . . . We all feed from his light."[40]

Extreme as this sentiment might be, it seems to me that it was indeed
by Juan's light that Evita was fed, though by now she was also feeding on
the fervor of their followers. Her style was still tense with emotion and a
sense of suffering, reflecting her years of radio performances, but her
speeches also conveyed hope and release. Though she has been criticized as
manipulative and insincere in these sentiments, it seems to me that it was

her very sincerity, empathy, and identification with her listeners that made her appeals so effective. These October 17 speeches and others on ceremonial occasions from the balcony of the Casa Rosada by the beautiful, glowing woman, herself a source of light among men dressed in dark colors, were almost spiritual, almost numinous. These epiphanies were filled with a rhetoric of love that resonated with the presence of that other Mother, that other mediator, so significant in the lives of believing Argentines, the Virgin Mary.[41] I think she believed in her role.

At the same time, her speeches emphasized Juan Perón as all-giving pater familias. Speaking to the Union of Streetcar Workers just before Christmas in the same year, immediately after a long discussion of her husband's good works, she emphasized the role of the proper father: to share whatever he had with his own. She then, referring apparently to Christ, asked that all stretch out their hands to Him, thanking Him for His love for those who suffered and for His "generosity without limits," but it is certainly possible that the listeners could have believed that she was referring to her husband. This rhetorical conflation of Christ and other religious figures by their juxtaposition to references to the Peróns became a frequent strategy in later years. She immediately returned the focus to Juan Perón, as she reminded her listeners of the well-being of Argentines under the leadership of her husband, "eating our bread, drinking our wine, secure, protected." The connection was immediate: each year she and her husband distributed a loaf of Christmas bread and a bottle of cidral, a popular local fermented beverage, to each working-class family. And then she asserted, "The present belongs to us, and the future is ours." She then returned to the Christmas story, declaring that "The child has been born in Galilee. On the road to Bethlehem, under the stars, the Kings are approaching." The implication was clear: Juan Perón, who had already provided so much, would provide an even brighter future. At the same time, he was further identified with the gift-laden three kings, who in Latin America bring presents to the children on the Día de los Reyes (Day of the Kings) in early January. Her rhetoric was profoundly nationalistic, defining her husband, workers, and Peronists as the genuine Argentines. General Perón was portrayed as bearing not only "our flag of blue and white" but also "the banner of happiness for the descamisados and workers of our Fatherland."[42] It was, moreover, the creation of a symbolic national family with Juan Perón at its head, united on this most significant Christian holiday.[43]

The identification of Evita Perón first with the Virgin and then later, as she became seriously ill and moved toward death, with Christ was one that I believe was profoundly satisfying to her psychologically. She had made sexual compromises early in order to make her way to stardom and then to political prominence. She carried a sense of shame and injustice that began to be remedied by her power both to get what she wanted, at least materially, and to provide it to others. Apparently unable to have children of her own (although at least one woman claims to be Evita's daughter from a secret pregnancy), she made it her business to perform miracles for others— but carefully emphasizing that she was the instrument of Perón's will.[44] This rhetorical strategy placed her firmly in the same spot emotionally as Mary—a loving and present Mother who would approach a more distant Father (and Juan Perón was definitely the Father, not the Son) to provide benefits for his children, that is, the Argentine people. When the time came, when she was suffering and dying, Evita herself would become the Christ figure, powerfully combining in one human woman resonances with both the Virgin Mary and her Son. The strategy was also useful in uniting the Argentine working class, including the immigrants from Spain and Italy and from the interior of the country, by using what Benedict Anderson has called a "sacred language," in this case not a written script but a highly resonant set of references and symbols of popular Catholicism that all could understand.[45] This previously heterogeneous, excluded group could unite behind the Peróns, especially Evita, and their idea of Argentina.

The role of loving and providing mediator, the fulfiller of dreams through her husband's political movement, led her to undertake extraordinary efforts that ultimately undermined her health. Working long hours, sometimes up to twenty-two out of the day's twenty-four, she lost weight and even began to lose touch with Juan himself. Later he wrote that in 1950 and 1951, "I had lost my wife." Even when they got away to the country to rest, she would spend much of her time on the telephone.[46] Her giving, reinforced by her glowing and increasingly powerful presence, made the bond between herself and the Argentine people enormously strong. Her behavior mirrored that of Roman Catholic saints, including overwork and physical deprivation and sometimes even a refusal to eat; her role as motherly provider emphasized her similarities to the Virgin; and, suddenly, her health snapped. Now she would move on to martyrdom, a Christlike figure, suffering and dying for her people.

She had uterine cancer. There are many stories about her illness, how she regarded it, and how it was (or was not) treated. One official in Perón's government, who happened to be a medical doctor, reported that he diagnosed her correctly after she collapsed while attending an official event in January 1950. He then, he said, advised a hysterectomy, but she refused, claiming that she was not seriously ill and that the diagnosis was a manipulation by her enemies who wished to remove her from politics.[47] If true, this incident was a foreshadowing of the significance her body would take on later; the implication that mutilating her body and endangering her health would destroy or diminish her power, at least in her mind, was a reflection of the profound relationship between her very womanhood and her political power. If not true, it showed the connection, at least in the mind of the teller of the story. What we do know is that this official resigned from Perón's cabinet only four months later, perhaps under pressure from Evita.

It was not the first time she had struggled with physical difficulties, suffering from faintness on several public occasions. One observer claimed that she had been diagnosed as anemic, another that she received regular blood transfusions. The doctor who would later embalm her body, Pedro Ara, reported that after having stood beside her at an October 17 celebration, probably the one in 1948, he believed her to be ill. After her extensive and rousing speech, he felt that he had witnessed "a case of inexplicable biological and physical resistance; a case of a colossal victory of willpower over bodily weakness."[48] He was clearly captivated by her beauty and rhetorical powers, saying of her mesmerizing performance, "When she finished, I could not have repeated, nor extracted, nor commented on the text of her speech. I wasn't in the word, but in the music; not in the idea, but in the rhythm."[49]

By August 1951, Evita was very weak and suffered from increasing abdominal pain. An examination by an Argentine physician showed that she had cancer of the cervix, and she received radium treatments that weakened her still further. Dr. George T. Pack, of Sloan-Kettering Cancer Center in New York, was called in for a consultation in October; he returned to Argentina in November to perform a hysterectomy. The surgery was extensive, as the disease had spread throughout her pelvic organs. The whole affair was kept secret because of fears that it might affect Juan Perón's reelection, which in the event went off smoothly. Evita was never told the nature of her illness, only that she had some sort of "female problems." It was standard practice at the time to withhold information from cancer patients; it was thought to be cruel and possibly medically unsound to reveal the truth. Nevertheless, she confided to her confessor, Father Benítez, that although the people around her were not being honest with her, she knew what was occurring. In any case, she seems to have had almost no control whatsoever over her treatment. She made a brief recovery after the surgery, but by February 1952 she was again suffering terribly. Chemotherapy turned out to be useless, and she died on July 26, 1952, perhaps without ever knowing for sure the nature of her illness.[50]

Her ailing health coincided with an enormous upsurge in her political popularity, connected to her work with the labor unions and the Peronist

Women's Party, along with her charity work. In August of 1951, just a few weeks before she was to undergo the secret surgery, a group of unionists visited President Perón to ask him to accept renomination for the presidential election. At the same time they asked that Evita accompany him as vice president on the ticket. He did not immediately refuse to permit her candidacy, and they and she were probably temporarily encouraged. Certainly she was not ready to believe that her health would disqualify her.

What followed was an extraordinary public acknowledgment of her charismatic bond with the people of Argentina. This event was the rally of August 22, 1951, to declare Juan Perón's candidacy. The day was beautiful, a typical "Peronist" day, as the weather seemed always to cooperate with the Peróns in their public political appearances. Huge portraits of the pair, each sixty feet high, dominated the display behind the speakers' platform on the Avenida 9 de Julio, a symbolic space named for Argentine Independence Day. The Plaza de Mayo in front of the Casa Rosada had been accurately deemed too limited to contain the expected crowds.

Perón entered first, surrounded by an exclusively male group of politicians and union officials, but speakers were continually interrupted by demands from the crowds that Evita appear. When she emerged, looking thin but beautiful, she delivered an impassioned speech, hands trembling, in which she emphasized that she had no political ambitions beyond supporting her husband and serving as the connection between him and the people of Argentina. Throughout the speech, she was interrupted by demands from the crowds that she accept the nomination immediately. As she began to make excuses and asked for more time to decide, the crowds became more insistent. The situation was slipping out of the Peróns' control, and Evita had become, suddenly, the center of fervor. Charisma involves an interactive bond, and the Peronist crowd was now taking the lead in defining that bond. Finally, she left the stage, stating, "Comrades, as General Perón has said, I will do what the people say." The crowd obviously believed that she had accepted.[51]

The truth was otherwise. Slightly more than a week later, she announced on the radio that she was declining the honor, relegating herself once again to the role of Juan Perón's helpmeet. This action failed to reestablish her in a secondary position, if that were the intention. August 22, 1951, became known as "the Day of Renunciation"—*renunciación*, a term that resonated with *Anunciación* and *Asunción*, the Annunciation to the Virgin that she would give birth to Jesus, and her bodily Assumption into heaven. The connection with these holy moments provided a symbolic significance that tied her even more closely to Mary. Nevertheless, she was still outside the government, still outside the official power structure. I believe this absence of institutional standing made it easier for the people of Argentina to relate directly to her, without the reservations that might have inhibited relating to someone in an official government position. And now Evita was associated with her own special sacrifice and her own Peronist day, August 22.

She continued to have her place in other established Peronist rituals, despite her now obviously failing health. Simultaneously with her decline, the Argentine military became increasingly restive, though a coup in late September failed. Juan Perón appeared on the balcony of the Casa Rosada to rally supporters on this occasion, but Evita did not, although she later went on the radio, audibly sobbing, to thank the descamisados for saving her husband. She also called several CGT leaders to her side to arrange for the purchase of arms that could be made available to the unions should another military insurrection occur. Her charitable foundation, the only direct source of funds that she had available, would pay the bill.[52] Large supplies of arms were purchased and stored in the foundation building, later to be confiscated after a military coup ousted Juan Perón in 1955.[53] In this action, she showed herself far more willing to give workers the means of physical force than was her husband.

October 17, 1951, was officially dedicated to the ailing First Lady, who was by now very ill, and to her Renunciation. On this occasion she was given a medal by the Peronist labor unions and another by Perón himself. His speech on this occasion was dedicated to exalting her role in the Peronist political project. He emotionally named her as "standard bearer in the struggle for this second independence. . . . She gave everything without asking for anything in exchange. Everything: her youth, her health, even her life."[54] Able to attend only with the use of a massive amount of painkillers, she was initially unable to speak. After her husband's extraordinary tribute, the first to this point to acknowledge her extensive contribution to his political movement and to himself, she fell into his arms, again sobbing. She then began to speak, her voice shaky and fragile, promising to be present each October 17, "even if I have to shed the tatters of my life to do so." Again she acknowledged that everything she had, everything she had become, was not hers but his. Becoming increasingly emotional, she insisted, "I am not anything because I renounced anything; I am not anything because I am somebody or have something. All that I have, I have in my heart, it hurts my soul, it hurts my flesh and it burns on my nerves, and that is my love for these people and for Perón." It was clear to the crowd that she was indeed burning her life away in their service, and her bodily sacrifice, so easily connected to Christ himself, was something that they believed themselves to be witnessing. Only two weeks later she underwent the secret surgery, but she had recovered sufficiently by November 11 to cast her ballot in the box brought to her on her sickbed. As the box was taken out of the residence, women keeping vigil on the sidewalk touched and kissed it, asserting their connection and support for the ailing First Lady.[55] At the same time, her foundation continued to provide benefits and material goods; around the end of the year, an Agrarian Plan, which provided equipment to the nation's farmers, was launched in her name.[56]

Her last major public appearance was at her husband's inaugural ceremony in June 1952, just over a month before her death. Despite her pain and frailty, she rode through the streets with him, standing in a convertible, waving at the crowds. A huge fur coat concealed her emaciated body and the framework of wire and plaster that kept her on her feet. Reactions to the process of her dying ranged from the understandable and spiritual to the bizarre. Psychiatrist Marie Langer, who catered to the elite who could afford such services, later recalled that many of her patients had wished Evita dead and then suffered horrible guilt, manifested in hypochondria and anxiety about their own possible spiritual punishments.[57]

At the same time, her supporters erected altars to her throughout the country, both in homes and public places, with her photograph beside images and pictures of the saints and especially of the Virgin Mary, often in her advocation as the patroness of Argentina, the Virgin of Luján. The Argentine Congress named her "the Spiritual Mother of the Nation" and gave her a massive necklace "of the Order of the Liberator, San Martín," thereby identifying her with both the Virgin and the hero of Argentine independence. Meanwhile, her husband and the Peronists made plans to memorialize her, designing a mausoleum and arranging for a prominent embalmer, the aforementioned Dr. Pedro Ara, to be on hand to begin the preservation of her body immediately upon her death. Even her time of death became symbolic: it was announced on July 26, 1952, that she had fallen into a coma in the morning and had expired at precisely 8:25 p.m. It was widely believed that she had in fact died earlier, but 8:25 p.m. was the moment of her marriage to Perón.[58] Thus she had been born anew as Juan Perón's wife and had died, at least officially, at the same hour and minute of the day.

Dr. Ara began his work immediately and spent the night preparing the body for public exhibition. The embalming was only temporary, designed to preserve the corpse temporarily so that it could be put on display immediately. For the moment, she was dressed in a white shroud, a rosary was placed in her hands, and—identifying her clearly with the Argentine nation—she was covered with the flag.[59]

The sense of urgency was significant and reflects the perceived political importance of Evita to the continuing rule of the Peronists. The body was first transported to the Ministry of Labor, where it was put on view for the public. White flowers surrounded the building and flowed over into the streets. Eight people were killed in the huge crowds of people that surrounded the ambulance transporting her. At the Ministry the lines to view her body stretched many blocks in each direction. Mourners waited patiently for hours in the rain, even the weather sharing the gloom that surrounded her demise. Later the body was taken to the headquarters of the CGT, highlighting her identification with and commitment to the workers. The move was accompanied this time by a huge parade symbolically featuring the descamisados, the nurses from her foundation, union members and officials, and military cadets. Black crepe covered the streetlamps. The crowds lining the route were kept under control by thousands of soldiers.[60]

Yet after Evita's death, Perón's political movement began to falter. Increasing economic difficulties, the exposure of corruption within the administration, an unwise attack on the Catholic Church, and the activities of Perón's security forces, including the use of torture on dissidents from the labor unions and academic institutions who might earlier have been expected to support him, led to widespread defections from his ranks, as well as to the further alienation of the armed forces. His attempt to create a kind of civic religion, with Evita at the center of devotion, to replace Roman Catholicism was heavy-handed and helped lead to the strong opposition of the hierarchical Church. Despite an attempt to equate Evita even more closely with the Virgin Mary by showing her associated with roses and other Marian symbols, putting out a primer for children in the Argentine schools that emphasized her position as "Spiritual Mother" of the Argentine people (and including close associations between Juan Perón himself, important Christian symbols, and the Argentine nation), and publishing poetry and songs eulogizing her and comparing her to Mary and to Christ, her death had removed from the Peronist movement her charismatic power.[61] In September 1955 her husband was forced from the country.

In the meantime, the body had remained in Dr. Ara's care, and he continued the meticulous embalming process until the fall of Perón's government. Evita's body lay outside the coffin for most of that period, hands crossed serenely over her chest, an image of the Virgin of Luján on the wall above her. Union members and employees in the building would come by to pay their respects, frequently kneeling, praying, and crossing themselves. When the military took over and ran Perón from the country, there was obvious concern that the body not become a rallying point for further Peronist political activity. Still, the sense of its power was so strong that they were afraid to destroy it. In fact, some of the military officers who came to see the body in the days before they decided what was to be done with it displayed the same kind of reverent behavior that CGT members had. Ara reported that when the military administrator of the CGT, Lieutenant Colonel Manuel Reimúndez, viewed the body, he wept, bent to kiss the rosary, given her by the Pope, which she held in her lifeless hands, and whispered, "This little medal should be that of the Immaculate. Poor little thing. Surely God has pardoned her."[62] He was associating her with one of the most pure (and most Spanish) aspects of the Virgin, the belief in Mary's freedom from sin from the moment of conception. Nevertheless, he ordered that the body be locked away, separated even from the devoted Dr. Ara. Sometime thereafter, military leaders in consultation with the Church resolved to remove the cadaver from the country. President Pedro Eugenio Aramburu was given a sealed envelope informing him of the location to which she was taken. His instructions were to have it delivered to whoever was the current president four weeks after his own death.

Strangely, this procedure led to his murder. Members of the urban revolutionary group, the Montoneros, kidnapped the former president in 1970 and killed him when he was unable to reveal the location of the cadaver. The letter was in due course turned over to his successor, who ordered Evita's remains recovered from an Italian cemetery and their return to Juan Perón, then living in exile in Spain. It is rumored that his third wife, Isabel, would lie on top of the coffin in hopes that the power and spirit of Evita would infuse her own body. If that indeed occurred, the attempt failed, as Isabel would never become politically effective.[63]

In fact, the return of Perón and Isabel to Argentina in 1972 turned into a political disaster. Though Evita was invoked immediately by the crowds welcoming them at the airport—the chant was, "We feel it, we feel it, Evita is present"—her power to support the old man Juan had become was gone.[64] With supporters on both the left and right, supporters who wanted and expected quite different things from the aging leader, political division and conflicts were inevitable. Perón himself was unable to do much about it; he had little energy and little understanding of the events that were transpiring. Despite becoming his vice president in 1973, Isabel never established any kind of resonance with the Argentine people. Evita, however, remained a vivid memory, and signs saying "*¡Evita vive!*" ("Evita lives!") proliferated. After Perón's death in 1974, Isabel succeeded to the presidency, but she herself was quickly overthrown by a repressive military regime that brought political horror to new heights in Argentina. Isabel's own plans for a monument to Juan and Evita, along with other prominent Argentines, were never brought to fruition. Finally, with Isabel's fall in 1976,

Figure 10.1. "I will return, and I will be millions. You will recover my name and use it as a flag of victory." Women's Branch, Metropolitan Division. 1983. Sam L. Slick Collection of Latin and Iberian Political Posters, University of New Mexico.

Figure 10.2. Eva Perón, Juan Perón, Isabel Perón. Political Secretariat of the Justicialist National Council, Justicialist Reorganizing Junta, Buenos Aires Province. 1983. Sam L. Slick Collection of Latin and Iberian Political Posters, University of New Mexico.

Evita's body was given to her sisters for burial and now rests in a discreet family crypt in Recoleta cemetery in Buenos Aires.

During the military repression that followed, images of Evita and most reminders of Perónism disappeared from the scene. She had become too dangerous to invoke, given the widespread disappearances (and often secret executions) of leftist and antigovernment activists—designated as "guerrillas" and thus enemies of the nation, according to those in power. However, after the disastrous defeat of the Argentine military in the Falklands/Malvinas War in 1982, and given increasing world attention to the repression, the military in 1983 began to prepare its withdrawal from power and the return to civilian government. The memory of Evita was again called upon by both political organizations and labor groups as political ferment increased. Several posters in the Sam Slick Collection at the University of New Mexico demonstrate the way in which she was used to reenergize the Peronist movement. As early as March 1983, one poster showed her with her arms extended and smiling radiantly, the text reading, "I will return, and I will be millions—you will recover my name and use it as a flag of victory."[65] Another, published by the Secretaria Política of the Consejo Nacional Justicialista (that is, the Peronist party), placed Evita and Isabel on either side of Juan Perón, all figures against the background of the Argentine flag. Juan and Isabel both wore the presidential sash, while Evita wore a pin of the flag itself.

Two other posters, one published by a railway workers group and the other by the Movimiento Nacional Justicialista, to commemorate the thirty-first anniversary of her death, indicated by the dates "1952—July 26—1983," presented far different yet iconic images. In the first, her hand is extended in exhortation, her appearance angry and strong; the text reads, "The era of privileges and of privileged minorities has ended, because the hour of the people has arrived."[66] The second, in contrast, shows her weeping into her husband's shoulder during the tributes to her and her renunciation at the October 17, 1951, appearance at the Casa Rosada. The theme, predictably, reads "Evita Lives!" This poster announced a religious ceremony and a parade with *antorchas*, the flaming torches that had lit nighttime Peronist celebrations since the original October 17.[67] Thus, in these two posters, both her strength in support of labor and her poignant refusal of special honors for herself were emphasized, the latter in a quasi-religious setting. The first showed her acting on her own as an inspiration to others, the second her tearful submission to her husband. And yet the

Figure 10.3. "Evita 1952—July 26—1983. The era of privileges and of privileged minorities has ended, because the hour of the people has arrived.'" Railroad Workers Group "Rafael Scalabrini Ortiz." Belgrano Railroad, Boulogne Section. 1983. Sam L. Slick Collection of Latin and Iberian Political Posters, University of New Mexico.

Figure 10.4. Justicialist National Movement. "Evita Lives! 1952—July 26—1983. 19:30 h., Plaza Primero de Mayo, Religious Ceremony and March with Torches." Council of Base Units of the Federal Capital. 1983. Sam L. Slick Collection of Latin and Iberian Political Posters, University of New Mexico.

message showed that this submission was born out of her physical sacrifice in support of her people. At least at that moment of ferment, Evita was again invoked in the ambiguous ways that had characterized her during her lifetime.

However, the Peronists lost the election to the much respected Radical party leader, Raul Alfonsín, Evita's powerful image unable to save them after revelations of secret pacts between the military and the political wing of the Peronist unions. Thereafter, though the evidence is sketchy, it seems that the militant and angry Evita was no longer the image that the party wished to portray. Although she continued to be used in subsequent years by political and labor groups, the usual treatment seems to have been less assertive and more neutral, either emphasizing her smile and femininity, as in the 1988 poster supporting the Peronist presidential candidate Cafiero de la Sota, or in the 1987 calendar published by a transportation workers union in which she appeared elegantly dressed and smiling at her husband's side. The text of the first reads, "So that all we women can have this smile again," while the second reads, "The two arms of Peronism are that of social justice and social aid. With them we give the people an embrace of justice and love."[68] Thus, Evita was emerging in a happier, loving image, the strong and angry personality disappearing behind a rhetoric of charm. This shift coincided significantly with the increasingly conservative nature of the Peronist (now usually referred to as the Justicialist) party. A 1995 poster commemorating the fiftieth anniversary of the first October 17 demonstration showed five photographs from the earlier era, with Evita, smiling, appearing in only one.[69] The party itself was moving away from the militant and self-sacrificing Evita defending her people to a beautiful woman at her man's side.

Yet the real Evita was remembered and continued to serve as a role model for women, as Doña María and others attest. In an interview conducted recently by sociologist Pablo Semán with a female evangelical minister in Buenos Aires, the minister said, "When I go up to the pulpit and face the congregation, I have in my mind what Evita did. She was . . . incredible. Because she brought much for women. . . . When some male preacher tells me that I am a woman and that I shouldn't be a pastor, I tell them that was before. But not now. *That I am like Evita.*"[70]

Of course, not everyone was always pleased with what Evita was doing, and she was not always selfless. She made difficult political decisions that hurt some of her followers and favored others. She helped Juan Perón destroy opposition to the leaders they selected within the labor unions and to bring the labor movement securely under their own control, a sometimes brutal process. Doña Maria, quoted at the beginning of this essay, suffered a personal political setback at Evita's hands when another, wealthier woman

Figure 10.5. "So that all we women can have this smile again. We are the guardians of the Peronist flags, and we are the hope of our people. Women forward to victory! Vote for Cafiero de la Sota." Sam L. Slick Collection of Latin and Iberian Political Posters, University of New Mexico.

Figure 10.6. Union of the Trolley Car Workers of the Argentine Republic. "Truth No. 10: The two arms of Peronism are those of social justice and social aid. With them we give the people an embrace of justice and love." 1987. Sam L. Slick Collection of Latin and Iberian Political Posters, University of New Mexico.

was chosen to run for provincial deputy, a nomination that she had expected for herself. Evita's lavish collections of gowns and jewels show that she enjoyed acquiring both personal possessions and adornments, along with supplying necessities to others. Nevertheless, the vast majority of Doña María's recollections focused on Evita's protection of and empathy with the disadvantaged, and she called her "a perfect human being, who loves the other, though she doesn't know her, she is another human being who suffers, though she doesn't think like her." Doña María recounted Evita's visits to the poor neighborhoods, the reverence that even prisoners had for her and her interventions in their behalf, the way that she "swept the multitude up." She found Evita's power a bit difficult to explain—"Supernatural; to tell the truth I have never seen anything like it. . . ." And she suggested that perhaps Evita's popularity was actually beginning to surpass Juan Perón's, and I believe that she was right.[71] His charismatic appeal may not have died with his wife, but it was severely diminished. After her death he was never able to reach the political heights they had achieved together.

Evita Perón combined her interest in laborers, women, and children; her gifts of communication, aided by her great physical beauty; her identification and empathy with the previously powerless and poor; her intense joy in giving, with all its material, psychological, emotional, and spiritual dimensions; and her position of honor—after a childhood and young womanhood of shame—as a powerful man's wife to become one of the most politically effective woman in Latin America in the twentieth century, and perhaps in its entire history. At the same time, she reaped great emotional and material benefits from what she did, and elites who faced relative declines in their power and wealth were quick to point in particular to what they regarded as her greediness. But with her death, even many of those who recognized her faults, as well as some of her bitter enemies, remembered her as a positive force in the lives of the unfortunate, as somehow cleansed by her good works. As General Reimúndez remarked, on seeing her body, "Poor little thing. Surely God has pardoned her." Or as Doña María commented, "when she died it was like Perón lost his arm. A woman who struggling [sic] until dawn in her office so that she could get the time to deal with all the tremendous pains of the republic."[72]

Notes

*The epigraphs for this chapter are from, respectively, Daniel James, *Doña María's Story: Life History, Memory, and Political Identity* (Durham, N.C.: Duke University Press, 2000), 78; Luisa Valenzuela, *The Lizard's Tail*, trans. Gregory Rabassa (New York:

Farrar, Straus, Giroux, 1983), 97; and Tomás Eloy Martínez, *Santa Evita* (Buenos Aires: Grupo Editorial Planeta, 1995), 300.

1. J. M. Taylor, *Eva Perón: The Myths of a Woman* (Chicago: University of Chicago Press, 1981), 128. In addition to Taylor's relatively short treatment, several biographies provide excellent data on Evita's story. Much of what exists in subsequent biographies comes initially from Otelo Borroni and Roberto Vacca, *Eva Perón* (Buenos Aires: Centro Editor de América Latina, 1970), which includes extremely valuable interviews about her early life. A careful and largely favorable view is Nicholas Fraser and Marysa Navarro, *Eva Perón* (New York: W. W. Norton, 1985); see also the somewhat more critical recent account, Alicia Dujovne Ortíz, *Eva Perón: A Biography*, trans. Shawn Fields (New York: St. Martin's Press, 1996). There is to date no full-scale biography of this major figure that uses extensive archival material, largely because the relevant archives have not been made available to researchers. The authors have been dependent on interviews and public documents, as I am, for their discussions.

2. Rodolfo Terragno, *La opinion*, July 29, 1971, 12, as quoted in Taylor, 128.

3. Interview with María Roldán, in James, *Doña María's Story*, 78.

4. Daniel James, *Resistance and Integration: Perónism and the Argentine Working Class, 1946–1976* (New York: Cambridge University Press, 1988), 8–9. David Rock, *Argentina 1516–1987: From Spanish Colonization to Alfonsín* (Berkeley and Los Angeles: University of California Press, 1987), 220, 283. Quotes from Bemberg appear in Julianne Burton-Carvajal, "Maria Luisa Bemberg's *Miss Mary*: Fragments of a Life and Career History," in *Redirecting the Gaze: Gender, Theory, and Cinema in the Third World*, ed. Diana Robin and Ira Jaffe (Albany: State University of New York Press, 1999), 340, 345.

5. Quotation from Ray Josephs, *Argentine Diary* (New York: Random House, 1944), 51–54, as quoted in Fraser and Navarro, 33.

6. Fraser and Navarro, 2–3. Dujovne Ortiz, 10–12.

7. Max Weber, *On Charisma and Institution-Building* (Chicago: University of Chicago Press, 1968), 48.

8. Dujovne Ortíz, 41. Borroni and Vacca, 56–57.

9. Fraser and Navarro, 24–26.

10. Dujovne Ortíz, 53. Taylor, 36–37.

11. Dujovne Ortíz, 59–62. Fraser and Navarro, 33. Borroni and Vacca, 71–74.

12. Fraser and Navarro, 42–43. Borroni and Vacca, 74–77.

13. Fraser and Navarro, 44–45.

14. Quotation from the interview by the authors with General Gerardo Demetrio, in Fraser and Navarro, 53–54. See also Dujovne Ortíz, 108.

15. The account of these events and much of the analysis is informed by Mariano Plotkin, *Mañana es San Perón: Propaganda, rituales políticos y educación en el regimen Peronista 1946–1955* (Buenos Aires: Ariel Historia Argentina, 1994), 88–103.

16. Fraser and Navarro, 64–65.

17. Dujovne Ortíz, 123.

18. Dujovne Ortíz, 123.

19. Quoted in Fraser and Navarro, 61. Another version of the quotation characterizes her as "unprotected." See Robert D. Crasswelder, *Perón and the Enigmas of Argentina* (New York: W. W. Norton, 1987), 165. Borroni and Vacca give the Spanish as "esta situación de desamparo. . . ."

20. Fraser and Navarro, 69–70, 91. Dujovne Ortíz, 123–133.

21. See photographs from these years in *Evita: Imagenes de una passion*, compiled by Fernando Diego García, Alejandro Labado, and Enrique Carlos Vázquez (Madrid: Celeste Ediciones), 27, 29, 31.

22. See the discussion and quotation in Dujovne Ortíz, 78–79.

23. A collection of newsreels at the National Archives in College Park, Maryland, containing both material that was actually used as well as outtakes, includes several of their early appearances together. The discussion of shared charisma is in Marysa Navarro, "Evita's Shared Charismatic Leadership," in *Latin American Populism in Comparative Perspective*, ed. Michael L. Conniff (Albuquerque: University of New Mexico Press, 1981), 47–49.

24. Dujovne Ortíz, 196–197.

25. Fraser and Navarro, 92–96. The authors do not list a source for the discussions with Guardo, but the Benítez information comes from an interview conducted by those authors. Dujovne Ortíz also reports the incident, 179.

26. Fraser and Navarro, 98. Dujovne Ortíz, 200.

27. Fraser and Navarro, 126–127. Dujovne Ortíz, 232–234.

28. Dujovne Ortiz, 260. Fraser and Navarro, 141. Taylor, 41, 51.

29. Taylor, 52.

30. Taylor, 51.

31. Frazier and Navarro, 183. *El Pregonero*, December 1998.

32. Taylor, 32.

33. Dujovne Ortíz, 153, 209. Taylor, 41.

34. Taylor, 47, 53.

35. Fraser and Navarro, 106–108. The discussion of Evita's urging the organizers of the Peronist Women's Party to engage in nontraditional activities while maintaining a traditional rhetoric of female subordination developed out of a conversation with Donna Guy. Dujovne Ortíz, 209.

36. Eva Perón, *Clases y escritos completes*, vol. 3, ed. Carlos E. Hurst and José María Roch (Buenos Aires: Editorial Megafón, 1987), 13.

37. Plotkin, 114, 118.

38. Plotkin, 117–118.

39. Eva Perón, *Discursos*, 297–299. See also Navarro, "Evita's Charismatic," 60–62.

40. See Fraser and Navarro, 110–113.

41. See Navarro, "Evita's Charismatic," 62. This identification of Eva Perón with the Virgin Mary is explored more thoroughly in Linda B. Hall, *Mary, Mother and Warrior: The Virgin Mary in Spain and The Americas* (Austin: University of Texas Press, 2004).

42. Eva Perón, *Discursos*, 304.

43. Eva Perón, *My Mission in Life* (New York: Vintage Press, 1953), 147–148.

44. On Evita's secret pregnancy, see "La aparición de una supuesta hija de Eva Perón reaviva en Argentina el debate sobre uno de sus grandes mitos," *Proceso*, April 5, 1998, 51–52.

45. See Benedict Anderson, *Imagined Communities: Reflections on the Origin and Spread of Nationalism* (London: Verso, 1991), 13.

46. See Fraser and Navarro, 138.

47. The official was Oscar Ivanissevich, Perón's minister of education. Joseph Page, *Perón: A Biography* (New York: Random House, 1983), 235. Taylor insists that Evita refused treatment, 58.

48. Page, 237. Ara, 46.

49. Ara, 44.

50. Lawrence J. Altman, "From the Life of Evita, a New Chapter on Medical Secrecy," *New York Times*, June 6, 2000. See also Dujovne Ortíz, 270.

51. Quotation from Fraser and Navarro, 146.

52. Fraser and Navarro, 149.

53. Ara, 176.

54. Plotkin, 127.

55. Fraser and Navarro, 150–154.

56. Taylor, 63.

57. Fraser and Navarro, 159.

58. Dujovne Ortíz, 277. Fraser and Navarro, 158.

59. Ara, 69–70. Fraser and Navarro, 164.

60. Fraser and Navarro, 166–167,170.

61. See, among dozens of examples, *El mundo Peronista*, June 15, 1964, cover and "Soneto a Eva Perón"; Graciela Albornoz de Videla, *Evita: Libro de Lectura para Primer Grado Inferior* (Buenos Aires: Editorial Luis Lasserre, 1953), 10, 28, and vocabulary sheet; *Cancionero de Juan Perón and Eva Perón*, ed. Dario Alessandro (Buenos Aires: Grupo Editor de SA, 1966), 261–285.

62. Ara, 241

63. Dujovne Ortíz, 298–300. Page, 424–425.

64. Fraser and Navarro, 190.

65. File ARGcc, Sam Slick Collection, University of New Mexico (UNM).

66. File ARGo, Sam Slick Collection, UNM.

67. File ARGn, Sam Slick Collection, UNM.

68. Files ARGbb and ARGc, Sam Slick Collection, UNM.

69. File ARGy, Sam Slick Collection, UNM.

70. María Julia Carozzi, "La religiosidad popular en las políticas del patrimonio cultural," *Estudios sobre religión: Newletter de la Asociación de Cuentistas Sociales de la Religión en el Mercosur*, no. 13, July 2002, 6. Emphasis in Carozzi.

71. James, *Doña María's Story*, 187–193, 76–77.

72. Ara, 241. James, *Doña María's Story*, 83.

Conclusion

Rethinking Latin American Heroes

SAMUEL BRUNK AND BEN FALLAW

Of what ingredients are heroines and heroes made? Comparisons between the ten subjects of this book are difficult because their lives were so distinct, because memories of them have been put to diverse uses, and because the authors of the different chapters have emphasized different themes. Still, though there is no single recipe for a Latin American hero, we would like to hazard some general comparative remarks.

Max Weber believed that charisma appears during periods of institutional breakdown, when individuals arise to fill power vacuums.[1] Though Charles Walker indicates that Gamarra's world was not bereft of functioning institutions, the independence period in which Bolívar and Gamarra participated was certainly, in relative terms, such a time, as was Santa Anna's post-independence Mexico. Indeed, the beginnings of nations, with their demand for creators, are inviting opportunities to acquire heroic stature. The Mexican Revolution—context for the heroism of Zapata, Carrillo Puerto, and Kahlo—was another era of new beginnings. Kahlo was born too late for her reputation to be a direct product of the revolutionary turmoil, but her art did contribute to Mexico's postrevolutionary search for a new national identity. Perón, meanwhile, gained her power in the wake of a military coup and used perceptions of institutional failure and sometimes extraconstitutional means to pursue her agenda. She too took what some have considered revolutionary steps to change political and social rules. Haya de la Torre never achieved political office, but his APRA movement met popular needs that the dysfunctional Peruvian state could not or would not address. Díaz, finally, was at least the product of a Mexico in which republican institutions had had a rocky history. As Victor Macías-González shows, he replaced those institutions in part with himself as embodiment of the state in the absolutist mode. Each of the heroes treated in this book, then, at some point in his or her career transcended bureaucratic structures, political allegiances, or cultural conventions that might have made him or her seem entangled, compromised, and thus less able to act heroically as an individual.

In some cases, of course, our heroes played leading roles in creating the unstable conditions in which their images could thrive. That is obviously true for Bolívar, Gamarra, Santa Anna, Zapata, Carrillo Puerto, and Sandino, and the same might be argued for Perón, Haya de la Torre, Kahlo (in the artistic realm), and even Díaz (who did, after all, first assume the presidency via armed rebellion). In such instances it is crucial either to convince the audience that the institutional breakdown preceded one's "revolutionary" actions or that institutions, though not obviously failing, were corrupt and thus nonfunctional—at least insofar as they did not serve the interests of "the people." Whatever the particulars, our data indicate that would-be heroes often cultivate the impression that they step into situations of crisis and do what is necessary to solve problems. This separation between institutions and heroes supports William Sater's contention that heroes are often oppositional figures who have virtues that many people admire but government officials rarely exhibit.[2] Here may lie much of the explanation for the heroism often found in bandits.

Although the status of heroes rises when institutions fail, would-be heroes do not have to break completely with the past. As Guzmán Blanco's and Hugo Chávez's uses of Bolívar and Evita Perón's evocations of the Virgin Mary demonstrate, heroes often look to previous heroes to enhance their status.[3] Indeed, in many nations there are chains of heroes, each engaging the legacies of those who came before. Leaping across the decades or centuries to associate oneself with a historical figure, however, is not an expression of cultural continuity. Rather, it generally makes a claim for a national (or more local) primordial identity that is purer, deeper, and more legitimate than prevailing institutions. It is an act of historical disjuncture, a means of looking to the idealized past for models of behavior to cure the ills of the present.[4]

The tendency to transcend institutions often allows heroes to bend ideologies to suit their needs. To be sure, all of our subjects had causes or ideals. Zapata and Carrillo Puerto fought for land reform and grassroots democracy, Sandino for similar goals plus an end to North American hegemony, Perón for workers and the downtrodden. Bolívar stood for independence and Latin America unity and Haya de la Torre for social justice for people marginalized by the Peruvian state. Kahlo "added a female viewpoint to artistic discourses" and adopted a highly personalized Marxism. In each of these cases our subjects were associated with causes that can be placed on the liberal, progressive, or radical half of the ideological spectrum—probably a good side to be on when one is being remembered from the twentieth or twenty-first centuries, with their mass politics. The same can also be said of Díaz, however conservative the revolutionaries would later consider him; he was, after all, a member of the Liberal Party, and his pursuit of progress fit perfectly into the liberal worldview. Only Gamarra and Santa Anna have strong associations with conservatism, and neither man generated lasting allegiances. Indeed, Gamarra's conservatism may have been a crucial factor in his failure to inspire a posthumous cult. Despite our ability to place them into broad categories, however, the subjects of this book were generally only loosely defined by or identified with political ideologies.

Because military and formal political spheres were reserved for men, it is not surprising that they dominate conventional lists of heroes across Latin America—and indeed the world. Eight of our ten subjects are male. Evita Perón and Frida Kahlo, however, have risen to iconic prominence greater than that of most of the men on our list. Indeed, both have developed international audiences, to the degree that residents of the United States are likely to be at least familiar with their names, which may not be true of any of the men discussed in this book save, perhaps, Santa Anna, the villain of the Alamo. Among Latin American men, perhaps only Che Guevara, Fidel Castro, and Pancho Villa can rival Kahlo and Perón for renown in this country, unless we consider media stars, such as baseball player Sammy Sosa, who have made their names in the United States.

Though they constitute a miniscule sample, Evita and Frida suggest that heroines are likely to be different from their male counterparts. One interesting difference is that we persistently refer to them by their first names. Men often use their first names or nicknames in populist campaigns, but few go through both life and posthumous career that way. Why might such a distinction exist? One possible reason is related to the notion that a major function of ancestors is to serve as mediators between this world and the next.[5] The greatest mediator in Latin American history is the Virgin Mary, whom Latin American Catholics ask to serve as their advocate with the more distant male figures of the celestial hierarchy. Her accessibility is connected in particular to her role as compassionate mother, and it has made her the region's prototypical heroine, to whom, as Linda Hall and Nancy Deffebach show, both Perón and Kahlo can be compared and with whom they at times identified themselves. Though neither Perón nor Kahlo was a biological mother, Perón acted as a sort of political mother to the *descamisados*, pleading their case and looking after their needs, while Kahlo's art often explored her childhood and her miscarriage.[6] In any event, the familiarity implicit in the use of their first names is surely a reflection of cultural expectations that women be more nurturing and may also reveal the expectation that they be, even in death, less detached, more motherly, and thus more effective, sympathetic intermediaries. Though they share this similarity to the Virgin Mary, in other respects the images of Kahlo and Perón are quite different. Perón's power was largely extra-official, but she was much more a politician and thus in some ways more similar to the men on our list. Kahlo's standing, on the other hand, reflects the fact that most prominent women will not achieve even unofficial political position.

Another important issue is the degree of success achieved by our subjects. Each of them had some triumphs, without which attaining heroic status would, of course, be unlikely. In fact, an alternative definition of charisma is being "near the heart of things," the political center, where the events that deeply affect the members of a society take place.[7] Our heroes managed to get there, in one way or another. Too many achievements, however, can threaten heroic stature in the long run if it means that a person comes to wield political power, because he or she then runs the risk of being blamed for actual policies and, ultimately, of being associated with the state and its shortcomings. Santa Anna, Bolívar, Gamarra, and Díaz all exercised executive power in their respective countries for substantial periods of time. Evita Perón enjoyed great power during her husband Juan's tenure as president of Argentina, but, as Linda Hall suggests, the unofficial nature of that power shielded her from close identification with the state apparatus. Carrillo Puerto achieved office—the governorship—only within his state, and many argue that he was killed before he could achieve his goals. Neither Sandino nor Zapata had authority that extended much beyond their regional movements, Haya de la Torre's clout was largely limited to his party, and Kahlo never entered the realm of formal politics. Five of our six subjects who did not rise to presidential office developed strong posthumous hero cults. The single possible exception is Haya, who has not, in David Nugent's opinion, enjoyed a powerful following since his death. Among those who did reach the presidency of their respective nations, only one of four, Bolívar, had a roughly comparable posthumous career. Díaz may simply have held too much power for too long to leave a heroic legacy, and Santa Anna surely took power too often. Gamarra's victories, meanwhile, seem to have permitted him to pursue policies that were not, in the long run, popular with the Peruvian people. They did allow him to demonstrate his managerial skills, but, as Walker indicates, there are few heroic administrators. Clearly, no amount of success enables one to create lasting iconic stature by fiat.

If defeat is often more memorable than triumph, that might explain why one of the most valuable attributes of a hero or heroine is a dramatic death, and preferably one that can be represented as a martyrdom for the benefit of a national community. William Sater proposes that dying in a way that reflects sacrifice for a larger cause helps make the contrast between oneself and the state (or the political status quo) clear, since self-sacrifice is one of those virtues that government officials rarely display.[8] Bolívar, Zapata, Carrillo Puerto, Sandino, Kahlo, and Perón all died deaths that boosted the heroic content of their images, and Santa Anna's dead leg was asked to carry the symbolic burden of sacrifice for the nation as well. Three of the men—Zapata, Carrillo Puerto, and Sandino—died violently in ways that could suggest they had been betrayed because they fought so steadfastly for the good of the many against powerful elites. Kahlo, Perón, and Bolívar, meanwhile, died after extended periods of poor health. Associated with the deaths of Bolívar and Perón, too, was the sense that they had sacrificed themselves and, at least in Bolívar's case, that he had been betrayed by those he sacrificed for: Bolívar had "plowed the sea" because his hopes were thwarted by rival politicians, and Perón sacrificed herself through overwork, "burning her life away" in the service of the Argentine people.[9] Kahlo, meanwhile, died at the age of 47, either of a pulmonary embolism or from an overdose, perhaps intentional, of painkillers. She had recently lost a leg in the latest of the many health problems that conditioned both her life and her art, and her death at such a young age easily lent itself to a tragic interpretation.[10] Among our other subjects, Gamarra's death might also have been construed as sacrificial had anyone been so inclined; the fact that no one was indicates that there were other problems with his candidacy for perpetual admiration. Santa Anna (the man, not the leg), Díaz, and Haya de la Torre did not suffer such deaths, though David Nugent reveals that APRA did frequently represent Haya de la Torre as a martyr. Coupled with their perhaps too successful political careers, these unromantic deaths may have doomed Díaz and Santa Anna, in particular, to less than heroic stature. Conversely, Bolívar could perhaps be pardoned his excessive success at least in part because of his appropriate death, which, after all, reflected a lack of ultimate success.

Why is death so crucial? It is one of the vivid moments in all lives, a rite of passage, a time that "will always baffle human understanding and fundamentally upset the emotional constitution of man."[11] It is a moment at which there is a passing connection between the earth and the heavens, when religion steps in to offer consolation and explanation.[12] It is a time when there is a reevaluation of the deceased, and as such a time when a person's life can become sacred—as did the lives of the many martyrs of the Catholic Church, who are familiar to most Latin Americans. Perhaps the death of a prominent person is particularly resonant because it confirms that not even the most charmed individual can escape this ultimate fate, that death is a universal condition that connects them with us.[13]

While death is clearly significant in the lives of individuals, it is also important in the lives of nations. As noted in the Introduction, ancestor worship has been practiced in most human cultures, and the structure of nations is often rhetorically patterned on the structure of families, so that nations have patriarchs and ancestors just as families do, and citizens are expected to venerate them. The Roman emperor Vespasian is said to have joked on his deathbed that he felt he was about to become a god; along those lines, we might see an appropriate death as the doorway heroes must pass through to become lasting members of their national pantheons.[14] Because of the sacrifices that dead heroes are understood to have made for nations, those who question the policies of national leaders—who are, as heads of state, usually seen as heads of national communities—may risk being charged not only with being antipatriotic but also with being irreligious or simply wicked, denying the godlike heroes that hold the community together. A fresh example is the period following the September 11, 2001, attacks on the World Trade Center in the United States. In the aftermath of that event, if only for a short time, to criticize the foreign policy of the president was akin to demeaning the sacrificed lives of the sacralized heroes who died on that day. Few were willing to speak out strongly under those circumstances.

Our sample, then, suggests that Latin American heroes are male, though there may be some advantages to being female when it comes to projecting heroic stature into the afterlife and the international sphere. Our subjects often made themselves known as resourceful leaders willing to face crises during unstable times. They were also, frequently, of vaguely liberal or leftist persuasion, though they were not often ideologically orthodox, and in general, personality seems to have been more important than doctrine. Many of them died in ways that evoked concepts of tragedy, self-sacrifice, and betrayal. Finally, we would recommend that if enduring heroism is the aim, it is best for a would-be hero not to rise to the office of the presidency. Of our ten subjects, those who best fit this description are Zapata, Carrillo Puerto, Sandino, and Perón. In the second tier we would place Bolívar, Kahlo, and Haya de la Torre, though Kahlo does not fall into the first group only because our criteria are skewed toward politicians. The rest—Gamarra, Santa Anna, and Díaz—largely fail to meet these criteria. These three groups correspond well with our rough impressions of how much resonance these individuals have at present in the hearts of their respective audiences, with two exceptions. After a promising start, Carrillo

Puerto's cult withered considerably, owing, it would seem, to the twists and turns of subsequent history, which cannot be discounted: both the manipulation of his memory and the misfortunes of his party undermined his image as the decades passed. As Ben Fallaw notes, however, some of its vestiges still exist, and it is not impossible that it will gain strength in the future. Based on our standards, Haya de la Torre, too, should probably have a greater presence today than David Nugent believes him to have. Why he does not remains unclear, but it may be that his fate, too, is bound to that of his party in ways that are not always beneficial to his memory.

Comparative Perspectives

DO LATIN AMERICA'S HEROES AND THEIR CULTS differ from those produced elsewhere? Many scholars have suggested that Latin Americans have had a greater number of personalistic leaders than some other societies, and have sought to explain why. One of the most common arguments, taking off from Weber's discussion of charisma, is that less stable nations need more such leaders because their institutions often fail.[15] A related notion is that charismatic—or at least autocratic—leadership is a response to the frustrations and turmoil that can come with modernization.[16] Putting those explanations together, one might see potential heroes rising to attempt to fix the economic and political problems spawned by independence, the rapid growth of the Gilded Age, and the Great Depression, and it is certainly true that those periods generated many such figures. Other historians have countered, however, that institutions have often failed precisely because ambitious individuals did not permit them to function. Brian Loveman adds that constitutional provisions for suspending individual rights and the separation of powers in times of emergency have been crucial in this regard.[17]

Another major category of explanation is what we would call cultural determinism, or the belief that personalistic leaders fulfill a deeply ingrained cultural archetype of the authoritarian leader. William Sater, for instance, sees in Latin America a valuing of self-sacrifice that inhabitants of the United States do not share, and suggests that the Catholic religion with its martyrs may be part of the explanation for the region's many heroes.[18] Arguments of cultural determinism often trace the historical roots of Latin American strongmen back to Roman Spain, and find them strengthened by medieval Catholic authoritarianism and the turbulence of Latin American independence. *Caudillos* and their charismatic offspring, this approach continues, both reinforce and reflect a widespread and deeply rooted mistrust of law, government, and democracy.[19]

We can also approach this question from other directions. Historians writing on memory and hero cults in the United States often argue that the United States has been exceptional in its treatment of heroes. Michael Kammen identifies a strong strain of ancestor worship in the United States and describes a myth of Abraham Lincoln that shares much with the cults we have seen in Latin America. On the other hand, he maintains that in the United States the private sector, not the government, has been the primary custodian of memory, and he makes a (rather provincial) distinction between free and unfree nations to argue that the citizens of the former are free to remember and forget as they choose while the latter are not.[20] More promising is John Bodnar's contention that World War II eroded "heroic nationalism" in England and Germany, and that the Vietnam War may have had a similar impact in the United States. This suggests that particular historical events affecting particular nations can shape the way inhabitants of those nations remember heroes in general.[21] In a similar vein, Maurice Agulhon asserts that France cannot have a cult of founding fathers similar to that of the United States because in France, revolutionary leaders turned bad once in power, not just undermining their own cults but immunizing the French against cults of "great men" in general.[22] Finally, in a book on V. I. Lenin, Nina Tumarkin develops an argument based on Russian exceptionalism. Russia's uniqueness, she claims, manifested in the new revolutionary regime's need for justification, combined with specific prerevolutionary cultural practices—the intelligentsia's worship of the nineteenth-century poet Alexander Pushkin, for example—gave Lenin's cult a distinct character.[23]

These arguments indicate that while all cultures may produce heroes, and while the use of those heroes may be roughly similar in different locations, there are also important variations because heroes are shaped by the unique historical trajectories of their communities. But some interpretations along these lines are less successful than others. Kammen's distinction between free and unfree nations is ineffective because it is a broad and naive generalization about political culture that dispenses with historical nuance. Explanations that focus on Latin America's large number of personalistic leaders often compare the region with the United States or Western Europe, and they are certainly correct that there has been a history of failed institutions in Latin America in comparison with those places, thus producing more leaders ruling extralegally. As we have seen, though, particularly in the case of Santa Anna, personalism does not necessarily make a hero. In any event, the number of heroes a society has is only one part of the story.

Sater's generalizations about culture are both risky and provocative. Latin American culture is and has been more Catholic than the culture of either the United States or Great Britain—his points of comparison—and it may be true, again in those specific comparisons, that Latin American hero cults are different as a result, more concerned with defeat, sacrifice, and death. Another source of some of that difference might be the contrasting views of the residents of different countries about the success of their nations on the international stage: the United States has been a world power in economic, military, and political terms; Latin American nations, historically, have not. But we have to be cautious here: sacrifice and a dramatic death, for example, are critical components of the Lincoln cult.

When settings besides the United States and Western Europe are brought into the comparative mix, arguments that Latin American heroes are unique become more difficult to sustain. Tumarkin shows that Lenin's posthumous cult matches anything Latin America can offer in terms of personalism, sacrifice, and concern with death. The main problem is that to make claims about what Latin America is like in general, one can only argue in terms of broad categories, as Sater does when he writes that Latin Americans are largely Catholic. The many different parts of the region do not share more specific cultural or historical attributes. And at that level of generalization, Latin America is not unique—it is not the only Catholic part of the world, nor is it the only part of the world in which institutions have often failed. In fact, if Sater reveals anything unique in comparing the heroes of Latin America and the United States, it is probably, inadvertently, some unique attribute of U.S. hero cults, because as Tumarkin and Bodnar seem to understand, the most promising unit of comparison is the nation. This is primarily because it is on the national stage that accounts of heroes have been most intricate during the past two centuries. As we mentioned in the Introduction, national communities have made particular uses of heroes. National politicians have sought to form unified audiences within their countries and to produce stories about national histories that would inculcate those audiences with shared values, give them greater unity, and ultimately, the politicians naturally hoped, make them both more governable and more productive. The makers of nations have also had some effective tools—educational systems, mass media, bodies of law—with which to pursue those ends.

Variations on a Latin American Theme: Is Mexico Different?

SO WHAT OF DIFFERENCES AMONG THE NATIONS of Latin America, and in particular, given the contours of this book, in what ways are Mexico's heroes distinct? Enrique Krauze's recent proposition that Mexican leaders have been uniquely sacred, powerful, and thus influential with regard to the nation's fate is unconvincing and has been effectively skewered by Claudio Lomnitz.[24] More promising are thoughts on Mexican exceptionalism offered by David Brading and Friedrich Katz. Brading demonstrates that around the time of Mexican independence, pro-independence intellectuals Carlos María de Bustamante and Servando Teresa de Mier linked insurgent priests Miguel Hidalgo and José María Morelos with Cuauhtémoc—leader of Aztec resistance to the Spanish conquest—as patriotic heroes. Another figure whose historical pedigree stretches back to the 1500s, the Virgin of Guadalupe, ranked as an even more important symbol of nationalism for Mexico's patriot rebels. Brading adds that only in Mexico, among the Spanish American nations, was this sort of deep history of nationalism evoked at the time of independence.[25] Katz, meanwhile, remarks that Mexico is unique because peasant uprisings have been crucial factors in important national transformations. He considers the conquest period—conceptualized not merely as the imposition of Spanish rule but rather as a broad rebellion against the Aztec state by other indigenous groups—and independence as two times when rural revolts profoundly shaped watershed events in Mexican history.[26]

If Katz and Brading are both correct, then we have at the birth of the Mexican nation the emergence of a unique set of patriotic heroes that coincides—again uniquely within Latin America—with peasant rebellion. What might such beginnings have to do with the Mexican heroes examined in this book? The easiest case to start with is that of Zapata. Katz's third example of the link between peasant uprisings and national transformation in Mexico is, predictably, the Mexican Revolution, in which Zapata was the most renowned peasant leader. In building their following, Zapata and his collaborators appealed to the patriotic legacy of the forebears mentioned by Brading—particularly Morelos and the Virgin of Guadalupe—and in the process constructed Zapata's image in part on the base of those heroes that preceded him. Surely the Zapatista leaders hoped that associating themselves and their cause with these figures would heighten their appeal, but they also seemed to have seen them as models establishing modes of honorable behavior that they should follow. In other words, they were connected not just by metaphor but by actions and practices: Zapata's home state was named for the caudillo Morelos, who had enjoyed one of his most important victories at Cuautla; the Virgin of Guadalupe was a prominent figure in the religious lives of many Zapatistas. In both image and deed, then, Zapata was prefigured: he was given his meaning and direction by a battery of cultural expectations that included historically conditioned concepts of leadership. The product was, and is, a hero unlike any

other in Latin American history, not just because of the fine balance of local
and national roots that Brunk's chapter discusses but because Zapata is a
peasant as national hero, one who even enjoys international renown.[27]
Adding a unique Zapata to the insights of Brading and Katz produces a
chain of heroes that suggests that Mexico has a distinct national story, some
of which seems largely rhetorical and some of which appears to have a basis
in fact.

To elaborate on what is peculiarly Mexican, we might focus on the role
of liberalism. After the reign of Emperor Maximilian during the 1860s, a
tradition of liberal control of the presidency began that continued virtually
uninterrupted until Vicente Fox came to power in the year 2000—at least
if we define liberalism broadly.[28] Liberalism enjoyed this extended (and
again, exceptional) period of supremacy in Mexico in part because the conservative cause was profoundly discredited by conservative support for the
French invasion that brought Maximilian to the throne. This produced the
pairing of liberalism and nationalism and of conservatism with the betrayal of the Mexican nation. As a result, since that time all national heroes
have been defined as liberals or progressives, and Benito Juárez, who wres-
tled Mexico's executive power away from Maximilian in 1867 to begin the
long liberal ascendancy, may be Mexico's most revered hero.

Another feature of Mexican liberalism is that many of its heroes have
either had Indian identities or have been otherwise associated with
Mexico's indigenous population. Aztec resistance leader Cuauhtémoc falls
into that category, of course, as do the dark-skinned Virgin of Guadalupe,
the priests Hidalgo and Morelos, who led partly Indian rebellions for independence, and the Zapotec Juárez. So do all three of the Mexican figures
covered in this book who achieved heroic standing. Carrillo Puerto championed the Mayan peasantry. In both art and life, Kahlo sought out indigenous culture as a source of inspiration, most famously in appropriating the
dress of Zapotec women from Oaxaca's Isthmus of Tehuantepec. Zapata,
finally, had a significant Indian following and has long been associated with
Indianness—though he considered himself a mestizo—in part because
urban Mexicans tend to identify all peasants, at least in central and southern Mexico, as Indians. With respect to this facet of Mexico's national tale,
then, the links in the heroic chain fit together as follows: independence pro-
pagandists utilized the Indianness of Cuauhtémoc and the Virgin of
Guadalupe; Juárez reaffirmed Mexican independence; and Zapata chose to
remember and honor not only the Virgin of Guadalupe and independence
heroes but Juárez, too, who presumably was valuable to him both for his liberalism and for his Indian ethnicity. The marked Indianness of this pantheon suggests that it may be more inclusive—and more representative of

resistance, rebellion, and revindication—than those of other Latin American countries, probably because those well-timed peasant rebellions demanded it.

This does not necessarily mean that Mexico has had in fact a more inclusive political system or society than other parts of Latin America. Mexico's liberal, Indian narrative has, of, course been manipulated by many who have not favored inclusion. Indeed, like Porfirio Díaz, most Mexican leaders who have projected themselves as liberals—and often as revolutionaries—have practiced authoritarian politics, hardly a hallmark of liberal ideology. Still, the narrative does exist, and elites do not have the option of throwing it out; it evolved, after all, in part out of their need to conciliate peasants, Indians, and other lower-class groups. And as long as the national story maintains its present form, the field for heroic action may be broader than it is in other nations. Zapata, Carrillo Puerto, and Kahlo, in other words—associated with Indianness and revolution—can open the way for other heroes in this mold. Here another quick look at the Zapatista Army of National Liberation (EZLN) might be instructive. Spokesperson Subcomandante Marcos has an urban background, an international perspective, and a flair for the use of the Internet, all making him a very different character from Zapata. The EZLN, though, has appropriated Zapata's name, and Marcos and his colleagues have found in Mexico's saga a host of other ingredients that are useful to their cause. They have tied their idea of Votán-Zapata (discussed in Chapter 5) to such national heroes as Hidalgo and Morelos, and by creatively placing the more local Votán together with national heroes, they have modified national myth to fit their situation. Because they have twisted that narrative effectively enough to capture the imaginations of many Mexicans, Marcos himself may be on his way to heroic stature.

In sum, we find that it is the interaction between individual leaders with all their personal idiosyncrasies and the structures of national history that gives Mexican heroes their uniqueness, and we presume that analysis of that dynamic in other Latin American nations would uncover exceptionalism in them as well. Focusing on the nation rather than the larger region allows for the way in which history moves, from one thing to the next, where individuals can and do make impressions on it. We therefore find it more satisfying than explanations, such as Sater's remark on Catholicism, that stress broad cultural characteristics that are conceptualized as more essential and unchanging. The charismatic link is embedded within these national histories, after the hero dies, through hero cults, which ultimately make charisma routine and thus something that can be passed from generation to generation.[29] Far from seeking to reduce national histories to the biographies of great men (or women), then, the authors of this volume merely insist that the dynamics between leaders, constituencies, and the stories they tell are significant. It is not so much that prominent individuals are of supreme importance as that people in many societies have been receptive to stories in which such individuals are central, and have sought to hang meaning on those extraordinary lives. Under those circumstances, heroes can tell us a great deal about the places from which they come.

Notes

1. Douglas Madsen and Peter G. Snow, *The Charismatic Bond: Political Behavior in Time of Crisis* (Cambridge, Mass.: Harvard University Press, 1991), 9.

2. William F. Sater, "Heroic Myths for Heroic Times," *Mexican Studies/Estudios Mexicanos* 4 (1988): 160.

3. On the influence of Bolívar on Chávez, see Richard Gott, *In the Shadow of the Liberator: Hugo Chávez and the Transformation of Venezuela* (New York: Verso, 2000), 97–108.

4. Mona Ozouf, *Festivals and the French Revolution*, trans. Alan Sheridan (Cambridge, Mass.: Harvard University Press, 1988), 276.

5. Elizabeth Carmichael and Chloe Sayer, *The Skeleton at the Feast: The Day of the Dead in Mexico* (Austin: University of Texas Press, 1991), 14.

6. For a demonstration of how motherhood can politically empower women, see Lorraine Bayardo de Volo, *Mothers of Heroes and Martyrs: Gender Identity Politics in Nicaragua, 1979–1999* (Baltimore: Johns Hopkins University Press, 2001).

7. Clifford Geertz, "Centers, Kings, and Charisma: Reflections on the Symbolics of Power," in *Culture and Its Creators: Essays in Honor of Edward Shils*, ed. Joseph Ben-David and Terry Nichols Clark (Chicago: University of Chicago Press, 1977), 151–152.

8. Sater, "Heroic Myths for Heroic Times," 154–155.

9. Death by betrayal is also the most common way bandit-heroes are understood to depart from the material world, since they are presumed to be too crafty to die in any other way. See Alan Knight, *The Mexican Revolution*, 2 vols. (Cambridge: Cambridge University Press, 1986), 2:369.

10. Hayden Herrera, *Frida: A Biography of Frida Kahlo*, reprint ed. (New York: HarperCollins, 2002), 429–432.

11. Bronislaw Malinowski, *The Foundations of Faith and Morals* (London: Oxford University Press, 1936), 28.

12. John Eade and Michael J. Sallnow, eds., introduction to *Contesting the Sacred: The Anthropology of Christian Pilgrimage* (London: Routledge, 1991), 6.

13. Dorothea Krook, *Elements of Tragedy* (New Haven: Yale University Press, 1969), 62–63.

14. Gaius Suetonius Tranquillus, *The Twelve Caesars*, trans. Robert Graves (New York: Penguin, 1957), 285.

15. Madsen and Snow, *The Charismatic Bond.* The most comprehensive study of early caudillismo, John Lynch's magisterial *Caudillos in Spanish America, 1800–1850* (Oxford: Oxford University Press, 1992), posits that the caudillos who arose after independence were the products of larger forces (pp. 403, 424–425). For Lynch, the caudillo "entered history as a local hero whom larger events promoted to military chieftains." Men such

as Rosas and Santa Anna tapped the resources of the colonial hacienda to fill the political vacuum created by the collapse of traditional colonial institutions.

16. Stephen Haber, ed., "Introduction: The Political Economy of Crony Capitalism," in *Crony Capitalism and Economic Growth in Latin America: Theory and Evidence* (Stanford, Calif.: Hoover Institute Press and Stanford University Press, 2002), xiii–xv.

17. Enrique Krauze, *Mexico: Biography of Power: A History of Modern Mexico, 1810–1996*, trans. Hank Heifetz (New York: HarperCollins, 1997); and Brian Loveman, *The Constitution of Tyranny: Regimes of Exception in Spanish America* (Pittsburgh: University of Pittsburgh Press, 1993).

18. Sater, "Heroic Myths for Heroic Times," 159. In a similar vein, David I. Kertzer, *Ritual, Politics, and Power* (New Haven: Yale University Press, 1988), suggests that the simplification that comes from hero cults may be most necessary for people unused to the idea of national identity (p. 178).

19. Octavio Paz, *El laberinto de la soledad* (Mexico City: Fondo de Cultura Económica, 1959), 110–111, 118; and Krauze, *Biography of Power*, 210–212.

20. Michael Kammen, *Mystic Chords of Memory: The Transformation of Tradition in American Culture* (New York: Knopf, 1991), 13, 128, 221, 700.

21. John Bodnar, *Remaking America: Public Memory, Commemoration, and Patriotism in the Twentieth Century* (Princeton, N.J.: Princeton University Press, 1992), 252. See also Marshall Fishwick, prologue to *Heroes of Popular Culture*, by Ray B. Browne and Michael T. Marsden (Bowling Green, Ky.: Bowling Green University Popular Press, 1972), 1–8.

22. Maurice Agulhon, *Marianne into Battle* (New York: Cambridge University Press, 1981), 183.

23. Nina Tumarkin, *Lenin Lives! The Lenin Cult in Soviet Russia* (Cambridge, Mass.: Harvard University Press, 1983), 3, 6–7, 12–13, 83.

24. Enrique Krauze, *Mexico: Biography of Power: A History of Modern Mexico, 1810–1996*, trans. Hank Heifetz (New York: Harper, 1997); and Claudio Lomnitz, *Deep Mexico, Silent Mexico: An Anthropology of Nationalism* (Minneapolis: University of Minnesota Press, 2001), 217, 225.

25. David A. Brading, *Mito y profecía en la historia de México*, trans. Tomás Segovia (Mexico City: Vuelta, 1988), 17–18.

26. Friedrich Katz, ed., "Introduction: Rural Revolts in Mexico," in *Riot, Rebellion, and Revolution: Rural Social Conflict in Mexico* (Princeton, N.J.: Princeton University Press, 1988), 16–17.

27. On the value of having a popular hero with whom the masses can identify, see Steven Palmer, "Getting to Know the Unknown Soldier: Official Nationalism in Liberal Costa Rica, 1880–1900," *Journal of Latin American Studies* 25 (1993): 47.

28. On liberalism becoming a "unifying political myth" during the Porfiriato, see Charles A. Hale, *The Transformation of Liberalism in Late Nineteenth Century Mexico* (Princeton, N.J.: Princeton University Press, 1989), 106.

29. On the routinization of charisma, see Weber, *On Charisma*, 54–61.

Bibliography

Archival Collections

Albuquerque, N.Mex.

Zimmerman Library, University of New Mexico
   Sam L. Slick Collection (SSC)

Brussels

Direction des Archives du Ministère des Affaires Étrangères, du Commerce Extérieur, et de la Coopération au Développement (AMAE-CECD)

College Park, Md.

United States National Archives

Cuzco

Archivo Departamental, Administración del Tesoro Público

El Paso, Tex.

Department of Special Collections, The Library of the University of Texas at El Paso
   Gertrude Fitzgerald Photograph Collection

Madrid

Archivo Histórico del Ministerio de Asuntos Exteriores, Palacio de Santa Cruz (AHMAE)

Managua

El Instituto de Historia de Nicaragua y Centroamérica, Universidad Centroamericana (IHCA)

Mérida

Archivo General del Estado de Yucatán (AGEY)
    Poder ejecutivo (PE)

Mexico City

Archivo del Cabildo Metropolitano de la Catedral de México (AHDF)
Archivo General de la Nación (AGN)
    Archivo de Emiliano Zapata (AZ)
    Archivo de Genovevo de la O (AO)
    Archivo del Cuartel General del Sur
    Fondo Presidentes
        Alvaro Obregón and Plutarco Elías Calles (OyC)
        Lázaro Cárdenas
Archivo Histórico de la Secretaría de Relaciones Exteriores (AHSRE)
Centro de Estudios de Historia de México, CONDUMEX
    Archivo José Yves Limantour (JYL-CONDUMEX)
Centro de Estudios Sobre la Universidad
    Archivo de Gildardo Magaña (AGM)
        Fondo Documental del Archivo de Rafael Chousal, 1860–1967,
Correspondencia de la señora doña Carmen Romero Rubio y Castelló de
Díaz (CRRCD)
Hemeroteca Nacional
    Fondo Silvino González (FSG)
Instituto Nacional de Antropología e Historia and Instituto de
Investigaciones Dr. José María Luis Mora
    Programa de Historia Oral (PHO)

Paris

Archives of the Foreign Ministry of the French Republic, Quai d'Orsay
(AMAE)

Washington, D.C.

National Archives and Records Administration (NARA)
    Mexican Historical Pamphlets 1820–1910
    Records of the United States Marine Corps (USMC)
    Department of State (DOS)
        Records Relating to the Internal Affairs of Mexico, 1910–1929

Newspapers

Diario del gobierno, Mexico City
El Boletin Oficial, Mexico City
El Campesino, Mexico City
El Demócrata, Mexico City
Excélsior, Mexico City
El Heraldo, Cartagena
El Imparcial, Mexico City
El Mundo Ilustrado, Mexico City
El Mundo Peronista, Buenos Aires
New York Times, New York
Nosotros, Mexico City
Novedades, Mexico City
El Pregonero, Buenos Aires
Proceso, Mexico City
La Tribuna, Lima
El Siglo XIX, Mexico City
El Universal, Mexico City.
Universal Gráfico, Mexico City

Books and Periodicals

Abascal, Salvador. *La revolución de la reforma de 1833 á 1848. Gómez Farías—Santa [Anna]*. Mexico City: Tradición, 1983.

Abel, Christopher, and Nissa Torrents, eds. *José Martí, Revolutionary Democrat*. Durham, N.C.: Duke University Press, 1986.

Aboites, Luis. *La Revolución Mexicana en Espita, Yucatán (1910–1940): Microhistoria de la formación del estado de la revolución*. Mérida: Maldonado Editores, INAH and SEP, 1985.

Adams, Jane Meredith. "In death, Mexican artist a cult figure." *Chicago Tribune*, November 8, 1992, sec. 1.

Ades, Dawn. *Art in Latin America: The Modern Era, 1820–1980*. New Haven: Yale University Press, 1989.

Aguilar, Anacleto Cetina. *Breves datos históricos y culturales del municipio de Hunucmá*. Mérida: n.p., 1990.

Aguilera, Carmen, Elena Vargas Lugo, Marita Martínez del Río de Redo, Jorge Loyzaga, Luis Ortiz Macedo, Teresa Castello Iturbide, Manuel Carballo, María Cecilia Martínez López, and Fernando Sánchez Martínez. *El mueble mexicano: Historia, evolución, e influencias*. Mexico City: Fomento Cultural Banamex, 1985.

Aguirre, Carlos, and Charles Walker, eds. *Bandoleros, abigeos, y montoneros: Criminalidad y violencia en el Perú, siglos XVIII–XX.* Lima: Instituto de Apoyo Agrario, 1990.

Aguirre Cinta, Rafael. *Lecciones de historia general de México desde los tiempos primitivos hasta nuestras días.* 16th ed. Mexico City: Sociedad de Edición y Librería Francoamericana, 1926.

Ake, Santos Domínguez. *La vida de Felipe Carrillo Puerto y su memoria en Muxupip.* Mérida: Maldonado, Consejo Nacional para la Cultura y las Artes, Culturas Populares, 1992.

———. *La historia de la sociedad ejidal de Muxupip.* Tlahuapan, Puebla, Mexico: Instituto Nacional Indigenista and Sedesol, 1994.

Alamán, Lucas. *Historia de Méjico desde los primeros movimientos que preparon su independencia en el año de 1808 hasta la época presente.* 2nd ed. Vol. 5. Mexico City: Editorial Jus, 1969.

Alayza Paz Soldán, Luis. *El Gran Mariscal José de la Mar.* Lima: Gil, 1941.

Albornoz de Videla, Graciela. *Evita: Libro de Lectura para Primer Grado Inferior.* Buenos Aires: Editorial Luis Lasserre, 1953.

Aldaraca, Bridget, et al. *Nicaragua in Revolution: The Poets Speak.* Minneapolis: Marxist Educational Press, 1980.

Alessandro, Dario, ed. *Cancionero de Juan Perón y Eva Perón.* Buenos Aires: Grupo Editor, 1966.

Aljovín Losada, Cristóbal. *Caudillos y constituciones, Perú: 1821–1845.* Lima: Pontificia Universidad Católica, Fondo de Cultura Económica, 2000.

Aljure Chalela, Simón. *Bibliografía bolivariana.* Bogota: Banco de la República/Biblioteca Luis Angel Arango, 1983.

Alonso, Ana Maria. "Gender, Ethnicity, and the Constitution of Subjects: Accommodation, Resistance, and Revolution on the Chihuahuan Frontier." PhD diss., University of Chicago, 1988.

Altman, Lawrence J. "From the Life of Evita, a New Chapter in Medical Secrecy." *New York Times,* June 6, 2000.

Alverez, Manuel Frances. *Los restos del Lic. Carlos María de Bustamante y el panteón de San Fernando.* Mexico City: Vida Gráfica, 1925.

Amado, Donato, and Luis Miguel Glave. *Periódicos cuzqueños del siglo XIX: Estudio y catálogo de Fondo de Archivo Departamental del Cuzco.* Madrid: Fundación Histórica Tavera, 1999.

Amendolla, [Luis]. *La revolución comienza a los cuarenta.* Mexico: n.p., n.d.

Anaya, Rudolfo. "'I'm the King': The Macho Image." In *Muy Macho: Latino Men Confront Their Manhood,* edited by. Ray González, 57–73. New York: Anchor Books, 1966.

Anderson, Benedict. *Imagined Communities: Reflections on the Origins and Spread of Nationalism.* Rev. ed. London: Verso, 1991.

Anderson, John Lee. *Che Guevara: A Revolutionary Life.* New York: Grove Press, 1997.

Angelis, Pedro de. Prologue to *Segunda campaña a la sierra del Perú en 1821,* by Jose I. Arenales. Buenos Aires: Vaccaro, 1920.

Anna, Timothy E. *The Fall of the Royal Government in Peru.* Lincoln: University of Nebraska Press, 1979.

————. *Forging Mexico, 1812–1835.* Lincoln: University of Nebraska Press, 1998.

Appleby, Joyce, Lynn Hunt, and Margaret Jacob, eds. *Telling the Truth about History.* New York: W. W. Norton, 1994.

Agulhon, Maurice. *Marianne into Battle.* New York: Cambridge University Press, 1981.

Ara, Pedro. *El caso Eva Perón.* Madrid: CVS Ediciones, n.d.

Archer, Christon I. "The Young Antonio López de Santa Anna: Veracruz Counterinsurgent and Incipient Caudillo." In *The Human Tradition in Latin America: The Nineteenth Century,* edited by Judith Ewell and William H. Beezley, 3–16. Wilmington, Del.: Scholarly Resources, 1989.

Arrom, Silvia Marina. *The Women of Mexico City, 1790–1857.* Stanford, Calif.: Stanford University Press, 1985.

El asesinato de Carrillo Puerto (discursos y articulos en elogio del ilustre Mártir, y protestas contra sus infames asesinos). Mexico City: n.p., 1924.

Aspúrua, Ramón. *Biografías de hombres notables de Hispanoamérica.* Caracas: Imprenta Nacional, 1877.

"La audiencia." *El Mundo Ilustrado* 4, no. 206 (1904): 789–790.

Azuela, Alicia. "*El Machete* and *Frente a Frente*: Art Committed to Social Justice in Mexico." *Art Journal* 52, no. 1 (Spring 1993): 82–87.

Baker, Shannon L. "Santa Anna's Legacy: Caudillismo in Early Republican Mexico." PhD diss., Texas Christian University, 1999.

Bancroft, Hubert Howe. *The Works of Hubert Howe Bancroft.* Vol. 13, *History of Mexico.* San Francisco: History Company, 1886.

Barnitz, Jacqueline. "Five Women Artists." *Latin American Literature and Arts* 75 (Spring 1975): 38–41.

Barrios de Chungara, Domitila. *Let Me Speak! Testimony of Domitila, a Woman of the Bolivian Mines.* New York: Monthly Review Press, 1978.

Barthes, Roland. *Mythologies.* New York: Hill and Wang, 1972.

Bartra, Armando. *Los herederos de Zapata: Movimientos campesinos posrevolucionarios en México.* Mexico City: Ediciones Era, 1985.

Basadre, Jorge. *Historia de la República del Perú.* 11 vols. 7th ed. Lima: Editorial Universitaria, 1983.

————. *La Iniciación de la república.* 2 vols. Lima: F. y E. Rosay, 1929.

Bayo, Alberto. *150 Questions for a Guerrilla*. Denver, Colo.: Panther Publication, 1963.

Beezley, William H. *Judas at the Jockey Club and Other Episodes of Porfirian Mexico*. 2nd ed. Lincoln: University of Nebraska Press, 2004.

———. "The Porfirian Smart Set Anticipates Thorstein Veblen in Guadalajara." In *Rituals of Rule, Rituals of Resistance: Public Celebrations and Popular Culture in Mexico*, edited by William H. Beezely, Cheryl English Martin, and William E. French, 173–190. Wilmington, Del.: Scholarly Resources, 1997.

Beezley, William H., and Judith Ewell, eds. *The Human Tradition in Modern Latin America*. Wilmington, Del.: Scholarly Resources, 1997.

Beezley, William H., Cheryl English Martin, and William E. French, eds. *Rituals of Rule, Rituals of Resistance: Public Celebrations and Popular Culture in Mexico*. Wilmington, Del.: Scholarly Resources, 1994.

Bendaña, Alejandro. *La Mística de Sandino*. Managua: Centro de Estudios Internacionales, 1994.

Benjamin, Medea, and Maisa Mendonça. *Benedita da Silva: An Afro-Brazilian Woman's Story of Politics*. Monroe, Ore.: Food First Books, 1997.

Benjamin, Thomas. *La Revolución: Mexico's Great Revolution as Memory, Myth, and History*. Austin: University of Texas Press, 2000.

Bergman-Carton, Janice. "Like an Artist." *Art in America* 81 (1993): 35–39.

Bertram, Geoffrey. "Peru, 1930–1960," chap. 7. In *Cambridge History of Latin America*, edited by Leslie Bethell. Vol. 8. Cambridge: Cambridge University Press, 1991.

Blanchard, Peter. *The Origins of the Peruvian Labor Movement, 1883–1919*. Pittsburgh, Pa.: University of Pittsburgh Press, 1982.

Blanco, Jose María. *Diario del viaje del Presidente Orbegoso al sur del Perú*. Lima: PUC, Instituto Riva-Agüero, 1974.

Blandón, Jesus M. *Entre Sandino y Fonseca*. Managua: Departamento de Propaganda y Educación Política de FSLN, 1982.

Bodnar, John. *Remaking America: Public Memory, Commemoration, and Patriotism in the Twentieth Century*. Princeton, N.J.: Princeton University Press, 1992.

Bolio, Edmundo. *De la cuña al parredón: Anecdotario histórico de la vida, muerte y gloria de Felipe Carrillo Puerto*. Mérida: Basso/Talleres de la Compañía Periodistica del Sureste, n.d.

Boorstin, Daniel J. *The Americans: The National Experience*. New York: Random House, 1965.

Booth, John A. *The End and the Beginning: The Nicaraguan Revolution*. Boulder, Colo.: Westview Press, 1985.

Borroni, Otero, and Roberto Vacca. *Eva Perón*. Buenos Aires: Centro Editor de América Latina, 1970.

Borsa, Joan. "Frida Kahlo: Marginalization and the Critical Female Subject." *Third Text* 12 (1990): 21–40.

Brading, David, ed. *Caudillo and Peasant in the Mexican Revolution*. Cambridge: Cambridge University Press, 1980.

Brading, David A. *Mito y profecía en la historia de México,* translated by Tomás Segovia. Mexico City: Vuelta, 1988.

Brown, Betty Ann. "The Past Idealized: Diego Rivera's Use of Pre-Columbian Imagery." In *Diego Rivera: A Retrospective*. New York: Founders Society of Detroit Institute of Arts/W. W. Norton, 1986.

Brunk, Samuel. *Emiliano Zapata: Revolution and Betrayal in Mexico.* Albuquerque: University of New Mexico Press, 1995.

———. "The Mortal Remains of Emiliano Zapata." In *Death, Dismemberment, and Memory,* edited by Lyman Johnson, 141–178. Albuquerque: University of New Mexico Press, 2004.

———. "Remembering Emiliano Zapata: Three Moments in the Posthumous Career of the Martyr of Chinameca." *Hispanic American Historical Review* 78 (1998): 457–490.

———. "'The Sad Situation of Civilians and Soldiers': The Banditry of Zapatismo in the Mexican Revolution." *American Historical Review* 101 (1996): 331–353.

———. "Zapata and the City Boys: In Search of a Piece of the Revolution." *Hispanic American Historical Review* 73 (1993): 33–65.

Burga, Manuel, and Alberto Flores Galindo. *Apogeo y Crisis de la República Aristocrática*. Lima: Instituto de Estudios Peruanos (IEP), 1979.

Burton-Carvajal, Julianne. "María Luisa Bemberg's *Miss Mary*: Fragments of a Life and Career History." In *Redirecting the Gaze: Gender, Theory, and Cinema in the Third World,* edited by Diana Robin and Ira Jaffe. Albany: State University of New York Press, 1999.

Bustamante, Carlos María de. *Apuntes para la historia del gobierno del General D. Antonio López de Santa Anna, desde los principios de octubre de 1841 hasta 6 de diciembre de 1844, en que fue dispuesto del mando por uniforme voluntud de la nación*. Mexico City: J. M. Lara, 1845.

———. *El gabinete mexicano durante el segundo periódo de la administración del Exmo. Señor Presidente Anastasio Bustamante, hasta la entrega de mando al Exmo. Señor Interino D. Antonio López de Santa Anna, y continuación del cuadro histórico de la revolución mexicana*. Vol. I. Mexico City: José M. Lara, 1842.

———. *Memorias para la historia de la invasión Española sobre la costa de*

Tampico de Tamaulipas, hecha en el año de 1829, y destruida por el valor y prudencia de los Generales D. Antonio López de Santa Anna, D. Manuel de Mier y Terán, en el corto espacio de un mes y quince dias. Mexico City: Alejandro Valdés, 1831, 3, vol. 763, ex. 8, CJML.

Bustillos, Carrillo, Antonio. *Yucatán al servicio de la patria y de la revolución.* Mexico City: Casa Ramírez, 1959

Butler, Judith. *Gender Trouble: Feminism and the Subversion of Identity.* New York: Routledge, 1990.

Cahuata Corrales, Fructuoso. *Historia del periodismo cuzqueño.* Lima: SAGSA, 1990.

Callcott, Wilfrid Hardy. *Santa Anna: The Story of an Enigma Who Once Was Mexico.* Norman: University of Oklahoma Press, 1936.

Camacho Navarro, Enrique. *Los Usos de Sandino.* Mexico City: Universidad Nacional Autónoma de Mexico, 1991.

Canales, Claudia. *El poeta, el marqués, y el asesino: Historia de un caso judicial.* Mexico City: Ediciones Era, 2001.

Caravedo, Baltazar. "Poder central y decentralización: Peru, 1931." *Apuntes* 5, no. 9 (1977): 111–129.

Cardenal, Ernesto. *Zero Hour.* New York: New Directions Books, 1980..

Carlyle, Thomas. "The Hero as King." Lecture VI, in *On Heroes, Hero-Worship, and the Heroic in History. The Works of Thomas Carlyle in Thirty Volumes.* Vol. 5. New York: AMS Press, 1969.

Carmichael, Elizabeth, and Chloe Sayer. *The Skeleton at the Feast: The Day of the Dead in Mexico.* Austin: University of Texas Press, 1991.

Carozzi, María Julia. "La religiosidad popular en las políticas del patrimonio cultural." *Estudios sobre religion: Newsletter de la Asociación de Cuentistas Sociales de la Religión en el Mercosur* 13 (July 2002): 6.

Carrillo Puerto, Acrelio. *La familia Carrillo Puerto de Motul, con la Revolución Mexicana.* Mérida: n.p., 1959.

Caso, Alfonso. *Thirteen Masterpieces of Mexican Archaeology*, translated by Edith Mackie and Jorge R. Acosta. Mexico City: Editoriales Cultura y Polis, 1938.

Castañeda, Jorge G. *Compañero: The Life and Death of Che Guevara*, translated by Marina Castañeda. New York: Alfred A. Knopf, 1997.

Castillo, Fernando Muñoz. *El teatro regional de Yucatán.* Mexico City: Universidad Autónoma Metropolitana, 1987.

Centeno, Miguel. *Blood and Debt: War and the Nation-State in Latin America.* College Park: Pennsylvania State University Press, 2001.

Centro de Estudios Históricos del Agrarismo en México. *El ejército campesino del sur (ideología, organización y programa).* Mexico City: Federación Editorial Mexicana, 1982.

Chambers, Sarah C. "Republican Friendship: Manuela Sáenz Writes Women into the Nation, 1835–1836." *Hispanic American Historical Review* 81, no. 2 (2001): 225–257.

Chasteen, John Charles. *Heroes on Horseback: A Life and Times of the Last Gaucho Caudillos.* Albuquerque: University of New Mexico Press, 1995.

Cleven, N. Andrew. "Dictators Gamarra, Orbegoso, Salaverry, and Santa Cruz." In *South American Dictators During the First Century of Independence*, edited by A. Curtis Wilgus, 289–333. Washington, D.C.: George Washington University Press, 1937.

Código Militar, Ley de organización de ejército y armada de la República Mexicana. Mexico City: Tipografía de "El Siglo XX," 1897.

Coerver, Don M. *The Porfirian Interregnum: The Presidency of Manuel González of Mexico, 1880–1884.* Fort Worth: Texas Christian University Press, 1979.

"Cómo emplea su tiempo el General Díaz: La audiencia." *El Mundo Ilustrado* 2, no. 2 (1895): 81.

"Cómo pasa su tiempo el Presidente de la República: Palacio Nacional." *El Mundo Ilustrado* 4, no. 206 (4 December 1904): 788.

Conde, Teresa del. *Vida de Frida Kahlo.* Mexico City: Secretaría de la Presidencia, Departamento Editorial, 1976.

Congreso del Estado Libre y Soberano de Chihuahua. "Reglamento Interior del Congreso." In *Nueva colección de leyes del Estado de Chihuahua.* Mexico City: Imprenta de Horcasitas Hermanos, 1880.

Conniff, Michael, ed. *Latin American Populism in Comparative Perspective.* Albuquerque: University of New Mexico Press, 1982.

———. *Populism in Latin America.* Tuscaloosa: University of Alabama Press, 1999.

Conor, Bonifacio Frias. *Divorcios celebres y amores fugaces: Historia auténtica de un famoso abogado especialista en divorcios.* Mexico City: Botas, 1939.

Conrad, Robert Edgar, ed. *Sandino: The Testimony of A Nicaraguan Patriot.* Princeton, N.J.: Princeton University Press, 1990.

Cosío Villegas, Daniel. "El barbero de Sevilla." In *Daniel Cosío Villegas: El historiador liberal*, edited by Enrique Krauze. Mexico City: Fondo de Cultura Económica, 1984.

Cossío del Pomar, Felipe. *Víctor Raúl.* 2 vols. Mexico City: Editorial Cultura, 1969.

Costeloe, Michael P. *The Central Republic in Mexico, 1835–1846:* Hombres de Bien *in the Age of Santa Anna.* New York: Cambridge University Press, 1993.

———. "The Junta Patriótica and the Celebration of Independence in

Mexico City, 1825–1855." *Mexican Studies/Estudios Mexicanos* 13 (Winter 1997): 21–53.

———. *La primera república federal de México (1824–1835): Un estudio de los partidos políticos en el México independiente.* 2nd ed. Mexico City: Fondo de Cultura Económica, 1996.

———. "The Triangular Revolt in Mexico and the Fall of Anastasio Bustamante, August–October, 1841." *Journal of Latin American Studies* 20 (November 1988): 337–360.

Covarrubias, Miguel. *Mexico South: The Isthmus of Tehuantepec.* New York: Alfred A. Knopf, 1947.

Crasswelder, Robert D. *Perón and the Enigmas of Argentina.* New York: W. W. Norton, 1987.

Craven, David. *Diego Rivera as Epic Modernist.* New York: G. K. Hall, 1997.

Cueva, Agustín. *The Process of Political Domination in Ecuador*, translated by Danielle Salti. New Brunswick, N.J.: Transaction Books, 1982.

Cumberland, Charles C. *Mexican Revolution: Genesis Under Madero.* Austin: University of Texas Press, 1952.

Cummins, Lejeune. *Quijote on a Burro: Sandino and the Marines.* Mexico City: La Impresora Azteca, 1958.

Cummins, Tom. "A Tale of Two Cities: Cuzco, Lima and the Construction of Colonial Representation." In *Converging Cultures: Art and Identity in Spanish America*, edited by Diane Fane. New York: Brooklyn Museum, 1997.

Curcio-Nagy, Linda A. *The Great Festivals of Colonial Mexico City: Performing Power and Identity.* Albuquerque: University of New Mexico Press, 2004.

de Jesus, Carolina Maria. *Child of the Dark: The Diary of Carolina Maria de Jesus*, translated by David St. Clair. New York: Dutton, 1962.

———. *The Unedited Diaries of Carolina Maria de Jesus*, translated by Nancy P. S. Naro and Cristina Mehrtens. New Brunswick, N.J.: Rutgers University Press, 1999.

de la Torre, Carlos. *Populist Seduction in Latin America: The Ecuadorian Experience.* Athens: Ohio State University Press, 2000.

de la Fuente, Ariel. *Children of Facundo: Caudillo and Gaucho Insurgency During the Argentine State Formation Process (La Rioja, 1853–1870).* Durham, N.C.: Duke University Press, 2000.

de Volo, Lorraine Bayardo. *Mothers of Heroes and Martyrs: Gender Identity Politics in Nicaragua, 1979–1999.* Baltimore, Md.: Johns Hopkins University Press, 2001.

Deffebach, Nancy. "Images of Plants in the Art of María Izquierdo, Frida Kahlo, and Leonora Carrington: Gender, Identity, and Spirituality in the Context of Modern Mexico." PhD diss., University of Texas at Austin, 2000.

————. "Pre-Columbian Symbolism in the Art of Frida Kahlo." Master's thesis, University of Texas at Austin, 1991.

Dellepiane, Carlos. *Historia Militar del Perú.* 2 vols. Lima: Librería e Imprenta Gil, 1931.

Derby, Robin. "The Dictator's Seduction: Gender and State Spectacle during the Trujillo Regime." In *Latin American Popular Culture,* edited by William H. Beezley and Linda Curcio-Nagy, 213–239. Wilmington, Del.: Scholarly Resources, 2000.

Deustua, José. *Intelectuales, indigenismo, y descentralismo en el Perú, 1897–1931.* Cuzco: Centro de Estudios Rurales Andinos "Bartolomé de las Casas," 1984.

Di Tella, Turcuato S. *National Popular Politics in Early Independent Mexico, 1820–1847.* Albuquerque: University of New Mexico Press, 1996.

Díaz Díaz, Fernando. *Caudillos y Caciques: Antonio López de Santa Anna y Juan Álvarez.* Mexico City: El Colegio de México, 1972.

————. *Santa Anna y Juan Alvarez: Frente a frente.* Mexico City: SEP/Setentas, 1972.

Díaz Soto y Gama, Antonio. *La revolución agraria del sur y Emiliano Zapata, su caudillo.* Mexico City: Imprenta Policromia, 1960.

Diccionario histórico y biográfico de la Revolución Mexicana. Tomo VII. Mexico City: Instituto Nacional de Estudios Históricos de la Revolución Mexicana and Secretaría de Gobernación, 1990.

Diccionario Porrúa: Historia, biografía y geografía de México. 6th ed. Mexico City: Editorial Porrúa, 1995.

Dik, Evgueni. "La percepción que el gobierno imperial ruso tenía del México porfirista: 1890–1911." *Signos Históricos* 5 (January–June 2001): 195–212.

Dospital, Michelle. *Siempre mas allá . . . reseña del movimiento Sandinista Nicaragua, 1927–1934.* Managua: Editorial Nueva Nicaragua, 1996.

Douglas, Eduardo de Jesús. "The Colonial Self: Homosexuality and Mestizaje in the Art of Nahum B. Zenil." *Art Journal* 57, no. 3 (Fall 1998): 14–21.

Dow, Thomas E., Jr. "An analysis of Weber's work on charisma." *British Journal of Sociology* 29, no. 1 (March 1978): 83–93.

Dujovne Ortíz, Alicia. *Eva Perón: A Biography,* translated by Shawn Fields. New York: St. Martin's Press, 1996.

Eade, John, and Michael J. Sallnow, eds. Introduction to *Contesting the Sacred: The Anthropology of Christian Pilgrimage*. London: Routledge, 1991.

Earle, A. Rebecca. *Spain and the Independence of Colombia 1810–1825*. Exeter: University of Exeter Press, 2000.

Elias, Norbert. *The Court Society*. New York: Pantheon Books, 1983.

Escandell-Tur, Neus. *Producción y comercio de tejidos coloniales: Los obrajes y chorrillos del Cuzco 1570–1820*. Cuzco: Centro de Estudios Rurales Andinos "Bartolomé de Las Casas," 1997.

Escoffie, Carlos. "Resumen Cronologico de 1930." *Diario de Yucatán*, 1 January 1931.

Escoffie Z., Manuel. *Bajo el sol de mi tierra*. Mérida: El Porvenir, 1950.

Espejel, Laura, Alicia Olivera, and Salvador Rueda, eds. *Emiliano Zapata: Antología*. Mexico City: Instituto Nacional de Estudios Históricos de la Revolución Mexicana, 1988.

Espinosa, Rafael. *Alacución que el ciudadano Rafael Espinosa dirijó el día 27 de Septiembre de 1842, aniversario de la gloriosa entrada de la ejercito trigarantia en México el ano de 1821*. Mexico City: Vicente G. Torres, 1842.

Esposito, Matthew D. "Death and Disorder in Mexico City: the State Funeral of Manuel Romero Rubio." In *Latin American Popular Culture: An Introduction*, edited by William H. Beezley and Linda A. Curcio-Nagy, 87–103. Wilmington, Del.: Scholarly Resources, 2000.

Evans, Albert S. *Our Sister Republic: A Gala Trip through Tropical Mexico in 1869–1870*. Hartford, Conn.: Columbian Book, 1873.

EZLN: Documentos y comunicados. Mexico City: Ediciones Era, 1994.

Fabela, Isidro, and Josefina E. Fabela, eds. *Documentos históricos de la revolución Mexicana*. Vol. 21. Mexico City: Editorial Jus, 1970.

Falcón, Romana, and Raymond Buve, eds. *Don Porfirio Presidente . . ., Nunca Omnipotente: Hallazgos, reflexiones, y debates, 1876–1911*. Mexico City: Universidad Iberoamericana, 1998.

Fallaw, Ben. "Dry Law, Wet Politics: Drinking and Prohibition in Revolutionary-era Yucatán, 1915–1935." *Latin American Research Review* 37, no. 3 (Summer 2002): 37–64.

———. *Cárdenas Compromised: The Failure of Reform in Postrevolutionary Yucatán*. Durham, N.C.: Duke University Press, 2001.

———. "The Life and Deaths of Felipa Poot." *Hispanic American Historical Review* 82, no. 4 (2002): 645–684.

Ferrer de M., Gabriel. *Nuestra Ciudad: Mérida de Yucatán (1542–1938)*. Mérida: Basso, 1938.

Fishwick, Marshall. Prologue to *Heroes of Popular Culture*, by Ray B.

Browne and Michael T. Marsden, 1–8. Bowling Green, Ky.: Bowling Green University Popular Press, 1972.

Flores Arellano, Nélida, and América Inces Román. *Doña María de la O, una mujer ejemplar.* Mexico City: Universidad Autónoma de Guerrero and Centro de Estudios Históricos del Agrarismo en México, 1992.

Flores Galindo, Alberto. *Buscando un Inca.* 4th ed. Lima: Editorial Horizonte, 1994.

Fonseca, Carlos. "Sandino: Proletarian Guerrilla." *Tricontinental* 24 (1971).

Fowler, Will. *Mexico in the Age of Proposals, 1821–1853.* Westport, Conn.: Greenwood Press, 1998.

———. *Tornel and Santa Anna: The Writer and the Caudillo, Mexico 1795–1853.* Westport, Conn.: Greenwood Press, 2000.

Frances, Manuel. *Los restos del Lic. Carlos María de Bustamante y el panteón de San Fernando.* Mexico City: Vida Gráfica, 1925.

Franco, Jean. *Plotting Women: Gender and Representation in Mexico.* New York: Columbia University Press, 1989.

Franz, David Arthur. "Bullets and Bolshevists: A History of the Mexican Revolution and Reform in Yucatan, 1910–1924." PhD diss., University of New Mexico, 1973.

Fraser, Nicholas, and Marysa Navarro. *Eva Perón.* New York: W. W. Norton, 1985.

Freud, Sigmund. *Moses and Monotheism*, translated by Katherine Jones. New York: A. A. Knopf, 1939.

Friedrich, Paul. *Agrarian Revolt in a Mexican Village.* Englewood Cliffs, N.J.: Prentice Hall, 1970.

Fuente, Ariel de la. *Children of Facundo: Caudillo and Gaucho Insurgency During the Argentine State-Formation Process (La Rioja, 1853–1870).* Durham, N.C.: Duke University Press, 2000.

Gage, John. "Colour and Culture." In *Colour: Art and Science,* edited by Trevor Lamb and Janine Bourriau. Cambridge: Cambridge University Press, 1994.

Gamboa, Federico. *Mi diario.* Vol. 1. Guadalajara: Imprenta de "La Gaceta de Guadalajara," 1907.

Gamarra, Agustín. *El Gran Mariscal Don Agustín Gamarra a los cuzqaueños.* Pamphlet. Cuzco, June 9, 1935.

García, Fernando Diego, et al. *Evita: Imagenes de una passion.* Madrid: Celeste Ediciones, 1997.

García, Genaro, ed. *Crónica oficial de las fiestas del primer centenario de la Independencia de México.* Mexico City: Talleres del Museo Nacional, 1911.

García Márquez, Gabriel. *The General in His Labyrinth,*. translated by Edith Grossman. New York: Alfred A. Knopf, 1990.

Garduño, Blanca, and José Antonio Rodríguez, eds. *Pasión por Frida.* Exhibition catalogue. Mexico City: Museo Estudio Diego Rivera, 1992.

Garner, Paul. *Porfirio Díaz.* Harlow, U.K.: Pearson, 2001.

Geertz, Clifford. "Centers, Kings, and Charisma: Reflections on the Symbolics of Power." In *Culture and Its Creators: Essays in Honor of Edward Shils,* edited by Joseph Ben-David and Terry Nichols Clark, 150–171. Chicago: University of Chicago Press, 1977. Reprinted in Clifford Geertz, *Local Knowledge: Further Essays in Interpretive Anthropology,* 121–146. New York: Basic Books, 1983.

"El General Díaz en las audiencias privadas." *El Mundo Ilustrado* 4, no. 206 (4 December 1904): 797–798.

Giddens, Anthony. *Modernity and Self-Identity: Self and Society in the Late Modern Age.* Stanford, Calif.: Stanford University Press, 1991.

Gill, Mario. "Zapata: Su pueblo y sus hijos." *Historia Mexicana* 2 (1952): 294–312.

Gilliam, Albert. *Travels over the Tablelands and Cordilleras of Mexico: During the Years 1843 and 1844; Including a Description of California, the Principal Cities and Mining Districts of that Republic and the Biographies of Iturbide and Santa Anna.* Philadelphia: John W. Moore, 1846.

Giménez, Catalina H. de. *Así cantaban la revolución.* Mexico City: Grijalbo, 1990.

Gobat, Michel. "Revisiting Revolutionary Nationalism: Sandinismo, Elite Conservatives and U.S. Military Intervention in Nicaragua, 1927–1933." Paper presented at the XXIII International Congress of the Latin American Studies Association, Washington, D.C., 2001.

Gómez, Marte R. *Las Comisiones Agrarias del Sur.* Mexico City: Porrua, 1961.

Gómez Pedraza, Manuel. "Oración encomiástica que dijo Manuel Gómez Pedraza el 16 de septiembre de 1842." In *Conciencia nacional y su formación: Discursos cívicos septembrinos (1825–1871),* edited by Ernesto de la Torre Villar and Ramiro Navarro. Mexico City: Universidad Nacional Autónoma de México, 1988.

González Navarro, Moisés. *La Confederación Nacional Campesina (un grupo de presión en la reforma agraria mexicana).* Mexico City: B. Costa-Amic, 1968.

González Padilla, Beatriz. *Yucatán: Política y poder (1897–1929).* Mérida: Maldonado, 1985.

González Pedrero, Enrique. *País de un solo hombre: El México de Santa*

Anna. Vol. 1, *La ronda de los contrarios.* Mexico City: Fondo de Cultura Económica, 1993.

González Prada, Alfredo. *Un crimen perfecto: El asesinato del Gran Mariscal Don Agustín Gamarra, Presidente del Perú.* New York: H. Wolff, 1941.

González Ramírez, Manuel, ed. *Planes políticos y otros documentos.* Mexico City: Fondo de Cultura Económica, 1954.

Gootenberg, Paul. *Between Silver and Guano: Commercial Policy and the State in Postindependence Peru.* Princeton, N.J.: Princeton University Press, 1989.

————. *Imagining Development: Economic Ideas in Peru's "Fictitious Prosperity" of Guano, 1840–1880.* Berkeley and Los Angeles: University of California Press, 1993.

————. "Population and Ethnicity in Early Republican Peru: Some Revisions." *Latin American Research Review* 26, no. 3 (1991): 109–157.

Gortari Rabiela, Hira de. "La política de la formación del Estado nacional." *Revista Mexicana de Sociología* 44, no. 1 (1982): 263–284.

Gott, Richard. *In the Shadow of the Liberator: Hugo Chávez and the Transformation of Venezuela.* New York: Verso, 2000.

Gould, Jeffrey. *To Lead as Equals: Rural Protest and Political Consciousness in Chinandega, Nicaragua, 1912–1979.* Chapel Hill: University of North Carolina Press, 1990.

Green, Stanley C. *The Mexican Republic: The First Decade, 1823–1832.* Pittsburgh, Pa.: University of Pittsburgh Press, 1987.

Griswold del Castillo, Richard, Teresa McKenna, and Yvonne Yarbro-Bejarano, eds. *Chicano Art: Resistance and Affirmation, 1965–1985* (CARA). Exhibition catalogue. Los Angeles: Wight Art Gallery/University of California, Los Angeles, 1991.

Grossman, Richard. "'Hermanos en la Patria', Nationalism, Honor and Rebellion: Augusto Sandino and the Army in Defense of the National Sovereignty of Nicaragua, 1927–1934." PhD diss., University of Chicago, 1996.

"Los Guardias de la Presidencia." *El Imparcial* 4, no. 1386 (1900): 1.

Guardino, Peter F. *Peasants, Politics, and the Formation of Mexico's National State: Guerrero, 1800–1857.* Stanford, Calif.: Stanford University Press, 1996.

Gruening, Ernest. "A Maya Idyl: A Study of Felipe Carrillo, Late Governor of Yucatan." *The Century Magazine,* April 1924, 832–836.

Guiol, Agustín. *La patria hoy el grito apolla, y así, es fuerza que arda troya.* Mexico City: Agustín Guiol, 1832.

Haber, Stephen, ed. "Introduction: The Political Economy of Crony Capitalism." In *Crony Capitalism and Economic Growth in Latin*

America: Theory and Evidence, xi–xxi. Stanford, Calif.: Hoover Institute Press and Stanford University Press, 2002.

Hale, Charles A. *The Transformation of Liberalism in Late Nineteenth Century Mexico.* Princeton, N.J.: Princeton University Press, 1989.

Hall, Linda B. "Alvaro Obregón and the Politics of Mexican Land Reform." *Hispanic American Historical Review* 60 (1980): 213–238.

———. *Alvaro Obregón: Power and Revolution in Mexico, 1911–1920.* College Station: Texas A&M University Press, 1981.

———. *Mary, Mother and Warrior: The Virgin Mary in Spain and the Americas.* Austin: University of Texas Press, 2004.

Hamill, Hugh, ed. Introduction to *Caudillos: Dictators in Spanish America.* Norman: University of Oklahoma Press, 1992.

Hamilton, Nora. *The Limits of State Autonomy: Post-Revolutionary Mexico.* Princeton, N.J.: Princeton University Press, 1982.

Hanighen, Frank C. *Santa Anna: The Napoleon of the West.* New York: Coward-McCann, 1934.

Hanley, Sarah. *The* Lit de Justice *of the Kings of France: Constitutional Ideology in Legend, Ritual, and Discourse.* Princeton, N.J.: Princeton University Press, 1989.

Haya de la Torre, Víctor Raúl. "Mis Recuerdos de González Prada." *Repertorio americano* (San José, Costa Rica) 15, no. 6 (1927).

———. *Obras Completas.* 7 vols. Lima: Juan Mejía Baca, 1977.

———. *Por la emancipación de América Latina: Artículos, mensajes, discursos 1923–1927.* Buenos Aires: Gleizer, 1927.

Hellman, Judith Adler. *Mexican Lives.* New York: New Press, 1994.

Herman, Edward, and Gerry O'Sullivan. *The "Terrorism" Industry.* New York: Pantheon Books, 1989.

Hernández Chávez, Alicia. *Anenecuilco: Memoria y vida de un pueblo.* Mexico City: El Colegio de México, 1991.

Herrera, Bartolomé. *Escritos y discursos.* 2 vols. Lima: Biblioteca de la República, 1929.

———. *Frida: A Biography of Frida Kahlo.* New York: Harper and Row, 1983.

Herrera, Hayden. *Frida: A Biography of Frida Kahlo.* Reprint ed. New York: HarperCollins, 2002.

Hershfield, Joanne. *Mexican Cinema/Mexican Woman, 1940–1950.* Tucson: University of Arizona Press, 1996.

Hispano, Cornelio. *Los cantores de Bolívar.* Bogota: Minerva, 1930.

———. *El libro de oro de Bolívar.* Paris: Garnier Hermanos, 1925.

Hobsbawm, Eric, and Terence Ranger, eds. "Introduction: Inventing

Tradition," *The Invention of Tradition*, 1–14. Cambridge: Cambridge University Press, 1983.

Hodges, Donald C. *Intellectual Foundations of the Nicaraguan Revolution*. Austin: University of Texas Press, 1986.

———. *Sandino's Communism: Spiritual Politics for the Twenty-First Century*. Austin: University of Texas Press, 1992.

Holmes, Barbara Ellen. "Women and Yucatec Kinship." PhD diss., Tulane University, 1978.

Hünefeldt, Christine. *Lucha por la tierra y protesta indígena: Las comunidades indígenas del Perú entre colonia y república*. Bonn: Bonner Amerikanische Studien, 1982.

Hunting, Gardner. "A Despot Has No Luck Nowadays: The Firing Squad Spoiled Carrillo's Dream." *Collier's*, April 26, 1924, 15–16, 37–38.

Irigoyen, Renan. *Felipe Carrillo Puerto: Primer gobernante socialista en México (semblanza interpretativa)*. Mérida: Ediciones de la Universidad de Yucatán, 1974.

Instituto de Estudio del Sandinismo (IES). *El Sandinismo: Documentos Básicos*. Managua: Editorial Nueva Nicaragua, 1983.

Iturribarría, Jorge Fernando de. *Historia de México*. Mexico City: Secretaría de Educación Pública, 1951.

———. "La política de conciliación del general Díaz y el arzobispo Gillow." *Historia Mexicana* 14, no. 1 (July–September 1964).

Jacobsen, Nils. "Liberalism and Indian Communities in Peru, 1821–1920." In *Liberals, the Church, and Indian Peasants: Corporate Lands and the Challenge of Reform in Nineteenth-Century Spanish America*, edited by Robert H. Jackson, 123–170. Albuquerque: University of New Mexico Press, 1997.

James, Daniel. *Doña María's Story: Life History, Memory, and Political Identity*. Durham, N.C.: Duke University Press, 2000.

———. *Resistance and Integration: Peronism and the Argentine Working Class, 1946–1976*. New York: Cambridge University Press, 1988.

Jiménez, Luz. *Life and Death in Milpa Alta*, translated and edited by Fernando Horcasitas. Norman: University of Oklahoma Press, 1972.

Johns, Michael. *The City of Mexico in the Age of Díaz*. Austin: University of Texas Press, 1997.

Johnson, John J. "One Hundred Years of Historical Writing on Modern Latin America by United States Historians." *Hispanic American Historical Review* 65 (1985): 747–749.

Jones, Oakah. *Santa Anna*. New York: Twayne, 1968.

Joseph, Gilbert. *Revolution from Without: Yucatán, Mexico, and the United*

States, 1880–1924. 2nd ed. Durham, N.C.: Duke University Press, 1988.

Joseph, Gilbert M. "Caciquismo and the Revolution: Carrillo Puerto in Yucatán." In *Caudillo and Peasant in the Mexican Revolution*, edited by David A. Bradling, 193–221. Cambridge: Cambridge University Press, 1980.

Joseph, Gilbert, and Daniel Nugent, eds. *Everyday Forms of State Formation: Revolution and the Negotiation of Rule in Modern Mexico.* Durham, N.C.: Duke University Press, 1994.

Josephs, Ray. *Argentine Diary.* New York: Random House, 1944.

Joyce, Thomas A. *Mexican Archaeology.* New York: G. P. Putnam's Sons, 1914.

Kahlo, Frida. "Hablando de un cuadro mío." *Así,* August 18, 1945, 70–71.

———. "Portrait of Diego" (translated by Nancy Deffebach [Breslow] and Amy Weisz Narea). *Calyx* 5 (1980): 92–108.

Kahlo, Frida, with Sarah M. Lowe, Essay and Commentaries, and Carlos Fuentes, Introduction, in *The Diary of Frida Kahlo: An Intimate Self-Portrait.* New York: Harry N. Abrams/La Vaca Independiente, 1995.

Kammen, Michael. *Mystic Chords of Memory: The Transformation of Tradition in American Culture.* New York: Knopf, 1991.

Katz, Friedrich, ed. *Porfirio Díaz frente al descontento popular regional (1891–1892): Antología documental.* Mexico City: Universidad Iberoamericana, 1986.

———. "Introduction: Rural Revolts in Mexico." In *Riot, Rebellion, and Revolution: Rural Social Conflict in Mexico,* 3–17. Princeton, N.J.: Princeton University Press, 1988, 16–17.

Katzman, Israel. *Arquitectura del siglo XIX en México.* 2nd ed. Mexico City: Editorial Trillas, 1993.

Keegan, John. *The Masks of Command.* New York: Penguin Books, 1988.

Kertzer, David I. *Ritual, Politics, and Power.* New Haven: Yale University Press, 1988.

Kettering, Sharon. *Patrons, Brokers, and Clients in Seventeenth-Century France.* New York: Oxford University Press, 1986.

Kinsbruner, Jay. *Independence in Spanish America: Civil Wars, Revolutions, and Underdevelopment.* Diálogos series. Albuquerque: University of New Mexico Press, 1994.

Kirk, John. *José Martí, Inventor of the Cuban Nation.* Tampa: University of Florida Press, 1983.

Klaiber, Jeffrey L. "The Popular Universities and the Origins of Aprismo, 1921–1924." *Hispanic American Historical Review* 55, no. 4 (1975): 693–715.

————. *Religion and Revolution in Peru.* South Bend, Ind.: University of Notre Dame Press, 1977.

Klaren, Peter F. "Modernization, Dislocation and Aprismo." *Latin American Monographs* 32. Austin: Institute of Latin American Studies and University of Texas Press, 1973.

Klingensmith, Samuel John. *The Utility of Splendor: Ceremony, Social Life, and Architecture at the Court of Bavaria, 1600–1800,* edited by Christian F. Otto and Mark Ashton. Chicago: University of Chicago Press, 1993.

Knight, Alan. *The Mexican Revolution.* 2 vols. Cambridge: Cambridge University Press, 1986.

Krauze, Enrique. *El amor a la tierra: Emiliano Zapata. Biografía del poder,* vol. 3. Mexico City: Fondo de Cultura Económica, 1987.

————. *Mexico: Biography of Power: A History of Modern Mexico, 1810–1996,* translated by Hank Heifetz. New York: HarperCollins, 1997.

————. *Místico de la autoridad: Porfirio Díaz.* Mexico City: Fondo de Cultura Económica, 1987.

————. *Siglo de caudillos: Biografía política de México (1810–1910).* Barcelona: Tusquets Editores, 1994.

Krook, Dorothea. *Elements of Tragedy.* New Haven: Yale University Press, 1969.

Krüggeler, Thomas. "El mito de la 'despoblación': Apuntes para una historia demográfica del Cuzco (1791–1940)." *Revista Andina* 16, no. 1 (1998): 119–137.

Kubler, George. *The Indian Caste of Peru, 1795–1940: A Population Study Based upon Tax Records and Census Reports.* Smithsonian Institution of Social Anthropology Publications, no. 14. Washington, D.C.: Smithsonian Institution, 1952.

Lamb, Trevor, and Janine Bourriau, eds. *Colour: Art and Science.* Cambridge: Cambridge University Press, 1994.

Lauretis, Teresa de. *Technologies of Gender.* Bloomington: Indiana University Press, 1987.

Lévi-Strauss, Claude. *The Savage Mind.* Chicago: University of Chicago Press, 1966.

Lewin, Linda. "The Oligarchical Limitations of Social Banditry in Brazil: The Case of the 'Good' Thief Antonio Silvino." In *Bandidos: The Varieties of Latin American Banditry,* edited by Richard W. Slatta, 67–96. New York: Greenwood Press, 1987.

Liévano Aguirre, Indalecio. *Bolívar.* Bogota: Oveja Negra, 1979.

Lindauer, Margaret A. *Devouring Frida: The Art History and Popular*

Celebrity of Frida Kahlo. Hanover, N.H.: Wesleyan University Press, 1999.

Lomnitz, Claudio. *Deep Mexico, Silent Mexico: An Anthropology of Nationalism*. Minneapolis: University of Minnesota Press, 2001.

Lomnitz-Adler, Claudio. *Exits from the Labyrinth: Culture and Ideology in the Mexican National Space*. Berkeley and Los Angeles: University of California Press, 1992.

Loveman, Brian. *The Constitution of Tyranny: Regimes of Exception in Spanish America*. Pittsburgh, Pa.: University of Pittsburgh Press, 1993.

Lynch, John. *Argentine Dictator: Juan Manuel de Rosas, 1829–1852*. New York: Oxford University Press, 1981.

———. *Caudillos in Spanish America, 1800–1850*. Oxford: Clarendon Press, 1992.

Macaulay, Neill. *The Sandino Affair*. Durham, N.C.: Duke University Press, 1986.

Macías-González, Víctor M. "The Mexican Aristocracy and Porfirio Díaz, 1876–1911." PhD diss., Texas Christian University, 1999.

———. "El ocaso de Júpiter: La crisis de representación simbólica de la dictadura porfiriana: México, 1890–1915." Paper presented at the VIII International Colloquium of the Centre Interuniversitaire de Recherche sur l'Éducation et la Culture dans le Monde Ibérique et Ibéro-Américain, "Texte et Image dans le Monde Ibérique et Ibéroaméricain." Tours, March 2002.

Maclachlan, Colin M., and William H. Beezley, *El Gran Pueblo: A History of Greater Mexico*. Upper Saddle River, N.J.: Prentice Hall, 1999.

Madariaga, Salvador de. *Bolívar*. Mexico City: Editorial Hermes, 1951.

Madsen, Douglas, and Peter G. Snow, *The Charismatic Bond: Political Behavior in Time of Crisis*. Cambridge, Mass.: Harvard University Press, 1991.

Magaña, Gildardo, and Carlos Pérez Guerrero. *Emiliano Zapata y el agrarismo en México*. 5 vols. Mexico City: Editorial Ruta, 1951–1952.

Malinowski, Bronislaw. *The Foundations of Faith and Morals*. London: Oxford University Press, 1936.

"Manifesto del Sindicato de Obreros Técnicos, Pintores e Escultores" (Manifesto of the Union of Technical Workers, Painters, and Sculptors). *El Machete*, June 24, 1924.

Martínez, Mariano R. *Simón Bolívar Intimo*. Paris: Casa Editorial Hispano-Americana, n.d.

Martínez, Miguel A. *El Mariscal de Piquiza, Don Agustín Gamarra*. Lima: Librería e Imprenta D. Miranda, 1946.

Martínez, Tomás Eloy. *Santa Evita*. Buenos Aires: Grupo Editorial Planeta, 1995.

Masur, Gerhard. *Simon Bolívar*. Rev. ed. Albuquerque: University of New Mexico Press, 1969.

Mayer, Brantz. *Mexico as It Was and as It Is*. New York: J. Winchester, New World Press, 1844.

McBeth, Brian. *Juan Vicente Gómez and the Oil Companies in Venezuela, 1908–1935*. New York: Cambridge University Press, 1983.

Melville, Roberto. *Crecimiento y rebelión: El desarrollo económico de las haciendas azucareras en Morelos (1880–1910)*. Mexico City: Editorial Nueva Imagen, 1979.

Méndez, Cecilia. *Incas sí, indios no: Apuntes para el estudio del nacionalismo criollo en el Perú*. Lima: IEP, 1993.

Mendiburu, Manuel de. *Biografías de generales republicanos*. Lima: Instituto Histórico del Perú, Academia Nacional de la Historia, 1963.

Merlo, Eduardo. *El Palacio Municipal de Puebla, una semblanza histórica*. Puebla: El Ayuntamiento Municipal Constitucional de Puebla, 1994.

Mexico. Secretaría de Comunicaciones y Obras Públicas. *Memoria presentada al Congreso de la Unión por el Secretario de Estado y del Despacho de Comunicaciones y Obras Públicasm General Francisco Z. Mena*. Mexico City: Tipografía de la Dirección General de Telégrafos, 1902, 1903.

Mexico. Secretaría de Guerra y Marina. *Código Militar, Ley de organización del ejército y armada de la República Mexicana*. Mexico City: Tipografía de "El Siglo XIX," 1897.

Mexico. Secretaría de Relaciones Exteriores. *La Secretaría de Relaciones Exteriores. Edificios que ha ocupado, 1821–1966*. Mexico City: Imprenta de la Secretaría de Relaciones Exteriores, 1966.

"Mexico: Fashion Notes." *Time*, May 3, 1946, 34.

Migdal, Joel S. *State in Society: Studying How States and Societies Transform and Constitute One Another*. New York: Cambridge University Press, 2001.

Millet, Richard. *Guardians of the Dynasty*. Maryknoll: Orbis Press, 1977.

Moreno, Salvador. *El pintor Antonio Fabrés*. Mexico City: Instituto de Investigaciones Estéticas-UNAM, 1981.

Mosquera, Tomás Cipriano de. *Memorias sobre la vida del General Simón Bolívar*. Caracas: 1983.

Muñoz, Rafael F. *Santa Anna: el dictador resplandeciente*. 4th ed. Mexico City: Fondo de Cultura Económica, 1996.

Murray, Pamela. "'Loca' or 'Libertadora': Manuela Sáenz in the Eyes of

History and Historians, 1900–c. 1990." *Journal of Latin American Studies* 33, no. 2 (2001): 291–310.

Navarro, Marysa. "Evita's Shared Charismatic Leadership." In *Latin American Populism in Comparative Perspective*, edited by Michael L. Conniff, 47–66. Albuquerque: University of New Mexico Press, 1981.

Navarro-Génie, Marco Aurelio. *Augusto "Cesar" Sandino: Messiah of Light and Truth*. Syracuse, N.Y.: Syracuse University Press, 2002.

The New Natural History of Tyranny in Peru. Cuzco, 1834.

Nicholson, Irene. *Mexican and Central American Mythology*. London: Paul Hamlyn, 1967.

Nieto Soria, José Manuel. *Ceremonias de la Realeza: Propaganda y legitimación en la Castilla Trastámara*. Madrid: Nerea, 1993.

North, Lisa. *Orígenes y crecimiento del Partido Aprista y el cambio socioeconómico en el Perú*. Lima: Pontificia Universidad Católica del Peru, 1975.

Nugent, David. *Modernity at the Edge of Empire: State, Individual and Nation in the Northern Peruvian Andes, 1885–1935*. Stanford, Calif.: Stanford University Press, 1997.

O'Leary, Daniel. *Bolívar and the War of Independence*, translated and edited by Robert F. McNerney, Jr. Austin: University of Texas Press, 1970.

Olivera de Bonfil, Alicia. "¿Ha Muerto Emiliano Zapata? Mitos y leyendas en torno del caudillo." *Boletín del Instituto Nacional de Antropología e Historia* 2, no. 13 (1975): 43–52.

O'Malley, Ilene V. *The Myth of the Revolution: Hero Cults and the Institutionalization of the Mexican State, 1920–1940*. New York: Greenwood Press, 1986.

Ortíz Macedo, Luís. *Los palacios nobiliarios de la Nueva España*. Mexico City: Seminario de Cultura Mexicana, 1994.

Ozouf, Mona. *Festivals and the French Revolution*, translated by Alan Sheridan. Cambridge, Mass.: Harvard University Press, 1988.

Páez, José Antonio. *Autobiografía del General José Antonio Páez*. New York, 1867.

Page, Joseph. *Perón: A Biography*. New York: Random House, 1983.

Palma, Ricardo. "Justicia de Bolívar." In *Tradiciones peruanas*, 178–181. Estella: Salvat Editores, 1984.

Palmer, Steven. "Getting to Know the Unknown Soldier: Official Nationalism in Liberal Costa Rica, 1880–1900." *Journal of Latin American Studies* 25 (1993): 47.

Pani, Érika. "El proyecto de estado de Maximiliano a través de la vida cortesana y del ceremonial público." *Historia Mexicana* 45, no. 2 (1995): 423–460.

Pardo y Aliaga, Felipe. "Semblanzas peruanas." *Boletín de la Academia Chilena de la Historia* 33 (1945): 6.

Pascal, Blaise. *Pensées,* translated by Martin Turnell. New York: Harper and Row, 1962.

Pasquali, Patricia. *San Martín: La fuerza de la misión y la soledad de la gloria.* Buenos Aires: Planeta, 1999.

Pasquel, Leonardo. *Antonio López de Santa Anna.* Técamachalco: Instituto de Mexicologia, 1990.

Paz, Octavio. *El laberinto de la soledad.* Mexico City: Fondo de Cultura Económica, 1959.

Paz, Octavio. *Labyrinth of Solitude: Life and Thought in Mexico,* translated by Lysander Kemp. New York: Grove Press, 1961.

Paz Solórzano, Octavio. *Hoguera que fue,* edited by Felipe Gálvez. Mexico City: Universidad Autónoma Metropolitana, 1986.

Peralta Ruíz, Víctor. *En pos del tributo: Burocracia estatal, elite regional y comunidades indígenas en el Cuzco rural (1826–1854).* Cuzco: Centro Bartolomé de Las Casas, 1991.

Peralta Ruíz, Víctor, and Marta Irurozqui Victoriano. *Por la concordia, la fusión y el unitarismo: Estado y Caudillismo en Bolivia, 1825–1880.* Madrid: CSIC, Departamento de Historia de América, 2000.

Pérez, Antonio Betancourt. *Carta peninsular confidencial: Episodios históricos. Carlos R. Menéndez y Felipe Carrillo Puerto: La destrucción de los talleres de la Revista de Yucatán en 1924.* Merida: Maldonado Editores, 1981.

Pérez Bermúdez, Carlos, and Onofre Guevara. *El Movimiento Obrero en Nicaragua: Primera y Segunda Parte.* Managua: Editorial El Amanecer, 1985.

Pérez Verdía, Luis. *Compendio de la historia de México desde sus primeros tiempos hasta la caida del segundo imperio.* Guadalajara, Jalisco: Author, 1883.

———. *Compendio de la historia de México desde sus primeros tiempos hasta los últimos años.* 17th ed. Reprint. Guadalajara: Editores Libreria Font, 1970.

Perón, Eva. *Clases y escritos completos,* edited by Carlos E. Hurst and José María Roch. Vol. 3. Buenos Aires: Editorial Megafón, 1987.

———. *Discursos completos 1946–1948.* Buenos Aires: Editorial Megafón, 1985.

———. *My Mission in Life.* New York: Vintage Press, 1953.

Pike, Frederick. *The Politics of the Miraculous: Haya de la Torre and the Spiritualist Tradition.* Lincoln: University of Nebraska Press, 1986.

Pilcher, Jeffrey. *Cantinflas and the Chaos of Mexican Modernity.* Wilmington, Del.: Scholarly Resources, 2001.

Planas Silva, Pedro. *Los orígenes del APRA: El joven Haya (mito y realidad de Haya de la Torre)*. 2nd ed. Lima: Okura Editores, 1986.

Platt, Tristan. *Estado boliviano y ayllu andino: Tierra y tributo en el norte de Potosí*. Lima: IEP, 1982.

Plotkin, Mariano. *Mañana es San Perón: Propaganda, rituals politicos y educación en el regimen peronista 1946–1955*. Buenos Aires: Ariel Historia Argentina, 1994.

Plotkin, Mariano. *Mañana es San Perón: A Cultural History of Perón's Argentina*, translated by Keith Zahniser. Wilmington, Del.: Scholarly Resources, 2002.

Polanco Alcántara, Tomás. *Simón Bolívar: Ensayo de interpretación biográfica a través de sus documentos*. Caracas: Academia Nacional de la Historia, 1994.

Prieto, Guillermo. *Memorias de mis tiempos, 1828 á 1853*. Puebla: Editorial José M. Cajica Jr., 1970.

Primer Congreso Obrero Socialista celebrado en Motul, Estado de Yucatán. Bases que se discutieron y aprobaron, 2nd ed. Mexico City: Centro de Estudios Históricos del Movimiento Obrero Mexicano, 1977.

Pruvonena (José de la Riva Agüero). *Memorias y documentos para la historia de la independencia del Perú*. 2 vols. Paris: Librería de Garnier Hermanos, 1858.

Ramírez, Gabriel. *El cine yucateco*. Mexico City: Filmoteca UNAM, 1980.

Ramírez, Sergio, ed. *Augusto C. Sandino: El pensamiento vivo*. 2 vols. Managua: Editorial Nueva Nicaragua, 1984.

Ranum, Orest. "Courtesy, Absolutism, and the Rise of the French State, 1630–1660." *Journal of Modern History* 52, no. 3 (September 1980): 426–451.

Raquillet-Bordry, Pauline. "Le milieu diplomatique hispano-américain à Paris de 1880 à 1900." *Histoire et Sociétés de l'Amérique Latine* 3 (May 1995): 81–106.

Rashkin, Elissa J. *Women Filmmakers in Mexico: The Country in Which We Dream*. Austin: University of Texas Press, 2001.

Ravines, Eudocio. *The Yenan Way*. New York: Charles Scribner's Sons, 1951.

Redfield, Robert. *The Folk Culture of Yucatan*. Chicago: University of Chicago Press, 1941.

———. *Tepoztlán, a Mexican Village: A Study of Folk Life*. Chicago: University of Chicago Press, 1930.

Reuque Paillalef, Rosa Isolde. *When a Flower Is Reborn: The Life and Times of a Mapuche Feminist*, translated and with an introduction by

Florencia Mallon. Durham, N.C.: Duke University Press, 2002.

"Reuniones de Carrillo Puerto. El cenote Sambulá, un lugar con valor histórico." In *Diario de Yucatán,* on-line. Available: http://www.yucatan.com.mx/especiales/motul/cenote2.asp.

Ricalde, Alvaro Gamboa. *Yucatan desde 1910.* Vol. 3. Veracruz: Imprente Standard, 1943.

Rivera, Diego. *Arte y política,* compiled by Raquel Tibol. Mexico City: Grijalbo, 1979.

Rivera, Diego, with Gladys March. *My Art, My Life.* New York: Citadel Press, 1960.

Rivera Cambas, Manuel. *Los gobernantes de México: Antonio López de Santa Anna.* Mexico City: Editorial Citlaltepetl, 1972.

———. *México pintoresco, artístico, y monumental.* 3 vols. Mexico City: Imprenta de la Reforma, 1882.

Rochfort, Desmond. *Mexican Muralists: Orozco, Rivera, Siqueiros.* San Francisco: Chronicle Books, 1993.

Rock, David. *Argentina 1516–1987: From Spanish Colonization to Alfonsín.* Berkeley and Los Angeles: University of California Press, 1987.

Rodríguez O., Jaime E. *The Independence of Spanish America.* Cambridge: Cambridge University Press, 1998.

Rodríguez Villa, Antonio. *Etiquetas de la Casa de Austria.* Madrid: J. Ratés, 1913.

Rojas, Ricardo. *San Martín, Knight of the Andes,* translated by Herschel Brickell and Carlos Videla. New York: Cooper Square, 1967.

Rojo, Alba C. de, Rafael López Castro, and José Luis Martínez. *Zapata: Iconografía.* Mexico City: Fondo de Cultura Económica, 1979.

Rourke, Thomas. *Man of Glory: Simón Bolívar.* New York: William Morrow, 1939.

Rugeley, Terry. "The Forgotten Liberator: Buenaventura Martinez and Yucatan's Republican Restoration." *Mexican Studies/Estudios Mexicanos* 19, no. 2 (December 2003): 331–366.

Ruz, Laureano Cardoz. *El drama de los Mayas: Una reforma social traicionada.* Mexico City: Editorial Libros de Mexico, n.d.

Saint Croix, Lambert de. *Onze mois au Mexique et au Centre-Amérique.* Paris: Librairie Plon, 1897.

Sala I Vila, Nuria. *Y se armó el tole tole: Tributo indígena y movimientos sociales en el virreinato del Perú, 1784–1814.* Lima: IER José María Arguedas, 1996.

Salado Álvarez, Victoriano. *Memorias.* Vol. I. *Tiempo Viejo.* Mexico City: EDIAPSA, 1946.

————. *Memorias.* Vol. II. *Tiempo Nuevo.* Mexico City: EDIAPSA, 1946.

Salas, Elizabeth. *Soldaderas in the Mexican Military: Myth and History.* Austin: University of Texas Press, 1990.

Saldarriaga Betancur, Juan Manuel. *Anecdotário del Libertador.* Medellin: Tipografía Olympia, 1953.

Sánchez, Luís Alberto. *Haya de la Torre o el político. Crónica de una vida sin tregua.* Santiago: Editorial Ercilla, 1934.

————. *Haya de la Torre y el Apra: Crónica de un hombre y un partido.* Santiago: Editorial del Pacífico, 1955.

Sánchez Azcona, Juan, Ramón Puente, and Octavio Paz Solórzano. *Tres revolucionarios, tres testimonios.* Vol. 2. Mexico City: Editorial Offset, 1986.

Sanger, Margarita. *La regulación de la natalidad: La brújula del hogar.* Mérida: Mayab, 1922.

Sarkisyanz, Manuel. *Felipe Carrillo Puerto: Actuacion y muerte del apostol "rojo" de los Mayas. Con un ensayo sobre hagiografía secular en la Revolución Méxicana.* Merida: Congreso del Estado de Yucatán, 1995.

Sarmiento, Domingo Faustino. *Life in the Argentine Republic in the Days of the Tyrants; or, Civilization and Barbarism.* New York: Collier Books, 1961.

Sater, William F. "Heroic Myths for Heroic Times." *Mexican Studies/Estudios Mexicanos* 4 (1988): 160.

Schodt, David W. *Ecuador: An Andean Enigma.* Boulder, Colo.: Westview Press, 1987.

Schroeder, Michael Jay. "'To Defend Our Nation's Honor': Toward a Social and Cultural History of the Sandino Rebellion in Nicaragua, 1927–1934." PhD diss., University of Michigan, 1993.

Seler, Eduard. *Collected Works in North and South American Linguistics and Archaeology: English Translations of German Papers from Gesammelte Abhandlungen zur amerikanischen Sprach- und Alterthumskunde,* translated by Theodore E. Gutman and Ingeburg Meinung Nagel. Lancaster: Labyrinthos, 2002.

Selser, Gregorio. *El pequeño ejército loco.* Managua: Editorial Nueva Nicaragua, 1983.

————. *Sandino.* New York: Monthly Review Press, 1981.

Sensores, William Brito. *Tizimín en la historia.* Mérida: Ediciones Salettianas, 1995.

Shaw, Lisa. *The Social History of the Brazilian Samba.* Brookfield, Vt.: Ashgate, 1999.

Sheesley, Joel E., et al. *Sandino in the Streets.* Bloomington: Indiana University Press, 1991.

Shils, Edward. "Charisma, Order, Status." *American Sociological Review* 30 (1965): 199–213.

Sierra, J. Adonay Cetina. *Mérida de Yucatán, 1542–1984: Historia Gráfica.* Merida: Secretaria de Educación Pública, 1984.

Sierra, Justo. *Historia patria.* Mexico City: Departamento Editorial de la Secretaría de Educación pública, 1922.

Sierra Brabatta, Carlos J. *Zapata: Señor de la tierra, capitán de los labriegos.* Mexico City: Departamento del Distrito Federal, 1985.

Sierra y Rosso, Ignacio. *Discurso que por encargo de la Junta Patriótica pronunció de el panteón de Santa Paula el ciudadano Ignacio Sierra y Rosso, en la colocación del pie que perdió en Veracruz el Ecsmo. Sr. General de División, Benemérito de la Patria D. Antonio López de Santa Anna, en la gloriosa jornada del 5 de diciembre de 1838.* Mexico City: Antonio Díaz, 1842.

Sims, Harold Dana. *The Expulsion of Mexico's Spaniards 1821–1836.* Pittsburgh: University of Pittsburgh Press, 1990.

Siqueiros, David Alfaro. *No hay más ruta que la nuestra: importancia nacional e internacional de la pintura mexicana moderna.* Mexico City, 1945.

Smith, Anthony D. *Myths and Memories of the Nation.* New York: Oxford University Press, 1999.

Smith, Peter. "The Search for Legitimacy." In *Caudillos: Dictators in Spanish America,* edited by Hugh M. Hamill, 87–96. Norman: University of Oklahoma Press, 1992.

Sobrevilla Perea, Natalia. "The Influence of the European 1848 Revolution in Peru." In *The European Revolutions of 1848 and the Americas,* edited by Guy Thomson, 191–216. London: Institute of Latin American Studies, 2002.

Sol, Hugo (Anastasio Manzanilla). *Bolchevismo criminal de Yucatán: Documentos y apuntes para la historia trágica del estado.* Mexico City: n.p., 1921.

Somoza García, Anastasio. *El verdadero Sandino, o el Calvario de las Segovias.* Managua: Robelo, 1976.

Sordo Cedeño, Reynaldo. *El congreso en la primera republica centralista.* Mexico City: El Colegio de México-Instituto Tecnológica Autónoma de México, 1993.

Sosa Ferreyro, Roque Armando. *El crimen del miedo: Reportaje histórico como y por que fue asesinado Felipe Carrillo Puerto.* Mexico City: B. Costa-Amic, 1969.

Sotelo Inclán, Jesús. *Raíz y razón de Zapata.* 2nd ed. Mexico City: Comisión Federal de Electricidad, 1970.

Spenser, Daniela. "Workers Against Socialism? Reassessing the Role of Urban Labor in Yucatecan Revolutionary Politics." In *Land, Labor and Capital in Modern Yucatan: Essays in Regional History and Political Economy*, edited by Gilbert M. Joseph and Jeffrey T. Brannon, 220–242. Tuscaloosa: University of Alabama, 1991.

Stein, Steve. *Populism in Peru: The Emergence of the Masses and the Politics of Social Control.* Madison: University of Wisconsin Press, 1980.

———. "Populism in Peru: APRA, the Formative Years." In *Latin American Populism in Comparative Perspective*, edited by Michael Conniff, 113–134. Albuquerque: University of New Mexico Press, 1982.

Stephen, Lynn. "Pro-Zapatista and Pro-PRI: Resolving the Contradictions of Zapatismo in Rural Oaxaca." *Latin American Research Review* 32 (1997): 41–70.

Sulmont, Denis. *El movimiento obrero peruano, 1890–1980: Reseña histórica.* 2nd ed. Lima: Tarea, 1980.

Taboada, Miguel Civeira. *Felipe Carrillo Puerto: mártir del proletariado nacional.* Mexico City: Comisión Editorial de la Liga de Economistas Revolucionarios de la República Mexicana, 1986.

Taibo, Paco Ignacio II. *Guevara, Also Known as Che*, translated by Martin Michael Roberts. New York: Thomas Dunne, 1997.

Tauro, Alberto. "Agustín Gamarra, fundador de la independencia nacional." In *Historia del Perú: Biblioteca de Cultura Peruana Contemporánea.* Vol. 7, 507–518. Edited by César Pacheco Vélez. Lima: Ediciones del Sol, 1963.

Taylor, J. M. *Eva Perón: The Myths of a Woman.* Chicago: University of Chicago Press, 1981.

Tello Díaz, Carlos. *El exilio: Un relato de familia.* 11th ed. Mexico City: Editorial Cal y Arena, 1994.

Tenenbaum, Barbara A. *The Politics of Penury: Debt and Taxes in Mexico, 1821–1856.* Albuquerque: University of New Mexico Press, 1986.

———. "Streetwise History: The Paseo de la Reforma and the Porfirian State, 1876–1910." In *Rituals of Rule, Rituals of Resistance: Public Celebrations and Popular Culture in Mexico*, edited by William H. Beezley, Cheryl English Martin, and William E. French, 135–146. Wilmington, Del.: Scholarly Resources Books, 1994.

Tenorio-Trillo, Mauricio. "1910 Mexico City: Space and Nation in the City of the Centenario." In *¡Viva Mexico! Viva La Independencia: Celebrations of September 16,* edited by William H. Beezley and David E. Lorey, 167–197. Wilmington, Del.: Scholarly Resources, 2001.

———. *Mexico at the World's Fairs: Crafting a Modern Nation.* Berkeley and Los Angeles: University of California Press, 1996.

Thelen, David. "Popular Uses of History in the United States: Individuals in History." *Perspectives* (American Historical Association Newsletter) 38, no. 5 (May 2000): 22–25.

Tibol, Raquel. Prologue to *Frida Kahlo: Crónica, testimonios y aproximaciones*. Mexico City: Ediciones de Cultura Popular, 1977.

Toro, Fermín. *La doctrina conservadora, Fermín Toro*. Caracas: Pensamiento Político Venezolano del Siglo XIX, 1960.

Torre, José Castillo. *A la luz de relámpago: Ensayo de biografía subjectiva de Felipe Carrillo Puerto*. Mexico City: Ediciones Botas, 1934.

Torre Diaz, Alvaro. *Cuatro años en el gobierno de Yucatán, 1926–1930*. Merida: n.p., 1930.

Tranquillus, Gaius Suetonius. *The Twelve Caesars*, translated by Robert Graves. New York: Penguin, 1957.

Tumarkin, Nina. *Lenin Lives! The Lenin Cult in Soviet Russia*. Cambridge, Mass.: Harvard University Press, 1983.

Valdelomar, Abraham. *La Mariscala: Doña Francisca Zubiaga y Bernales de Gamarra*. Lima: Taller de la Penitenciaría, 1914.

Valega, José María. *República del Perú*. Lima: Librería e Imprenta Don Miranda, 1927.

Valenzuela, Luisa. *The Lizard's Tail*, translated by Gregory Rabassa. New York: Farrar, Straus, Giroux, 1983.

Valverde, Sergio. *Apuntes para la historia de la revolución y de la política en el estado de Morelos*. Mexico City: n.p., 1933.

Van Young, Eric. "Recent Anglophone Scholarship on Mexico and Central America in the Age of Revolution (1750–1850)." *Hispanic American Historical Review* 64 (1985): 733–734.

Vanderwood, Paul J. *Disorder and Progress: Bandits, Police, and Mexican Development*. Rev. ed. Wilmington, Del.: Scholarly Resources, 1992.

Vargas, Oscar-René. *Sandino: Floreció al filo de la espada*. Managua: Centro de Estudios de la Realidad Nacional, 1995.

Vasconcelos, José. *Breve Historia de México*. Mexico City: Compañia Editorial Continental, 1976.

Vaughan, Mary Kay. *The State, Education, and Social Class in Mexico, 1880–1928*. DeKalb: Northern Illinois University Press, 1982.

Vega-Centeno B., Imelda. *Aprismo popular: Cultura, religion y política*. Lima: CISEPA y Tarea, 1991.

Verdery, Katherine. *The Political Lives of Dead Bodies: Reburial and Postsocialist Change*. New York: Columbia University Press, 1999.

Verea de Bernal, Sofía, ed. *Un hombre de mundo escribe sus impresiones: Cartas de José Manuel Hidalgo y Esnaurrízar, Ministro en París del Emperador Maximiliano*. 2nd ed. Mexico City: Editorial Porrúa, 1978.

Verges, José F. *Recuerdos de Méjico*. Barcelona: Imprenta de Henrich y
　　Cía., 1903.

Villanueva Urteaga, Horacio. *Gamarra y la iniciación de la república en el
　　Cuzco*. Lima: Banco de los Andes, 1981.

Viramontes, Guillermo Sandoval, and Jorge Mantilla Gutiérrez. *Felipe
　　Carrillo Puerto: Ensayo biográfico (vida y obra.)* Merida: Universidad
　　Autónoma de Yucatán, 1994.

Walker, Charles F. "La orgía periodística: Prensa y cultura política en el
　　Cuzco durante la joven república." *Revista de Indias* 61, no. 221 (2001):
　　7–26.

———. *Smoldering Ashes: Cuzco and the Creation of Republican Peru,
　　1780–1840*. Durham, N.C.: Duke University Press, 1999.

Warren, Richard A. *Vagrants and Citizens: Politics and the Masses in Mexico
　　City from Colony to Republic*. Wilmington, Del.: SR Books, 2001.

Webb, Simon. "Masculinities at the Margins: Representations of the
　　Malandro and the Pachuco." In *Imagination Beyond Nation: Latin
　　American Popular Culture*, edited by Eva P. Bueno and Terry Caesar,
　　238–248. Pittsburgh: University of Pittsburgh Press, 1998.

Weber, Max. *Economy and Society*, edited by Guenther Roth and Claus
　　Wittich. 2 vols. Berkeley and Los Angeles: University of California
　　Press, 1968.

———. *Economy and Society: An Outline of Interpretive Sociology*. Berkeley
　　and Los Angeles: University of California Press, 1978.

———. *On Charisma and Institution-Building*. Chicago: University of
　　Chicago Press, 1968.

Weeks, Charles A. *The Juárez Myth in Mexico*. Tuscaloosa: University of
　　Alabama Press, 1987.

Wharton, Clarence R. *El Presidente: A Sketch of the Life of General Santa
　　Anna*. Austin: Gammel's Book Store, 1926.

Wharton, Edith, and Ogden Codman. *The Decoration of Houses*. New
　　York: Charles Scribner's Sons, 1902.

Whitaker, Arthur Preston. *The Western Hemisphere Idea: Its Rise and
　　Decline*. Ithaca, N.Y.: Cornell University Press, 1954.

Widdifield, Stacie G. *The Embodiment of the National in Late Nineteenth-
　　Century Mexican Painting*. Tucson: University of Arizona Press, 1996.

Williams, Dion. "The Nicaragua Situation." *Marine Corps Gazette*, 15, no.
　　3 (1930): 19–20.

Wise, George S. *Caudillo: A Portrait of Antonio Guzmán Blanco*. Westport,
　　Conn.: Greenwood Press, 1951.

Wolfe, Bertram D. *The Fabulous Life of Diego Rivera*. New York: Stesin
　　and Day, 1963.

Womack, John, Jr. *Zapata and the Mexican Revolution.* New York: Vintage Books, 1970.

Wünderich, Volker. *Sandino: Una biografía política.* Managua: Editorial Nueva Nicaragua, 1995.

Yañez, Agustín. *Santa Anna: Espectro de una sociedad.* Mexico City: Ediciones Oceano, 1982.

Zamora, Martha. "Por qué se pintaba Frida Kahlo." *Imagine* 2, no. 1 (1985): 1–19.

Zimmermann, Matilde. *Sandinista: Carlos Fonseca and the Nicaraguan Revolution.* Durham, N.C.: Duke University Press, 2000.

Zoraida Vázquez, Josefina. *Nacionalismo y educación en Mexico.* Mexico City: El Colegio de México, 1970.

About the Contributors

SHANNON BAKER teaches Mexican and Mexican American History at Texas A&M University-Kingsville. She is currently completing a book manuscript, "Pomp and Scorn: Public Ceremonies in the Age of Santa Anna," and is coediting a primary documents reader in Mexican American history with James Garza and Victor Macias-González.

SAMUEL BRUNK teaches Mexican, Latin American, and world history at the University of Texas, El Paso. He has published a biography of Emiliano Zapata, *Emiliano Zapata: Revolution and Betrayal in Mexico* (1995) and is finishing work on a book manuscript, "The Myth of Emiliano Zapata and Mexico's Twentieth Century." He plans to turn his attention next to the environmental history of the Chihuahuan desert.

JOHN CHARLES CHASTEEN teaches Latin American history at the University of North Carolina at Chapel Hill. His interest in hero myths dates back to his first book, *Heroes on Horseback: A Life and Times of the Last Gaucho Caudillos* (1995).

NANCY DEFFEBACH is assistant professor of art history at San Diego State University specializing in modern and contemporary Latin American art. She is currently working on a book manuscript titled, "Other Routes: The Art of María Izquierdo and Frida Kahlo in Postrevolutionary Mexico."

BEN FALLAW teaches history and Latin American Studies at Colby College in Waterville, Maine. He published his first book, *Cárdenas Compromised: The Failure of Reform in Yucatan*, in 2001, and is completing a study on the connections between revolutionary politicians and the Church, business, and the press in Mexico in the 1920s and 1930s.

RICHARD GROSSMAN is an instructor in history at Northeastern Illinois University. He contributed a chapter, "The Blood of the People: The Guardia Nacional de Nicaragua's Fifty Year War Against the People of Nicaragua, 1927–1979," to *When States Kill: Latin America, the U.S., and*

Technologies of Terror, edited by Cecilia Menjívar and Néstor Rodríguez. He continues to research Sandino and the relationship between Nicaragua and the United States.

LINDA B. HALL is professor of history at the University of New Mexico. She has also taught at the Universidad de los Andes in Bogota, Colombia; Southern Methodist University; Trinity University; and the University of California at Los Angeles. Her most recent book is *Mary, Mother and Warrior: The Virgin in Spain and the Americas* (University of Texas Press, 2004). In 2000, she was named University Research Lecturer, the University of New Mexico's highest research honor.

VÍCTOR M. MACÍAS-GONZÁLEZ teaches history at the University of Wisconsin at La Crosse. He is presently working on two projects, an edited anthology on Mexican masculinities and a monograph on the Mexican aristocracy in the age of Porfirio Díaz.

DAVID NUGENT is professor of anthropology at Colby College. He is the author of *Modernity at the Edge of Empire: State, Individual and Nation in the Northern Peruvian Andes,* the editor of *Locating Capitalism in Time and Space: Global Restructurings, Politics and Identity,* and the co-editor (with Joan Vincent) of *A Companion to the Anthropology of Politics.* He is currently working on a project that examines underground processes of state formation and alternative democracies in twentieth-century Peru.

CHARLES WALKER is the author of *Smoldering Ashes: Cuzco and the Creation of Republican Peru, 1780–1840,* as well as two edited volumes in Spanish. He is finishing a book on a massive earthquake/tsunami that struck Lima and Callao in 1746. He teaches Latin American history at the University of California, Davis.

Index

CPSIA information can be obtained at www.ICGtesting.com
Printed in the USA
BVOW04s1603110314

347309BV00001B